The Crisis of Russian Autocracy

Studies of the Harriman Institute
COLUMBIA UNIVERSITY

Founded as the Russian Institute in 1946, the W. Averell Harriman Institute for Advanced Study of the Soviet Union is the oldest research institution of its kind in the United States. The book series *Studies of the Harriman Institute*, begun in 1953, helps bring to a wider audience some of the work conducted under its auspices by professors, degree candidates, and visiting fellows. The faculty of the Institute, without necessarily agreeing with the conclusions reached in these books, believes their publication will contribute to both scholarship and a greater public understanding of the Soviet Union. A list of the *Studies* appears at the back of the book.

The Crisis of Russian Autocracy

NICHOLAS II AND
THE 1905 REVOLUTION

Andrew M. Verner

PRINCETON UNIVERSITY PRESS

PRINCETON, NEW JERSEY

Copyright ©1990 by Princeton University Press
Published by Princeton University Press, 41 William Street,
Princeton, New Jersey 08540
In the United Kingdom: Princeton University Press, Oxford

Library of Congress Cataloging-in-Publication Data

Verner, Andrew M., 1949–
The crisis of Russian autocracy : Nicholas II and the 1905
Revolution / Andrew M. Verner.
p.   cm.
Includes bibliographical references.
1. Nicholas II, Emperor of Russia, 1868–1918. 2. Soviet Union—
Kings and rulers—Biography. 3. Soviet Union—History—Revolution
of 1905. I. Title.
DK258.V44   1990   947.08′3—dc20   89-10710

ISBN 0-691-04773-1

Publication of this book has been aided by the Whitney Darrow
Fund of Princeton University Press

This book has been composed in Linotron Caledonia

Princeton University Press books are printed
on acid-free paper, and meet the guidelines for
permanence and durability of the Committee on
Production Guidelines for Book Longevity of
the Council on Library Resources

Printed in the United States of America by Princeton University Press,
Princeton, New Jersey

10 9 8 7 6 5 4 3 2 1

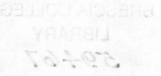

*To the memory of
my mother and father
and especially my grandmother*

Contents

Acknowledgments

FOR ALL the lonely hours spent in archives, libraries, and the privacy of one's study, the historian's craft is not a solitary enterprise. I speak not of the characters from the past, some dull, some fascinating, in whose presence the historian has decided to dwell, but of one's fellows in the profession. As historians we are engaged in a constant dialogue with the past and with ourselves—and with each other. History is very much a collective effort involving our predecessors on whose work we build, our teachers whom we emulate, our peers and, yes, our students. Consciously or not, we are tied to each other by a web of relationships and obligations that usually go unrecognized except on occasions such as this. I therefore happily seize this opportunity to acknowledge a number of special debts in addition to those already confirmed in the body of my work in accordance with scholarly conventions.

This book grew out of a dissertation written at Columbia University under the auspices of Leopold Haimson, that incomparable teacher of several generations of Russian historians who taught us the importance of language. The dissertation itself took on form amid a remarkable circle of fellow students whose uninhibited criticisms and soaring free associations made each seminar at once intimidating and exhilarating. The personal closeness and intellectual crossfertilization of our *kruzhok* at times may have blurred the boundaries between individual contributions and yet enriched us all. Other graduate students should have the good fortune of such an experience. Composed originally of Jonathan Sanders, Ron Petrusha, Frank Wcislo, William Duggan, Dwight Van Horn, David MacDonald, and Philip Swoboda, this seminar attracted visiting fellows from near and far and has since been institutionalized as the Russian History Workshop. And my work would have been immeasurably poorer but for the teaching of Marc Raeff and Daniel Field.

My research could not have proceeded, of course, without the cooperation of the following libraries and archives and their staffs: the Butler Library of Columbia University, the Russian and East European Archive, since renamed the Bakhmetev Archive, at Columbia University, the New York Public Library, the International Law Library of Harvard University, the Lenin Library in Moscow and its manuscript division, the Library of the Academy of Sciences and the Saltykov-Shchedrin Public Library in Leningrad, the Central State Archive of the October Revolution in Moscow, and, finally, the Central State Historical Archive in Leningrad, whose thoroughly professional and wonderful *sotrudnitsy* did everything in their power to make my stays productive. While in the Soviet Union, I also received help from Professor E. D. Chermenskii in Moscow and could always count on the gracious guidance and warm solicitude of Professor B. V. Anan'ich, whose command of archival materials in my area of interest is matched only by that of his colleagues in the Institute of History of the Academy of Sciences in Leningrad.

For financially supporting my research and writing I am most beholden to the International Research and Exchanges Board, the Fulbright-Hays Program, the Mrs. Giles Whiting Foundation, and the W. Averell Harriman Institute for Advanced Study of the Soviet Union at Columbia University, which is also sponsoring this book.

I also wish to thank a number of friends and colleagues who found time in their busy schedules to read all or parts of previous versions of this study: Ronald Suny, who brought the manuscript to the attention of Princeton University Press; Richard Wortman, who may know more about my subject than I do; Richard Hellie, who gave me the benefit of his blunt advice; Margaret Anderson, Robert Bannister, and Robert DuPlessis, whose non-Russian perspectives sought to protect me from narrow parochialism; and Lauren Glant, who as a student made Russian history in general, and my work in particular, her avocation. The book, whatever its merits, owes much to their combined substantive criticisms and stylistic suggestions.

I am grateful to my editors at Princeton University Press: Gail Ullman, who may yet regret acquiring this tome; Beth Gianfagna, who is orchestrating the effort; and Adrienne Shirley, who diligently cleansed my language of any sexist overtones and all other offenses against good taste and convention. Last but not least, I wish to thank the historian's ideal factotum and the soul of any history department, Eleanor Bennett, for her assistance in typing and for her unfailing good cheer.

While it is customary at this point to express one's gratitude to family who have suffered blamelessly and silently for so many years, more than mere form moves me to do so. Although I have often envied the monastic scholars of another time, I am profoundly aware that I could not have made it without the unstinting and uncomplaining support of my wife Susan and the uncritical acceptance of my sons, Christopher and Michael.

Note on Translations, Transliterations, and Dates

ALTHOUGH I have provided a glossary designed to help the non-Russian-speaking reader with unfamiliar terms, the problem remains that many very important words lack precise equivalents not only in our language but in our very experience. Acutely aware of linguistic subtleties and the conceptual nuances behind them, I have made every effort to capture these differences in English. *Obshchestvo*, for example, is conventionally translated as "society," and its adjectival derivative, *obshchestvennyi*, as "social." In fact, obshchestvo cannot boast the value-neutral, all-encompassing meaning of the English word. Rather, it refers to civil society in a politically active and privileged sense. Hence its adjective has usually been rendered here as "societal," not "social." Other attempts at elucidating such differences are considerably more prolix, if less awkward, perhaps. It would be impractical, of course, to repeat such lengthy explanations every time the Russian term recurs in an original document. In these cases, the glossary can serve only as the crudest of reminders.

Needless to say, all translations from Russian are my own, unless otherwise noted. I have sought to remain as faithful as possible to the peculiarities of the original, including style and spelling. Any emphasis in the citations is to be found in the original, too, again unless otherwise indicated.

I adhere to the system of transliteration used by the Library of Congress, except that I dispense with diacritical marks and usually observe the postrevolutionary conventions of modern Russian orthography. For certain well-known names, such as Nicholas, Alexander, or Witte, the English form has been retained.

All dates, unless followed by "N.S.," refer to the Julian or Old Style calendar used in Russia until February 1918. This calendar lagged behind the Gregorian by twelve days in the nineteenth century and by thirteen in the twentieth.

Abbreviations

GBL OR	Gosudarstvennaia biblioteka im. V. I. Lenina, otdel rukopisei
ILLHU	International Law Library, Harvard University
KA	*Krasnyi Arkhiv*
KFZ	*Kamer-fur'erskie zhurnaly*
MIA	Ministry of Internal Affairs
REEACU	Russian and East European Archive (now Bakhmetev Archive), Columbia University
TsGAOR	Tsentral'nyi Gosudarstvennyi Arkhiv Oktiabr'skoi Revoliutsii
TsGIA	Tsentral'nyi Gosudarstvennyi Istoricheskii Arkhiv

The Crisis of Russian Autocracy

Introduction

SURELY, yet another study purporting to deal with the crisis of Russian autocracy demands some justification. The 1905 Revolution, it is widely agreed, marked a watershed in Russian history; yet the precise meaning and implications of that divide remain very much in dispute. Whatever one's personal vantage point or stake in the outcome, 1905 heralded the coming-of-age of Russian society as a whole. Some of its constituent groups, such as workers, students, rural intelligentsia, urban professionals, liberal gentry, or factions thereof, had been mobilized before, but never in concert. They finally came together when Russian autocracy proved incapable of living up to the most basic and essential task of any state—the preservation of its territorial integrity during the Russo-Japanese War of 1904–5. The fact that these unexpected defeats on land and at sea came at the hands of a non-European enemy previously deemed inferior made them all the more humiliating. Although the groups participating in the so-called All-Nation Struggle against Absolutism differed in their interests, timing, and ultimate objectives, they were united in their opposition to the inefficient, corrupt, overweening, and repressive bureaucracy. This concerted challenge, however short-lived, made for a crisis of authority that came to pervade the entire system of autocracy.

This crisis has to be distinguished from the chronic problems and latent conflict that preceded it. To speak of a crisis before then, as some Soviet historians have done in discussing various aspects and phases of Alexander II's rule, or in describing the entirety of Nicholas II's reign, to say nothing of the sixty-year span from the Crimean War to World War I, is to confuse the first signs of a life-threatening illness with its acute, critical phase. Difficult though it may be to avoid entirely the perspective of 1917, such a sweeping characterization is excessively teleological. It not only tends to belittle the uniqueness and significance of individual events, but it runs the real risk of being meaningless; the more protracted the crisis, the more normal and ordinary it becomes. Applied exclusively to the events of 1905–6, on the other hand, the crisis of Russian autocracy indeed describes the state of limbo between life and death, the crucial moment when its fate hung in the balance. It was in this very vein that the eminent Russian historian, Pavel Miliukov, leader of Russia's liberals and himself an active participant, explained the revolution to his Western audience in *Russia and Its Crisis*.

The story of the main revolutionary events has been told repeatedly, of course, by Soviet and Western historians through general accounts and as part of more specialized studies dealing with the liberal movement, the nobles, commercial and industrial circles, the professions, workers, peasants, and political parties—Social Democrats, Socialist Revolutionaries, and others. To the extent that scholars deal at all with Russian autocracy in the 1905 Revolution, they have focused on the technical preparations and prehistory of individual reforms, their legal implications, implementation, and effects, or on the government's relations with certain social and political groups or the Duma, or on outstanding individuals such as Witte or Stolypin. The role of the autocrat and of Nicholas, however, has not received the critical attention that it deserves.

If we discount sensationalist or hagiographic treatments, popular biographies, and traditional-idealist histories, this role has been taken for granted or largely ignored. Although Nicholas II may seem to have been weak, narrow-minded, or otherwise forgettable, his role was by no means a negligible one. He still happened to be the tsar and as such was both apex and linchpin of the entire autocratic system. Whether regarded as passive or active, Nicholas played a key role by virtue of his position. And if the tsar's role was important, so was his personality, no matter how unremarkable it might have appeared.

Nicholas's personality emerges in the opening chapter, which deals with his upbringing as heir to the Russian throne. The drawn-out socialization of his childhood and youth not only decisively influenced his personality, but also determined the image of his future role and hence its exercise. Through the examples of his grandfather and father, the teachings of his tutors, and the sheltered environment of his family, Nicholas was initiated into the theories and practices of autocracy.

In emphasizing the importance of the tsar's personal qualities, I do not wish for a moment to return to the idealist interpretations of the past. Obviously his personality did not exist in a vacuum, but had to operate instead within equally important constraints, ideological as well as structural. The very significance of these two dimensions derived from Nicholas's personal makeup, which was directly affected by them and thus served to reinforce them. For this reason, the second and third chapters, respectively, address the practice and theory of prerevolutionary autocracy.

Nicholas's upbringing, it turns out, coincided with the attempts of various autocratic apologists to meet society's growing challenges by formulating theoretical justifications in defense of autocracy. Far from being unanimous or coherent, these autocratic apologia reflected different and even irreconcilable values, traditions, and conceptions. Although many of the differences remained confined to the theoretical realm for the time being, these ideas would serve as Nicholas's ideological compass. By the same token, it is essential to understand the daily routine and practice of autocratic rulership, which helped define the tsar's role in the normal decision-making process of government. The way in which Nicholas related to family members, bureaucratic servitors, and outsiders as part of his official responsibilities was as much a function of traditional practices and institutional precedent as of personal predilections. In this sense, personal idiosyncrasies combined with those other factors to determine Nicholas's role as autocrat.

Events, too, directly affected this role. If the tsar's position was important, indeed crucial, during normal times, it was even more so during abnormal ones. In 1905–6 Nicholas found himself in the calm eye of the revolutionary hurricane that tore across his empire. Belying his eerie detachment from the surrounding turmoil, his role was both central and subject to change as the storm swept up different elements of society and altered the political landscape. Not only was Nicholas's very position at stake during this revolutionary upheaval, but in the face of a rapidly disintegrating political and social order, as powerful conventions were shattered and traditional reference points disappeared, members and factions of bureaucracy and society alike appealed to him as the ultimate authority, the referent of last resort. The fact that they had not done so before served to heighten the importance of the autocrat's role.

From a methodological point of view, these developments also helped to cast Nicholas's role into sharper relief. It is during the crisis of 1905–6 that Nicholas, his courtiers, and bureaucrats, as well as individuals and groups within society, chose or were compelled to act according to their respective beliefs, tenets that otherwise might have remained little more than wholesome ideological platitudes. Theories were put into practice or discarded when challenged by reality. Desperately seeking the sovereign's ear as events appeared to be spinning out of control, members of his entourage, government, and society invoked different and often conflicting views and expectations of autocracy and the autocrat's function. These in turn forced the tsar to declare himself, to enact whatever notion of his role appealed or was suggested to him.

Nicholas's response, or failure to respond, to these competing and complementary impulses determined the course of government policy and the outcome of the reforms of 1905–6 that take up the remaining parts of this discussion. A comparison of the conceptions and execution of the autocrat's role before and after the introduction of quasi-constitutional forms of government in late 1905 and early 1906 sheds light on the nature of those measures. Instead of being construed simply in legal-technical terms, these changes have to be seen as the result of conflicting and evolving ideas about the meaning of autocracy. If the revolutionary din itself seems but a faint echo at times, this is how reality was perceived by the tsar. It was filtered through the different strands and layers of autocratic ideology and the practices of autocratic administration before being registered by Nicholas. Indeed, from the vantage point of the autocrat and his government the revolutionary conflict between autocracy and democracy, both in its liberal and socialist variant, was transformed into a conflict between different conceptions of autocracy, none of them democratic, of course.

This book not only hopes to contribute to an understanding of autocratic theory and practice under Nicholas II, but also takes its place in the long-standing historical and historiographical controversy that dates back to the 1905 revolution itself. What looked like a dress rehearsal for the real drama soon to be staged by Lenin and other revolutionaries, or like opening night from a hopeful liberal-constitutionalist perspective, was the final performance of the tragedy of Russian autocracy. It was the swan song that would soon ring down the curtain on the autocratic stage of Russian history. Given the nature of autocratic government at the time, in particular the role and personality of Nicholas II, there was no realistically conceivable way after 1906 that autocracy could have reformed and adapted itself enough to the demands of society in order to avert a revolutionary outcome—hence the growing social polarization on the eve of World War I, hence the debacle of the war, and hence, too, the February Revolution of 1917. Russian autocracy was doomed, or rather, had doomed itself. With the crisis of 1905–6, its ultimate fate had been decided; the ten years remaining until 1917 were little more than a death rattle.

CHAPTER I

The Making of an Autocrat

"WHAT AM I going to do? . . . What is going to happen to me, to you, to Xenia, to Alix, to mother, to all of Russia? I am not prepared to be a Czar. I never wanted to become one. I know nothing of the business of ruling. I have no idea of even how to talk to the ministers. Will you help me, Sandro?"[1] With these tearful words Nicholas II, the new Tsar of All the Russias and ruler over one-sixth of the earth, is said to have turned to his cousin, brother-in-law, and closest childhood friend, the Grand Duke Alexander, on the very day that Nicholas's father died. Born May 6, 1868, the oldest child of the Tsarevich Alexander Alexandrovich and his Danish-born wife, Maria Fedorovna, Nicholas was twenty-six years old when he succeeded his father to the throne on October 20, 1894.

It was only natural that the young emperor should experience an acute sense of personal loss. His personal diary, which only rarely displayed such deep emotion, bore moving testimony to his overwhelming grief: "My God, my God, what a day. The Lord called away our adored, dear, warmly beloved Papa. My head spins, one refuses to believe it—it still seems like improbable, awful reality. . . . This was the death of a saint! Lord, help us in these hard days! Poor dear Mama!"[2] Nicholas, his bride, his family, all of Russia had lost their father, their center of stability. Life without him was simply inconceivable; woe to them all in the future!

The dread with which Alexander's son contemplated this bleak future was heightened by the fact that he felt inadequate and unprepared for his new role. As he told his foreign minister during their first audience: "I don't know anything. The late Sovereign did not foresee his end and did not initiate me into anything."[3] While it remains to be seen to what extent this confession was accurate, worse than this admitted ignorance

---

[1] The Grand Duke Alexander, *Once a Grand Duke* (New York, 1932), pp. 168–69.

[2] *Dnevnik Imperatora Nikolaia II* (Berlin, 1923), p. 85, October 20, 1894.

[3] "Dnevnik V. N. Lamzdorfa," *Krasnyi Arkhiv (KA)* 46 (1931): 10, November 4, 1894. For the time being, I shall not address the impression the new emperor made on others. Instead, I intend to look at Nicholas and his upbringing as seen through his own eyes, his own perceptions and feelings. Thus I hope to elucidate the emotional and affective impulses, the psychological tensions and adaptation, which shaped Nicholas's mentality, not their rationalizations and ideological justifications. The latter, for the most part, were revealed only in his subsequent actions as autocrat when challenged. This approach should give some indication as to how Nicholas perceived the world around him and thus should suggest the range of attitudes he would display later in specific situations.

of practical government matters was his apparent lack of any psychological preparation for his new responsibilities. As a result the new tsar was gripped by panic. Suddenly and irrevocably, his sheltered and carefree existence had come to an end. The family idyll that had comforted him for so long had been rudely shattered, and out of this private world he found himself flung onto the unfamiliar public stage of Russian history, cast into an alien role to which he had never before given any conscious thought.

DAILY ROUTINE AND FAMILY LIFE

Lest Nicholas's own feelings of despair and inadequacy be attributed entirely to his momentary bereavement, the young emperor's childhood and youth must be examined in detail for clues concerning the development of his personality, his mentality, values, and outlook. Among the sources that shed light on this crucial phase of Nicholas's life, his own diary is certainly the most illuminating, even though it contains scarcely a hint of his future role. In part, this apparent absence of any real introspection and substance reflected a particular style of diary writing that eschewed any displays of emotion and thought in favor of plain facts and a simple listing of one's daily schedule. Nicholas's uncle, the Grand Duke Sergei, and his own brother, the Grand Duke Michael, kept their diaries in much the same way; obviously they had all been told to write in this manner. Nowhere is this more evident than in Nicholas's first diary, begun at the age of thirteen in 1882.[4] Very fastidiously the boy chronicled the details of his daily routine, including the exact times of rising, meals, and going to bed, the names of lunch and dinner guests, the regiments reviewed by his father, and the uniforms he himself wore on those occasions. No matter how repetitive this routine, Nicholas took great care to remember the morning coffee with milk, the cleaning of the bird cages, his daily studies and readings, indoor games and outdoor activities, as well as many of his parents' obligations.

Nicholas was still a boy, of course, too young and impressionable to develop his own style of diary writing and to escape the influence of his first tutor. General Danilovich, who had been charged with supervising the heir's and his younger brother George's education, was better known for his military discipline and plodding uprightness than for the brilliance of his mind or breadth and tolerance of his views.[5] Not surprisingly,

[4] Tsentral'nyi Gosudarstvennyi Arkhiv Oktiabr'skoi Revoliutsii (TsGAOR), fond (f.) 601, opis' (op.) 1, delo (d.) 217.
[5] Alexander Iswolsky, *Recollections of a Foreign Minister* (Garden City, N.Y., 1921), pp. 257–58; A. A. Mosolov, *At the Court of the Last Tsar; Being the Memoirs of A. A. Mosolov, Head of the Court Chancellery, 1900–1916* (London, 1935), p. 6.

Nicholas's diary, then as well as later, often reads like a military log and lacks critical reflection.[6] Thus the factual blandness and uncritical perspective of Nicholas's early diaries can partly be blamed on his tender age and the inhibiting example and disciplinary influence of others.

Indeed, by 1883 these daily diary notations were becoming briefer, describing only the more important or unusual events instead of every detail; for some days there is no entry at all. At the same time, Nicholas's own interests and emotional reactions, such as his love for physical activities of all kinds or his generally favorable opinions of various forms of entertainment, were beginning to manifest themselves.[7] And yet, the same style, the same formal enumeration of his daily calendar, the same absence of analysis continued to characterize his diary throughout his life. Clearly, this emphasis on form rather than substance was the direct consequence of an upbringing that cultivated such qualities. They therefore bespeak the writer's more permanent values and traits.

Not only was the regularity and repetitiveness of Nicholas's daily routine mirrored in his diary, but this routine also left an indelible imprint on his outlook and behavior. In reading page after page of this diary, especially the parts dealing with Nicholas's youth, the reader is overwhelmed by boredom and monotony. This routine must have had the same stupefying impact on the writer. Virtually unrelieved by any critical thought, interesting insights, or engaging observations, the daily pattern rarely varied. Even the diary's language is repetitive, as we encounter identical expressions and qualifiers, the same stock phrases. This is not to suggest that the daily life of a more ordinary youth would have been any less routinized or any more interesting—quite the contrary. But aside from the fact that the average youth did not grow up to become an autocrat and was not groomed to that end, it is unlikely that he would have recorded the details of his routine with the same pedantry and numbing regularity as did the heir to the Russian throne.

In adolescence as well as in later life, Nicholas was likely to list painstakingly the ordinary, everyday occurrences more often than any unusual happenings. While those routine events and their timing, such as getting up and going to bed, eating, studying, skating, and walking, may have had a special meaning for Nicholas that is not immediately apparent to today's reader, he himself did not explain their significance. In fact, he was not totally unaware of the irrelevance of many of his daily activities,

---

[6] Whether in fact Nicholas had to submit this log for inspection is not clear. While there is no direct evidence to support such a hypothesis, the use of abbreviations and euphemisms during his adolescence and his evident unwillingness to share his most intimate concerns with his diary suggest both a prudishness and certain doubts as to the confidentiality of his remarks.

[7] TsGAOR, f. 601, op. 1, d. 218 passim.

as this remarkable and strangely contradictory admission indicates: "The reason I am writing so briefly is because I have to get up early tomorrow morning, although I know, too, that it will be boring later to read these lines again."[8] In other words, he felt compelled to write in spite of the irrevelance of what he wrote. Routine had conditioned him to do so.

Nicholas's recordings of facts, then as well as later, rarely revealed any critical reflection. During his reign, for example, we encounter tantalizing references to meetings, audiences, reports, conversations, but we seldom learn what was said by whom, or how a particular decision came about. Substance and content were foresaken for the formal and superficial. Both as youth and as ruler, Nicholas was content to account for his use of time; *what* he did, said, and thought was far less important than *that* he did something, anything. The purpose of the diary was to prove that he had been busy or occupied—*zaniat*—the term Nicholas preferred above all others. In this sense, empty routine assumed real meaning for Nicholas; by shaping and dominating his life, it became the ultimate purpose of his existence. At the same time, its very monotony and superficiality bred a subliminal sense of boredom and alienation that came to undermine his interest in and identification with his role as tsarevich and future tsar.

The activity that most satisfied Nicholas was physical exercise. Almost every day he spent several hours outdoors, and he chafed under any restrictions from the weather or his schedule. In winter, Nicholas, together with his parents, the other children, and relatives, skated and sledded, shoveled snow, cleared ice, built snowmen and snow-mountains, engaged in snowball fights, or chopped and sawed wood. During the summer, they played ball, walked, rode, and fished. As he grew older, he went horseback riding or boated on the ponds of the imperial winter residence at Tsarskoe Selo or off the beach at the summer quarters in Peterhof. After learning to shoot a rifle at age fifteen, he became an avid huntsman. Apparently he derived particular pleasure from fencing, for each day that he fenced he marked with consecutive Roman numerals, a habit that started in 1885 and reached the number of 136 by January 1889.[9] This love for the outdoors and for physical exertion, acquired in early childhood, remained with Nicholas throughout his life. It gave rise to amateur meteorological studies and also accounts for the prominence,

---

[8] *Das Tagebuch des letzten Zaren* (Berlin, 1923), p. 57, November 27, 1891. I have used the published portions of Nicholas's diary in both their Russian and German variants, since these excerpts do not always coincide chronologically. As for the cited archival portions of his diary, most of these are not part of the public record. These citations are usually identified here by date rather than by page, because most pages bear multiple page numbers as a result of repeated archival repaginations.

[9] TsGAOR, f. 601, op. 1, d. 223; for the preceding, see d. 219–20 passim.

regularity, and detail of weather observations in his diary. One of the reasons he would find military life so appealing was the manifold opportunities it afforded for exercise. Physically and psychologically, Nicholas was simply dependent on these outdoor activities, which became an essential part of his daily routine and were recorded with exacting diligence.

Time spent outdoors was more than a relaxing diversion, however, more than a necessary complement to mental labors and indoor engagements. As an integral part of his daily routine, it became a purpose of Nicholas's life and thus at least as important as his official duties. In fact, this penchant for physical exercise made him resent his public responsibilities still more. There is even some indication that he viewed physical labor as the only worthwhile form of work, his official tasks and the mental effort involved being no more than vexing, worthless distractions. In his physical work of sawing wood, breaking up ice, shoveling snow, and digging up the ground, Nicholas felt that he was making a real contribution in which, as his clothing and occasional comments would suggest, he even went so far as to identify with other toilers of the land, the Russian peasants.

Nicholas's routine evolved strictly within the confines of the imperial family; his diary is very much a chronicle of this family life. He lunched regularly with his parents, younger siblings, and other relatives. He attended classes with his brother George. In the afternoons the children were joined by their first and second cousins on the skating rink and ball field, or they rode out with their mother, or took walks, shoveled snow, and sawed wood with their father. The evenings, too, were spent en famille, be it at home or at the theater. Trips abroad invariably involved large family reunions.

If the frequency with which the word *semeistvo* (extended family) crops up on virtually every page of his diary is any indication, the family was very important to Nicholas. It not only gave him comfort and security, but also provided a collective identity that overshadowed his own individual identity. Instead of the first person singular "I" he often used the plural "we" to describe many of his childhood activities, which always included his brother George. In addition to countless military reviews and other official engagements, Nicholas faithfully recorded each of his father's hunts with precise data on what and how much they bagged. Clearly, his interest in his parents' goings and doings was as much vicarious as it was a sign of his filial attachment and devotion.

The family sphere was identical with Nicholas's world. It defined his horizons to such an extreme degree that he resented any intrusion or reminder of another, less familiar, more public world. With evident impatience he repeatedly mentioned people who held up his father with their official reports.[10] On one occasion he was annoyed with a visiting German prince who dared to interrupt the family get-together celebrating the birthday of his maternal grandfather, the Danish king.[11]

The fact that many official obligations and functions were performed within the family context made it possible to ignore their public character and political implications. Foreign state visitors, many of whom were close or distant relatives or their personal emissaries, would be welcomed, feted, and seen off by the whole family. State visits abroad were largely family occasions marking christenings, weddings, anniversaries, and funerals of relations. Military reviews and maneuvers brought together younger and older family members. In short, being tsarevich or, for that matter, a tsar was very much a family affair.

Outside the family, the young heir was painfully shy at first. He developed headaches when he had to face some public function, such as his father's coronation in 1883, his first balls, or the celebration of his seventeenth birthday, during which he had to receive a Cossack delegation and answer many congratulatory telegrams.[12] Not infrequently he suffered nosebleeds as well. To be sure, after a time he did begin to relax and even enjoy those engagements that were strictly social and essentially private. Whereas in 1885 he was still praising his lucky stars whenever he did not have to attend a ball, two years later he was dancing up a storm at those same functions.[13] Yet headaches continued to beset him during his reign in periods of stress and strain. Moreover, long after assuming office, he often was so terrified of speaking in public that he would forget the text of his remarks in mid-speech.

Nicholas's confinement to the family sphere made him a poor judge of people. His diary conveys the impression that he was growing up in a rather small, closed circle consisting of relatives and a few friends from the military and from families close to the court. They constantly saw each other during meals, indoor games and outdoor activities, visits, balls, birthdays, and anniversaries. These social situations were the primary and sole focus of their lives. Nicholas did not choose these persons as his friends and social partners; instead they were chosen for him by virtue of their birth. During his own reign, many of the people at court who were personally close to Nicholas and his family came from that very group or had been his parents' friends. By contrast, some of the individuals whom Nicholas and Alexandra themselves chose stand out for their very lack of high birth and positive qualities.

The heir's social isolation and sheltered upbringing narrowly circum-

[10] TsGAOR, f. 601, op. 1, d. 217 passim.
[11] TsGAOR, f. 601, op. 1, d. 221.
[12] TsGAOR, f. 601, op. 1, d. 218; d. 220, May 6, 1885, July 28, 1885, and passim.
[13] TsGAOR, f. 601, op. 1, d. 221, January 1887.

scribed his world. Even when Nicholas was able to venture beyond the family sphere, he usually did so in the company of attendants and guards, effectively barred from real contact with the outside world. Hence he was delighted to be able to walk through the streets of a large town without such restrictions, as happened in Denmark in 1887 for the first time in his life; he and his two cousins simply took the train into Copenhagen and went window-shopping. When he and relatives did the same thing without even being recognized, during a brief visit to Sweden, he was utterly amazed.[14] At home, where tradition and caution dictated otherwise, such direct exposure to the public was out of the question. The arrest of five "scoundrels," found with dynamite charges on them as Nicholas was accompanying his father to a service commemorating the sixth anniversary of his grandfather's assassination, served as a vivid reminder of the dangers facing them in public. The nineteen-year-old heir was horrified: "During this time something terrible could have happened, but through God's kindness everything went well."[15] So impressed was he by the danger from which they had escaped that he made a particular point of noting the occasion on which his father rewarded the secret police agents, who were responsible for the arrest of the alleged student terrorists, with "medals and awards, fine fellows." As for the arrestees, there was no doubt in Nicholas's mind that they were guilty.[16]

In the absence of any direct evidence, we can only imagine the trauma suffered by the twelve-year-old in confronting the bomb-torn body of his grandfather, Alexander II, in 1881. This fear of terrorism and hostile social forces was certainly very real and not altogether unfounded. For years Alexander III and his family lived as virtual prisoners in their palaces outside of the capital; thus the young heir grew up physically cut off from the real world to a greater degree than any of his predecessors. As the physical dangers and barriers reinforced the social isolation and private orientation of his youth, the temptation was great to identify this narrow world with reality and to mistake it for the whole world.

So sheltered was this environment, so limited was Nicholas's outward horizon and introspection, that we find scarcely a hint of his being the future tsar. Nicholas was fifteen years old at the time of his father's coronation in 1883, but we look in vain for any diary comments reflecting the significance of the event or any realization that he would be the next ruler to be crowned. Except for the occasional headache, the coronation was essentially good, clean fun allowing Nicholas and his relatives to see some exciting places.[17] Nor did this awareness intrude as he grew older.

[14] Ibid., August 25, 1887.
[15] Ibid., March 1, 1887.
[16] Ibid., March 9, 1887.
[17] TsGAOR, f. 601, op. 1, d. 218, May 23, 1883.

Such lack of maturity and introspection might not be that unusual or noteworthy for a fifteen-year-old lad; it does come as somewhat of a surprise, however, when encountered at a later age. Many of his pursuits and reactions remained those of a child. At the age of seventeen he was still taking drawing lessons and painting birthday, name-day, and other gifts for his parents.[18] During a visit to Denmark at this time, we find the tsarevich hiding under the beds of his English cousins to scare them. He and his friends continued corresponding in secret codes and vanishing ink. Two years later *Schnitzeljagd*—a game in which the "prey" would leave a trail of paper for the "hunters" to follow—was still very much in vogue.[19] Even then the favorite pastime of Nicholas and his young dinner companions was to bombard each other with bread pellets at the dinner table.[20] The clique of cousins and friends that gathered daily in early 1890 for tea, gossip, and outdoor games went under the name "potato"; words like "tussling" and "chasing about" described their daily get-togethers.[21] In November 1892, during a visit to his ailing brother George in the Caucasus, Nicholas wrote to his mother that they "were overcome by awful fits of laughter, we simply couldn't stop," as they listened to lectures by several professor-astronomers.[22] Clearly, the closed family atmosphere and continued peer association prolonged Nicholas's childhood and retarded his maturation.

PUBLIC DUTY, PRIVATE FEELINGS

Unabashed sentimentality as well as genuine affection and devotion characterize the relationships between Nicholas, his parents, and younger siblings. He quite obviously adored his father. He prized the time that Alexander III managed to wrest from his official schedule in order to lead the children in their outdoor activities, and he recorded with unconcealed glee how his father kept smashing the palace windows during their ball games.[23] Yet the omnipotence and majesty of Alexander's position, the burdens of his duties, and his imposing, not to say overbearing, physical presence combined to make him a more remote person than the tsarina. It was Nicholas's mother who seems to have been responsible for raising him and his younger brothers and sisters. Nicholas was deeply attached to his mother, as their lifelong correspondence reveals; whenever Maria Fedorovna and her eldest son were separated, they wrote to

[18] TsGAOR, f. 601, op. 1, d. 220 passim.
[19] TsGAOR, f. 601, op. 1, d. 221 passim.
[20] *Tagebuch des letzten Zaren*, p. 36, March 15, 1890.
[21] TsGAOR, f. 601, op. 1, d. 224, January–March 1890.
[22] *The Letters of Tsar Nicholas and Empress Marie* (London, 1937), pp. 68–69.
[23] TsGAOR, f. 601, op. 1, d. 220 passim.

each other regularly and at length. Apparently Nicholas and his father never corresponded. Though Nicholas's letters before his accession rarely ventured beyond family life or descriptions of maneuvers and the weather, they depict their author as an obedient son who always deferred to his parents' wishes.

Nicholas's letters, like his diary, betrayed no cognizance of his present and future roles, whereas his mother's epistles occasionally did. As he grew older, she reminded him that he and his actions were subject to constant public scrutiny. Therefore he was not to behave in public as he pleased, but as his public duties demanded. When he left for his first military summer camp at the age of nineteen, she admonished him: "Never forget that everyone's eyes are turned on you now, waiting to see what your own first *independent* steps in life will be." And she added these words of advice: "Always be polite and courteous with everybody, see that you get along with all your comrades without discrimination, although without too much familiarity or intimacy, and *never* listen to flatterers."[24] Nicholas's promise to heed her advice missed the point: "I will always try to follow your advice, my dearest darling Mama. One has to be cautious with everybody at the start."[25] Oblivious to the particular implications of his elevated position as heir, he instead embraced caution and suspicion as a universally applicable rule of conduct.

During Nicholas's eight-month world cruise from October 1890 until June 1891, the world received its first close impression of the future tsar. Maria Fedorovna seemed more mindful of this fact than Nicholas himself. With growing misgivings she noted that her son's travel accounts were preoccupied with personal pleasure. Revealing a disturbing lack of awareness of his public responsibilities, he objected to anything that might interfere with his enjoyment. In India where Nicholas was the guest of the British viceroy he had to endure his mother's criticism:

> I quite see that the balls and other official doings are not very amusing, espe-
> cially in that heat, but you must understand that your position brings this with
> it. You have to *set your personal comfort* aside, be doubly polite and amiable
> and, above all, never show you are bored. You will do this, won't you, my dear
> Nicky. At balls you must consider it your duty to *dance more* and *smoke less* in
> the garden with Vladimir Grigorievich and the officers just *because it is more
> amusing*. One simply cannot do this, my dear, but I know you understand all
> this *so well*, and you know my only wish is that *nothing* can be said against you,
> and for you to leave a good impression with everybody everywhere![26]

[24] *Nicholas-Marie Letters*, p. 32.
[25] Ibid., p. 34.
[26] Ibid., p. 47.

Conceived as his public debut, the world tour brought the Tsarevich face-to-face with the conflict between private pleasure and public duty. Quite obviously Nicholas chafed under this dichotomy and even managed to elicit sympathy from his mother; thus she was glad that he could at least savor his visit on the island paradise of Ceylon, without "being hampered by receptions and other official functions which so often spoil one's enjoyment of a voyage like yours." Yet she was quick to remind her almost twenty-three-year-old son of his duty. Softening her admonition by using the more childlike, less confrontational third-person singular, she wrote: "I hope my Nicky will do everything to be friendly and charming with everybody and will be ready to carry out his personal duties *even* if they are *boring* at times." Then, more emphatically, she added: "This *must* be done as a duty, and you know how to do it *well* if you want to."[27] No matter how onerous the obligation or painful the interruption of personal pleasure, a sense of duty was to compel Nicholas to carry out his responsibilities.

Maria Fedorovna, too, experienced the tug between the summons of public duty and of private feelings. If her well-intentioned advice sought to instill in her eldest son such a sense of duty, she herself undermined these efforts through her own possessive and protective maternal instincts. As a mother she found it hard to let Nicholas pass out of her constant care; her letters betrayed her misery and anguish whenever she was separated from him. Their farewells, no matter how short-lived, were inevitably tearful, her letters full of references to how much she missed her "dear Nicky." She was beside herself with sorrow and anxiety during the world cruise of her two oldest boys:

> The impression of the painful parting . . . weighs on my mind like a horrible nightmare. It was too awful! I cannot think of it without tears, and your dear face, so sad and bathed in tears, is constantly before my eyes, although your tears made me happy and soothed my suffering heart; for some reason I had imagined you were not very sorry to leave us, so that seeing your deep and acute grief I was almost pleased, for this at least reassured me and was balm to my heart.

She imagined him everywhere, even hearing his footsteps and expecting him to enter—only to be disappointed every time.[28] Naturally, the grave illness that forced her son George to abandon the tour and the assault by a saber-wielding Japanese fanatic on Nicholas only compounded her fears and worries. Although Nicholas escaped serious injury thanks to the timely intervention of his Greek cousin George, he was ordered to break

[27] Ibid., pp. 53, 57–58.
[28] Ibid., p. 42.

off his visit immediately and return home by way of Siberia. So impatient was the empress for her son's return that she asked him to shorten his intended stay in Uralsk: "What are you going to do there for so long? It is not too far—you could always return there another time."[29] The pangs of her maternal heart here prevailed over any considerations of duty.

Maria Fedorovna's evocation of duty, moreover, had a rather hollow ring, preoccupied as it was with ceremonial, often purely social, tasks and responsibilities. The empress, in appealing to her son's sense of duty, was concerned above all with external appearance and impressions. From her point of view, the way others should or might perceive Nicholas's actions was more important than the actions themselves. This formal conception of duty is evident throughout her written exhortations, as, for example, in her reaction to the possibility that Prince George of Greece might accompany Nicholas on the Siberian leg of their world tour:

> It would be nice for you to have his company in your *free* moments, but don't let him play his little jokes in front of *others* or do things that might shock people, because *you* must remember what you represent, and I don't want the *smallest* thing to be held up against you. So you must impress on him quite *seriously* not to play the clown there. I am sure you understand, my beloved Nicky, all this really means a lot to me. On board ship it was quite different. You were, so to speak, all more or less among yourselves; but in *Siberia* it is *official*, and you must not forget that for a moment. Think how *many eyes* are turned on you.[30]

Reminders such as these posited a dichotomy between private and public behavior and thus heightened Nicholas's anxiety and misgivings concerning official functions. In private he could act as unrestrainedly, childishly, and willfully as he pleased, but in public he was to conform with the accepted norms of propriety and with the expectations of a future ruler. Under the watchful gaze of his audience he was to act the role that was his by reason of birth, regardless of whether or not it accorded with his own preferences and needs. This stress on appearances engendered a spirit of dishonesty and dissimulation, since Nicholas simply had to go through the motions of his public role—without internalizing it, however. The obvious danger was that such a performance would be less than convincing, both to himself and to his audience, i.e., his entourage and Russian society.

Maria Fedorovna, a woman of royal blood, whose own upbringing undoubtedly had centered on the issue of propriety and appearance and whose duties as empress were largely formal, can hardly be faulted for

[29] Ibid., p. 64.
[30] Ibid., p. 58.

subscribing to a formal notion of duty. Furthermore, considerations of propriety, external appearances, and perceptions were indeed of crucial importance, and Nicholas was well advised to take to heart his mother's insistent admonishments. Many of the tsar's responsibilities would be strictly formal, and ritual was a vital aspect of kingship. But it was not the only one, nor could it be effective without the emotional content and message that derived from the ruler's identification with the ritual role. Maria Fedorovna's conception of duty equated the performance of ceremonial functions and trivial official tasks with the fulfillment of duty. Once Nicholas had been conditioned to conform dutifully to formal standards and external expectations, even if these conflicted with his internal feelings, the execution of formal routine and the observance of formal conventions would come to be the exclusive source of meaning in his existence.

Duty, as implied by his mother's definition, was something alien that had been imposed by fate; one therefore had no choice but to submit. The more onerous the task, the more acute the conflict with one's private predilections and hence the more pronounced the personal sense of alienation from the burdens of office, the more this notion was confirmed. At the same time, the very superficiality of this concept, which commanded and justified the execution of the most trivial and formal chores, was bound to aggravate this alienation and rule out any meaningful identification with the role that required such duties. Such an understanding at once appealed and contributed to Nicholas's fatalism; he tended to see himself as the object or victim of fate—a view encouraged, incidentally, by basic tenets of Russian Orthodoxy which came to assume still greater significance in his later life.

The exclusive emphasis on formal behavior and appearances that helps account for the shortcomings and idiosyncrasies of Nicholas's upbringing cannot be blamed on his mother alone. Instead, it bespoke the absence of real power and substantive responsibility that was the fate of any heir to the Russian throne, not just Nicholas's. His father, the autocrat, was by definition all-powerful. As God's anointed and the symbol of Russia's greatness, he towered in his majesty and splendor over his subjects, including his own son and heir. Like these other subjects, the son was utterly powerless. He felt simultaneously drawn to and kept distant from his father. As son he sought to emulate and to identify with his father, yet as his heir and inferior he was not permitted to do so. He might even become a father himself, yet could not take his father's place as the omnipotent ruler or be like him, as long as the father was alive. At the same time, the son remained a potential rival, as history had demonstrated bloodily on several occasions; hence the father's need to keep the son out of positions of real power and real responsibility and to prevent him from feeling equal to the task. This need had to be balanced, however, against the indisputable necessity of preparing the heir for his future role, when he would exercise the same unlimited power and responsibility that his father now possessed.[31]

As a result, the heir's training tended to stress the external, ceremonial elements of the autocratic role, without entrusting him with any real measure of responsibility. This upbringing discouraged identification with and internalization of this role, and it acted to check any assertions of individual identity that might give rise to nonconformist values and conflicting political aspirations. Substituting external norms and group identities instead, the drawn-out socialization of his adolescence conditioned the tsarevich to submit to formal routine and convention, social isolation and parental fiat. This crude behaviorism precluded any independent choice—an essential prerequisite for the development of a firm individual identity. This process was all the more effective and insidious in Nicholas's case because it was not achieved by brute force and coercion, which might have provoked resistance and rebellion, but took place in an atmosphere abounding with sympathy, affection, and protection. For these very reasons Nicholas's upbringing and education did not differ markedly from that of his younger brothers, George and Michael, or of many other grand dukes, for that matter. He and George grew up in the same family environment, had the same friends and tutors, and ventured everywhere together until George's illness separated them.

Yet it was Nicholas alone who was tsarevich and faced a unique future. As his parents' oldest son, he had become the heir-apparent to his father—who at that time was still tsarevich—at the very moment of his birth.[32] By contrast, both his father and his great-grandfather Nicholas I had been grown men when they advanced into the immediate line of succession; they had spent their entire childhood and adolescence unencumbered by the awesome prospect of taking their father's place on the throne some day. In addition, Nicholas I's immediate predecessor had been his older brother Alexander I, not his father Paul, whom he hardly knew. The formation of their identities during childhood and adolescence had taken place undisturbed by the critical scrutiny and wide-ranging expectations, both private and public, that inevitably greeted an heir; their personality development was unhampered by the oppressive psychological conditions just described. Unlike Nicholas, moreover, all of his male forerunners since Peter III had become fathers and thus had a

[31] A similar argument is presented by Richard Wortman in his unpublished paper "Power and Responsibility in the Upbringing of the Nineteenth Century Russian Tsars."

[32] The Grand Duke Alexander was mistaken in blaming fate and medical negligence for making Nicholas the heir; the unfortunate "elder brother, a lusty infant named Alexander," had in fact been born a year after Nicholas; cf. *Once a Grand Duke*, p. 165.

chance to establish that part of their identity before ascending the throne.

From early childhood on Nicholas had to come to terms, consciously or not, with his singular, solitary, and uncertain destiny at a time when, as we shall see, autocracy and the autocrat's role were the focus of fundamental disagreements among the very adherents of the autocratic order. Even for an adult such an adjustment, i.e., the reconciliation of identity, personal needs, predilections, and values with the duties and requirements of the new role, whatever these might be, would have been problematical at best. This was all the more true for a maturing adolescent like the sensitive Nicholas, who, far from being a father himself, was still in the process of asserting his male sexuality and of affirming his independent individual identity. How could he possibly succeed, in Erik Erikson's words, in "convincing himself that he has *chosen* his past and is the *chooser* of his future"[33] under conditions that precluded such choice, stifled initiative and individual identity, consigned the boy to the protective ministrations of his mother, and made the normally threatening paternal presence a forbidding, emasculating one?

FORMAL EDUCATION AND PRACTICAL TRAINING

Nicholas's native intelligence and formal education, while not remarkable in themselves, far exceeded his father's; whether judged by historical precedent or contemporary standards, they were certainly sufficient for a future tsar. Instead of seeking to develop critical faculties, encourage self-assertion, or awaken and stimulate the quest for knowledge and truth, however, his studies were designed merely to impart the facts and teach the skills required of a ruler. According to one of his teachers, they were told to lecture, but not to ask any questions of the tsarevich.[34]

Like any youth in educated society, Nicholas was expected to be proficient in several languages. As soon as he had learned to read and write in Russian, he started to study English, French, and German, all of which he mastered. With the notable exception of German, these languages also were represented in his reading, though haphazardly and belatedly. In early 1882 his diary has him reading *Uncle Tom's Cabin*, in 1885 Jules Verne, Dickens, Tolstoi (*War and Peace*), Dostoevskii (*The Possessed*), the historians Karamzin and Solov'ev, as well as a number of

---

[33] Erik H. Erikson, *Young Man Luther. A Study in Psychoanalysis and History* (New York, 1958), pp. 113–14. Without examining the applicability to the Russian context of Erikson's model, which, as I have been reminded by Jan Goldstein at the University of Chicago, is both culture- and class-specific, I maintain that the evidence of Nicholas's own musings very much points to the dilemma painted so eloquently by Erikson.

[34] S. Iu. Witte, *Vospominaniia*, 3 vols. (Moscow, 1960), 3:59.

lesser-known authors; unfortunately, his own opinions and reactions remain a mystery. Nicholas's early schooling also included arithmetic, religion, drawing, and music. He was almost fifteen years old when he had his first lessons in physics and Russian history, followed by geography in 1885 and chemistry in 1887.[35]

The heir's introduction to the affairs of state began at age seventeen, when his education diverged for the first time from the usual training given to grand dukes and thus hinted at his future responsibilities. His legal studies with the procurator-general of the Holy Synod, K. P. Pobedonostsev, commenced in 1885 and were soon supplemented by Finance Minister N. Kh. Bunge's lectures on the basics of economics and state finance. These lessons elicited no reactions or comments in Nicholas's diary, which simply noted his "ministerial day" on Fridays.[36] By the time he first mentioned reading newspapers, Prince Meshcherskii's reactionary *Grazhdanin* (The Citizen) and Suvorin's conservative *Novoe Vremia* (The New Time), he was almost twenty-one years old.[37] Nicholas's diary leaves the reader with the definite impression that the tsarevich derived little joy and satisfaction from his studies and regarded them instead as unavoidable chores. On April 28, 1890, a week before his twenty-second birthday, he registered with evident relief the end of his formal education: "Today I concluded my studies finally and forever."[38]

If there was an exception to this apparent indifference—apart from his enthusiasm for all things military, which will be described shortly—it was to be found in his historical studies. There can be little doubt that the subject excited his interest. Like thousands of Russian students before him, Nicholas studied European history according to Ilovaiskii's textbooks, while Solov'ev's epic initiated him into the history of his own country.[39] Nicholas's readings in his spare time had a definite historical bent, too. He read "historical journals,"[40] and joined the Imperial Historical Society at the age of sixteen. His diary evinced great personal interest in the affairs and publications of this group, and he continued to take part in its sessions throughout his reign.[41]

The tsarevich impressed many of his contemporaries by his knowledge of historical facts and his recall of details concerning their own ances-

[35] For preceding, see TsGAOR, f. 601, op. 1, d. 217–21 passim.

[36] TsGAOR, f. 601, op. 1, d. 220, October 11, 1885; d. 221, January 9, 1887, March 6, 1887.

[37] TsGAOR, f. 601, op. 1, d. 223, January 1889.

[38] TsGAOR, f. 601, op. 1, d. 224.

[39] TsGAOR, f. 601, op. 1, d. 180, l. 17.

[40] *Tagebuch des letzten Zaren*, p. 26, January 26, 1890.

[41] TsGAOR, f. 601, op. 1, d. 220, February 18, 1885, and d. 221, February 23, 1887; "Dnevnik A. A. Polovtsova," *KA* 3 (1923): 121.

tors.[42] After his promotion to colonel in the Preobrazhensky Regiment and his appointment as commanding officer of its first battalion in late 1892, Nicholas arranged tours of historical places and monuments in St. Petersburg for small groups of his soldiers. By then Nicholas had formed some definite opinions about Russia's history. On one occasion he invited the historian S. F. Platonov to lecture on the history of the regiment; when Platonov praised Peter the Great as the great founder without equal before or since, his host is supposed to have voiced this objection, a criticism he would repeat subsequently: "Emperor Peter the Great, in clearing the cornfield of Russian life and eradicating the weeds, did not spare the healthy shoots. Not everything before Petrine Rus' was bad, not everything in the West was worth imitating. Empress Elizaveta Petrovna sensed that and, with the help of such a naturally gifted native as Razumovskii, she made some corrections."[43]

Although this view was far from original, it revealed a historical awareness that could be useful to a future ruler. The heir's teachers had good reason to encourage such a historical perspective and look towards tradition. History provided a collective identity which Nicholas readily embraced and assimilated; it established precedents and guideposts for future action. It is no coincidence that historians of Kliuchevskii's caliber were invited to participate in the 1905 reform commissions and that historical arguments played such a prominent role in their discussions. As Nicholas wrote to Queen Victoria two years after his accession, "history is one's real positive teacher" in politics.[44] Implicit in this view was the notion of historical laws that determined historical development independent of individual human efforts, thus limiting, if not denying, personal choice.

To the extent that one can speak of a consuming interest of Nicholas's, however, it was the military. From the very outset of his diary, military matters attracted his attention and elicited the most detailed observations of all. Whenever his father attended a military review, young Nicholas would be sure to list each participating regiment as well as the uniform he himself had worn. In spring he invariably noted the day that frigates and sailboats were refitted for the season. Military studies were the only subjects of his education he cared to describe; tactics lessons began in 1884, supplemented by artillery lessons the following year.[45] Even in

[42] "Zapiski F. A. Golovina," KA 19 (1926): 114–15.

[43] "Vospominaniia byvshago ofitsera Sv. Gv. Preobrazhenskago Polka i Minskago Gubernatora A. F. Girsa o svoikh vstrechakh s Gosudarem Imperatorom Nikolaem II," manuscript, Russian and East European Archive, Columbia University (REEACU), pp. 13–14.

[44] TsGAOR, f. 601, op. 1, d. 1111, l. 36.

[45] TsGAOR, f. 601, op. 1, d. 217–19 passim; d. 220, February 8, 1885.

adult life, his diary continued to express his fascination with military affairs.

Nicholas was genuinely ecstatic when he received his father's permission to begin his military service in 1887.[46] With his uncle, the Grand Duke Sergei, commanding the Preobrazhensky Regiment, Nicholas's first summer camp only added to his delight: "I am now happier than I can say to have joined the army, and every day I become more and more used to camp life." Writing to his mother, he then described at length his new quarters, daily regimen, and social life, all of which he relished.[47] After camp he joined the family for a visit to Denmark where he felt like "an officer on leave."[48] Nicholas's excitement was boundless when he was named an imperial aide-de-camp on the eve of his twenty-first birthday: "Was beside myself with joy," he exulted in his diary. From his point of view, the honor was definitely not an automatic or empty gesture.[49]

Nicholas's preoccupation with military matters was hardly unusual. It reflected the pervasive militarist spirit and ethos of the time. Given the large military component of the autocrat's role, moreover, military subjects figured prominently in the upbringing of the heir, as it did in that of all grand dukes. At the moment of birth the heir was named an honorary commander and member of numerous regiments and Cossack detachments. As a child he would wear the uniforms of these units. On name days and birthdays he received delegations of officers and enlisted men bearing gifts of icons, food, uniforms, and models. During parades and audiences he was exhibited to troops and officers. He grew up surrounded by military uniforms, and military functions crowded the family calendar. The emperor and his extended family had to take part in an unending series of parades, reviews, inspections, guard changes, troop arrivals and departures, changes of command, commissionings, flag presentations, blessings and services, salutes, maneuvers, regimental holidays and dinners, anniversaries of battles, weapons tests, christenings, and launchings. All grand dukes were expected to undergo military training and select a military career; a nonmilitary education in universities and institutes as well as civilian careers and appointments were proscribed by tradition. Outside of largely honorific positions in the arts, sciences, and charities and membership in the State Council, only posts related to military service were open to the male members of the imperial family.

Although Nicholas's upbringing and interests were very much in keeping with this tradition, the particular attraction that military life held for

[46] TsGAOR, f. 601, op. 1, d. 221, January 18, 1887.
[47] *Nicholas-Marie Letters*, p. 33, June 25, 1887.
[48] TsGAOR, f. 601, op. 1, d. 221, August 23, 1887.
[49] TsGAOR, f. 601, op. 1, d. 223, May 5, 1889.

him demands to be explored further. For the first time in his life, it would appear, he had himself chosen his own calling, when in fact traditional expectations and his militarist conditioning had merely created an illusion of choice. By providing a group identity and collective security, military life compensated for the lack of a firm individual identity. He seized on that facet of his education that was the least unique part of the heir's upbringing, since it was shared by all male relations and did not prepare him for the exclusive, nonmilitary responsibilities of his future office. Indeed, by transcending the family context, the universality of military life erased, or at least obscured, the distinction of being the heir and thus allowed him to escape its onerous psychological implications. He was just another officer, and first and foremost an officer. Heretofore shy and ill at ease with strangers, Nicholas enjoyed the company of his fellow officers: the camaraderie and familiarity, social license and revelry, lack of inhibition and restraints. For the most part, this world was also functioning smoothly. Based on an easily understood hierarchy of command and obedience and comprised of externally defined relationships and norms, this carefree order was appealingly devoid of psychological dilemmas and moral choices. Duties and responsibilities were narrowly circumscribed and largely formal. Nicholas was free to indulge his pedantic attention to detail and his penchant for appearances.

From the moment he entered military service at the age of nineteen until his accession, Nicholas very much led the life of a junior guards officer from a socially prominent and well-connected family, a life more remarkable for its social than its professional exploits. Military service was a way of life and a state of mind, rather than a purposeful activity. Nicholas savored this life to the extent that the restrictions and demands imposed by his other duties as tsarevich allowed. With these exceptions, his life revolved around parade grounds and riding rinks, camp life and maneuvers, balls, dinners and picnics, theater and ballet, smoking, drinking and hangovers, gambling gains and losses, controversial bachelor parties, balalaika orchestras, and gypsy dancers.[50]

Although indubitably genuine, Nicholas's interest in military affairs and his celebration of its social conventions betray elements of superficiality and unreality. His knowledge of military matters was dilettantish, his understanding of strategy and generalship woefully inadequate. Forever preoccupied with numbers and raw data and enchanted by inconsequential details, he failed to gain a comprehensive overview of any military activity. His vague diary entries are most revealing: "We executed some kind of avoidance maneuver," or "Confusion and running back and forth until the end!"[51]

[50] TsGAOR, f. 601, op. 1, d. 223–24, 226–31 passim.
[51] *Tagebuch des letzten Zaren*, pp. 37–47, especially p. 43, July 14, 1890, and p. 45, July 23, 1890.

The military exercises that elicited such muddled comments from Nicholas seemed populated by toy soldiers; they were mere interludes in the social life of the participating officers: a few moves and attacks which would be over after three hours, followed invariably by big dinners, theater performances, and spirited parties. Such a routine, with its anachronistic emphasis on parade-ground formation and formal appearance, may not have been unusual for a royal scion. Indeed, it was representative of military science, at least as practiced in Russia at the time. Still, Nicholas's reactions cast additional light on his mentality. Once again there is no hint of his future role as Russia's commander in chief. His outlook was that of an unaspiring junior officer content to follow rather than to lead. He willingly carried out orders but made no effort to understand the plans on which they were based. He went through tactical motions without any awareness of strategy or purpose. Passive experience substituted for active apprehension.

Nicholas's outlook as a military man was profoundly conservative. Typically, it was the trifling issue of uniforms which prompted him to reflect on the general question of innovation and reform. After inspecting new prototypes of Cossack uniforms and saddles on the thirty-first anniversary of the Emancipation—a coincidence of which he was unaware—the tsarevich wrote:

> Generally I oppose all such innovations and I cannot understand the addiction of our military to replacing practically tested results by new untested ones. In my opinion one must be above all conservative and try to preserve as long as possible old traditions and institutions; of course, that doesn't mean bringing back the gauntlet or flint rifles. No, there is a limit to everything.[52]

Clearly, he equated the preservation of forms and appearances with the maintenance of the status quo and the conservation of cherished traditions and institutions.

As a minor Nicholas evidently remained excluded from governmental business. While he participated in numerous official functions, such as the funeral of the German emperor Wilhelm I in March 1888,[53] these were strictly ceremonial and included him in his capacity as officer and representative of the imperial family. Only with the official beginning of adulthood and the rendering of the prescribed loyalty oath to Alexander III on his twenty-first birthday did Nicholas become entitled to take part in the affairs of state. If he recognized the momentousness of this passage, he did not confide it to his diary. In contrast to the euphoria with which Nicholas greeted his simultaneous promotion as aide-de-camp, his appointment to the State Council and the Committee of Ministers, the

[52] Ibid., p. 73.
[53] TsGAOR, f. 601, op. 1, d. 222, March 3–4, 1888.

two highest and most important government institutions, was acknowledged the next morning without any emotion at all.[54]

Whereas the former appointment had had real meaning for the tsarevich, the latter two did not. From Nicholas's point of view, membership in the two government bodies was little more than a chore, an onerous obligation which took him away from his social life but could not be shirked. Although he attended regularly, he was far from unhappy when a session was canceled[55] and he did not have to read in advance the thick sheaves of papers that were prepared for each meeting. Once, after receiving a veritable mountain of such materials, Nicholas reacted in exasperation: "I simply do not understand how one can manage to read such a mass of papers in one week. I constantly limit myself to one or two of the most interesting matters, but the rest go straight to the fireplace."[56]

Nicholas's membership in the two highest councils of the land was a formality devoid of real responsibility or authority. Above all, it was a training exercise designed to acquaint him with the workings of these two institutions and their members. There certainly is no evidence to suggest that he or others viewed his new duties in any other light. Conceivably, he might have played a more active part in the deliberations of those two august bodies, but the fact is that he did not nor was he expected to do so. He remained a passive participant, an onlooker who refrained from taking a position in the actual proceedings and who reserved his occasional observations, mostly brief and general, for his diary.[57]

The problems discussed evidently failed to stir the tsarevich's imagination. They neither awakened his interest in state affairs nor encouraged any reflection about his future role in government. Instead, his own lack of authority, when combined with the mounds of paperwork and the nature of the agenda, merely confirmed in Nicholas's eyes the onerousness of his task. Thus, practical experience not only failed to overcome his lack of identification with his official duties, but also served to compound it. He resented the interference of these obligations with his private life; for example, after being forced to commute between Tsarskoe Selo and St. Petersburg for several days in a row, he complained: "I must admit that this is an ordeal in its own right which is beginning to wear me out very much. . . . By evening I had sunk into a virtual stupor as a result of these constant trips from one place to another."[58]

The world tour on which Nicholas embarked in late October 1890 was part of his preparation for his future responsibilities in state affairs. He

[54] TsGAOR, f. 601, op. 1, d. 223, May 6, 1889.
[55] TsGAOR, f. 601, op. 1, d. 224, January 29, 1890.
[56] TsGAOR, f. 601, op. 1, d. 227, December 15, 1891.
[57] *Tagebuch des letzten Zaren*, p. 36, April 24 and May 28, 1890.
[58] TsGAOR, f. 601, op. 1, d. 227, December 18, 1891.

was not at all eager to leave his family, friends, and familiar surroundings. After learning of the plan from his father on January 7, 1890, Nicholas thought about it the whole day, and when shown a preliminary schedule for the ten-month cruise, he groused: "That's too much."[59] As much as he dreaded his departure, the pain of parting was eased by the fact that he found himself in the company of his brother George and several friends and fellow officers. He could also look forward to joining up with a number of relatives en route. The very composition of his entourage and itinerary demonstrates the representational and 'apolitical' character of his journey; shunning Germany, France, England, and the United States, the voyage would take them from Greece to the English and French colonial possessions in Egypt, India, Ceylon, and Indochina, as well as to Japan. Having visited Scandinavia, Germany, France, and England on earlier trips, Nicholas was simply to be shown other parts of the world. The primary purpose of this cruise was not to conduct concrete government business but to promote a sense of duty in Nicholas, test his social skills, broaden his horizons, and heighten his awareness of Russia's international position.

On all these counts Nicholas's diary remains silent. Limiting himself to cursory listings of trivial routine and bare facts, such as the details of tropical weather and tiger hunts, he exhibited little fascination with the numerous new sights and impressions. As they sailed eastward, he liked each new country better than the preceding one. Egypt and India were his least favorite—"It's unbearable to be surrounded once again by Englishmen and to see their red uniforms everywhere"[60]—while Japan elicited the most favorable reactions, the attempt on his life notwithstanding.[61]

Nicholas was touched by the reception that awaited him in Siberia after he had survived the attack in Japan. He was the first member of the imperial family to visit this part of the Empire in many years. Making his way back to European Russia by coach and train, Nicholas was greeted enthusiastically everywhere by military and civilian administrators, Cossack and army units, railroad workers and the local population. The affection of "all the workers and Chinese, too," who ran alongside his train,

---

[59] TsGAOR, f. 601, op. 1, d. 224, January 8 and March 16, 1890.

[60] *Tagebuch des letzten Zaren*, p. 59.

[61] TsGAOR, f. 601, op. 1, d. 225 passim. In his memoirs (*Vospominaniia*, 1:439–40) Witte would later claim—unconvincingly—that the attack in Japan instilled in Nicholas a deep-seated antipathy, even hatred, towards the Japanese, which proved a fertile medium for the suggestions of those favoring expansionist policies in the Far East. Witte also contends that the world tour as a whole had a tragic influence on Nicholas's reign, giving him an exaggerated notion of his own future role and its greatness and leaving him preoccupied with the East and Far East as opposed to the Balkans and the West.

moved him; he also remembered with particular fondness the "unceremoniousness" of Cossack farmers on the Chinese border.[62] The spontaneity and simplicity of his future subjects, in marked contrast to the stiff protocol and reserve that he had just encountered on his journey abroad, made a lasting impression on the tsarevich. These scenes, moreover, gave visual expression to the personal bond between the ruler and his people, providing Nicholas with an ideological reference point for the future.

Within months after his return, Nicholas's official duties were further extended. On November 17, 1891, Alexander III appointed him to the chairmanship of the Special Committee on Famine Relief, which had been established to deal with the devastating effects of recent crop failures.[63] Three months later Nicholas became a member of the Finance Committee. While his reaction to this second appointment was almost predictable—"A great honor, but little satisfaction. . . . I must admit I never even suspected its existence"[64]—this lack of enthusiasm may have stemmed more from his ignorance of the highly technical and complex questions of state finance than from any general hostility towards his new duties. These included, by February 1893, the chairmanship of the Special Committee that was to supervise construction of the Trans-Siberian Railroad, a post to which he allegedly was appointed on Finance Minister Witte's recommendation and in which he revealed himself to be a quick and interested student.[65]

Undoubtedly Nicholas took his new responsibilities seriously and even derived some satisfaction and sense of accomplishment from them, despite occasional annoyances. Indeed, in his capacity as head of famine relief Nicholas displayed considerable enthusiasm for the proceedings and affairs of his committee. He was appalled by the extent of popular suffering. His diary contains greater detail about the decisions and sessions of this body than about any of his previous official activities. Although he presided—not without initial trepidation—over each meeting, he did not take active charge of his committee. Instead, he relied heavily on and consulted frequently with Assistant Minister of Internal Affairs Pleve. Nicholas was a thorough and attentive student of the papers prepared for the committee's sessions, and he did not hesitate to speak his mind on occasion. One of his first recorded comments is revealing for its suspicion of established institutions and officials, and for its reliance on

[62] TsGAOR, f. 601, op. 1, d. 226, May 28, 1891.

[63] *Tagebuch des letzten Zaren*, p. 75. The original rescript is in TsGAOR, f. 601, op. 1, d. 812.

[64] TsGAOR, f. 601, op. 1, d. 227, February 25, 1892.

[65] Witte, *Vospominaniia*, 1:434–36.

trusted individuals who were to be dispatched to the suffering provinces in order to ascertain needs and verify deliveries.[66]

No matter how diligent and conscientious Nicholas tried to be, however, the novelty of his assignments, which had helped fuel his interest and the short-lived prolixity of his diary, soon began to wear off. By late 1893 and 1894 the various sessions of the Siberian Railroad, Famine, and Finance Committees as well as those of the State Council and Committee of Ministers had become integral parts of his daily routine. Apart from vague references to excessively long, boring, or, on occasion, important and interesting sessions and apart from information on their duration, Nicholas rarely revealed what was discussed.[67] Other, more important concerns were on his mind.

LOVE AND MARRIAGE

Like any self-respecting young officer, Nicholas had a mistress, the ballerina Mathilda Kshesinskaia. He had met her during a graduation performance and dinner of her Imperial Ballet School class on March 23, 1890.[68] That year he repeatedly watched her perform at the summer theater in Krasnoe Selo as well as on stage in St. Petersburg. As he confided to his diary two years after he first made her acquaintance, he "fell passionately in love (platonically) with little K." during the 1890 summer camp.[69] The romance did not really flourish, however, until he returned from his world cruise in mid-1891. By the spring of 1892 Nicholas was seeing the ballerina almost daily, often visiting her and her sister at home: "Our conversations are happy and animated! I really enjoy these meetings."[70] Then travels and various commitments intervened, but their relationship survived. "She has become still prettier and I like her still more," he wrote on January 4, 1893. His regular visits resumed, rarely ending before five or six o'clock in the morning. His diary entry of January 25, 1893, was euphoric: "In the evening I flew to M. K. and spent the best evening with her to date. As I am under her spell—the pen trembles in my hand!" When the two Kshesinskaia sisters moved to their own comfortable two-story house on the English Quay the following month, the liaison appears to have reached its climax. Hardly a day passed without Nicholas visiting the house he liked so much. After

[66] *Tagebuch des letzten Zaren*, pp. 75–76, November 22 and 29, 1891; D. N. Liubimov, "Russkaia smuta nachala deviatisotykh godov. 1902–1906. Po vospominaniiam, lichnym zapiskam i dokumentam," manuscript, REEACU, p. 83.

[67] TsGAOR, f. 601, op. 1, d. 231 passim.

[68] TsGAOR, f. 601, op. 1, d. 224, March 23, 1890.

[69] TsGAOR, f. 601, op. 1, d. 228, April 1, 1892.

[70] Ibid., April 16, 1892.

spending the time with her alone or with her sister and their friends and returning home only at sunrise, he would exult: "Spent the night ideally."[71]

As passionately as he may have felt about the ballerina, Nicholas never entertained the thought of marrying her. She was clearly his mistress and not a potential bride. It was this fact which sanctioned their intimate involvement. The word "platonically," which Nicholas used to describe his relationship with the younger Kshesinskaia, signalled a lack of serious intentions on his part rather than a want of sexual intimacy. In fact, even before his first meeting and throughout his romance with Kshesinskaia, his diary bore witness to his frustrated affection for Princess Alix of Hesse, the granddaughter of Queen Victoria. There is absolutely no truth to the long-standing and near-universal contention that Nicholas's parents were so concerned about his amorous dalliances with the ballerina that they sent him on the world tour; that decision was made a full two months before his very first meeting with Kshesinskaia.

Despite occasional flirtations and his affair with Kshesinskaia, marriage to a Russian woman, aristocrat or commoner, was out of the question.[72] Nicholas understood that as heir to the throne he would have to marry a woman belonging to a foreign ruling house. As a teenager he had had a mad crush on the British Princess Victoria and had exchanged countless letters with her; this correspondence continued long after both had found spouses. Nicholas's interest in Alix was first aroused in 1887 during a family reunion in Denmark, and it had grown perceptibly by the time she visited St. Petersburg for six weeks in January–February 1889. Upon her arrival he observed how she had matured and become even more beautiful since their last meeting. His mood during this visit oscillated sharply[73]; he was anxious whether his love was reciprocated. As Nicholas would explain two years later, Alix's stay had only deepened his affection and left him determined to marry her: "My dream—to get married one day to Alix of Hesse."[74]

There were two serious obstacles, however: the possibility of her engagement to the Duke of Clarence, oldest son of the Prince of Wales, and her unwillingness to convert to Russian Orthodoxy as required by law.

[71] TsGAOR, f. 601, op. 1, d. 229, January 4, 1893; d. 230, January 25, February 20, and March 13, 1893, and passim.

[72] TsGAOR, f. 601, op. 1, d. 223 passim; *Tagebuch des letzten Zaren*, p. 27, February 4, 1890.

[73] TsGAOR, f. 601, op. 1, d. 223: "neither sad nor happy"—January 18, 1889; "angry"—January 25, 1889; "heavy- and empty-hearted"—January 31, 1889; "particularly gay"—February 10, 1889; "very excited"—February 14, 1889; "headache"—February 16, 1889; "melancholic"—February 27, 1889.

[74] TsGAOR, f. 601, op. 1, d. 227, December 21, 1891.

By December 1891 the first stumbling block had ceased to exist, as Alix had not proved receptive to the Duke. In fact, it appears that Nicholas's love had struck a responsive chord: "I am almost convinced that our feelings are mutual," he wrote. Yet the intractable issue of religion loomed ever larger: "the only obstacle or chasm between her and me is the question of religion."[75] As early as July 1890 he had discussed this matter with his father.[76] Evidently Alix let it be known that she was unwilling to abandon her Protestant faith. Alexander III, on the other hand, refused to suspend the requirement. A year and a half later, Nicholas would write: "since then nothing has changed, either for better or for worse." There was little left to do but pray: "Everything according to God's will! Relying on His Mercy I calmly and obediently anticipate the future."[77]

From a dynastic as well as the personal point of view of Nicholas's parents, the dim marital prospects of the twenty-three-year-old tsarevich became a source of growing concern. There is no evidence whatsoever to substantiate the widespread contention that Alexander III and Maria Fedorovna so disliked the Hessian princess that they refused to agree to the match, and relented only when the tsar's declining health left them no other choice.[78] Had the parents really disapproved of Alix, Nicholas most certainly would have heeded their wishes, however reluctantly. If his parents began to intimate other possibilities, they did so not because they disliked Alix but because the chances of her consent did not look bright. Thus in early 1892 Maria Fedorovna hinted at Hélène, daughter of the Count of Paris. Nicholas, according to his own admission, found himself in "a strange position" at a "crossroads," wanting to go one way, his mother "apparently" another. "What will happen?"[79]

Nicholas was confused. While he was very much in love with Alix and still hoped to marry her some day, he also had found daily joy and diversion in his affair with Mathilda Kshesinskaia, which by now was in full bloom. Indeed, the very bleakness of his marriage prospects might have made him turn to the ballerina with even greater enthusiasm and energy. This circumstance in turn might have prompted his parents to look around for other suitable candidates. Whatever the case may be, the tsarevich was puzzled by his own contradictory sensations: "I never imagined that two identical feelings, two loves simultaneously could coexist in one's soul. . . . Our heart is a wondrous thing!"[80]

[75] Ibid.

[76] TsGAOR, f. 601, op. 1, d. 224, July 22, 1890.

[77] TsGAOR, f. 601, op. 1, d. 227, December 21, 1891; d. 228, May 6, 1892.

[78] Cf., for example, S. S. Oldenburg, *Last Tsar. Nicholas II, His Reign and His Russia*, trans. Leonid I. Mihalap and Patrick J. Rollins (Gulf Breeze, Fla., 1975), 1:39.

[79] *Dnevnik Imperatora*, p. 25, January 29, 1892.

[80] TsGAOR, f. 601, op. 1, d. 228, April 1, 1892.

Undiminished by his "platonically" passionate affair with the ballerina, his love for Alix endured. More than a year later he discussed with an aunt the possibility of meeting with Alix again. He went to Denmark, but apparently nothing came of it. By late fall 1893 he heard from Alix that she could not change her faith. Nicholas's hopes appeared to have been shattered:

> Before this inexorable obstacle all my hope, my very best dreams, and most sacred desires for the future come tumbling down. Only recently it still seemed bright and tempting and even within close reach—but now it appears indifferent!!! Sometimes it is difficult, indeed, to submit to God's will! I walked around the whole day as if in a trance; it's awfully hard to appear calm and happy when the question of one's entire future life has been decided in this way and so suddenly.[81]

He began visiting Kshesinskaia again as a substitute for the permanent female companionship that had so far eluded him. As the old year of 1893 drew to a close, he wrote wistfully: "I personally had hoped to be a bachelor no longer. But everything is the will of only God Almighty!"[82] Miraculously, Nicholas's prayers were soon to be fulfilled.

Undaunted by Alix's letter of refusal, the two families had not given up on the idea of a match between Nicholas and Alix. It is not clear what happened in the three intervening months, but on April 2, 1894, we find Nicholas journeying to Germany to plead his case in person with the Hessian princess.[83] The formal occasion was the wedding of her brother, the Grand Duke Ernst Ludwig of Hesse, to Princess Victoria of Coburg-Gotha in Coburg. The celebrations attracted, among other visitors of royal blood, Alix's grandmother, Queen Victoria, and Alix's first cousin, Kaiser Wilhelm II. Nicholas was accompanied by three of his uncles, one of whom was married to Alix's older sister Elizabeth. Clearly, all favored the match and were determined to bring their persuasive powers to bear on the intended bride, whose religious loyalty so far had proven stronger than her personal regard for the tsarevich.

The morning after his arrival Nicholas went to talk to Alix in the presence of her brother Ernst Ludwig, an opportunity, Nicholas wrote, "for which I had very much longed for a long time, but which at the same time I had feared very much." She had become "extraordinarily beautiful, but she looked very sad." They talked for two hours. She cried a lot and persisted in her refusal to convert. When he saw her again the next day, he avoided the subject altogether. The fact that she was at all willing

---

[81] TsGAOR, f. 601, op. 1, d. 231, August 8 and November 18, 1893.
[82] Ibid., December 31, 1893.
[83] *Tagebuch des letzten Zaren*, pp. 78–79.

to meet and talk with him still left him hopeful.[84] Then came her brother's wedding day.

Finally, after another heart-to-heart talk on the following day, April 8, 1894, Alix relented—to everyone's relief. Nicholas's joy and rapture knew no bounds: "A beautiful, unforgettable day of my life. The day of my engagement to dear, beloved Alix. . . . O God, what a relief it was! What joy for dear Papa and dear Mama. The whole day I was as if in a trance, could not imagine what was happening to me."[85] Countless congratulatory telegrams poured in, church services, concerts, breakfasts, lunches, teas, and dinners followed, but above all Nicholas savored the time he could spend with his bride. Neither these social engagements nor the miserable weather could mar the idyllic happiness of the young couple. They strolled, visited, and wrote verses and comments in each other's diaries—something they would continue to do for the rest of their lives. When they finally had to bid farewell for six weeks, they commenced another lifelong custom of corresponding daily and intimately whenever separated.

Although Nicholas's daily routine back in St. Petersburg for the most part continued as of old, official concerns were not permitted to interfere with his newfound private bliss; his thoughts during this time were entirely given to his longing for Alix, to their correspondence, and to the anticipation of their reunion in June. With his parents' permission he spent five heavenly weeks in England, chaperoned by their Victorian "Granny" and numerous relatives.[86] Nicholas's diary celebrated their new relationship, chronicling every shared moment, no matter how trivial, and recording his feelings of joy and contentment. These pages also contain Alix's declarations of undying love, invocations of God's blessings, and whimsical verses in English, German, and French: "Love is caught. I have bound his wings, love! No longer will he roam or fly away. Within our two hearts forever love sings."[87] Even after his departure from England such homilies continued to grace Nicholas's diary, for his bride had taken care to enter them on the blank pages.

They utterly abandoned themselves to each other. Nicholas went so far as to confess all his past sins and transgressions to her, delivering himself into her mercy and forgiveness. She, in turn, was deeply touched:

What is past, is past and will never return. And we can look back on it with calm—we are all tempted in this world and when we are young, we cannot always fight and hold our own against the temptations, but as long as we repent

[84] Ibid., pp. 80–81, April 5–6, 1894.
[85] Ibid., p. 82, April 8, 1894.
[86] Ibid., pp. 91–107.
[87] Ibid., p. 106.

and come back to the good and straight path, God forgives us, if we confess our sins. He is faithful and just to forgive us our sins. God pardons those who confess their faults.[88]

Being frank and unburdening oneself had been elevated to sacraments of confession and repentance. Marital fidelity and faith, personal morals and religious beliefs had become indistinguishable. Both warranted the same feverish degree of intensity and ecstasy, as sexual and religious fervor merged. Invoking God's blessings, Alix prayed that "His Love caress you." "God" and "Love," both His and hers, recurred in the same breath, haunted at times by the strange image of death: "Ever true and ever loving, faithful, pure and strong as death."[89]

A sense of guilt born of deserting her deeply held Protestant faith, on the one hand, and of resisting Nicholas's entreaties for so long, on the other, inspired and cemented Alix's commitment. To the new faith and new relationship she brought the fanaticism and obsessive possessiveness of a religious convert. Her decision to marry Nicholas was the fruit of a religious experience, their marriage its continual reaffirmation. He as well as their children became the sole purpose of her earthly life. This preoccupation and the fact that she was a foreigner who was slow and hesitant to speak Russian contributed to her isolation at court.

Nicholas, in turn, was totally absorbed with Alix. After more than five years of nightly prayers,[90] of emotional peaks and valleys, wrenching anxiety and dashed hopes, his dream of marrying the Hessian princess was finally coming true. The endless frustration of his fondest wish had driven him further into his bride's arms; more importantly, it had intensified his private orientation and thus had accentuated his lack of identification with his public role. For the first time in his life Nicholas had made a choice and prevailed; henceforth his marital happiness was to be the primary focus of his existence. Nicholas and Alexandra were clearly intoxicated with and would grow ever more dependent on each other.

"THE DEATH OF A SAINT"

If anything could penetrate Nicholas's absorption in his newfound happiness, it was the growing concern for his father's physical condition. By August 1894 the tsarevich had returned home to attend the wedding of his sister Xenia and his cousin and childhood friend, the Grand Duke Alexander. As yet no definite plans had been made for his own wedding.

[88] Ibid., p. 104.
[89] Ibid., pp. 101, 103.
[90] This is what he confided to his mother on April 16, 1896; see *Nicholas-Marie Letters*, p. 114.

These arrangements depended in part on Alexander III's health. Throughout the summer of 1894 the tsar had looked and felt unwell, and the doctors had recommended a long rest in the drier Crimean climate. Unwilling to deviate from his established annual routine, however, Alexander had ignored his doctors' advice. He attended large military maneuvers and went to hunt in the imperial game preserve in Poland. His deteriorating state of health and the pleas of his family finally persuaded him to consult an eminent German specialist, who confirmed the earlier diagnosis of nephritis and urged that the patient be transferred immediately to the Crimea. Nicholas had little choice but to cancel his intended journey to Alix in Germany and accompany his family to Livadia, where they arrived on September 21.[91]

Nicholas's diary still betrayed little awareness of how serious his father's illness really was. If he was in a downcast mood at times, that had more to do with the separation from his bride and the disappointment of not receiving mail from her every day. Walks and climbs on the beach and in the gardens, rides on horseback and in carriages, swimming, dining, and music-making en famille formed the daily routine—a carefree idyll, had it not been for Alexander's worrisome health. Nicholas's Greek cousin and namesake Niki accompanied him on many of his excursions, and they staged fights in which they pelted each other with chestnuts and pine cones.

Two weeks after their arrival, the tsar's condition, which had already attracted five physicians, took a turn for the worse. Nicholas's parents allowed him to summon his fiancée to the Crimea. Nicholas's diary begins to read like a medical bulletin; he noted any changes in the patient's sleep pattern, appetite, appearance, behavior, and anxiously looked for the slightest sign of improvement. The next day, on October 6, the tsar for the first time let his oldest son see official papers and dispatches.[92] As other relatives started arriving, Nicholas continued to study government reports and papers.

Alix's arrival on October 10 made him feel as though half of his worry and sorrow had been taken from him. They spent all their waking moments with each other. They dined, walked, and prayed together. Nicholas attended to official business in her company, while she prepared herself for her first Orthodox communion. In his diary she assured him that God and she were always near him, especially at this time. She also exhorted him to have Alexander's physicians report directly to him with their findings and requests: "Be firm . . . see that you are the first always to know. . . . Don't let others be put first and you left out. You are Father

[91] *Tagebuch des letzten Zaren*, pp. 111–14.
[92] Ibid., pp. 115–17.

dear's son and must be told all and be asked about everything. Show your own mind and don't let others forget who you are. Forgive, my love."[93] He was the tsarevich and, with his father's condition steadily deteriorating, soon to be the new tsar. Nicholas, however, cared little for this, hoping instead—as was only natural—for a miraculous recovery.

Divine intervention must have been on his and everyone else's mind when the family attended a thanksgiving service to commemorate their miraculous escape during the railway disaster in Borki on October 17, 1888. The next day brought new trials as the family was awakened and called to Alexander's bedside. Later that morning Nicholas had to attend "a serious conference" at his Uncle Vladimir's; "horrible," he wrote. Undoubtedly, they discussed the imminence of death and the transfer of power: "The only hope is God's mercy; may His holy will be fulfilled." The daylight hours of October 19 appeared to offer new hope, but by evening the tsar had grown weaker still. As Alexander received oxygen to assist his labored breathing, the family spent the next morning at his bed. Around 2:30 in the afternoon he was given communion. The end came soon thereafter. "The death of a saint," his son was to write that day, "I felt as if I had been struck dead." Yet even at this moment of shock and grief, Nicholas did not forget his bride: "My precious Alix again had pains in her legs."[94] Her well-being was more on his mind than that of the country which he now ruled.

Nicholas's sorrow, as we observed at the outset, was overwhelming, his sense of loss excruciating. The yawning personal void was in part filled by his wife-to-be, whose love, sympathy, and encouragement was balm and solace for his pain. Nicholas realized that he was to take his father's place, both in private and on the public stage of Russia. Worse, he was expected to assume a role for which he felt unprepared and with which he could not identify. The sudden impact of this realization was traumatic.

So stunned was the new emperor that he acted almost as if nothing had changed. Seeking to escape into his own private world with Alix and deferring to his mother and uncles on family matters, he went through the motions of official routine and duties and clung desperately to the personnel and policies of his late father. In this sense, Nicholas's adaptation to his new position was purely formal or superficial—the result of the extensive conditioning and socialization of his youth, which had succeeded in containing his individuality as heir and which had prevented him from internalizing his future role.

On the second full day of Nicholas's reign, the imperial family dis-

---

93 Ibid., p. 121.
94 Ibid., pp. 121–22.

cussed the arrangements for his wedding. The day before Alix had officially converted to the Orthodox faith and henceforward was to be known as Alexandra Fedorovna. Nicholas, his mother, and a few others favored an immediate and quiet wedding while they all still were under the same roof with Alexander, whose body already had begun to decompose in the subtropical climate of the Crimea. All uncles were opposed, however; they wanted the wedding to take place in St. Petersburg after the funeral. "This to me seems completely inappropriate," Nicholas wrote. Three days later his uncles prevailed.[95]

The week following Alexander's death was filled with services, walks, receptions of arriving relatives, the answering of condolence telegrams, and the reading of official papers. Then the family accompanied Alexander's remains to Moscow where the coffin was exhibited in the Archangel Michael Cathedral. During the procession from the station to the Kremlin, Nicholas was cheered by the "exemplary order" of thousands upon thousands of troops and people. The Kremlin itself was full of pleasant memories for the new tsar, making it even harder "to manage the whole task instead of dear Papa." The next morning he awoke "terrified" because he was to say a few words to the estate representatives who had gathered in one of the halls. "Thank God all went well," he noted with relief.[96] In the meanwhile, Alexandra sought to console Nicholas on virtually every page of his diary, reassuring him that God was with him and that He loved and protected him: "God gives thee strength to bear as surely He lays the burden on you. God crowns thy patience as soon as He takes the burden from thee."[97] Although she did not say so, her comments suggested Job on whose day Nicholas had been born.[98]

Back in St. Petersburg Nicholas received the court, State Council, Senate, and diplomatic corps, as well as countless other delegations; each time he "had to speak again." The new tsar felt overwhelmed, preferring instead to be left alone with his grief and his bride. The funeral on November 7 only heightened this feeling. He wished that the various foreign guests would leave as soon as possible, since "their presence only further increases the burden" of work. He had his first ministerial audiences, but gave no hint in his diary as to what was discussed. He winced at "having to answer all kind of questions. One totally loses one's head and balance." His downcast mood almost made him break out in tears when he had to give a big dinner for all visiting foreign dignitaries and

---

[95] Ibid., pp. 124–25.
[96] Ibid., pp. 126–27.
[97] Ibid., p. 127.
[98] Alexander, *Once a Grand Duke*, p. 186.

make the rounds of the two hundred guests. When Sunday finally left his schedule free of reports and audiences, he was greatly relieved.[99]

Private and public spheres clashed more than ever. Whereas Nicholas's grief rendered public functions and meetings with virtual strangers a painful experience, his whole private inclination, particularly his desire to be with his bride, made him resent these duties outright. The fact that his assumption of office and the start of married life coincided—Alix arrived only ten days before Alexander's death and they were publicly married five weeks later on November 14—would have tended to accentuate the conflict between personal preference and official obligations which Nicholas had always perceived. As a result, his alienation from his role grew still further. The day after their wedding Nicholas was glad not to be bothered by official, i.e., nonfamily, visitors.[100] Two days later he noted regretfully: "Too bad business takes up so much time, for I would prefer to spend the whole time with her only." After a week the two newlyweds took off for a brief, four-day honeymoon at Tsarskoe Selo.[101] Their ecstasy at being together without any interruptions was supreme, all the more so since the dowager empress let them stay a day longer. "No more separations," Alexandra exulted; they were united forever in this world and eternity.[102]

With their return to the capital, life finally resumed a more regular course. The young emperor settled into his official routine of ministerial reports, committee meetings, military receptions, and document reading, balanced by meals, rides, walks, and evenings with wife and family. Such a predictable and established routine should have made these official commitments more natural and palatable to Nicholas. Yet he continued to complain about the amount of work and time spent on them. In fact, his new role was the source of much tension and anxiety, judging by his repeated fits of nerves in public and by the good-natured complaint of his wife: "It isn't good that you grind your teeth at night, your Aunt cannot sleep then."[103]

The new emperor's attitudes towards his official duties are best characterized as resentful but conscientious. He found little satisfaction in attending daily audiences and committee sessions, reading reports, signing legislation, answering dispatches, and issuing orders. Still, day after day Nicholas submitted to this disliked routine. His sense of duty and his fatalistic belief in providence compelled him to do so but could not over-

[99] *Dnevnik Imperatora*, pp. 90–92.

[100] Ibid., p. 94, November 14, 1894.

[101] There Nicholas found it "strange to spend the night in the bedroom of dear Papa and Mama where I was born"; ibid., p. 96.

[102] *Tagebuch des letzten Zaren*, p. 136.

[103] Ibid., p. 139. Alexandra was also the sister of the wife of Nicholas's Uncle Sergei.

come his lack of enthusiasm and his preconceived notion of official tasks as being onerous and boring. Indeed, the more trivial and burdensome these obligations were, the more they tended to confirm his formal sense of duty and appeal to his fatalism. This fatalistic attitude expressed itself in stark religious utterances. Rooted in Orthodoxy and encouraged, no doubt, by Alexandra's extreme religiosity, this fatalistic leaning reflected Nicholas's alienation from the responsibilities and demands of his role. Clearly, he had not chosen this role; it had been chosen for him, thrust on him by fate. At the same time, such fatalistic rationalization and externalization made this burden more bearable. The possibility of avoiding it altogether by abdicating had not yet entered Nicholas's mind.

One of Nicholas's first official acts as tsar was to ask Pobedonostsev—conceivably at the very suggestion of the procurator general himself—to instruct Assistant Minister of Foreign Affairs Count Lamzdorf to prepare a circular to all foreign courts and governments, announcing the new tsar's determination to remain true to his father's ideals and policies of peace.[104] It was perfectly natural for the son to honor and revere the memory of his beloved father in such a way, especially during the first moments of acute grief. The personal wound which time should have been expected to heal, however, was constantly reopened as the son found himself in situations that contrasted sharply with earlier, more carefree times. Whenever he took his father's place at church services, for instance, Nicholas was painfully reminded of the void left by Alexander III.[105] After paying his old Preobrazhensky Regiment the first visit of his reign, he confided to his mother: "it was wonderfully touching and I felt inexpressibly sad and sorrowful! I even cried in the railway carriage, this scene had such an effect on me. It was the first time that I saw my men and spoke to them!" So distraught and tense was he that during the final review of all participating units acute stomach pains "almost prevented [him] from saluting."[106] In another letter to his mother, Nicholas spoke of moments when "old beautiful memories crowd into my brain all the more powerfully, and at times such sadness and dreariness overcomes me that I don't know how it all would end were I not married." After thanking providence for Alix, he continued: "We talk each day, I of dear Papa, she of her father. I want to teach her to know him better and more thoroughly and I hope I will succeed in this completely."[107] As the first anniversary of those dark October days in the Crimea approached— a subject on which his mother's letter from Denmark had dwelt at some

---

[104] "Dnevnik Lamzdorfa," p. 8. This happened even before Nicholas learned of his father's secret agreements with France.

[105] *Tagebuch des letzten Zaren*, pp. 132, 145.

[106] *Nicholas-Marie Letters*, p. 99, August 13, 1895.

[107] Ibid., p. 102, September 3, 1895.

length—Nicholas described a tearful walk with his Uncle Sergei, during which they talked only about Livadia and the "hopes and fears" they had had at the time.[108]

Going beyond mere sentimentality, Nicholas's veneration of his father's memory assumed extreme proportions. On October 21, 1895, the day after the first anniversary of Alexander's death and thus officially the anniversary of his own accession, the young tsar made the following revealing notation: "Also not one of the happy days. What a shame and pity to take off mourning: it still served as something of a visible bond with the dear past."[109] Nicholas was psychologically dependent on his father's memory. The trauma of being cast out of a familiar sheltered world and of acceding to a position for which he felt unprepared made him cling to his father. After a whole year of mourning and ruling Nicholas was unwilling to cut loose the anchor steadying him in the unfamiliar and threatening seas of state.

Unable to sever this emotional tie, the new emperor looked to his father for legitimation of his own role and actions. He expected Alexander to confer the authority that he himself lacked both personally and politically. In almost every respect Nicholas was the very antithesis of his father. Small and fine-featured in contrast to Alexander's sheer physical bulk, Nicholas was also shy, soft-spoken, and controlled where his predecessor had been outgoing, boisterous, and tempestuous. Nicholas's charming, polite, and indirect ways were at variance with his father's gruff and blunt demeanor. In both his appearance and his stereotypically feminine traits, Nicholas resembled his mother, not his father. While growing up in Alexander's overbearing presence, he, no doubt, had become painfully aware of this profound contrast. Alexander had done little to let Nicholas forget his inferiority; he allegedly called his son a girl, *devchonka*,[110] and had kept him out of positions of real responsibility because he thought of him as immature and inexperienced.[111] As we have seen, Nicholas's entire upbringing had acted to retard his independence and maturation and to inhibit his will and self-assertion. Not surprisingly, Nicholas considered himself weak and excessively kindhearted. "Your

[108] Ibid., p. 107, October 5, 1895.
[109] *Dnevnik Imperatora*, p. 108.
[110] Wortman, "Power and Responsibility," p. 11.
[111] When Witte put forth Nicholas's name for the chairmanship of the Siberian Railroad Comittee, for example, Alexander III seemed perplexed and asked his minister whether he had ever had a serious conversation with the heir. Witte's negative reply brought this reaction from the tsar: "That's just it, he is very much a boy, he has totally childish opinions: how could he possibly be chairman of a committee?" Witte admitted that Nicholas was still young and he might never have given any serious thought to state affairs, but that it was time for him to learn and receive his first introduction to state affairs; Witte, *Vospominaniia*, 1:434–36.

own poor little huzzy with no will Nicky," he would write later to Alexandra, and she, in turn, admonished him time and again to be firm, strong, assertive, and to let others know with whom they were dealing.[112] In another instance, he was furious with himself for letting his Uncle Vladimir talk him out of his personal choice for the command of the Guards Corps and for agreeing to Vladimir's candidate instead. Reversing himself after due reflection, the tsar blamed the incident on "*my kindness, yes, I insist, my stupid kindness.* Just to avoid quarreling and straining family relations, I constantly make concessions and finally end up a dolt, without will and without character."[113]

Both in Nicholas's impressionable mind and in the eyes of others, Alexander's particular attributes had become identified with those demanded and typical of any autocrat. Thus Nicholas's personal qualities not only fell short of his father's in his own self-estimation, but, worse, they did not meet the requirements and expectations of an autocratic ruler in general. The very importance that his upbringing had placed on external forms and appearances only served to heighten this perceived discrepancy and the feeling of shortcoming it engendered in Nicholas. No matter how determinedly the son had tried to emulate his father personally—witness the vicarious interest in everything Alexander was doing—he obviously could not acquire his father's attributes. At the same time, he could not boast the personal authority, i.e., the self-assurance, sovereignty, and legitimation, that comes from a developed sense of identity and that would have enabled him to strike out on his own. Alienated from the role that had been his father's and that he had inherited against his will, but lacking a personally internalized and comfortable concept of his role, the new tsar sought instead to retreat into the private world of his youth and into his chosen relationship with his wife.

Yet his strong sense of duty and obligation, born of the behavioral training in his adolescence and the expectations of others, constantly urged Nicholas to overcome this alienation. He was intent on imitating his father and copying his autocratic formula. Formally and mechanically he adhered to Alexander's definition of autocracy—or at least to what he imagined or what others persuaded him this definition to be. Since these interpretations of autocracy diverged sharply, as we shall soon see, Nicholas was left only with the personal example of his father and the psychological dilemmas that it posed. Adherence to words, form, and appearance was often more important than the preservation of substance and real power. The literalness and dogmatism of this imitation bespoke Nicholas's own distance and insecurity and masked his conceptual void.

[112] TsGAOR, f. 640, op. 2, d. 137.

[113] TsGAOR, f. 652, op. 1, d. 619, ll. 54–55, November 26, 1896.

The result was an often superficial and exaggerated copy of the ideal represented by Alexander—until Nicholas encountered serious resistance and a changing consensus on how the autocratic formula should be defined.

Alexander's perceived or suggested example became Nicholas's universal frame of reference; in fact, it provided literal and concrete guidance. As he told "Granny" Victoria two years after his accession, in addition to the positive teachings of history, "I have always got the sacred example of my beloved Father and also the result and proof of all His Deeds!"[114] The very spelling of these lines elevated Alexander III to divine heights. Far from being mere hyperbole, this vow reflected the son's sacred fealty to his father. Encouraged and exploited by Alexander's advisors and Nicholas's former tutors such as Pobedonostsev, it was this quasi-religious worship and psychological dependence, not a coherent or clearly enunciated view of his own, that account for the shocking insensitivity and intransigence with which the new tsar greeted society's modest aspirations for a political voice in national affairs. Meeting with the representatives of local self-government on January 17, 1895, Nicholas affirmed his determination in the concluding sentence of his brief prepared remarks: "May all know that I, who will devote all his strength to the well-being of the people, will maintain the principles of autocracy as firmly and inviolably as my unforgettable Father did." Anyone who thought or expected otherwise was entertaining "senseless dreams."[115]

Regarding himself as the faithful administrator and trustee of his father's estate and legacy, Nicholas discharged both his private and public responsibilities as a caretaker. Nicholas imagined himself to be carrying out his father's wishes and bequest, which Alexander's advisors would help him identify. These counsellors formed as much a line of continuity with Alexander's reign as did Nicholas's personal memories, and he was unwilling and sad to part with them. He sincerely mourned the passing of Foreign Minister N. K. Giers on January 14, 1895, and that of his former tutor and Chairman of the Committee of Ministers N. Kh. Bunge, "an experienced and faithful advisor," on June 3, 1895.[116] By the same token, he would repeatedly justify his faith in Finance Minister Witte and others by reference to the confidence shown them by his father.[117]

The paternal bequest and precedent was also on Nicholas's mind when he had to contend with the opinions and requests of his relatives. Typical

[114] TsGAOR, f. 601, op. 1, d. 1111, l. 36, October 10, 1896.
[115] *Tagebuch des letzten Zaren*, p. 147. Aside from his usual stage fright and "terrible excitement" before addressing the deputies, Nicholas's only recorded reaction to the event itself was: "A tiring day!" Ibid.
[116] Ibid., pp. 149–50.
[117] *Nicholas-Marie Letters*, pp. 97–98, November 14, 1894.

was the following rebuke he gave to his Uncle Vladimir for inviting guests to the imperial box and dining room in the Marinskii Theater without the tsar's permission: "Under Papa nothing of the kind would have happened; and you know how I maintain everything as it was under Him."[118] Even Nicholas's mother was not exempt from such reminders, as in the following, albeit more tactful, variation on the "senseless dream" theme. Maria Fedorovna had implored him to cancel the nearly half-million-ruble debt of the Lopukhin-Demidov family to the State Bank and have the bank issue a new one-million-ruble interest-free loan; she also asked him not to consult Witte in this matter, since it was his policies that had placed the landed nobility as a whole in dire straits and in need of assistance.[119] Nicholas's answer was a firm "No": "I must tell you honestly that this is impossible. I should have liked to see how [Princess Demidova] would have dared even to hint at such a thing to Papa; and I can certainly hear the answer he would have given her." Nicholas did agree to cancel the debt, obviously to salve his mother's feelings, but he refused the loan:

> But to make her an additional present of a million is sheer madness, and, darling Mama, just because I know Papa's attitude toward such requests, I will *never* agree to this. . . . It would be a fine state of affairs indeed at the Treasury if, in Witte's absence (he is at present on holiday) I were to give a million to one, two million to another, etc. All that has been accumulated—and what forms one of the most brilliant pages in the history of dear Papa's reign is the sound condition of our finances—would be destroyed in the course of a few years! I am sure, darling Mama, that you understand me, and will not be angry with me for having told you this quite frankly. This is not only my opinion, but my deepest conviction, and I repeat that I know this would have also been the conviction of our dearly beloved Papa.[120]

In the resolution of both major and minor problems during the first decade of Nicholas's reign, such references to his father's sacred legacy abound.

Nicholas's dependence on an external, in this instance the paternal, definition of the autocrat's role, his lack of an internalized and firm concept of his own, and the alienation he felt from his official duties did not prevent him, of course, from exercising this role. Many of its elements were purely ritualistic and symbolic, others routinized and trivial. Simply by virtue of rightfully occupying the throne and by going through the

---

[118] TsGAOR, f. 652, op. 1, d. 619, ll. 61–62, January 29, 1897.
[119] *Nicholas-Marie Letters*, pp. 93–95, August 3, 1895.
[120] Ibid., pp. 97–98, August 13, 1895.

prescribed motions, no matter how onerous and resented, Nicholas satisfied those dimensions.

Still, there was the obvious danger that Nicholas's lack of identification would communicate itself to his environment: his family, courtiers, ministers, bureaucrats, and members of society. Mechanical and formal ritual devoid of substance would lose its suggestive powers and the symbol would turn into an empty shell. With authority perceived as weak, even nonexistent, the political process would be deprived of legitimacy, and the government apparatus would become disorganized. In addition, the very definition of the autocrat's role was subject to profound disagreement, manipulation, and change. Some of those dangers and developments manifested themselves even before the onset of Russia's revolutionary crisis.

CHAPTER II

Autocratic Administration and Nicholas II

IN SUCCEEDING Alexander III, Nicholas inherited long-established practices of autocratic government. These administrative traditions, i.e., the day-to-day functioning and decision making of autocratic bureaucracy and its interactions with the autocrat, constituted the structure of autocracy within which the ruler had to operate. Here the congruence between administrative reality and some of the pretensions of autocratic ideology is striking, as we shall learn in the next chapter. Given the centrality of the ruler myth and the pervasiveness of personal and arbitrary elements in this system, much depended, of course, on the person and personal attributes of the sovereign. While it may have been difficult for any tsar to escape the restrictions or alter the role definitions imposed by autocratic structure, Nicholas's lack of any firmly internalized conception of autocracy and the autocrat's role would make it still more so. Instead of counteracting the idiosyncrasies of autocratic government, Nicholas's personality served to accentuate them. The resulting shortcomings, so readily apparent even in normal times, would become a still greater liability during Russia's first revolutionary crisis.

ADMINISTRATIVE STRUCTURE

Russian bureaucracy has attracted a lot of scholarly attention over the last fifteen years, but to date the emphasis has been on bureaucratic personnel, changes in their social origin, service background, property status, and educational qualifications, and on the relationship of these changes to particular institutional affiliations and to their reflection of a growing professional ethos.[1] By contrast, the actual workings of Russian bureaucracy in addressing the problems that confronted Russian autocracy have not been scrutinized comprehensively. Neither legal theory, such as institutional blueprints, organization charts, and formal definitions of responsibility, nor social investigations have shed much light on the functioning of autocratic government at its apex—the crucial "interface" between the tsar and his senior bureaucrats. Thus understood, the ad-

---

[1] Cf., for example, the pioneering works of S. M. Troitskii and P. A. Zaionchkovskii in the USSR and of H. J. Torke, W. M. Pintner, W. B. Lincoln, S. F. Starr, and R. Wortman in the West.

ministrative *practice* of autocracy is still waiting to be explored systematically.

At its highest level, autocratic government for the most part assumed
the form of regular written and oral reports by the tsar's senior servitors.
This tradition went back to Nicholas I, who had thus sought to stay
abreast of and retain control over all matters that came within the purview of each government agency.[2] Besides satisfying Nicholas I's need to
be personally involved in all aspects of government, this innovation was
to have enhanced the accountability and improved the workings of Russia's growing administrative apparatus; its ultimate effect, however, was
quite different.

In their so-called *vsepoddanneishie doklady* (most humble or loyal reports) ministers and agency heads were to address themselves to those
matters that exclusively or directly concerned their own institutions. As
a result, narrowly circumscribed, less important everyday affairs tended
to predominate in the ministerial reports. Any problem or issue, no matter how minor, that affected the interests of more than one agency was
referred to special interagency conferences or the Committee of Ministers, which in turn submitted their collective conclusions and proposals
to the tsar. Yet here, too, the same limitations prevailed.

Indeed, the extreme specificity of virtually all reports boggles the
mind. Almost invariably, the ministerial accounts and proposals per-
tained to particular cases and individuals. Each appointment, business
trip, or vacation extension of officials above a certain rank, every extra-
budgetary allocation, salary bonus, award, debt cancellation, administrative sentence, or tax deferment had to be expressly approved by the tsar,
who served as the director of personnel for his unwieldy bureaucracy and
as a personal referee for each and every one of his 130 million subjects.

Autocratic government, as inherited and practiced by Nicholas II, was
little more than the sum of innumerable ad hoc decisions. Even the highest deliberative body of the land, the State Council, was not immune to
such narrow specificity. Not only did the legislative projects considered
there all originate with the ministries, but the Council itself consisted of
the ministers and of former high-ranking bureaucrats. There is every indication that the bureaucratic apparatus was only equipped to handle
such personal and particular problems, to the obvious detriment of
larger, more important issues and unforeseen circumstances. The latter
inevitably had to reach the critical stage before autocratic government
would begin to address their resolution by establishing yet another conference or commission specifically for this purpose and personally involv-

---

[2] W. Bruce Lincoln, *Nicholas I. Emperor and Autocrat of All the Russias* (Bloomington,
Ind., 1978), p. 103.

ing the autocrat. A general lack of perspective and a myopic predisposition against decisions on matters of principle characterized the day-to-day administrative process.

The twofold purpose of the vsepoddanneishie doklady was to inform and, in most cases, to solicit the tsar's approval or resolution. As for this second category, the writer's recommendations usually fell into two general, though often indistinct, categories: those requiring the sovereign's confirmation under the law, and those calling for a temporary suspension of or specific exemption from existing law. Laws and tradition demanded, for example, that the tsar personally sanction the erection of monuments or the endowment of scholarships honoring members of the imperial family. Likewise, he had to confirm many appointments, all name changes, citizenship requests, or divorce applications. On the other hand, the tsar personally had to suspend or temporarily amend laws and traditions that did not anticipate a particular problem or did not permit the desired resolution. Thus he had to lift the legal prohibition against publicly owned companies whenever such a firm wanted to go public—an increasingly common phenomenon of Russia's capitalist development. He also had to defer the military obligations of a twenty-two-year-old student in a state school, or extend the deadline for fishing herring on the Volga. The traditional monarchic privilege of dispensation, as in the commutation of death sentences or pardoning of political and criminal offenders, also implied a legal exemption.

No matter how many such dispensations he issued, however, the underlying law or regulation remained in effect. Although he would have been free to nullify or amend such laws, the tsar and his ministers evidently were unwilling or unable to rewrite Russia's laws. Several considerations account for this reticence. From a short-term perspective—and there is no reason to believe that tsarist ministers acted with more foresight than today's politicians—it was simply easier to request and authorize countless legal exemptions than to draft new laws that would accommodate changed or more complex circumstances and thereby eliminate the need for these exceptions. The reports of each agency, it will be recalled, were to confine themselves to such matters as came within its purview or exclusively affected its interests. The revisions of many laws, on the other hand, invariably concerned more than one institution and therefore had to be taken up by a specially constituted interagency conference (*Osoboe Soveshchanie*), the Committee of Ministers, and, as a rule, the State Council before being submitted for imperial approval.

Regardless of the institution involved, the procedure for drawing up new legislation was extremely cumbersome and time-consuming. Weeks, even months, would pass while a particular agency prepared a draft proposal, which, together with supporting materials, was then submitted to other agencies. These institutions in turn, required more time to consider the proposal and to make their own comments, corrections, and suggestions, sometimes prompting detailed responses from the officials who originally had drawn up the project. This sizable body of materials then was discussed during the weekly or bi-weekly meetings of the collective body that had been charged with the task. The chancellery staff drafted preliminary summaries of the proceedings and conclusions of each meeting and referred them to each participant for review and additional corrections. These changes were collated and incorporated into the final summary of the proceedings and draft legislation, sometimes in several majority and minority versions. The State Council presented its proposals directly to the tsar, whereas the legislative recommendations of a Special Conference or the Committee of Ministers might first have to run the gauntlet of the State Council before reaching the sovereign. Clearly, this process was drawn out, especially since the State Council did not even meet for a third of the year during the summer, to say nothing of the multitude of official holidays that together with Sundays closed all government offices for one-fourth of the entire year.[3]

Nor did such delays necessarily guarantee the desired result, as many a legislative project fell prey to conflicting institutional interests, petty personal rivalries, and vague oppositional tendencies among some State Council members. Not surprisingly then, such formidable obstacles to legislative review and innovation only further encouraged ministers to concentrate on specific cases and palliative measures, which could be quickly approved and carried out by imperial fiat.

There was no firm and ironclad rule, of course, stipulating that every new piece of legislation follow such a lengthy and laborious route. In theory at least, the tsar had the right to choose a less circuitous path, abrogating old and issuing new laws by the stroke of his pen and without much advance preparation. Still, the fact remains that he did so only rarely, when extreme circumstances left him little choice, as would happen with the manifestos of October 17 and November 3, 1905. Even these sudden and dramatic measures did not spring full-blown from Nicholas's head, but were preceded by collegial consultations, much soul-searching, and widespread and protracted agitation in their favor. Moreover, much like the December 12, 1904, ukase and February 18, 1905, rescript, the October Manifesto only promised general political reforms and rights, the precise extent and implementation of which still had to await legislative definition.

Not only was it often less troublesome and time-consuming in light of those practical difficulties to issue individual legal exemptions, but this

---

[3] See, for example, *Pridvornyi kalendar'* for 1905.

time-honored approach emphasized the tsar's right of dispensation, his role of personally granting favors and deciding the fates of each of his subjects. In eliminating the need for such exemptions, any modernization of the law would have tended to automate and standardize administrative decision making, thereby circumscribing the tsar's authority and obscuring his personal role. Ironically, although inspired by the desire to preserve the autocrat's freedom of action, such resistance to legislative change and innovation had the very opposite effect of limiting it, for the tsar would find himself mired in a swamp of anachronistic practices and senseless specificity.

Also militating against any genuine legislative improvements was a peculiar understanding of law that bordered on perverse infatuation. Russia could boast a voluminous body of laws in the form of the *Polnoe Sobranie Zakonov* (Complete Collection of Laws) and *Svod Zakonov* (Code of Laws). Irrespective of original intent, import, or subsequent shortcomings and contradictions, any order, statute, or regulation, once part of the public record, acquired a sacrosanct aura and therefore was not to be tampered with lightly.

Law, in the Russian historical context, had not evolved out of the interaction and conflict of existing socioeconomic groups and institutions; there was no common-law tradition to shape and determine state laws. Instead, the development of law mirrored the separate evolution of state and people in Russia, during which the state had sought to regulate every detail of social life for its own purposes and in its own image. Law only served to extend central government control to all aspects of its subjects' existence, yet it remained an alien, arbitrary force that rarely entered into the common consciousness of these subjects and could not become an end in itself. Imposed from above, the law merely expressed the state's organizational goals and economic interests; for this reason, government servitors clung to the legal system all the more determinedly, if superficially, as a profession of faith and intent rather than as a set of firm rules that might define and limit their own actions.[4] The unchangeability of law was equated with the stability of public and social order. Any permanent change in law not only drew into question the state's original purpose, but also threatened its organizational accomplishments to date and thus order itself. By contrast, specific legal suspensions maintained the illusion of legal order without tying the hands of the autocrat and his servitors.

Such a self-serving and one-sided affirmation of law helped thwart leg-

[4] For a similar argument, see George L. Yaney, "Law, Society and the Domestic Regime in Russia in Historical Perspective," *American Political Science Review* 59 (June 1965): 380–86.

islative change and instead called forth countless individual exemptions. Although such decisions carried the force of law, they were not law themselves, for they lacked the very criteria we have come to associate with law: universality and permanence. Laws, at least theoretically, apply to all individuals in a group, i.e., part or all of the population, within a given context or set of circumstances that may recur as long as a particular law is in effect. The ruler's decisions, however, applied only to specific individuals in particular circumstances and therefore had to be repeated for another person in the same circumstances, or even for the same individual in another, even if identical, set of circumstances. As a result, the tsar's resolutions rarely reflected any firm legal principles or set any precedents. Singularity and transience were the hallmarks of virtually every case requiring imperial sanction.

The widespread use of the tsar's dispensational power as a matter of common administrative practice[5] reflected a lack of respect for and thus undermined the inviolability and supremacy of the law, revealing just how superficial the understanding of law really was. Law became inseparably linked with considerations of expediency and was observed mostly in the breach. To demand innumerable specific suspensions in the name of the law was to make a travesty of the law.

Autocratic government was caught up in a vicious circle. Many of its laws were simply inadequate; they did not meet the requirements of modern life nor did they reflect social changes. Considerations of principle and practical obstacles, as we have seen, stood in the way of legislative improvements and encouraged government by dispensation. On the other hand, this tendency only further compounded the deficiencies of existing legislation; by requiring ever more exemptions it rendered legal revisions still more difficult. *Zakonnost'*, i.e., legality, had lost all meaning.

Such practices constituted a harsh indictment of tsarist bureaucracy and government. Minor administrative matters dominated government routine, taking up time and seizing control of ministers and other officials. These men, regardless of their personal attributes and beliefs, were trapped in the traditional habits and arbitrary particularism of the bureaucratic process. Whatever might be said about the qualities and performance of individual servitors, a look at the most senior bureaucrats and their dealings with the tsar and with each other reveals the backwardness of Russian bureaucracy as a whole: a hollow legalism that saw laws honored mainly in their breach and that ignored legal precedent, an

---

[5] The eminent legal scholar, N. I. Lazarevskii, confirms that such dispensations were the "normal form of government"; *Lektsii po russkomu gosudarstvennomu pravu* (St. Petersburg, 1910), 1:206–7.

utter lack of administrative generalization, the nondelegation of responsibility under uniform and systematic operational rules and procedures—in short, the extreme retardation of institutionalized authority in the Weberian sense.

Instead, it was personalized authority that permeated the tsarist administrative apparatus and caused those egregious shortcomings. This personalized notion of government was reflected in the specificity of bureaucratic practice and in the requirement that the emperor personally authorize a myriad of actions, each bearing on the personal fate of particular individuals; ultimately, it doomed all attempts at systematization as it refused to submit to either legal definitions or institutional limitations. Neither the legal code nor administrative practice made a clear and convincing distinction between executive and legislative rules or between different legal forms, whether classified as *ulozhenie, nakaz, ustav, uchrezhdenie, gramota, polozhenie, manifest, ukaz,* or State Council opinion (*mnenie*).[6] More importantly still, these statutes provided little assurance as to how a particular problem might be resolved. The differentiation between "public" and "private" law remained incomplete, since "this conceptual separation," as Max Weber explains, "presupposes the conceptual separation of the 'state,' as an abstract bearer of sovereign prerogatives and the creator of 'legal norms,' from all personal 'authorizations' of individuals."[7] In the Russia of Nicholas II, sovereignty and government authority continued to reside exclusively in the person of the ruler.

Government was equated with grantsmanship—the bestowal of privileges and favors by the tsar on his subjects. Most vsepoddanneishie doklady and countless petitions illustrate this point. Petitions even more than normal ministerial reports served the exclusive purpose of directly soliciting personal favors from the sovereign; the petitioners were not permitted by law to discuss matters or request favors outside of their own private sphere. As a general rule, only positive recommendations, i.e., those urging approval, reached the tsar's desk. Comparatively few contained negative conclusions or offered a choice of options. To be sure, imperial approval was by no means a foregone conclusion; the many instances in which Nicholas withheld his approval or modified the proposals prove that he considered each case, no matter how trivial or commonplace, conscientiously and on its own merits. Still, the heavy

---

[6] As Lazarevskii demonstrated so persuasively in his lectures on Russian constitutional law, all efforts to establish formal and substantive criteria for laws as opposed to administrative rules in pre-1905 Russia always had been and would be futile. No consistent and logical separation existed; *Lektsii,* 1:404–13.

[7] *From Max Weber: Essays in Sociology,* ed. H. H. Gerth and C. Wright Mills (New York, 1958), p. 239.

preponderance of affirmative recommendations leaves no doubt that it was the tsar himself who personally had to sanction every grant of favor, while it usually fell to his subordinates to reject or deny it.

This practice granted the tsar's ministers and the bureaucrats below them considerable freedom, one virtually untempered by legal responsibility. The crucial question was whether a particular matter reached the tsar or not, for it was this decision that really determined the outcome of a case. A negative judgment, i.e., a denial of favor, could be rendered on several subordinate levels of administration; it simply meant that the matter would not be referred to a higher bureaucratic echelon. For a positive resolution by the emperor, on the other hand, a case first had to survive the uncertainties of the administrative maze. In both instances, the officials involved were relieved of firm and final responsibility for their actions. Rejections were not usually subject to superior review, while approvals meant merely that the item in question would be passed on, with the final decision yet to be made.

This procedure, revealing just how pervasive personal and arbitrary authority really was, might suggest a practical limitation of the monarch's own power. Despite claims that he alone decided the personal fates of each of his 130 million subjects, it was his bureaucrats who made most of the actual decisions by rejecting some matters out of hand and passing others on for the tsar's confirmation. The ruler, it seemed, did little more than approve the recommendations submitted to him. This apparent limitation was haphazard and incomplete, however. Of two identical problems or cases, one, two, or none might come to the attention of the tsar, depending mainly on chance, influence, or the personal views and moods of the officials concerned. The very arbitrariness of this negative filtration, the utter lack of legal and institutional systematization, guaranteed that the autocrat's power was not circumscribed in any systematic way. Moreover, rejections were tantamount to inaction and thus had the added advantage of preserving the status quo, whereas the initiative for action and change was reserved for the sovereign.

Subaltern officials might also have been reluctant to make indiscriminate use of their right to reject. In the absence of uniform rules and procedures and in the face of bureaucratic rivalries and jealousies, the possibility that a negative decision might be revealed to higher authorities at some later point could never be ruled out with any certainty. It was easier and less dangerous to pass on a particular request to a higher level than to reject it outright. In fact, the very petitioning process was designed to bypass normal institutional channels. These petitions reached Nicholas either directly or by way of only a few intermediaries; many of them sought a satisfaction or relief that subordinate officials so far had refused or that the petitioners had no hope of obtaining by regular means. Very often the mere fact that the tsar, without taking a stand on the matter, personally referred these petitions to the respective agencies for investigation and recommendations sufficed to assure a positive resolution. In this sense, extrainstitutional and personal recourse and decisions not only engendered arbitrariness but helped contain it.

The possibility that the positive recommendations and countless cases that did get through to the tsar were based on incomplete or deliberately distorted information cannot be ruled out, of course. Face to face with the emperor and without witnesses of any kind, a minister presumably was free to present each case so as to anticipate objections, eliminate options, and effectively influence the final outcome.[8] This danger was all the more real since the tsar's approval was almost automatic. On the other hand, as the only one to receive the ministers' reports as well as scores of telegraphic dispatches, newspapers, and other visitors, he stood at the hub of this information network and, at least in theory, commanded a comprehensive perspective. Most ministerial reports, moreover, were recorded in writing and therefore could be verified at any time, while petty bureaucratic rivalries and fast-grinding rumor mills acted as effective checks to personal excesses and deceptions at the top. Even if one were to allow for occasional distortions, however, the overwhelming majority of these reports was so trivial that the potential damage would have been limited to isolated displays of personal favoritism.

Nor did the tsar's bureaucratic servitors possess any independent power base or represent an autonomous constituency which could have competed with the ruler's autocratic pretensions. All power and authority issued from the sovereign; state officials were utterly dependent on his favor and mercy, and they had little reason to bite or paralyze the hand that fed them. The tsar, as we have noted, personally acted as the director of government personnel, approving all appointments in the first five ranks, authorizing their salaries, pensions, bonuses, nonfinancial awards, and vacation requests, as well as exempting lower officials from existing civil service regulations. As Theodore Taranovski concluded in his study of bureaucracy under Alexander III, "the autocrat had a number of positive means at his disposal to shape the composition and character of top officialdom and ensure compliance with and fulfillment of his decisions and policies."[9] Given the want of firm legal guarantees and systematic organizational procedures, the monarch's generosity offered the best promise for security and advancement, to say nothing of the fact that the

---

[8] Lazarevskii, *Lektsii*, 2:167–68, sees in this potential for abuse one of the major shortcomings of the vsepoddanneishie doklady.

[9] Theodore Taranovski, "The Politics of Counter-Reform: Autocracy and Bureaucracy in the Reign of Alexander III, 1881–1894" (Ph.D. diss., Harvard University, 1976), p. 158.

wider state and ruler's interests they were supposed to safeguard were identical to their own.

Potential abuses notwithstanding, the practice of the ministerial reports was to permit the ruler to exercise personal control over his administration. Through this arrangement the monarch, himself not an expert, could play off one expert against another in order to gain a thorough overview and avoid arbitrary decisions. Weber's observation that "often the prince expects to assure himself a maximum of personal influence less from personally presiding over the collegiate bodies than from having written memoranda submitted to him"[10] certainly applied to the Russia of Nicholas or his father, where the one body that was chaired by the emperor himself, the Council of Ministers, had long before ceased to function. The occasions on which the sovereign convened and personally presided over a meeting of his senior servitors to discuss government business were rare indeed and inevitably brought on by extraordinary circumstances. Instead, the tsar usually received his ministers individually or read their written memoranda.

Personal relations were a substitute for institutional relationships, whether between sovereign and government agencies or between and within the various administrative branches.[11] The absence of institutionalized coordination and unity left the field wide open for personal jealousies and intrigues. Not only did every minister occupy his post by virtue of the tsar's trust in him, but his particular policies continued at the ruler's sufferance. Therefore, political disagreements were inevitably fought out in personal terms. This battle demanded that political opponents be personally denigrated and that suspicions about their qualifications, philosophies, and even loyalties be raised. Correctly or not, specific policies were identified with or blamed on certain persons and could be undermined or promoted indirectly by challenging or backing their sponsors. Since a change of personnel often meant a change in policy, a rapid turnover could lead to vacillations and a failure of political will reminiscent of the ancien régime under Louis XV and XVI.

The legitimation for this constant backbiting derived from the assumption that one had the emperor's trust, that one's own opinions and political proposals most accurately mirrored those the tsar harbored in his impenetrable inner sanctum, and that one was faithfully carrying out his stated or unstated wishes. Any proposal, moreover, had to be phrased and explained as conservative, as defending the autocrat's position, preserving the status quo, or eliminating threats to both. Here is how Interior Minister Pleve described the rules of the game, which he himself,

---

[10] *From Max Weber*, p. 236.
[11] Cf. Taranovski, "Politics of Counter-Reform," p. 51.

with the assistance of others, was so adept in playing: "On the surface autocrats hear out their ministers, but outsiders almost always find a way into their hearts, or implant in the Sovereign distrust toward the ministers by depicting them as encroaching on autocratic rights." Such practices encouraged vagueness and deliberate obfuscation and at the same time created considerable uncertainty. "Hence the duality of [the tsar's] actions," as Pleve explained.[12]

It also follows that this operating premise, which provided the framework for autocratic politics—the constant jockeying and jostling, the bureaucratic infighting and court intrigue—fell or rose with the perception that others had of the autocrat's personality and qualities. A ruler with a defined sense of self, who conveyed the impression of having firm opinions, unbending will, and consistency, was the foundation needed to stabilize this framework,[13] while a tsar viewed as weak-willed, vacillating, passive, and distrustful undermined it by giving rise to confusion, insecurity, and hesitation. Without assurance of the emperor's personal trust and determination, the legitimizing principle of autocratic government evaporated. The effectiveness and power of a ministerial servitor depended entirely on imperial favor; without it he was unable to function, much as a fish without water. The most striking illustration of this phenomenon was to be the former finance minister and new chairman of the Council of Ministers, Count Witte, who in 1905–6 would be driven to near-despair and eventual resignation in his untiring quest for and anxiety over imperial approval.

The tsar's position of superiority and impartial control, it would appear, depended on just such contradictions and rivalries. Indeed, it can be argued that personalized autocratic government presupposed government disunity. In this sense, the notion of the autocrat as standing above selfish and diametrically opposed interests and as mediating petty partisan squabbles had been turned on its head. In order to retain and justify his pre-eminent position, the autocrat had to exploit or even manufacture conflict and opposition. Hence a unified ministry and government, in which the first minister would inherit some of the monarch's prerogatives, was not necessarily in the ruler's own best interests. Although such a ministry could give coherence and purpose to government policies and expedite the implementation of the sovereign's orders, its very unity might deny him the opportunity to play off different factions against each other and in fact might run counter to the notion of personal arbitrage. Thus, the task that fell on the tsar's shoulders was immense and fraught

[12] "Dnevnik A. N. Kuropatkina," *KA* 2 (1922): 45.
[13] See, for example, Witte's praise for Alexander III's "tsarist" character and qualities; Witte, *Vospominaniia*, 2:280, 305.

with contradictions, for by divisive means he was to effect concerted government action.

NICHOLAS'S ROLE

The personal nature of autocratic government put a premium on personalities, their attributes and interaction. This, too, was the belief of Konstantin Pobedonostsev, tutor of the last two tsars; individuals, not laws or institutions, constituted the essence of autocratic government.[14] Success, therefore, greatly depended on the personal qualities of the monarch, his mentality, vision, and determination, and on the way these in turn were perceived by others. Only a forceful ruler with a firmly developed identity and conception of his role could restrain the disruptive and discordant tendencies and lack of unity inherent in this system and impose on it a sense of direction and coherence, whatever the underlying program and ultimate objectives might be.

Long before Russia's first revolutionary crisis, the signs of government disunity were readily apparent to contemporaries and were blamed by many for its worsening problems. Korkunov, in his standard reference work on constitutional law, spoke of the "disorderliness and confusion that exist in all parts of the organization"; as a constitutional lawyer he naturally attributed this problem to the lack of a "body established for the general consideration of state problems in all their legislative aspects."[15] The diaries of former Imperial Secretary Polovtsev and of War Minister Kuropatkin for 1901–3 vividly portray the interminable bureaucratic infighting; individual bureaucrats seemed more concerned with protecting their own positions and scoring victories over their opponents than with resolving Russia's problems. Given the spate of rumors, the endless succession of committee sessions and State Council meetings, the fruitless bureaucratic wranglings, and, inevitably, the establishment of new commissions to collect additional materials or to restudy a given problem, it is a wonder that anything ever got done at all.[16] S. E. Kryzhanovskii, who would have an important hand in preparing the Council of Ministers reform of October 1905 that sought to bring about ministerial coherence, bemoaned the lack of unity and defended the emperor as being simply unable to look after everything: "The ministers undermined

[14] Robert F. Byrnes, *Pobedonostsev. His Life and Thought* (Bloomington, Ind., 1968), p. 239.

[15] M. N. Korkunov, *Russkoe gosudarstvennoe pravo* 2:72, as quoted in George L. Yaney, *The Systematization of Russian Government. Social Evolution in the Domestic Administration of Imperial Russia, 1711–1905* (Urbana, Ill., 1973), p. 283n.107.

[16] "Dnevnik A. A. Polovtseva," *KA* 3 (1923): 75–172 passim; "Dnevnik Kuropatkina," *KA* 2 (1922): 5–117 passim.

one another around the throne, defamed each other in society, exchanged polemical tracts and even carried their disagreements into the pages of the periodical press."[17] On the other hand, Vladimir Gurko, an influential bureaucrat and one-time assistant minister of internal affairs who himself was not entirely innocent of Kryzhanovskii's charges, put the blame squarely on Nicholas for failing to assume firm control and for delivering the country into the hands of a constantly changing group of agency chiefs "who were united by no common political opinion and therefore were in continual opposition to one another."[18]

In the case of Nicholas II, the image of a quixotic, passive, suspicious, fickle ruler came embarrassingly close to a feminine stereotype and compared unfavorably with the impression left by his father. Nicholas shunned open disagreements or confrontation.[19] A minister, so the story went, might have the friendliest of chats with Nicholas, only to find his dismissal notice on his desk upon returning home. The following observation by the head of the imperial court chancellery is typical: "He could part with the greatest ease even from those who had served him for a very long time. The first word of accusation breathed in his presence against anybody, with or without evidence, was enough for him to dismiss the victim, though the charge might have been a pure fabrication. . . . He was distrustful, like all weak persons."[20]

When it came to choosing a servitor, more important than particular views or professional qualifications were personal virtues, or rather how Nicholas perceived them and personally felt towards the man. Nicholas's choice of his bureaucratic associates was almost entirely based on personal trust, a foundation that emphasized style, manners, appearances, and loyalty over programmatic considerations and accomplishments. Unassuming and shy himself, he valued modesty and humility in others, or what he viewed as such. Unfortunately, he was a poor judge of character and had a weakness for feigned displays of personal devotion and obedience. By the same token, he was liable to mistake self-assurance, outspokenness, and determination in others for arrogance and lack of respect.[21] It was all the worse if an official, no matter how competent, really was arrogant and abrasive. Nicholas's alleged explanation of how he came to doubt Witte's motives and sincerity is as good an example as any that may be found. Witte had only just left the tsar's presence after one of

[17] S. E. Kryzhanovskii, *Vospominaniia* (Berlin, [1938]), p. 205.

[18] V. I. Gurko, *Features and Figures of the Past: Government and Opinion in the Reign of Nicholas II* (Stanford, Calif., 1939), pp. 21, 30–31.

[19] A. N. Naumov, *Iz utselevshikh vospominaniia, 1868–1917*, 2 vols. (New York, 1954–55), 2:533–34.

[20] Mosolov, *At the Court*, p. 7.

[21] Witte, *Vospominaniia*, 2:18–19, 312.

their audiences when Nicholas decided to call him back and pursued him into the antechamber. There he came upon a totally changed person. Instead of the polite and deferential servant who always demonstrated his deep devotion and affection for his imperial master, Nicholas encountered what he now saw to be the real Witte: proud, arrogant, self-important, and scornful of others. The story may well be apocryphal, but it reveals clearly how both men, the tsar and his minister, were perceived among the highest echelons of government.[22]

Competence, programs, and success apparently counted for less than personal devotion and trustworthiness. Thus, in April 1902 Nicholas mourned the assassinated Sipiagin, his sycophantic and intellectually limited minister of internal affairs, as a true personal friend. On the other hand, he dismissed Witte as minister of finance in 1903, although he could ill afford to dispense with his services and technical understanding and had to ask him to conduct the crucial negotiations on a new trade agreement with Germany.[23] To add insult to injury, Nicholas would have little choice but to make Witte his chief peace negotiator and then his prime minister in the gravest moment of peril for Russia and himself, even though he remained suspicious of the man. Other appointments are equally revealing. Twice he picked generals to head up the Ministry of Education, without first ascertaining their views.[24] The man in charge of his own education had been a military officer, it will be recalled, as were several of the teachers who taught his favorite subjects; obviously Nicholas felt comfortable with the two generals, Vannovskii and Glazov, and expected them to instill some military discipline in Russia's schools, universities, and rebellious youth.

Nicholas's personal confidence and a particular candidate's trustworthiness might well help explain the apparent contradictions in his ministerial appointments. These changes often seem to have been made with little concern for the appointees' political views and the dramatic programmatic consequences. As we shall see, an enlightened and relatively moderate man like Sviatopolk-Mirskii would succeed the universally hated and repressive Pleve in 1904, to be replaced in turn by Bulygin who as deputy to the governor-general of Moscow was identified with the obscurantist regime of the Grand Duke Sergei. Such paradoxes abound; without belittling the events and changed circumstances that might have influenced these appointments and that are still to be examined, it is clear that these decisions were due in large part to personal considera-

---

[22] Kryzhanovskii, *Vospominaniia*, pp. 67–68n.

[23] Witte, *Vospominaniia*, 2:299.

[24] The first was Vannovskii, a former minister of war, whose main distinction was that he had effectively dealt with student demonstrators. After Vannovskii's turn and the brief tenure of Zenger, Nicholas offered the position to General Glazov.

tions—which is not surprising, given the personal nature of autocratic government.

At the same time, the capriciousness of appointments mirrored the passivity of Nicholas's role. Unlike his father, he did not seek to assert his own political program or actively fashion a consensus. He clearly was unable or unwilling to reconcile conflicting opinions and advice himself. Ambiguities and inconsistencies are so pervasive in all of Nicholas's appointments as to appear almost purposeful. While the notion of personal confidence goes some way toward explaining them, there is also the suggestion that Nicholas was unconsciously balancing personalities, pairing off appointees to assure his own control and superiority as mediator, and delaying policy decisions until a new consensus had emerged.

A host of evidence lends credibility to this suggestion. Russia's slide into the disastrous war with Japan may well have been the result of such a balancing act between Nicholas's official and unofficial advisors.[25] In that instance the tsar appointed War Minister Kuropatkin and Viceroy Alekseev as rival commanders, who effectively paralyzed each other in the Far Eastern theater. As the nominal commander in chief, incapable both of acting this role from afar and of following his urge to join his troops in the field as he would do in World War I, he evidently did not want anyone else to take his place. Second, the February 18, 1905, rescript, which called on the interior minister to draft plans for a consultative assembly, and the ukase, which invited public suggestions, were accompanied and partly discredited by a harshly worded manifesto denouncing recent public demonstrations. Third, Witte's Conference on the Needs of Agricultural Industry, although close to a consensus on drastic agrarian reforms by March 1905, was replaced by another body chaired by Goremykin and including officials who were opposed to such reforms. Fourth, the Special Conferences at Peterhof and Tsarskoe Selo, which under Nicholas's chairmanship discussed the crucial political reforms of 1905–6, were carefully balanced with spokesmen for contrasting views. And finally, left with no choice but to name Witte chairman of the new Council of Ministers in October 1905, Nicholas wished to appoint an acknowledged enemy of his, Goremykin, to the cabinet, but was dissuaded at the last moment by Governor-General Trepov.

Such personal suspiciousness to the contrary, Nicholas was not incapable of lasting personal relationships with members of his entourage. Some of these friendships predated his accession to the throne or were inherited from his parents. Baron Frederiks, the minister of court who held this position from 1897 until his death in 1917, was by all accounts

[25] David M. MacDonald, "Autocracy, Bureaucracy, and Change in the Formation of Russia's Foreign Policy, 1895–1914" (Ph.D. diss., Columbia University, 1987), ch. 3.

the official closest to the imperial couple. He saw the tsar between his two weekly audiences, lunched regularly with Nicholas, Alexandra, and their children, participated in all court ceremonies, was a regular member of the emperor's hunting party, and attended family occasions like birthdays and Christmas. He was an upright, faithful, and discreet family servant and counselor, totally devoid of political ambition and opinion, well-liked and trusted even by the shy and reclusive empress.[26] Frederiks's predecessor, Count Vorontsov-Dashkov, had been a close friend of Alexander III and remained on good terms with his son, despite his forced departure in the wake of the catastrophe on Khodynka Field during the coronation festivities in 1896 and irrespective of his liberal views, which often encountered imperial resistance and open disapproval during his tenure as viceroy in the Caucasus. Likewise, Nicholas's fondness for many members of his military suite went back to his days as tsarevich and junior officer.[27] He obviously felt comfortable with men of military background, as his relations with War Minister Rediger, Naval Minister Birilev, the court commandants Gesse and Trepov, and others attest.

Even among civilian officials and ministers, i.e., those outside the military and court hierarchy, there were men with close personal ties to Nicholas, including Interior Minister Sipiagin, Minister of Communications Prince Khilkov, and Minister of Agriculture Ermolov. They were privileged enough to accompany the tsar on his hunting excursions and they retained his confidence. In fact, it was personal bonds that permitted such moderate and unconventional men like Ermolov and Khilkov to voice their disagreements and criticisms so openly vis-à-vis the tsar and that help account for their ministerial longevity—ten years for Khilkov (1895–1905) and twelve for Ermolov (1893–1905). Naturally, Nicholas also valued their technical expertise and background, which set them apart from the average tsarist bureaucrat.

Witte, too, brought these qualifications to his work as minister of finance. After inheriting him from his father, Nicholas kept him on for nine years and even later was unable to dispense with his financial know-how. Indeed, this specialized knowledge and reputation as a financial wizard might well have been responsible for Witte's appointment as chief peace negotiator and then as chairman of the Council of Ministers, despite Nicholas's lack of trust in him. Russia was in dire financial straits at the time. Only a Witte had any chance of restoring the confidence of its foreign creditors and potential lenders. Thus it should come as no surprise

[26] Witte, *Vospominaniia*, 2:107–8.

[27] E.g., Naval Captain Lomen had commanded the *Pamiat' Azova* during Nicholas's world cruise, while Admiral Dubasov, who would play such a crucial role in subduing the December 1905 uprising in Moscow, had been in charge of the accompanying naval squadron.

that Witte would leave the government right after the successful conclusion of a new French loan, and that Nicholas would consider this accomplishment the main one of Witte's tenure. The complexities of state finances and economy were beyond Nicholas's understanding and were better left in the hands of experts like Witte or Kokovtsev (1904–5, 1906–14), even though the latter fit the traditional bureaucratic mold better than Witte. Both men owed their long political tenures more to their technical expertise than to any particularly affectionate feelings on Nicholas's part, an observation that also appears to apply to N. V. Murav'ev and I. G. Shcheglovitov, who directed the Ministry of Justice from 1894 to 1905 and from 1906 to 1915, respectively.

How then are we to explain the brief terms of so many other ministers and Nicholas's near-universal reputation as suspicious and distrustful? That which was perceived as a negative trait of Nicholas's personality was in reality his estrangement from the autocratic role in general and his disenchantment with his bureaucracy in particular. Even a military man such as Kuropatkin was not immune to this "principled distrust of ministers"; as he proffered his resignation as war minister in August 1903, he told Nicholas somewhat paradoxically that his "trust in me would grow only when I ceased to be a minister." In a rare insight, the tsar had to agree: "It is strange, you know, but maybe that is psychologically true."[28] Alienated from his bureaucratic role, Nicholas found the daily government routine onerous, was always glad to escape from it by going on vacation or inspection trips, and inevitably hated to return to it.[29] Yet the conditioning of his youth, a sense of duty, and the security he derived from this detested routine compelled him to abide by it.

Nicholas's daily and weekly schedule was regular and predictable enough to permit a fairly accurate generalized description.[30] After dressing, breakfasting, and taking a stroll, Nicholas usually commenced his

[28] *Dnevnik A. N. Kuropatkina* (Moscow, 1923), pp. 57–58.

[29] Gurko, *Features and Figures*, p. 130.

[30] The original handwritten court logs (*kamer-fur'erskie zhurnaly* [*KFZ*]), which were kept by the duty officer, provide a detailed chronology of Nicholas's daily routine, recording the exact time and length of meals, walks, ministerial reports, audiences, ceremonies, inspections, and excursions as well as identifying almost everyone involved. This chronology is confirmed, sometimes supplemented, but rarely contradicted by Nicholas's own daily diary entries.

As for any information going beyond such formal details, the court logs are of no use and Nicholas's diary only of infrequent use to the researcher. To the limited extent that the tsar confided any substantive descriptions and personal reactions to this diary, these invariably concerned his private life or military and ceremonial matters and almost never dealt with political affairs. Instead, we have to turn to the thousands of ministerial reports, to bureaucratic communications and minutes, and to correspondence and memoirs, in order to determine the substance of Nicholas's government routine.

official workday about 10 A.M. by receiving brief reports from his aide-de-camp on duty, the palace commandant, and the lord chamberlain who supervised all dining arrangements and social functions at the court. These gentlemen in turn would be followed by one or more of Nicholas's ministers with their weekly reports, each lasting anywhere from twenty to forty-five minutes, sometimes even longer. Any time remaining before lunch (1 P.M.) was reserved for audiences, during which recently promoted, transferred, or otherwise honored military officers and civil servants, such as governors, vice-governors, nobility marshals, ministerial councellors and department chairmen, Senators and State Council members, were presented to their emperor and, on occasion, their empress. After lunching en famille or with members of the court, Nicholas often continued to receive or review for thirty to sixty minutes. With these exceptions, he invariably spent the early afternoon till teatime (5 P.M.) engaged in some form of physical exercise, such as boating, bicycling, riding, chopping wood or ice, but above all walking, either by himself or with his wife, children, and guests. Such activity had to last at least one-and-a-half hours lest Nicholas complain in his diary that it was "brief" or "too short." Often Nicholas took off more time for this purpose between tea and dinner (8:00 P.M.) and again after dinner with Alexsandra. Occasional reports by aides-de-camp and ministers punctuated the late afternoon, which also found Nicholas reading official government documents. Those evenings not filled with family gatherings and social or private pursuits afforded Nicholas opportunity for the perusal and annotation of additional materials.

This crude outline needs to be qualified and refined, of course, for Nicholas's daily calendar also had to accommodate an unending string of parades, military reviews, church services, diplomatic and memorial ceremonies, and the vast spectrum of social engagements. Military inspections, maneuvers on land and at sea, hunts and vacations, and foreign state visits would interrupt the usual schedule for days and weeks at a time. Still, those occasions, far from being exceptional or unusual, were an integral part of the autocratic routine.

At the heart of this routine lay Nicholas's daily audiences with his ministers and other select officials. Most of them reported to their sovereign on a certain day of the week, just as their predecessors had done and as their successors would continue to do. Nicholas had inherited this weekly routine from his father and evidently had seen no reason to change it. On Mondays Nicholas received jointly the naval minister and, until his retirement in 1905, his uncle Aleksei, the lord admiral; then he met with the minister or chief administrator of agriculture. On Tuesdays the tsar heard the reports of his foreign minister and the war minister accompanied by the chief of staff. Wednesdays were set aside for the minister of justice, Thursdays for the minister of internal affairs, the head of His Imperial Majesty's Chancellery for Petitions, and—on an irregular basis—the minister of the court. The procurator general of the Holy Synod and minister of communications visited the imperial residence every Friday, as did the minister of finance, with the mysterious exception of Kokovtsev, who in 1905 rendered his weekly report on Thursdays. Saturdays witnessed the tsar's audience with his minister of education as well as the second weekly report of the ministers of court and of war. On the seventh day Nicholas usually rested from his governmental labors.

The other agency chiefs and key officials reported to the tsar less frequently, often only once or twice a month, although it would appear that they, too, preferred or were assigned certain days of the week. Among those not reporting on a weekly basis were the chairman of the State Council, the imperial secretary, who played an important role in the State Council and in the drafting of new legislation in general, the chairman of the Committee of Ministers, the state comptroller, the heads of Nicholas's Private Chancellery, the crown land administration, and the charity institutions of the Empress Marie, as well as the governor general of Finland and the state secretary for Finnish affairs. The minister of trade, whose department was created in October 1905, made his pilgrimage to Tsarskoe Selo or Peterhof about every other Monday. Thus, in addition to the ten to twelve weekly meetings with his ministers, Nicholas received another nine officials every two to three weeks, an average of about twelve to fifteen such audiences a week.

These weekly têtes-à-têtes were cancelled or rescheduled, of course, when Nicholas's other commitments so demanded or when the ministers themselves were taken ill or were out of town on inspection trips, or when they had nothing to report—which rarely happened. Sometimes a deputy filled in for a vacationing minister. Occasionally, a summons from the emperor or a request from a minister with dramatic news or pressing business resulted in an audience outside the regularly scheduled times. Finally, the regularity and frequency of ministerial reporting was affected by the identity of the particular reporter in question. Thus, Procurator General K. P. Pobedonostsev, for obvious health and less obvious political reasons, met with Nicholas only very rarely and irregularly in the last years of his stewardship of the Holy Synod up to October 1905; his immediate successors, on the other hand, Prince A. D. Obolenskii and, after July 1906, P. P. Izvol'skii, made a point of seeing Nicholas virtually every Friday. V. K. Pleve and P. N. Durnovo, ministers of internal affairs from April 1902 till July 1904 and from October 1905 till April 1906, respectively, reported to their imperial master virtually every Thursday, whereas Prince P. D. Sviatopolk-Mirskii and A. G. Bulygin, the two men to occupy this post between Pleve and Durnovo, did not. Or, to provide another example, S. Iu. Witte, first chairman of the new Council of Ministers, was received by Nicholas far less frequently than P. A. Stolypin, who succeeded to this position after the brief Goremykin interlude of April–July 1906.

Despite these personal variations in reporting patterns and any other deviations from the general norm of ministerial reports, there can be little doubt as to the regularity of this routine. Had Nicholas ever forgotten what day it was, the particular ministerial reporter would have served to remind him: "It's the Minister of Justice," for example, "so it must be Wednesday." This regularity imposed itself on Nicholas and those who reported to him in much the same way that its predictability and endless repetition numbs the latter-day observer. The ministers and agency heads embarked on their weekly or bi-weekly pilgrimages to the imperial residence on their appointed days, less because of actual need or pressing matters than because of custom and habit. Although he often found these audiences wearying, Nicholas did not question and even derived comfort from their mechanical habitualness which suggested the illusion of normality and of a smoothly functioning government. During those feverish days of October 1905, for example, when revolution gripped the whole country and autocracy teetered on the brink of collapse, Nicholas did not fully grasp the extreme gravity of the situation until it disrupted his own daily routine and prevented his ministers from reporting at the appointed hour.

The very content of these reports further reinforced the numbing regularity of Nicholas's government routine. While some of the information submitted to the emperor was significant and of direct concern, much of it definitely was not. Day in, day out, quite independent of the officials' identities, the agencies they represented, and of events, he had to endure an unending succession of trivial details and mostly minor administrative matters, all of which were submitted for his enlightenment and approval. The overwhelming impression left by most of these reports is one of repetitiveness, specificity, triviality, even frivolity. There were scores of such items every week, never fewer than a hundred and sometimes twice as many. A typical audience with the minister of education, for instance, would contain a dozen items, with the minister of interior sometimes twice or three times that many, and with the minister of justice or the head of H.I.M.'s Chancellery for Petitions rarely fewer than that.

Nicholas, however, did nothing to stem the deluge of excessive and inconsequential details, or of totally frivolous information—quite the contrary. There can be little doubt that he was well-informed about the daily events and goings-on in his realm, too much so perhaps; the compulsive detail and inclusion of minor matters tended to obscure and distract from more consequential developments, thus blinding the imperial reader to the forest for all the trees. Sometimes the news that reached Nicholas was redundant, although he might not have been aware of this fact. During the revolutionary turmoil of 1905, for instance, the tsar learned of the latest unrest through the daily dispatches of the St. Petersburg Telegraphic Agency, the almost daily reports and a weekly summary from the police department, as well as accounts from the ministers of finance, agriculture, education, and communications. The steady barrage of such cumulative horror stories, the ceaseless repetition of bad tidings, made each individual event appear less significant and urgent than it often was, while their aggregate effect may have numbed and paralyzed Nicholas instead of stirring him to action. The bad became routine and thereby more acceptable.

To be sure, the trivial content of many ministerial reports at times appears to have been a bone of contention. Thus, one of his aides-de-camp who accompanied him on his walks in Livadia, the imperial residence in the Crimea, claims that the tsar voiced his unhappiness with the reports of the naval minister. These hour-long resumés, complained Nicholas, were filled with all sorts of irrelevant information, such as recent retirements, pension awards, and current business, but failed to provide detailed insights into the real conditions of the fleet or the qualifications of new recruits, for example. An important matter, such as improving the provisioning of ships, would be referred to a newly appointed committee which never finished its work. Nicholas even spoke of actions taken without his knowledge or approval, or of documents, bearing his signature, that were subsequently amended. On occasion, Nicholas would also vent his frustration on the interminable bureaucratic delays and the slow responses to his orders and queries, but these expressions of dissatisfaction had little effect.[31]

Nicholas gave the impression of having no confidence in his bureaucrats and of considering himself trapped and isolated. The petty jealousies, begrudging comparisons of favors, and constant infighting among their entourage reportedly upset Nicholas and Alexandra and contributed to their sense of isolation: "Somebody needs only to approach us for them immediately to begin talking evil about this person."[32] The tsar clearly disliked the slanderous rumormongering and personal disagreements, but was incapable of countering them. This inability and apparent passivity reflected his alienation from his role. Instead he merely complained idly, waiting for the disharmony to resolve itself and for the new or old

[31] S. S. Fabritskii, *Iz proshlago. Vospominaniia fligel'-ad'iutanta Gosudaria Imperatora Nikolaia II* (Berlin, 1926), pp. 104–5.

[32] Ibid., pp. 106–9.

consensus to emerge. And he did little or nothing to alter the form and content of bureaucratic practice, despite the fact that he resented it bitterly and criticized it openly.

Naturally, the question arises whether there was anything he possibly could have done to effect a change. Was he not the victim of traditional institutional habits, which had their origin in the notion of personalized government? Given these traditions and the absence of firm legal concepts, any attempt at reform, to be sure, would have faced uncertain odds at best. Nicholas, however, did not even make a serious effort. He continued to go through the motions of his routine and endorse hundreds of trivial reports while his resentment grew. Ironically, his disaffection and suspicion of bureaucracy made him zealously defend his prerogatives and insist on continued direct and personal supervision of ordinary and minor matters—the very experience that had contributed to his hostility in the first place. Returning from a provincial inspection, one of his ministers was disturbed by Nicholas's predilection for detail incidental to the business at hand. How and by whom had he been received, did they hold church services and ring the bells, how was the weather, were there children and did they carry flowers—the tsar wanted to know all this as though he might through it be able to avoid weightier, more troubling issues and their difficult resolution.[33] On several occasions ministers proposed that the large number of cases requiring Nicholas's approval be reduced by having the ministers on their own authority dispose of a few of the most insignificant categories. Although he responded favorably to some of these suggestions, more than once he rejected them indignantly.[34]

By contrast, when Prince Khilkov, his trusted minister of communications, went to Siberia during the Russo-Japanese War to supervise the laying of temporary tracks and the movement of troop transports across frozen Lake Baikal, Nicholas gladly granted him the broad authority Khilkov had requested in order to make on-the-spot decisions that normally would have required the tsar's approval.[35] Whereas Nicholas generally was unwilling to relinquish the least bit of his power and prerogatives to bureaucratic institutions on a permanent basis, he had no qualms about granting unusual liberties to personal confidants like Khilkov or even broader license to personal emissaries like the governors-general. All military men, these local satraps epitomized personal rule; they were the tsar's firefighters against the revolution and were endowed with virtually unlimited powers.

[33] Naumov, *Iz utselevshikh vospominanii*, 2:515.
[34] E.g., Tsentral'nyi Gosudarstvennyi Istoricheskii Arkhiv (TsGIA), f. 1284, op. 241, d. 119, ll. 119–20.
[35] TsGIA, f. 446, op. 31, d. 10, ll. 39–40 obratno (ob.), January 16, 1904.

So suspicious was Nicholas of bureaucrats and bureaucratic interference that he did not even suffer a private secretary to help him with the mounds of paperwork and routine business. He personally wrote the notes summoning officials to audiences, and he himself answered the countless congratulations and condolences he would receive on numerous occasions, such as birthdays and name days, the birth of the heir, or the death of a family member; yet each time he would record with relief the ebbing wave of such messages and the end of his latest chore.[36] Not infrequently, the tsar himself made up the seating charts for dinners, and he always went over them and the guest lists for church services with the lord chamberlain, Count Benckendorf, who came to see him several times a week.[37] Simple logistical instructions, such as the readying of a motorcar, yacht, or cutter for a certain time, also bear Nicholas's handwriting.[38] Every evening he read the numerous private petitions and summaries of oral requests received that day[39] and on them recorded his orders to his chancellery. With evident exasperation the chancellery chief noted that his imperial master "himself sealed the envelopes containing his decisions." As Mosolov explains, "it would have been necessary to take a third party into his confidence and the Tsar hated to confide his ideas to anybody. There was another danger—the secretary might magnify his position, impose his own personality, try to influence his master . . . who was not prepared to consult anything but his own conscience. . . . He wanted to be alone. Alone with his Conscience."[40]

Although Nicholas socialized regularly with members of his extended family and the court hierarchy and felt comfortable and relaxed with them, these occasions were entirely given to private pleasure and enjoyment, not political discussions.[41] His suite, confirms Mosolov, "had no part in determining His Majesty's policy, [and] was incapable of bringing him fresh ideas concerning what was going on in his country, of suggesting political ideas independently of the reports from his ministers."[42] As a rule, the tsar was reluctant to discuss any substantive political matters, preferring instead to talk about tennis, horses, weather, the view, or not to talk at all.[43] To those relatives who ventured opinions and asked to be given positions in government so as to assure the execution of his orders and to serve as living links between him and his subjects, Nicholas is said

[36] TsGAOR, f. 601, op. 1, d. 247, e.g., August 1 and 3, 1904.
[37] E.g., TsGIA, f. 516 KFZ, op. 1, Sdatochnaia op. 219/2728, d. 20–21, 1905 passim.
[38] E.g., TsGAOR, f. 601, op. 1, d. 1118, ll. 13, 15.
[39] Fabritskii, Iz Proshlago, p. 89.
[40] Mosolov, At the Court, pp. 12–13.
[41] Iswolsky, Recollections, pp. 300–2.
[42] Mosolov, At the Court, pp. 127–28.
[43] Ibid., p. 14.

to have insisted: "For nearly three hundred years it was a habit of my ancestors to insist upon military careers for their relatives. I am not going to break this tradition. I will not permit my uncles and cousins to interfere with my Government."[44] Nicholas insisted on segregating the private sphere of his family from the public sphere of government.

There were, of course, several men notorious for having the tsar's ear, among them his uncle Sergei; the reactionary editor of the weekly *Grazhdanin*, Prince V. P. Meshcherskii; the military adventurists Bezobrazov and Alekseev; the Court Commandants Gesse and Trepov; and not least the mystic healers Philippe and Rasputin. The very fact that these people stood outside the regular government bureaucracy or acted entirely in a private capacity attracted Nicholas to them, which further confirmed the separation between his private and his official role and his distance from the latter. As bureaucratic outsiders and moral outcasts— for example, both the Grand Duke Sergei and Prince Meshcherskii were well-known homosexuals, while Philippe's and Rasputin's sexual habits were the object of much gossip and indignation—these people were exempted from Nicholas's suspicious guarding of his prerogatives and from his bureaucratic disaffection.

He had a veritable weakness or affinity for private individuals who seemed untainted by any official associations, although tainted in other respects. His contacts with them allowed him, or so it seemed, to break through the bureaucratic wall that he sensed around him and escape the perceived restrictions of his official role. The mythical union between tsar and people appeared to come alive in such unofficial relationships. Only in such a way would he learn of and do justice to the interests of his subjects. Hence the importance of the petitioning process and the interest he took in it; hence, too, his fascination with outlandish ideas that went against common sense and the grain of bureaucratic thinking. His Foreign Minister Izvol'skii cites the examples of adventurers and inventors, whose harebrained schemes struck the tsar's fancy. One wanted to build a bridge across the Bering Straits, another an electrical fence along Russia's entire western frontier to ward off attacks.[45] Gurko, too, commented on "the tendency of Nicholas II to become captivated by new persons and new ideas."[46] Arguably the most pernicious example of this tendency was the tsar's support for the adventurism of Bezobrazov and his associates, which eventually propelled Russia onto the path of war and revolution.

Nicholas's credulity in such matters, his susceptibility to holy men and

[44] Alexander, *Once a Grand Duke*, p. 154.
[45] Iswolsky, *Recollections*, p. 283.
[46] Gurko, *Features and Figures*, p. 221.

adventurers, and his penchant for conspiratorial secrecy represented in part a rebellion against officialdom and against his government role. And yet the very estrangement and suspiciousness that had fostered these un-official relationships usually—with the possible exception of the so-called *Bezobrazovshchina* (Bezobrazov Affair)—limited the influence that they could exert on him and invariably made them short-lived. His relation-ship with Meshcherskii, for example, blew hot and cold over the years, and even the ten-year connection with Rasputin owed more to the tsari-na's faith than to her husband's trust. Instead of trading bureaucratic tu-telage for unofficial connections, the tsar used one to escape the other. In view of Nicholas's wait-and-see attitude and his preference for consen-sus on important problems, moreover, any such unofficial influence was more likely to remain confined to particular and personal cases, i.e., tra-ditional acts of personal favoritism.

In the final analysis, of course, Nicholas's efforts to flee from his role as the head of autocratic administration were as ineffective as the routine and practices that defined this role and that had originally inspired those escape attempts. He was indeed trapped, a prisoner of the administrative structure. He chafed under the external restrictions imposed by his ad-ministrative responsibilities, and he rebelled against them. Yet, lacking a firmly internalized and personally comfortable conception of his role through which to assert himself and his views, he had no choice but to submit. Such resignation only heightened the estrangement that he had felt in the first place. It also made him appear weak-willed and passive, though he was neither in any personal sense. He was mild-mannered, to be sure, but there were plenty of examples of persistence and stubborn-ness on his part. What was perceived as indecision, vacillation, and pas-sivity was in fact the result of his being contained by a structure with which he could not identify and which therefore became still more im-posing, alienating, and constraining.

CHAPTER III

The Ideology of Prerevolutionary Autocracy

ONE OF Nicholas II's first acts, his "senseless dreams" speech of January 1895, suggested that for him only the model of autocracy represented by his beloved father existed and that he was prepared to defend it at all costs. On both counts appearances lied, however. Although emotionally drawn to the personal example of Alexander III, whose physique and demeanor exuded strength and resolve, Nicholas lacked the personal makeup to emulate it. To make matters worse, there were several competing conceptions of autocracy, and the new tsar had failed to internalize any of them. Nicholas's youth and upbringing as heir to Alexander III happened to coincide with a period of profound ideological ferment among the adherents of Russian autocracy. The very absence of any ideological consensus and consistency around him only served to aggravate his personal distance.

If we conceive of ideology as a self-consciously argumentative, pseudo-rational system of defenses to justify and make explicit one's own beliefs, values, and expectations as they are being challenged from without, i.e., as rationalization both in the Marxist and the Freudian senses of the word, then it stands to reason that autocracy would find its most divergent—and persistent—ideological apologists when it came under attack politically in the face of changing socioeconomic realities.[1] In the late 1870s, as the reign of Alexander II was drawing to its violent close, prerevolutionary autocratic ideologists began to wrestle with the legacy of the peasant emancipation and the Great Reforms. Reacting to the political and social unrest that preceded the death of the Tsar-Liberator and the accession of Alexander III in 1881, the defenders of autocracy in their manifold incarnations repeatedly rejected, modified, affirmed, or developed the conceptions of rulership, state, and society implicit in the reform legislation of the 1860s and early 1870s. The ideology of autocracy was neither unchanging nor rationally coherent any more than people's feelings and psychological needs are immutable or free of logical contradictions. Autocracy, as we shall see, meant different things to different people at different times.

---

[1] Some writers even go so far as to speak of the virtual absence of a well-developed formulation of autocratic theory until this time; cf., for example, Richard Pipes's introduction to *Karamzin's Memoir on Ancient and Modern Russia* (Cambridge, Mass., 1959), pp. 12–13.

On the one hand, then, ideology consists of the consciously articulated reflections of particular political actors in particular conjunctures. Yet when taken together or when employed unconsciously, these divergent formulations make for an anonymous and collective structure that transcends individual personalities and circumstances. Ideology as structure is, in the words of William Sewell, at once enabling and constraining, an unconscious mechanism by which we interpret and make sense of the world around us and which limits our choice of theoretically conceivable actions. In this structural sense, ideology is indeed "constitutive of the social order."[2] Thus the conflicting formulations of autocratic ideology not only bespoke the difficulties of apprehending changing realities, but also interfered with ideology's function of binding together the social and political community and of organizing the personality of a maturing individual such as the heir to the Russian throne. One of the results was the so-called "role strain" engendered by different expectations of the role to be played by the emperor.

This chapter is concerned primarily with the varied ideological conceptions that affected the workings of autocracy and were part of Nicholas's environment, both during his youth and in the early part of his reign. My aim here is not to trace the history of autocratic ideology or to attempt any comparisons with Western theories of kingship.[3] While there are enough parallels and similarities to suggest occasional borrowings, the ideologists of Russian autocracy also reacted consciously *against* Western developments. The multifaceted picture of autocratic ideology that follows is akin to a hypothesis, to be developed and tested in subsequent chapters when this ideology, or fragments thereof, becomes the catalyst, creed, and guide for action. Only then will it be possible to distinguish between operative principles and Gramsci's atavistic "traces" or "passive beliefs . . . which are asserted or acknowledged but which do not lead to action or conscious inaction."[4]

As the sociologist Nigel Harris points out, "men sometimes cling to the symbol for other reasons even though the single substance has gone."[5] While it remains to be seen to what extent the main protagonists of autocracy really were conservatives in the sense of seeking to preserve the status quo, conservative doctrines, in particular, are characterized, in

---

[2] William H. Sewell, Jr., "Ideologies and Social Revolutions: Reflections on the French Case," *Journal of Modern History* 57, no. 1 (March 1985): 61. My own position is obviously closer to Sewell's than Theda Skocpol's, though perhaps the two are not nearly as far apart as their debate suggests.

[3] For such an attempt, although one not uniformly well-received, see Michael Cherniavsky, *Tsar and People. Studies in Russian Myths* (New York, 1969).

[4] Nigel Harris, *Beliefs in Society. The Problem of Ideology* (London, 1968), pp. 64–65.

[5] Ibid.

Harris's words, by "a peculiarly high proportion of non-operative beliefs, traces from the past that have little or no relevance for immediate practice." For the most part satisfied with the way things are and opposed to a general reconsideration of system and society that might open the flood gates of change and instability, conservatives will formulate broad theory only in response to a universalist radical challenge. In more ordinary, peaceful times, the place of theory is taken instead by the concrete and the particular, by those "traces" as "embodied in ritual, in lovingly conserved details detached from the context where it was originally created, in pageant and ceremony, detached from the meaning of the objects ostensibly symbolized." Hence the conservative emphasis on form as opposed to content.[6] When taking up the universalist challenge of the radicals, conservatism "frequently retreats into an assertion of mystery; the final justification is unknowable. Beneath the appearance of reality lurks divine mystery, original sin and divine grace, heredity or blood, ethnic or family charisma, national spirit or fate."[7]

The point of this discussion, however, is not the conservatism of autocratic ideology, but the difficulties in identifying commonalities and contradictions of the various conceptions, by no means all conservative. Some of the ideological differences emerged in full relief only when Nicholas, his court, bureaucrats, and individuals or groups within society had to act according to their beliefs.[8] It is one thing to mouth ideological platitudes that have their source in one's own psychology and perception of reality, quite another to reconcile these ideological notions and postulates with an intrusive and hostile reality of another sort. The fact that the central character of this study, Nicholas II, remained largely silent and declared himself only when compelled to do so by events and an overwhelming consensus does not make our task an easy one.

THE NATURE OF AUTOCRATIC POWER

In theory, autocracy represented the concentration and monopolization of all political power and authority in the hands of one person, the auto-

---

[6] Ibid., pp. 233–34.

[7] Ibid., pp. 233–34 and 240. Cf., too, Karl Mannheim, "Das konservative Denken," *Archiv für Sozialwissenschaft und Sozialpolitik* 57 (1927): 68–142, 470–95.

[8] Remarking on the inevitable elasticity and plasticity of any major orthodoxy, Harris, *Beliefs in Society*, pp. 47–48, warns of the difficulties in analyzing any ideology:

> In relationship to one group, some of the ambiguities may *not* have been clarified or inconsistencies may exist, simply because the people concerned have not had to act—that range of problems has not occurred yet, so that the clarification which action needs or entails has also not occurred. Looking at ideologies from the outside, it is extremely difficult to see always what elements are really operative—would in fact guide action in the event of a challenge—and what are elements merely carried along because they originally occurred in the same context as the operative element.

crat. As late as 1910, the liberal legal historian N. I. Lazarevskii would write: "Autocracy is a form of government which concentrates the entire power of the state in the hands of one man—the tsar, king, emperor—in such a manner that no power exists in the state standing above him or of equal rank. The power of such a ruler has the character of an autonomous power."[9] According to an earlier definition by Chicherin, a legal scholar and member of the Statist historical school,[10] autocratic power was "indivisible, constant, sovereign [*derzhavna*], sacred, inviolate, responsible to nobody, omnipresent, and the source of any state power,"[11] a formula that would also fit our current understanding of popular and national sovereignty.

Autocratic power had become virtually synonymous with unlimited and arbitrary power by the sixteenth and seventeenth centuries, i.e., even before the advent of Peter the Great with whom this development is often associated. In his thorough study of Russian kingship in the seventeenth century, Douglas Bennet agrees that by this time any restraints that might be invoked were merely moral, admonitory, and "measures of the purity of the sovereign's reign."[12] Thus Tsar Aleksei Mikhailovich was known as The Most Gentle or Pious (*Tishaishii*), notwithstanding the fact that he, in Bennet's words, "seems to have believed that the authority of God and the authority of the Tsar were combined in a homogeneous sovereignty which gave divine sanction to each act of the ruler. The Tsar's will and God's were, for Aleksei, virtually indistinguishable."[13]

The notion of a divine mandate, of the tsar as God's viceroy on earth, by this time did little more than mask the thoroughly secularized character of autocratic power. This secularization had begun much earlier with the reigns of Ivan III (1462–1505) and his grandson Ivan IV, also known as the Terrible (1533–84). Not only did the Muscovite grand princes take the credit for the unification of Russia, but they used the fall of Constantinople in 1453 to elevate Muscovy to imperial rank and to claim for themselves "the attributes, privileges, status, and functions" of the Byzantine Basileus, as Michael Cherniavsky has demonstrated.[14] While the theory of a Third Rome served as religious sanction, claims of dynastic descendance from the first two Romes provided secular justification for the continuity and legitimacy of the Russian ruler and state.

---

[9] Lazarevskii, *Lektsii*, 1:61.

[10] For brief description, see below, p. 100.

[11] Cited in L. A. Tikhomirov, *Monarkhicheskaia gosudarstvennost'* (Buenos Aires, 1968), p. 42.

[12] Douglas Joseph Bennet, Jr., "The Idea of Kingship in 17th Century Russia" (Ph.D. diss., Harvard University, 1967), p. 96.

[13] Ibid., p. 77.

[14] Cherniavsky, *Tsar and People*, pp. 36–39.

Whether we look at Ivan IV's correspondence with the renegade Prince Kurbskii or his establishment of the *oprichnina*, the realm of terror within his realm, we find him justifying his absolute power on secular as well as divine grounds. Moreover, the tsar ruled the territory as his personal, hereditary property—*votchina*—from which derived the legitimacy of his sovereignty. The fiction of a divine mandate was thus imputed to any ruler who was the legitimate and designated heir of a legitimate predecessor and his property.[15] During the Nikon controversy of the 1650s and 1660s, Russia's rough equivalent of the investiture conflict, Bennet finds non-Russian churchmen using classic, non-Christian sources to furnish the theoretical underpinnings for the secularization of the ruler-myth. Although the state or, for that matter, the Orthodox faith continued to depend on the person of the ruler, state and ruler existed for their own sake now that the latter had been elevated to the position of a god on earth beyond human or divine judgment.

At the same time there was a change in the Russian idea of kingship which Bennet explains

> as a by-product of increasing realism in the Russian view of the terrestrial responsibilities of government prompted by a pressing need for reform and by increasing contact with Western Europe. . . . By the time Peter the Great came to the throne . . . terrestrial well-being, rather than salvation, had become the stated objective of Russian statecraft. The practical, rather than spiritual, needs of human society provided the justification for royal authority. . . . Once this process was in motion, however, it gained momentum from the Nikon controversy, of which it was both cause and effect. . . . Russians had begun to turn from Orthodox theology to Aristotle for political ideas.[16]

Hand in hand with this reorientation from spiritual salvation to physical well-being went a redefinition of government's proper functions from conservative and regulatory ones discouraging change and innovation, such as the protection from evil and temptation, defense against attack, the preservation of justice, and adherence to tradition, to a more broadly conceived, activist, innovative, expansionist role that recognized few, if any, limits and traditions.

Contrary to the assertions of Cherniavsky and others, the secularization and redefinition of the ruler's role, which gave rise to "true absolutism,"[17] were essentially complete by the time of Peter the Great's accession in 1682. Yet this transition remained obscured by the continued obeisances to traditional forms and Orthodox ritual or the invocation of

---

[15] Bennet, "The Idea of Kingship," pp. 2–3, 5.

[16] Ibid., pp. iii–iv, 267.

[17] Cherniavsky, *Tsar and People*, pp. 75–78.

familiar rhetoric. Peter had no such compunctions, however, about rudely breaking with cherished customs; indeed, he seemed to take a particular delight in brazenly defying traditional strictures and making a mockery of church and court ritual to the point of turning it into a burlesque or bacchanalia. In tearing off this protective veil, Peter brought Russia face to face with naked arbitary power; hence the tendency of his contemporaries and posterity to regard his reign as a turning point marking the advent of secular autocratic absolutism. But Peter's reforms, by demonstratively doing away with old customs and traditions and by highlighting the secular aims of the state, merely ratified changes in the conception of autocratic power that had already occurred.

Although the absolute and unlimited nature of autocratic power was expressly affirmed by Nicholas I in the 1832 revision of Russia's Fundamental Laws—"The All-Russian Emperor is an autocratic and unlimited monarch"—most of its subjects remained reluctant to recognize the absence of limits.[18] Even the most fervent defenders of autocracy, while rejecting any formal legal-constitutional limitations, were loath to admit that the autocrat's power was totally unrestricted and blatantly arbitrary. Such unlimited, willful, and inherently selfish power, one writer wanted to believe, was typical of absolute monarchies, not of Russian autocracy.[19] History, tradition, religious and moral norms such as those of the Orthodox faith, the knowledge of absolute truth, responsibility before God, and the prescription of charity and impartiality, were seen as defining the intrinsic limits of the autocrat's power. Although such norms were purely subjective and unenforceable, with only the Last Judgment promising restitution and consolation, they were routinely affirmed in ritual and ceremonial gestures of autosuggestion that masked the absence of effective limitations. Reality was no match for wishful thinking, which instead created realities of its own.

No matter how important the differences dividing them, all adherents of autocracy were agreed that the ruler's power, while juridically unlimited, carried definite moral connotations. As even Chicherin had argued a scant half-century before, "any limitations may only be moral, not juridical. Juridically unlimited, the supreme power finds its limits both in

---

[18] Indeed, the debate on the question of limitations was as old as autocracy itself; its history and historiography is to be found in Vladimir Val'denberg, *Drevnerusskie ucheniia o predelakh tsarskoi vlasti. Ocherki russkoi politicheskoi literatury ot Vladimira Sviatago do kontsa XVII veka* (Petrograd, 1916).

[19] Ibid., pp. 426–27 and passim. This assertion was obviously erroneous; as Perry Anderson points out, "absolute monarchy in the West was . . . in fact, always doubly limited: by the persistence of traditional political bodies below it and the presence of an overarching moral law above it"; *Lineages of the Absolutist State* (London, 1974), p. 51.

its own moral consciousness and in the conscience of the citizens."[20] Such power not only was founded on truth, *pravda*, but this truth, as the other component meaning of pravda—i.e., justice—indicates, was objective and absolute, not subjective or relative. "Truth is absolute," Konstantin Petrovich Pobedonostsev, tutor and advisor to the last two tsars and long-time procurator-general of the Holy Synod, wrote anonymously in 1896, "and only the absolute may be the foundation of human life."[21]

In this view, autocratic power did not represent the product of superior force, the victory of the stronger over the weaker, or the predominance of one interest over another. Absolute in every respect, such power was antithetical to and utterly irreconcilable with parties (*partiia*), i.e., selfish factional interests. "Our Autocratic power is the only incorruptible power in the world, standing outside of any evil, partiality, or party."[22] Only absolute power, as embodied in the autocrat, could be impartial; he alone stood above partisan interests and social groups as the sole and final arbiter, judging according to truth and his conscience. Autocracy, according to a newspaper panegyric on Alexander III, was "the subordination of interests and desires to the absolute truth," "the reconciling power" of which constituted the very essence of autocratic government: "For him neither the wise nor the fool, neither the strong nor the weak, neither majority nor minority exist. For him there is only conscience and pravda."[23]

The autocrat, in the well-nigh perfect embodiment of Alexander III eulogized here by Lev Tikhomirov, a revolutionary turned reactionary,[24] takes on a definite resemblance to Christ. The tsar is not only the arbiter for his people, but the mediator and go-between (*posrednik*) between his people and God: "In his conscience he hears only the voice of God's will. . . . His self-rule is not a privilege, not the mere 'concentration' of human power, but it is a heavy sacrifice [*podvig*], the great service above human selflessness, a 'cross,' not enjoyment." Through the hereditary principle all human choice is excluded and God's will reigns supreme.[25]

[20] Quoted approvingly in Tikhomirov, *Monarkhicheskaia gosudarstvennost'*, p. 42.

[21] Pobedonostsev, *Reflections of a Russian Statesman* (Ann Arbor, Mich., 1965), p. 139. This is the English translation of his *Moskovskii sbornik* (Moscow Journal).

[22] P. N. Semenov, *Samoderzhavie kak gosudarstvennoi stroi* (St. Petersburg, 1906), p. 12.

[23] *Moskovskiia Vedomosti*, October 30, 1894.

[24] A Populist implicated in the assassination of Alexander II, Lev Tikhomirov was exiled to Siberia whence he escaped abroad. After repenting of his sins, he was welcomed back to the fold. He went on to serve the autocracy with the fanatical zeal of a late convert—as an editorialist for the staunchly reactionary *Moskovskiia Vedomosti*, as a member of the Ministry of Internal Affairs under Stolypin, and as a participant in discussions on the subject of church reform in 1907–8, services that attracted the personal attention of the last two tsars.

[25] Ibid.

Power was selfless and so was its imperial bearer who sacrificed himself for his people in dutiful obedience to God's unfathomable will or the cruel quirks of fate. "Power is understood as burden, not privilege—this is the cornerstone of Christian Autocracy," exclaimed another theorist.[26] So immense was the weight of this power, so intimidating its responsibilities, that ordinary mortals did not seek it but were content to see it exercised by their tsar. In return, they accorded him the honor and love merited by the greatness of his sacrifice, without forgetting, of course, that all the external trappings of glory and splendor did not begin to compensate for this burden.[27]

The very language of autocratic ideology mirrored this peculiar understanding of autocratic power, for the Russian term *vlast'*, which is usually translated as "power," denotes "authority" as well. Power, in the strict sense, is the ability to control and determine human activity, and rests on coercion or at least the threat of force. In Max Weber's definition, "power (*Macht*) is the probability that one actor within a social relationship will be in a position to carry out his own will despite resistance, regardless of the basis on which this probability rests."[28] Authority, by contrast, is power sanctioned by historical precedent, tradition, social convention, habit, or law: "What clearly distinguishes authority from coercion, force, and power on the one hand, and influence on the other hand, is legitimacy. Superiors feel that they have a right to issue commands; subordinates perceive an obligation to obey."[29]

Both meanings, physical-coercive power and legitimate power, were contained in Article I of Russia's Fundamental Laws, according to which "to obey his power [vlast'], not only out of fear but also for conscience's sake, is commanded by God himself." In linking the negative, deterrent-proscriptive component of fear and the positive, normative-prescriptive notion of conscience, the law appeared to stress that the absolute power it reserved for the tsar did not simply rest on superior force but was in fact legitimate, i.e., accepted and voluntarily obeyed by the tsar's subjects.

Exactly how is legitimacy to be understood here? Doubting the longevity of power based on coercion alone, Lazarevskii observed in 1910: "The real source of any state power in the final analysis lies in the peo-

[26] D. Khomiakov, *Samoderzhavie (Opyt' skhematicheskago postroeniia etogo poniatiia)* (Moscow, 1903), p. 41.

[27] Ibid., pp. 33–34.

[28] Max Weber, *The Theory of Social and Economic Organization*, ed. Talcott Parsons (New York, 1964), p. 152.

[29] Robert L. Peabody, "Authority," *International Encyclopaedia of the Social Sciences* (New York, 1968), 1:474.

ple's recognition of its necessity."[30] Making legitimate power or authority contingent on the acceptance of those subject to it, a condition manifestly absent from pure power with its implication of superior force, is a thoroughly Western notion, however. Here is how the sociologist Robert Michels relates the two: "Authority presumes faith in some power, present or future, or in a man who possesses or is believed to possess either power or special gifts of competence, wisdom and reasonableness. . . . Whether authority is of personal or institutional origin, it is created and maintained by public opinion, which in turn is conditioned by sentiment, affection, reverence, or fatalism," or, for that matter, the fear of force.[31]

In combining the meanings of both power and authority, vlast', on the other hand, was—and remains—ipso facto legitimate from the point of view of those governing. The subjects' obedience was *not* a precondition of its legitimacy; instead it was a necessary fiat and consequence. To make the legitimacy of autocratic power dependent on the voluntary recognition of the people, as Lazarevskii did or as George Yaney does in his ambitious analysis of Russian administrative transformations,[32] may be to describe reality accurately, but it fails to define the correct meaning of *vlast'* as used by autocratic ideologists then—and now. Indeed, it should have become amply clear that any ideological pronouncements on autocracy and the nature of tsarist power say little or nothing about the actual extent and character of this power or of the entire system.[33] Instead, the language itself structured and constrained the perceptions of its users.

MODELS OF AUTOCRATIC RULERSHIP

Although the proponents of autocracy held diverging and sometimes diametrically opposed views of government and the ruler's role, virtually all of them were drawn to the vision of absolute, selfless power standing above and mediating among all interests. There were at least five such differing conceptions, as we shall see presently. For the moment, they can be summarized as the personalized notion of pre-Petrine *votchina* paternalism; the depersonalized view of the Petrine service class state; the *Rechtsstaat* principles of Legal Autocracy, which sought to combine the personal with the abstract; the organic conception of an amorphous

---

[30] Lazarevskii, *Lektsii*, 1:62.

[31] Robert Michels, "Authority," *Encyclopaedia of the Social Sciences* (New York, 1930), 1:319–21.

[32] George L. Yaney, *The Systemization of Russian Government. Social Evolution in the Domestic Administration of Imperial Russia, 1711–1905* (Urbana, Ill., 1973), p. 285: "Its supposed absoluteness," Yaney writes in reference to the tsar's absolute power, "is not the ruler's own; it resides in the attitudes of those who recognize it."

[33] This discrepancy is also recognized by Anderson, *Lineages of the Absolutist State*, p. 220.

community contained by pure power; and, finally, the model of a modern bureaucratic state joining an activist, interventionist bureaucracy with a dynamic society. Whatever the very real and important differences in these distinct models of rulership, they all incorporated the superordinate pretensions of moral and impartial autocratic power. In fact, it was this vantage point and the perceived chance to put into practice their respective blueprints with the sanction and means of autocratic power that brought together and made strange bedfellows out of many autocratic servitors. Sergei Iulevich Witte, who as minister of finance was the architect of Russia's forced-draft industrialization in the 1890s, and Pobedonostsev, for example, though so dissimilar in many of their convictions, were united in their regard for Alexander III as the incarnation of true autocratic power, an agreement that helps explain the respect in which they always held each other, no matter how they disagreed on other issues.

The abstract, impersonal ruler and state images, which had emerged by the time of Peter the Great, were reflected in the foreign and impersonal title *Gosudar' Imperator* (Sovereign Emperor). The autocrat was, according to Peter, merely the first servant of the equally abstract state or *gosudarstvo* which all subjects had to serve, each in their own station as defined by the state. As such, the new title was at odds with, indeed antithetical to, the traditionally used, personal and popular appellation *Tsar' Batiushka* (Little Father Tsar), who stood in a direct personal relationship to each of his subjects unmediated by the new state structure and its various agencies.[34] This contrast highlighted the contradiction between the Petrine bureaucratic service state based on the notion of impersonal administration (*upravlenie*) and the pre-Petrine prikaz order based on personal leadership (*rukovodstvo*). The first represented pretensions to system and standardization, in which uniformity and regularity were enforced through rules rather than personal caprice. The latter stood for personal ties and rule which depended entirely on the all-pervasive personalized image of the tsar amidst a bewildering array of chancellories with conflicting and overlapping territorial and task-specific responsibilities. Institutionalized authority, which included the concept of a well-organized bureaucracy with clearly delineated tasks and rights, conflicted with personal authority. Peter had sought to routinize and institutionalize the sovereign's personal authority through far-reaching bureaucratic reforms and reorganizations. Yet, by virtue of his larger-than-

---

[34] Cherniavsky, *Tsar and People*, pp. 82–84, comments on this contrast in similar terms and goes on to write: "The husband-tsar (*Batiushka Tsar'*) carried the burdens of Russia (*Matiushka Rus'*) on his shoulders, acting because of his personal qualities as mediator between his children and God as his model, Christ, had done. The emperor, however, was the father of *his* country (*Otets Otechestva*)."

life persona, the nonsystematic character of the reforms, and the shortage of qualified bureaucratic servitors, his innovations remained, in Cherniavsky's words, mere "executive extensions of [his] personal will" that served to reassert his personal authority and the notion of personal as opposed to institutional rule.[35] Thus the very prominence of the ruler-myth with its exaltation of the tsar's person and power prevented the resolution of this conflict.

The irreconcilability of the two conceptions, evident in theory but still more so in practice, confronted the apologists of autocracy in the late nineteenth century with a stark choice between returning to a real or alleged *status quo ante* or embracing a course of reform that might in time lead to a limitation of the tsar's power. Henceforth these conflicting views would exist side by side, to be invoked singly by those who preferred one over the other or jointly by those who sought to make the real and the ideal accord with each other.[36] While these alternative conceptions were certainly apparent in the preparation and discussion of the so-called Counter-Reforms of the 1880s and early 1890s, they emerged in full relief during the early reign of Nicholas II.

Here is how the conflict between personal and impersonal notions of rulership found expression in the writings of Lev Tikhomirov during this very time. Classifying government either as *sluzhiloe* (service, executive) or *predstavitel'noe* (representative), Tikhomirov explained that autocracy belonged to the first, absolute monarchy (!) and parliamentarism to the second category. In the first case, the tasks and responsibilities of each government servant supposedly were clearly defined; he acted on precise instructions from his superior or according to specific laws. The ruler in turn exercised "control and supervision," but relinquished neither his unlimited power, nor its claim to universality, nor his moral responsibility for all actions taken by government agencies. In the second case, on the other hand, each government official acted in the name of a higher authority, even when its prior will or decision was unknown. Acting only "in the name" of the tsar—or, for that matter, of the people—government servants and agencies became independent and thus created bureaucratic government. Although the fiction of executing the supreme will was preserved, absolute power in fact passed on to the bureaucracy.[37] The function of government, according to Tikhomirov, was to transmit the sovereign's will; since this "transmitting mechanism" consisted of people and their organizations, it had begun to exhibit a will, desire, and logic of its own. As a result, bureaucracy had come to distort, even coun-

[35] Ibid., pp. 85–87.
[36] Ibid., pp. 93–95, makes a similar point.
[37] Tikhomirov, *Monarkhicheskaia gosudarstvennost'*, pp. 53–59.

termand, the will and instructions of the ruler, usurping his power and interposing itself between him and his subjects.[38]

What then were to be the precise relationships between the sovereign and his subjects, between government and citizens, and among government institutions, Tikhomirov asked, and what were the proper definitions of personal and civil rights? These questions, he claimed, had gone unanswered since the Petrine reforms, which instead had given birth to absolutist monarchy, the diseased aberration of an autocracy devoid of ethical substance.[39] Russian autocracy therefore had little choice but to give precise answers to the questions raised. It had to issue laws to which all would be subject and which would be observed by all, spelling out and codifying the rights and responsibilities of officials and citizens alike while leaving the autocratic ruler free to control and supervise.

Men far less enamored of autocracy than Tikhomirov might have agreed with his criticisms—for reasons he could hardly have intended. His solution, if carried to its radical conclusion, would appear incompatible with the autocrat's personal authority, for the very concept of a well-organized bureaucracy with clearly delineated tasks and rights rested on the assumption of institutional authority, and it expressed aspirations to system and legal universality that flatly contradicted the autocratic understanding of law and authority. Nothing could have been further from Tikhomirov's mind.

In preferring "service" to "representative" government, he favored a personal over an impersonal conception, i.e., "servants" carrying out the personal and specific commands of the sovereign as opposed to officials acting according to impersonal and general guidelines or rules in his name. In theory at least, these distinctions coincided with the pre-Petrine prikaz and the Western-inspired collegiate bureaucratic system, and Tikhomirov left no doubt where his sympathies lay. In an editorial written on the occasion of Nicholas's accession, he emphasized this same personal element, the need for personalized as opposed to institutionalized authority:

> Only a personality has conscience, only a personality bears responsibility before God. . . . [A]ny limitation of the tsar's power by people would relieve him of his answerability before his conscience and before God. Surrounded by limitations, he would no longer be subordinate to the truth but to these or those interests, this or another force of the land.[40]

Autocratic power, as understood by Tikhomirov, had to be personal, indivisible, and unlimited.

---

[38] Ibid., pp. 52–53.
[39] Ibid., pp. 272–73.
[40] *Moskovskiia Vedomosti*, October 30, 1894.

Tikhomirov was not the first, of course, to give expression to the myth of the bureaucratic barrier between ruler and ruled, pitting the monarch against his own bureaucracy. This myth followed directly from the irreconcilability of the personal and impersonal notions of rulership, and it endured until the very end of the tsarist regime, if not beyond. Indeed, such was the hold and persuasiveness of this myth that the tsar's subjects, be they peasants or members of the intelligentsia, usually blamed disastrous government policies and harmful official actions on ignorant, selfish, and corrupt bureaucrats, who allegedly had obstructed the ruler's true intentions or had deliberately kept him in the dark. Positive reforms and concessions, on the other hand, were attributed to the personal efforts and persistence of the sovereign himself. Even a man like Herzen, an icon of the Russian intelligentsia and someone who cannot be accused of harboring excessive sympathies for autocracy, was under the spell of this myth when he greeted the intended emancipation of the serfs as the personal achievement of Alexander II against odds that might have overwhelmed an ordinary mortal: "Thou hast conquered, Galilean!" Countless popular sayings, to say nothing of tens of thousands of petitions to the emperor by people from all walks of life, testified to this deep-seated belief in the personal goodness and power of the tsar and the sinister role of his servitors.[41]

In their actions and statements, the tsars themselves, whether we speak of Nicholas I, Alexander III, or Nicholas II, revealed a similar and ever-increasing hostility toward their bureaucrats. Suspecting bureaucratic ineffectiveness and ineptness, the autocrat often felt compelled by the ruler-myth to ignore institutional restrictions and precedent and to assert his personal will to the point of regulating and intruding into the personal lives of his subjects.[42] Yet, as if to illustrate the spell of the bureaucratic myth, those affected by these capricious intrusions would often persist in blaming the hated officialdom, not the emperor.

By obscuring the discrepancies between the personal and institutional dimensions of autocratic government, between rhetorical aspirations and administrative realities, the myth of the bureaucratic barrier functioned as an ideological smoke screen protecting the exalted image and role of the ruler. For this reason, even the harshest criticisms of bureaucratic bungling and lawlessness rarely provoked the censor's ire or police retaliation, provided such attacks were careful not to question the institution of autocracy or implicate the tsar himself. For example, a eulogy on Alexander III delivered in 1894 by a leading member of the Society for the Assistance of Commercial Shipping explicitly distinguished between the

[41] See, for example, V. Dal', *Poslovitsy russkogo naroda* (Moscow, 1957), pp. 243–44.
[42] Cf. Cherniavsky's observations about Nicholas I, *Tsar and People*, pp. 152–53.

late sovereign's personal achievements and the more debatable actions of his bureaucrats:

> Everything which originated with him *directly* was wise and for the good and glory of Russia. . . . Thus, a dispassionate examination of what was accomplished during the past reign in this or that sector of state administration can only provide an assessment of the activity of the tsar's associates and determine the level of public understanding and knowledge; but it will not add one single aspect to the radiant image of the late Monarch, which is already clearly defined and deeply imprinted in Russian hearts.[43]

Autocratic rule, the will and direct actions of the tsar, were contrasted with the bureaucratic regime whose universally noted arbitrariness and other shortcomings were the bureaucrats' fault, not the sovereign's.

The myth of the bureaucratic barrier could not serve indefinitely as such a buffer, however. Sooner or later the unresolved contradiction between personal and depersonalized notions of government, which suffuses autocratic ideology and had given birth to the myth, was bound to erupt. The tsar could not divorce himself entirely from his administrative apparatus. The growing isolation and ineffectiveness of his bureaucracy, which were very real, adversely affected the ruler's ability to exercise his role, to assert his leadership pretensions and thus his very authority.

It was at this point that the myth showed itself from a less positive side, for it implied a criticism of the status quo. It is no coincidence that the most fervent adherents of autocracy as well as its sharpest opponents found themselves in the same antibureaucratic camp. Unanimous in their condemnation of bureaucratic administration, on which they blamed many, if not all, of Russia's woes, both sides directed their volleys against the same target, albeit from diametrically opposed vantage points. Whereas some self-proclaimed defenders of autocracy such as Tikhomirov criticized the distortions of the tsar's will and the restriction of his personal power by petty bureaucratic rules and foreign institutional practices, its opponents inveighed against the excess of personal power and arbitrariness, which they blamed on the absence of bureaucratic systematization and a superficial sense of legality (zakonnost') in Russia. The latter diagnosis was shared even by those autocratic loyalists who believed in Legal Autocracy; in their eyes, the best guarantee for the preservation of autocratic power was the establishment of clearly delineated bureaucratic responsibilities and civil rights. In all cases, whether seen as an idea and institution alien to autocracy and Russia or as the very incarnation of this hated system, bureaucracy per se (or as then constituted) symbolized a status quo in need of drastic change.

[43] *Russkii Vestnik* 235 (November 1894): 311.

At its most extreme, of course, the myth of the bureaucratic barrier became a powerful incentive as well as a radical dispensation for unrest and revolution. Manipulable almost at will, as Daniel Field has shown us,[44] it served to sanction acts of popular disobedience and violence against bureaucrats and landlords, though not against the ruler. "The Russian tsar, in the eyes of the people, is not at all the chief bureaucrat," the Slavophile Ivan Aksakov wrote. "In Russian history . . . there had been uprisings against voievodas, boyars, gentry, but in popular eyes the Tsar was never identified with them,"[45]—that is, unless this tsar was considered an illegitimate usurper, in which case the rebels invariably would be led by a pretender claiming to be the real tsar. Such behavior was rooted both in personal suspicion of the tsar's agents and in a deep-seated hostility toward the institutions and agencies of the abstract state.

A profound antagonism not only towards the abstract state but also towards formal definitions and theoretical abstractions of any kind characterized those conservatives who adhered to the personalized conception of autocracy. "Faith in abstract principles is the prevailing error of our time," Pobedonostsev wrote in 1896.[46] His buzzwords were "external," "artificial," "formal," and "mechanical." He denounced science, philosophy, logic, formalism, institutions, mechanical regularity, and theory, since they were irreconcilable with faith, feeling, organicity, history, spirituality, personal morality, ethics, the idiosyncrasies and aspirations of human nature—in short, living reality. Time and again Pobedonostsev returned to this contrast:

> Abstract generalities have set up science itself in opposition to life and its phenomena. . . . [T]hey have fettered, hand and foot, the living organism of social life with artificial formulas imposed by force. . . . Life is not a science, or a philosophy, but a living organism. Neither science nor philosophy, as external forces, can rule our lives. . . . [I]t would be vain to think that they can exhaust and comprehend life in all its infinite manifestations, endow it with new elements, or reconstruct it upon new foundations. . . . On earth we walk by faith and not by sight. . . . The infinity of the universe and the principle of life cannot be expressed by any logical formula. . . . [T]he recognition of an immortal self, faith in the only God, the consciousness of sin, the yearning for perfection, the sacrifice of love, the feeling of duty: these are the truths in which the soul may trust—not in the idols of formula and theory.[47]

Autocratic power, despite its ethical connotations and absolute pretensions, was not an abstraction, but a living reality, a reflection of life's

[44] See Field's *Rebels in the Name of the Tsar* (Boston, 1976), *passim*.

[45] Cherniavsky, *Tsar and People*, pp. 183–84.

[46] Pobedonostsev, *Reflections*, pp. 99–100.

[47] Ibid., pp. 137–38.

mysteries. "Such truth is absent," Pobedonostsev claimed, "where the ruling principle of power is abstract theory, detached from life with its manifold conditions and needs."[48] The people's deep-seated faith in the ideals of truth, justice, and moral order required "a living incarnation of the principle of order and of truth"[49] in a single person, not some impersonal system, for which Pobedonostsev had nothing but contempt. Tikhomirov's editorial on the occasion of Nicholas's twenty-eighth birthday echoed this thought: "Our system of government is not maintained by written agreements, not by innumerable compromises between opposing parties nor by a complicated artificial mechanism, but only by deep faith in the Tsar."[50] With this mystical worship of feeling and faith and with this organicist emphasis on the community and its history, Pobedonostsev, Tikhomirov, and other like-minded conservatives were taking up the battle cry of Burke, De Maistre, and Taine against the rational-mechanical world view of the Enlightenment and its offspring, the French Revolution, which by making a fetish of the individual and his rights, they charged, had unleashed the Hobbesian "war of all against all" (*bellum omnium contra omnes*).

Though Pobedonostsev was a jurist by training and had been involved in preparing the enlightened reforms of Alexander II, his experiences with the superficial legalism of Russia's bureaucracy made him deny the supremacy of the law altogether. The reforms of Peter and his successors, Pobedonostsev explained, had sought to introduce bureaucratic institutions and to reorder the state along Western lines; to this end they had promoted foreign notions of law that had given rise to an increasingly confusing and contradictory maze of rules and regulations. These so-called laws ignored human nature and historical conditions. Instead of protecting the people's real freedoms, they limited them, delivering the common people into the clutches of advocates who picked the rule or law that best suited them and their argument. Such law possessed neither a necessary spiritual element nor moral authority. Applied purely formally and technically, law was no more than "the regulation of external action, the preserver of mechanical equilibrium of the diverse operations of human activity in their juridical relations."[51] Law in the context of autocratic government met with Pobedonostsev's boundless scorn:

> When wickedness and violence have to be exposed, the injured to be justified, order to be restored, and his due to be given to each, most necessary of all things is a powerful exercise of will, inspired by ardor for justice and for the

[48] Ibid., p. 260.
[49] Ibid., p. 255.
[50] *Moskovskiia Vedomosti*, May 6, 1896.
[51] Pobedonostsev, *Reflections*, pp. 85–88.

welfare of the people. But if at every step the executor of the law finds in the law itself restrictive prescriptions and artificial formulas, if at every step he fears to transgress the limits of law established, if in addition the jurisdiction of coordinate institutions is obscured by detailed limitations, then all authority is lost in doubt, weakened by the laws which ought to be the source of its strength, and crushed by the fear of responsibility in that moment when not fear but the consciousness of duty and right should be the only guide and impulse. The moral influence of the law is sapped by a multitude of provisions and definitions . . . and, as a result, the law in the popular conception assumes the aspect of a mysterious power, existing for a purpose inexplicable, and everywhere restricting and paralyzing the operations of life.[52]

Clearly, the supreme power of the autocrat was not subject to the law; in fact, law was seen as incompatible with real authority and the exercise of free will. Instead, the law was to be an expression of the autocrat's free will and thus free to be changed, to serve the autocratic power which Pobedonostsev saw as absolute truth and justice incarnate.

Since the ruler could not govern the immense Russian Empire by himself, he had to rely on countless assistants who together constituted the government apparatus. Were they to stand above the law, too? Pobedonostsev's criticisms suggest that the tsar's agents should indeed be free to ignore the law's "restrictive prescriptions" and be guided instead by their "consciousness of duty and right." Since autocratic government, in Pobedonostsev's opinion, was a government of men, not laws, the personal qualities and views of these men were of vital importance. The autocrat was to surround himself with capable and trustworthy servitors, "men of truth, of clear intellects, of strong understandings, and of sincere speech," simple yet dignified, like him "a mirror and example for all . . . subordinates."[53] Every official, it would appear, had to be a carbon copy of the monarch, infused by the same moral qualities and desire for absolute truth and justice. Naturally, the ruler could not personally appoint all of his agents, but was to leave the appointment of those in secondary and less important positions to his trusted aides. Similarly, it would be a mistake for the tsar to "pay the same attention to trifling details of routine work as to those essential questions which it is his duty generally to direct. His place is above all work, whence he may survey the whole horizon of subordinate activity."[54] While this last remark was at variance with and therefore may have implied a criticism of contemporary practice, Pobedonostsev left little doubt that personal authority, issuing from the autocrat himself and compelled by a sense of duty and moral responsibility,

[52] Ibid., pp. 88–89.
[53] Ibid., pp. 257–59.
[54] Ibid., pp. 260–62.

not legal-institutional and abstract-mechanical imperatives, was to drive the administrative machinery of autocracy.

Those who sought "to replace power [vlast'] with the authority of the law" were condemned to failure, Pobedonostsev insisted, for "to live without power is impossible."[55] It is here that he departed from the traditional understanding of autocratic power. Where others saw vlast' as *resting on* pravda, i.e., truth/justice, Pobedonostsev *equated* vlast' with pravda. If truth was absolute and indivisible, so was vlast'; if justice was universal, so was vlast'. Where others derived reassurance from the personal qualities of the autocratic power, Pobedonostsev also worshipped power for its own sake. Though couched in traditional terms, the glorification of power with which he concluded his book was decidedly nontraditional and stands in a category by itself: "To power belongs the first and last word—it is the alpha and omega of human activity," he intoned, building toward a rapturous climax. "Great and sacred is the vocation of power. . . . To see such power, to feel its inspiring influence, is a great happiness for every man who loves truth, and yearns for light and virtue."[56]

Far from adopting Witte's utilitarian view of autocratic power, Pobedonostsev went so far as to claim—and was seconded by Tikhomirov[57]—that the very psychology of human beings impelled them toward subordination to authority and a higher principle: "The natural instinct of man seeks for power in unbroken activity, to which the mass, with its varied needs, aspirations, and passions, may submit . . . in which it may find amid all the subversions of willfulness a standard of truth."[58] Human beings, it would appear, instinctively craved the chastening brunt of power. Indeed, this spiritual need for subordination to power was second only to the need for communion with God. Because of the eternal conflict between good and evil, justice and injustice, "there has been no salvation save to seek sustenance and reconciliation in a high judge of this conflict, in a living incarnation of the principle of order and truth." In their quest for good and truth and in their own helpless ambivalence, people "can never cease to believe in the ideal of power," the constant suffering and humiliations at the hands of that power notwithstanding.[59] Pobedonostsev's sobering glorification of power went hand in hand, as we shall see, with a pessimistic assessment of the Russian people and of human nature in general.

[55] Ibid., pp. 254–55.
[56] Ibid., p. 254.
[57] Tikhomirov, *Monarkhicheskaia gosudarstvennost'*, pp. 16–17.
[58] Pobedonostsev, *Reflections*, p. 253.
[59] Ibid., p. 255.

Since "power is the depository [*sic*] of truth"[60] and therefore indivisible, it could not be shared with anyone, least of all the people. The idea that the people were sovereign, that they equally possessed power and thus were entitled to equal voices or votes, was denounced as "the great falsehood of our time. . . . [T]his apparently equal distribution of 'freedom' among all involves the total destruction of equality. Each vote, representing an inconsiderable fragment of power, by itself signifies nothing; an aggregation of votes alone has a relative value." Much as in a shareholding company, the person who controlled the most shares or votes would exercise real power, giving rise to bribery and manipulation, party conflict and demagogic sloganeering, and creating the illusion of majority rule or popular will.[61] "Parliament is an institution for the satisfaction of the personal ambition, vanity, and self-interest of its members. . . . Parliamentarism is the triumph of egoism—its highest expression."[62] Power atomized was no power at all, for it could exist only in totality and as an absolute; power divided was inherently selfish and devoid of truth. Real vlast', Pobedonostsev insisted, was divine, disinterested, and onerous: "Power exists not for itself alone, but for the love of God; it is a service to which men are dedicated. Thence comes the limitless, terrible strength of power, and its limitless and terrible burden."[63]

Reality, however, was more prosaic. In fact, Pobedonostsev's very worship of power might well have reflected the sense of impotence conveyed by the incumbent tsar. In what was most certainly meant as an unfavorable comparison between Alexander III and Nicholas II, Pobedonostsev professed his chagrin at seeing "power lost to the sentiment of duty and to the knowledge of its calling; power fulfilling its work unconsciously and formally, under the shield of its dignity. The same forms of procedure remain, the wheels of the mechanism turn as before, but the spirit of life is not in them . . . till men are no longer chosen at all, but appointed at random through casual impulses and fortuitous interests."[64] At the same time, Pobedonostsev was reacting against what he regarded as the mistaken emphasis on legality (zakonnost') and an independent abstraction of the state inherent in the Great Reforms of Alexander II or those of his predecessors. The belief in the supremacy of the law, either as a check on the arbitrariness of the bureaucratic servitors who were to remain subservient to the tsar's personal authority, or as the driving principle of the professionally organized, disinterested bureaucratic state mechanism

---

[60] Ibid., p. 256.
[61] Ibid., pp. 26–27, 32.
[62] Ibid., pp. 34–35.
[63] Ibid., p. 254.
[64] Ibid., pp. 266–67.

(Max Weber's Rechtsstaat) that was to contain and institutionalize the tsar's personal authority, clearly was abhorrent to Pobedonostsev.

NAROD AND SOCIETY

Whatever the understanding of autocratic power and government, it rested on the alleged uniqueness of the Russian *narod*—a word used in reference to the simple people or folk, as distinct from educated and privileged society. Pobedonostsev, for example, praised the masses for their natural suspicion of all things new and for their stubborn resistance to change, their "precious virtue of steadfastness, which has hitherto sustained society." Behind this inertia stood the obdurate convictions and unconscious beliefs of the common people, which were immune to rational persuasion:

> The obstinacy of the simple man in opinions which he holds on faith proceeds, although for the most part without recognition by himself, from instinctive but in the highest degree logical impulses. The simple man instinctively feels that the change of opinions, which is thrust upon him by arguments apparently irrefutable, would involve the modification of his whole system of outlook upon life, a system for which, perhaps, he has no justification, but which is indissolubly bound up with his being, and constitutes his spiritual life.[65]

In the same vein, Pobedonostsev glorified traditional structures and practices as "precious and indispensable" expressions of a national spirit and thus as inviolate and sacred:

> Often in the depths of the old institutions there is embodied some profoundly true idea which springs directly from the spirit of the people. . . . They cherish their institution with its excrescences, sometimes ugly and often objectless, because their instinct is to guard the hidden germs of truth against shallow attack. These germs are all the more precious because they symbolize the immemorial needs of the soul, protecting the truth hidden in their depths.[66]

Good or bad, the existing social order, its institutions, conventions and ritual observances, reflected the unique way of life (*byt*) of the Russian people.

Accentuating the positive, the Slavophiles and their heirs idealized the spiritual quality of the masses, their unselfish rejection of power, and their sensible acceptance of reality. According to this interpretation, Russian autocracy had its origins in the very character and psychology of the Russian people whose "absolute ethical element"[67] distinguished them

---

[65] Ibid., p. 82.
[66] Ibid., pp. 184–85.
[67] Tikhomirov, *Monarkhicheskaia gosudarstvennost'*, p. 373.

from others. Even such a sober-minded westernizer as Chicherin claimed to have discovered an essential difference between Russia and the West in the Russian people's "readiness to sacrifice everything for the tsar and the fatherland directly opposite to the spirit of personal liberties."[68] Clearly, autocracy was rooted in the uniquely positive qualities of the Russian narod, which could boast a host of proverbs testifying, in Tikhomirov's words, to "the unity of the people with the tsarist [ideal]." Writer after writer adduced homilies, such as "the narod is the body, the tsar its head" or "without the tsar the people are orphans," to document the popular attitudes toward autocracy. In addition to confirming the people's affinities and affections for their ruler, these sayings dramatized the centrality of the ruler-myth by affirming the tsar's role as God's representative on earth, the supremacy of his will, and his inherent wisdom, justice, and goodness as opposed to the fickleness and corruption of laws and officials.[69]

History provided proof. According to the Normanist myth popularized in the early nineteenth century by Nicholas Karamzin, Russia's first modern historian, the people had selflessly proffered the unwanted burden of power and voluntarily entrusted themselves to their equally unselfish rulers and to God's mercy. Describing the invitation extended to the Varangian overlords in 826, Karamzin wrote:

> The Slavs voluntarily destroy their ancient popular government and request sovereigns from the Varangians. . . . [E]verywhere else the sword of strong men, or the cunning of ambitious men, brought in absolute power . . . [but] in Russia it was sanctioned by the general consent of the citizens. [The Varangians] *did not conquer* our home-land, rather they were chosen by the Slavs to govern the state.[70]

This idealization of the narod had several implications, not always easily reconciled. On the one hand, this idyllic view of the people and their personal bond with the tsar went hand in hand with and even reinforced the myth of the bureaucratic barrier standing between the ruler and his subjects. For this reason, ways had to be found to break through this wall and thus to restore the mystical union. Some sort of mechanism was required in order to bring the people's needs directly to the personal attention of the tsar. However circumscribed and ineffective in practice, the right of individuals and groups to petition the tsar personally was one

---

[68] J. L. Black, *Nicholas Karamzin and Russian Society in the Nineteenth Century. A Study in Russian Political and Historical Thought* (Toronto, 1975), p. 184. Actually, the fatherland was a very un-Russian notion that had been introduced only by Peter the Great.

[69] Cf. Tikhomirov, *Monarkhicheskaia gosudarstvennost'*, pp. 247–54; *Novoe Vremia*, May 15, 1896, p. 2.

[70] Black, *Nicholas Karamzin*, p. 105.

such attempt at piercing the ruler's isolation. A consultative assembly along the lines of the sixteenth- and seventeenth-century Assemblies of the Land (*zemskie sobory*), as proposed by followers of the Slavophile tradition under the motto "It is for the people to counsel, for the tsar to decide," was another. To make sure that the tsar's decrees were faithfully implemented, his bureaucrats also had to be made to recognize their own legal accountability as well as minimal civil liberties or rights on the part of the ruler's subjects. This, in brief, was the platform of Legal Autocracy. Inasmuch as these ideas were at variance with the reality of autocracy, they of course put in question the status quo.

On the other hand, the mythical picture of the narod was reflected in various assumptions by the autocratic bureaucracy and landowning nobility about the loyalties and interests of the peasant masses, assumptions equally far removed from reality. Identification with the good narod would also prompt Nicholas II to wear peasant blouses and a simple soldier's tunic in private. Clearly, the narod's idealization of the tsar, as echoed in its own words, and autocracy's idealization of the narod and its qualities were two sides of the same ideological coin.[71] Needless to say, peasant behavior during the revolutionary crisis of 1905–6 would subject these romantic suppositions to their sternest test yet.

Indeed, previous tests had already left their mark, injecting a darker, negative strain into this idealized picture. This more sober, though perhaps no more realistic, estimation treated the narod as immature, yet largely innocent, children. Thus Pobedonostsev, in his most benign moods, regarded human beings as impulsive children without reason, ruled by emotions and unable to assume responsibility, but in need of loving care and a firm parental hand. Russia was one large family in which an impartial and solicitous father, the tsar, exercised absolute parental control and responsibility over his obedient, loving, well-intentioned, if not always accomplished, children-subjects.[72] The idea of the tsar speaking or appealing to his children like a father was a common one in official pronouncements and ceremonies. As children, the tsar's subjects had no legal rights as such, but at least they were entitled to protective care and guidance; in this sense, the notion of family presupposed definite obligations on the part of both father and children.

Less charitably, these children were reduced to perpetually drunk, gullible, ignorant, anarchic sloths—in short, mere animals. Pobedonostsev, this time more in keeping with his character, railed against the "decomposition and weakness and untruth" of his compatriots and found that

---

[71] See, too, Field, *Rebels in the Name of the Tsar*, p. 213.

[72] Robert F. Byrnes, *Pobedonostsev. His Life and Thought* (Bloomington, Ind., 1968), p. 320.

"inertness and laziness are generally characteristic of the Slavonic nature." Human nature, in Pobedonostsev's gloomy estimation, was "weak, vicious, worthless, and rebellious"; not surprisingly, Russia, excepting perhaps "the aristocracy of intellect," was "but an icy desert and an abode of the Bad Men."[73] On government documents, "the dark people" (*temnyi narod*) was a ubiquitous ephithet for the peasant masses, presumably referring to their lack of culture and enlightenment, or, more ominously, to the ever-present threat of disorder and rebellion that they posed.

Such deep-seated fears, coexisting uneasily with sentimental idealization, were rooted in concrete historical precedents. Rebellions led by Stenka Razin and Emilian Pugachev, to name only the most prominent, had left an indelible scar on the national psyche. In fact, the dread of unrest and anarchy and, correspondingly, the insistence on shows of strength that pervaded the thinking of officials and landlords alike bespoke the haunting memories of jacqueries (*bunty*) and spontaneous acts of insubordination and defiance too numerous to mention. Even more immediate and searing, though not as spectacularly memorable, were the experiences of serfdom and its aftermath, during which landlords and peasants had intimately learned of each other's shortcomings and sins, a long and lasting lesson not at all conducive to an optimistic assessment of human progress and perfectability. Since human nature left to its own devices could be expected to follow its own worst instincts, it was the task of the authorities to exercise firm control and thus check these natural tendencies; otherwise, the result would be total chaos.[74]

This wary attitude toward the narod had religious sources as well. Orthodoxy stressed the corrupt and sinful nature of human beings and treated the miseries of their earthly existence as the natural and unavoidable, albeit temporary, consequences of their fallen state. The peasants and workers themselves shared this view, if Lukashevich's experiences during the To-the-People movement of the 1870s are any indication. While the people he encountered resented their miserable living conditions and the cruel abuse visited upon them by government agents and noble landlords, they appeared resigned to their fates, blaming these conditions instead on the fact that "they were drunkards and had forgotten God."[75] Such an outlook both encouraged a profound fatalism and

[73] Ibid., pp. 291–93. While Byrnes fails to state his source, Father Georgii Florovskii in his *Puti russkago bogosloviia* (Paris, 1937), p. 413, quotes the following aphorism about Russia, one ascribed to Pobedonostsev: "An icy desert, and in it walks evil man."

[74] For a similar conclusion in a more contemporary context, see Robert G. Kaiser, *Russia. The People and the Power* (New York, 1976), p. 218.

[75] Leopold H. Haimson, *The Russian Marxists and the Origins of Bolshevism* (Boston, 1953), p. 14.

gave rein to human foibles and vices; hence the authorities could never relax their guard over the people.

Above all, what was altogether absent from this conception of the narod and from popular peasant culture was the notion of the individual. In this view, the narod was essentially an amorphous collective, bereft of any individuation or individualism. As if to demonstrate that the collective is qualitatively different from a mere multiplication of individuals, the singular and plural nouns for human being or "man" in Russian, *chelovek* and *liudi*, are derived from two completely different roots. Missing, too, were any notions of conscience and guilt, which are predicated precisely on such individualization. The admission of sinfulness described above is a reflection not of individual guilt but of shame before others, of actively violating external rules of personal or group conduct sanctioned by the collective. Guilt, by contrast, is the passive product of the individual conscience or superego, i.e., an internalized conception of a universal, depersonalized order. Thus understood, the narod indeed seemed to represent an elemental, chaotic, anarchic, formless force of nature, on which order and form had to be imposed from above. Hence the constant preoccupation of the authorities with *stikhiinost'* ("elementalness" or "spontaneity"), *bezporiadok* ("disorder" or, more literally, "without order"), or, in the case of Nicholas II, with *bezobrazie* ("nonsense," but literally, "without form").

It was precisely this lack of individualism and of form that required and justified the concentration of all power in the hands of one man, who in turn would use his theoretically unlimited power to create order out of chaos, hierarchy out of anarchy. In this hierarchically organized service class state, the position of each social stratum within the body politic said little about the actual power and collective consciousness of each group. Instead of being the result of centuries of social conflict, this social structure was the handiwork of the autocratic state, designed to serve only its interests. Social groups, such as the *dvorianstvo* (nobility), *krest'ianstvo* (peasantry), *dukhovenstvo* (clergy), *kupechestvo* (merchantry), and *meschchanstvo* (townspeople), both in reality and in ideology were the creations and handmaidens of autocracy, *service* classes or estates (*sosloviia*) that were expected to carry out the tasks that their royal taskmaster had assigned to them in a hierarchical division of labor. It was the state's designation of these obligations and corresponding awards that identified and separated the members of each service class. They did not represent autonomous sociopolitical forces welded together by a common identity and awareness of interests, as in the West, but derived their legitimacy and very identity from the autocratic state and the fulfillment of their state-defined duties.

One's place in the service class structure identified one's particular relationship to the impersonal autocratic state as well as to the autocrat himself, an identification expressed in personalized terms through the myth of the personal bond between each member of the amorphous narod and the person of the ruler. Society was but a fiction in the sense that the various service classes and their members were accorded neither rights nor interests, neither power nor identity, independent from and outside of the autocratic order. The very concept of society was missing from traditional and traditionalistic autocratic ideology. Lacking individuation, the narod was also atomized, united only by its common ties with and faith in the tsar. Only absolute power could give coherence and order to this formless mass.

Since the acceptance of the autocratic order depended on the powerless equality and homogenization of its subjects, any changes in this socio-ideological foundation threatened the political system and the absolute pretensions of the ruler. Ideological incantation alone could not ward off such a threat, however, as the traditional service class system was becoming increasingly anachronistic toward the end of the nineteenth century. Many individuals had lost their identification based on state definition or personal relationships with the ruler. In effect, they now stood outside of the existing order. New groups remained excluded. Thanks to a growing individualization within diverse service classes or segments thereof, a new sense of self-worth and shared identity and an expanding awareness of collective interests opposed to those of the state or of other groups began to challenge the denial of society and hence autocracy itself. A gradually emerging sense of power, purpose, and possibility provided the stimulus and justification for active self-help instead of the traditional appeals to the tsar for redress and protection. Sooner or later, these social changes—themselves the product of Russia's economic development—were bound to conflict with the ideological claims and practical policies of autocracy.

The first indications of this conflict led to the establishment of the so-called Kakhanov Commission during Interior Minister Loris-Melikov's "Dictatorship of the Heart" in the late 1870s. Taking their cue from the Emancipation and the Great Reforms of the 1860s with their insistence on partial civic equality and the mingling of service estates, the Commission proposed far-reaching reforms of local government that aimed at nothing less than the full civil and political integration of all social groups and the harmonious interaction between emancipated society and the modern bureaucratic administration.[76] The violent death of Alexander II

[76] For a more thorough examination of the Kakhanov Commission and of the Counter-Reforms discussed below, see Francis Wcislo's forthcoming work, *The Dilemmas of Reforming Rural Russia.*

and the accession of his son doomed these proposals, however, which instead had to yield to the so-called Counter-Reforms of 1889–92. Evidently, the flash point, when the ideology, or strains thereof, could no longer accommodate or be reconciled with the social and administrative reality, when the lack of a social and political consensus would become apparent to all, had not been reached yet.

It was these growing individualist tendencies and their disturbing consequences that prompted Pobedonostsev, as we have seen, to embrace the amorphous collective of the narod and its "absolute powerlessness," which was extolled as the precondition of true and universal equality. Notwithstanding the great diversity and glaring material and social inequalities among them, before the all-powerful tsar all were without power and therefore truly equal. Such equality was not only more genuine and perfect than the alleged equality of citizens in Western democracies whose individual votes were meaningless illusions of power, Pobedonostsev insisted, but it was more important than the physical conditions of their lives with which he was well acquainted. His nihilistic asceticism had little intrinsic respect for the spendthrift nobility or, for that matter, any of the other service estates. Instead, he viewed the service-class system as a useful means of organizing the people, much in the same way that he valued religion not for any inherent qualities but as the cement holding together the body politic.

This utilitarian view of the estate system clashed with the paternalist conception of A. D. Pazukhin, the chief architect of the Counter-Reforms, which equated the participation of private landowners in local affairs with noble status and put the communal peasantry at the mercy of an all-powerful land captain or miniature tsar. Reacting to the same danger signals as Pobedonostsev and completely repudiating the liberal bureaucratic perspective of the Great Reforms and the Kakhanov Commission, Pazukhin persisted in excluding everyone belonging to urban society—whether *raznochinets* (a declassé member of a traditional service estate), *intelligent* (a member of the intelligentsia), worker, Jew, or industrialist—from the largely rural, organic hierarchy composed of the two main sosloviia, i.e., a paternalistic nobility and their peasant-children. By seeking to close off the noble estate to newcomers and making it into a virtual caste, Pazukhin's proposals not only denied the problems caused by increasing social mobility but also threatened the autonomy and power of the autocrat.

Neither Pobedonostsev nor Alexander III himself were prepared for such a sacrifice. In fact, even Dmitrii Tolstoi, Pazukhin's nominal superior as minister of internal affairs, failed to embrace his subordinate's proposals in their entirety. Instead, Tolstoi sought to combine a return to the nobiliary, particularistic, paternalist model on the local level with a reassertion of the state's protective, controlling, supervising role, i.e., its police functions. As a result, the Counter-Reforms in their final version did more to bolster the position of the tsarist bureaucracy than the power of the nobility, all appearances to the contrary notwithstanding.

Yet given the simultaneous defeat of the proposals prepared by the Kakhanov Commission, this bureaucratic victory did nothing to promote the notions of zakonnost', Legal Autocracy, or of a modern bureaucratic state backed by the power of the autocrat. These ideological alternatives remained below the surface and never even registered in Nicholas II's consciousness. They were resurrected only at a time of extreme peril—the revolutionary crisis of 1904–7.

For the time being, the harmony-by-design or organicist models of autocracy embraced by traditionalist and pseudo-traditionalist ideologues alike did not even concede the possibility of political and social conflict or the resolution of the disputed issues through compromise. The very concept of public opinion, not to mention public will, was altogether absent. Since society did not exist in this official view, it could not be entitled to the expression of political views. Such opinions and decisions were the sole preserve of the autocratic power instead. Interests by definition were subjective and self-centered, possessing no legitimacy whatsoever in the eyes of autocracy. The very word *interes* was of foreign origin, symptomatic of Western egotism and individualism, and therefore not to be trusted. Interests spelled conflict, endangering the harmony and unity of the whole edifice. Such conflict ended either with the victory of the stronger over the weaker party or by compromise. Both these outcomes were unacceptable to autocratic ideology and practice.

The concerns of autocracy superseded any selfish, partisan interests; they alone were legitimate. Only the autocrat could assume a detached, universal, transcendent vantage point from which to resolve matters to the benefit of the whole. He was not bound by the interests of individuals or social groups, nor by their opinions and recommendations, even if they belonged to a numerical majority. He was free to side with a minority of one or substitute his own opinion. Since such a decision reflected absolute truth and was in the interest of the whole, it also was in the interest of a particular faction. Instead of the interests of a nonexistent "society," this absolute vantage point acknowledged only the "needs" of individuals and state-defined groups. Needs, in contrast to the subjective and negative connotation of interests, had an objective ring; needs could be ascertained and met by the autocratic power. Unlike interests, needs were not in conflict with each other or with the underlying harmony of the autocratic polity.

Reality looked different, of course. Ultimately, needs were defined by the bureaucracy and thus considerably less objective than claimed. Time and again, individuals, social groups, and even the tsar himself complained that real needs had been ignored, distorted, and were yet to be satisfied. Without effective safeguards, moreover, there was always the danger that the tsar would make a particular view representing special interests his own and thus enshrine it as official policy.

THE ROLE OF HISTORY

Such affirmations of objective needs, harmony, and impartial transcendence should not be dismissed, however, as transparently self-serving obfuscations designed to mask the selfish, arbitrary, and voluntarist nature of autocratic power; they were grounded instead in an organicist understanding of history not unlike that of Burkean conservatism or of the nineteenth-century "historical school" in Germany. According to this view, which in Russia was first articulated by Karamzin under the influence of German idealism, the evolution of autocracy was the organic result of Russia's unique historical conditions and geography as well as its people's physical and spiritual needs, character, and Byzantine heritage; what is more, it was sanctioned, indeed objectively prescribed, by the primacy, autonomous organicity, and wholesome integrity of the historical process. As history was absolute and good, its inevitable outcome was good and harmonious. Whether viewed as the expression of the Creator's will and eternal law, to which all human beings were subject, or as the logical workings of an impersonal principle, history had objectively determined the institution and policies of autocracy.

Contrary to what his glorification of power with its implied extreme voluntarism might lead one to expect, Pobedonostsev, too, affirmed the primacy and inevitability of historical development: "History cannot be changed or evaded; and history itself, with its actions, its actors, and its complex polity, is the product of the national spirit, as the history of the individual is the product of the living soul."[77] While such a conception tended to justify any existing institutions and conditions, it did not preclude changes in the status quo, as long as they were gradual, orderly, and in keeping with what came before. Since history was an organic, ongoing process, the ruler had to act in consonance with it, neither precipitously nor obdurately.[78] The final decision as to whether a change contemplated or demanded was artificial or organic rested with the autocrat, of course, and was inherently subjective.

[77] Pobedonostsev, *Reflections*, p. 211.

[78] Karamzin, too, had professed his belief in the necessity of peaceful evolution; the main theme of his *Zapiski o drevnoi i novoi Rossii* was his contention that the rulers ought to be guided by the requirements of the times and make changes only when their subjects were ready; cf., too, Black, *Nicholas Karamzin*, pp. 49, 89.

The very emphasis on Russia's uniqueness and on the organic and inevitable emergence of autocracy suggested that Russia was unlikely to
evolve into a constitutional monarchy along Western lines. Yet the forward march, whatever its direction, could not be resisted and required
timely adjustments, as Pobedonostsev was quick to concede:

> There are periods when reform is the ripe fruit of social evolution, the expres-
> sion of a necessity felt by all, when it loosens the knots bound by immemorial
> social relations; then the reformer appears a prophet who speaks with the voice
> of the public conscience, and realizes the thought which all bear in themselves.
> His words and his works master all because they witness to the truth, and all
> who are of the truth echo and emulate them.[79]

As this observation implies, there were times when reform was necessary, even unavoidable. Such reforms were not the artificial schemes of
human fantasies, ambitions, and emotions, but the natural result of social
change and consensus, as the references to "a necessity felt by all," to
"public conscience," to "thought which all bear in themselves" attest. At
the same time, Pobedonostsev's opinion appeared to rule out measures
that would anticipate or even bring about social transformation. In this
sense, the reformer was seen less as an active agent than as the obedient
instrument of history. While such a notion of historical development
might have encouraged a passive wait-and-see attitude and fatalistic inaction on the part of the ruler, this certainly was not true for the autocrats
Pobedonostsev most revered: Peter I and Alexander III.

By the same token, Pobedonostsev's active involvement in the
Counter-Reforms was not an attempt to turn back the clock of history. As
we have observed already, the interpretation of history and the perception of social change which in turn would necessitate political reforms
ultimately depended on human, all too human judgments. Alexander III
and the men he chose as his government servitors strongly felt that the
Great Reforms of the 1860s had gone too far in that they had outpaced
Russia's historical development and artificially injected foreign ideas and
theories of government, including the ideals of the Rechtsstaat and of
individual autonomy.[80] The mounting wave of popular agitation and terrorism that had crested with the assassination of Alexander II was blamed
on the alleged antihistorical excesses of the Great Reforms. Hence the
Counter-Reforms were designed as a necessary corrective, so that Russia's political system might conform once again to its social structure and
national spirit.

[79] Pobedonostsev, *Reflections*, p. 114.
[80] Cf. Pobedonostsev's program for court reform of October 30, 1885; P. A. Zaionchkovskii, *Rossiiskoe samoderzhavie v kontse XIX stoletiia* (Moscow, 1970), pp. 236–39.

This firm belief in the organicity and primacy of history suffused the autocratic conception of government then in vogue, as expressed in the notions of *popechitel'stvo* and *opeka*, i.e., "guardianship." Reflecting its superordinate and universal pretensions, autocracy claimed with these concepts a higher and broader view that both transcended and chose between the more restricted partisan and immature vantage points of various social groups and their members. Yet, while reserving all political and final decisions for the autocratic power, these terms excluded the possibility of actively fostering or forestalling social change in the manner of Peter's *reguliarnoe gosudarstvo*. "Guardianship," whether in the more nurturing, encouraging meaning of *popechitel'stvo* or the more patronizing, restrictive interpretation of *opeka*, denoted government control, supervision, responsibility, sponsorship, and moderation, not active interference or sudden transformation; it suggested detached guidance rather than immediate intervention. The autocrat was no longer the architect and builder of the social order, as Peter I had been or at least claimed to be, but its administrator or caretaker who was bound by its structure, requirements, and spirit. The system was not to be tampered with until its inadequacies had become obvious to all or until, overtaken by spontaneous changes within its midst, it had ceased to function. Anachronism rather than progress was the rationale for reform. When the time was ripe, however, autocracy, with its concentration of power in the hands of one man, so the argument went, would be the ideal system for the implementation of all innovations and changes.[81]

Far from contradicting the omnipotence and the voluntarist aspirations of the ruler, this understanding of history was indissolubly bound up with a belief in the organic evolution of autocracy. Russia's history, its creation as a state and its emergence as a world power, was seen as the personal achievement of its individual rulers against well-nigh insurmountable obstacles and odds. D. I. Ilovaisky, whose textbook on Russian history was republished thirty-five times between 1860 and 1912[82] and was read by virtually every Russian schoolchild including the last tsar, said of autocracy: "It gave political unity to the hitherto divided Russian lands and bound the tribes, dispersed over the plains of Eastern Europe, into one compact mass; it gave the Russian people a state structure . . . [which] directed the national forces toward serving one goal—the state."[83] Autocracy was at once the product, agent, symbol, and guarantor of Russia's historical greatness. Autocracy was history personified. It was in this vein

---

[81] Tikhomirov, *Monarkhicheskaia gosudarstvennost'*, pp. 426–27; on this last point, Tikhomirov was in agreement not only with Pobedonostsev but also with Chicherin.

[82] Black, *Nicholas Karamzin*, pp. 164–65.

[83] D. I. Ilovaiskii, *Kratkie ocherki russkoi istorii. Kurs starshago vozrasta*, 9th ed. (Moscow, 1868), p. 212.

that Karamzin had reminded Alexander I that he was not free to change what he had inherited from his ancestors: "Sire! You exceed the limits of your authority. . . . You may do everything, but you may not limit your authority by law!"[84] Given the identification of autocracy and history, the autocratic power was paradoxically limited in the sense that it ought not violate its own unlimitedness.

This personalized view of history, identifying the ruler with the state, became an integral component of traditional autocratic ideology. Karamzin's *History of the Russian State*, first published in 1818, went through half of its fourteen editions between 1889 and 1903, to say nothing of the repeatedly reissued school texts of Ilovaiskii, Abaza, and El-pat'evskii.[85] The following example illustrates the subservience of much popular historical writing to practical considerations of autocratic ideology. In his textbook for intermediate grades, Ilovaiskii said not a word about the violent ends of Peter III and Paul I, or about the possibility that their respective successors, Catherine II and Alexander I, were complicit in their murders. Peter merely had to yield power to Catherine and died soon thereafter, while Paul simply died and was succeeded by Alexander. While correct technically, this account certainly did not reveal the full story.[86]

Despite the fact that these popular historians and autocratic apologists often invoked the Statist school of Russian history founded by Sergei Solov'ev and that Solov'ev's own textbook was republished thirteen times before 1915[87], their personalized conception was at odds with the Statist notion of progress based on the growing depersonalization of the state. The abstract state, according to Solov'ev, had evolved out of the personal, family- or clan-based votchina model of absolute rule. As altruism writ large and thus antithetical to the universal egotism of society, this Hegelian understanding of the state signified the self-liberation of the individual from a constraining environment. By voluntarily recognizing, i.e., by internalizing, objective historical necessity, human beings consciously achieve freedom in and through this abstract state ruled by laws. This universal conception of historical progress denied the uniqueness of Russia's development and was difficult to reconcile with essential tenets of autocratic ideology, whether in their Slavophile, official, or traditionalistic manifestation. By contrast, the liberal-constitutional ideals of a Chicherin, Kliuchevskii, or Miliukov grew directly out of the Statist school of thought.

[84] Pipes, *Karamzin's Memoir*, p. 139.
[85] Black, *Nicholas Karamzin*, pp. 132–33, 155, 175.
[86] D. I. Ilovaiski, *Rukovodstvo k russkoi istorii. Srednyi kurs*, 44th ed. (Moscow, 1916), pp. 134, 150.
[87] Black, *Nicholas Karamzin*, p. 175.

As for the adherents of autocracy, however, who persisted in identifying Russia's history with autocracy and its imperial representatives, the centrality of the tsar's person and the absoluteness of his position as impartial arbiter uniquely reflected the ethnic, social, cultural, and religious heterogeneity of the immense Russian empire. The tsar was both symbol and agent of the empire's unity; he was, in Katkov's definition, "the unity and power of Russia incarnate in one person."[88] In a practice long since abandoned in most of western and central Europe, the territorial diversity of Russia and the autocrat's historical accomplishments and symbolic function were expressed in his official title, which, when not abbreviated to "etc., etc.," enumerated the geographical regions and former political entities that made up the empire. Only autocratic power, the single will of the tsar, could forge these disparate components and interests into a unified whole. Only one impartial and truthful authority could ascertain the true interests of the commonwealth and serve as the common focus of his subjects' diverse aspirations and loyalties.[89] Democracy and parliamentary institutions in heterogenous and multinational states, Pobedonostsev insisted, had proved unable to contain the explosive demands for national independence, and had instead aggravated national and racial disharmony. "Autocracy," on the other hand, "succeeded in evading or conciliating such demands and outbreaks, not by means of force alone, but by the equalization of rights and relations under the unifying power. . . . Providence has preserved our Russia, with its heterogeneous racial composition, from like misfortunes."[90]

In this view, the autocrat was the main, if not the only, communal tie of the multinational empire. He was allied with each of his subjects in personal communion, and the subjects in turn shared a common identification through their faith in the tsar and this personal relationship. This theme of the quasi-mystical union between ruler and ruled, of the tsar's role as the symbol and guarantor of national unity and hence of historical greatness, was sounded again and again in political pronouncements, autocratic ritual, administrative practice, and popular sayings. Revealing a

[88] Tikhomirov, *Monarkhicheskaia gosudarstvennost'*, pp. 311–12.

[89] There were, however, dissident nationalist voices who saw the heterogeneity and multinational character of this empire as inimical to a genuine *Russian* autocracy. The imperial idea, claimed Khomiakov, *Samoderzhavie*, pp. 13–14, made the tsar the leader of some twenty different peoples, equally distant from him regardless of their nationality. The monarch had become "anything for everybody [*vsiacheskaia dlia vsekh*]; he consciously ceases being only a Russian Tsar, or rather, he is emancipated from his dependence on the spirit of the Russian people." Instead of living the life of the people to whom he owed his very existence, he lived above them. Whereas the narod still maintained its faith in an Orthodox and above all Russian tsar, it had no sympathy or understanding for the strange-sounding title of "emperor" or "monarch" which the clergy (!) insisted on using.

[90] Pobedonostsev, *Reflections*, pp. 48–49.

deep-seated unease and insecurity, the term *edinstvo* (union, unity) was repeated countless times—as if to turn it into reality through usage. Tikhomirov derived reassurance from the great outpouring of grief at the death of Alexander III, seeing in the common sorrow of the humble and poor as well as the great and powerful a reflection of a unified Russian people and nation. "Only in the Autocratic Ruler," he wrote, "surrounded by the boundless devotion of his subjects, does the narod find its unity. Only by closing ranks around their national Sovereign, the Chosen One of God's Providence, do the popular masses become a great nation."[91]

From this thesis it followed that any attempts to limit the autocrat's power, to encroach on his central position as a supernational, disinterested mediator, or to give a political voice to parts or all of the population, posed a direct threat to the territorial integrity, unity, and social peace of the empire. As one ideologist warned in the face of growing unrest and crisis: "For the people to renounce [autocracy] is tantamount to a renunciation of their own history, centuries of labors and efforts *on behalf of the gathering of the Russian land and its unification into one whole* powerful state."[92] In this sense, the continued insistence on the unlimited and personal nature of the monarch's power sprang in part from anxiety lest the social, ethnic, religious, and other differences described above erupt and destroy the empire in the absence of its unifying agent and symbol.

By the same token, any threat to this unity and integrity posed by foreign powers and war, national minorities, or social revolutionaries highlighted the unifying role of the tsar. Those who had reason to fear and oppose the social and territorial disintegration of the empire appealed to his absolute authority and insisted on its preservation in one form or another, while others who promoted disunity or hoped to gain

[91] *Moskovskiia Vedomosti*, October 23, 1894. Robert G. Wesson, *The Imperial Order* (Berkeley, Calif., 1967), pp. 77–78, makes the same point. Wesson, however, goes so far as to assert a necessary causal relationship between universal empires and an autocratic system such as Russia's. Thus it was Russia's character as a multinational, far-flung, and heterogeneous empire that gave rise to autocracy. About this assumption Wesson admits to the following doubt: "If the universal empire makes for unlimited government, it may also be that strong government makes for universal empires" (ibid., p. 53); yet he proceeds to make Russian autocracy the model for his imperial order. Autocracy is held to be the natural and inevitable product of a universal empire. Ideological claims and rationalizations in effect become statements of historical fact. Stripped of its questionable premise, Wesson's seemingly persuasive account is no more than a simple reductionist description of doubtful analytic significance.

[92] Semenov, *Samoderzhavie*, p. 10.

from it attacked the central symbol and demanded far-reaching restrictions on its powers and prerogatives, even its outright abolition. For friend and foe alike, the symbol of unity and guarantor of order assumed a greater importance at the very moment when the essence symbolized and guaranteed by it was in dispute or lost.

CHAPTER IV

To Reform or Not

WHEN NICHOLAS II attended a performance of Wagner's *Götterdämmerung* in St. Petersburg on January 8, 1904, it did not dawn on him that the curtain was about to open on another drama of equally tragic and cosmic dimensions: the life-or-death struggle of his own reign and empire, one in which he was destined to play the leading role in a cast of millions. Within three short weeks Russia would find itself in a war with Japan for which it was ill-prepared and which in turn would set the stage for the more consequential war between Russian autocracy and society, commonly known as the First Russian Revolution.

While Nicholas did not actively seek war, he was supremely confident of the righteousness of Russia's cause and of its every success and had done nothing to prevent it. The actual hostilities, it is true, commenced with the Japanese surprise attack on Russia's Pacific fleet at Port Arthur on January 27, 1904, but the real cause of the conflict lay in the mutually exclusive imperialist designs of the two countries in Manchuria and Korea. On the Russian side, these ambitions had been promoted for a variety of reasons, some of them contradictory, by a wide coterie of officials that included S. Iu. Witte, the minister of finance until August 1903 and architect of Russia's industrialization; Minister of Internal Affairs V. K. Pleve, Witte's implacable foe who allegedly anticipated with relish the salutary effects of "a successful, little war"; and a group of military adventurists who enjoyed Pleve's protection. Even Nicholas's cousin, the German Kaiser, had encouraged Russia's expansion in the Far East, urging the "Admiral of the Pacific" not to yield to what he considered the insolence of the Japanese and their British allies. Neither the collapse of negotiations in mid-1903 nor the counsel of more prudent advisors could persuade Nicholas to stem the inevitable slide toward war.

Temporarily at least, the outbreak of hostilities put a damper on the demands of the growing opposition within society, demands that Nicholas had sought to banish so unsuccessfully eight years earlier when he dismissed even the most modest aspirations for some form of national representation and a modicum of civil liberties as "senseless dreams." Now the tsar was able to report "from all quarters touching manifestations of unanimous excitement and displeasure at the impudence of the Japanese" as well as "touching expressions of popular feelings and in complete order."[1] Even some of the leaders of the so-called liberation movement did not remain immune to the patriotic fever sweeping Russia within the first days of the war. Whether out of conviction or pragmatic calculation, they urged a suspension of their agitation until a successful conclusion of the war. Some went so far as to offer their organizational talents and services to help the wounded and the families of those killed in action.

The organizational backbone of the movement had been the *zemstvos*, institutions of limited self-government created in 1864 to help fill the void left by the abrogation of the noble landlords' (*pomeshchiki*) sweeping patrimonial powers over the persons and property of their serfs. Elected by private landowners, propertied townspeople, and communal peasants in thirty-four of the fifty provinces of European Russia, the district (*uezd*) and provincial (*guberniia*) zemstvos were given considerable responsibilities in the establishment and maintenance of local infrastructure and services, yet constantly had to contend with the unfriendly presence and suspicious control of various agents of the central bureaucracy, such as the minister of internal affairs or his emissaries, from the governor down to local police officials. As a result of their growing involvement in local and provincial affairs through the zemstvo assemblies and their executive boards, elected zemstvo members (*zemtsy*), most of them nobles, increasingly came to resent what they regarded as the unwarranted interference and manifest incompetence of the tsarist bureaucracy. As early as 1878 some of the most outspoken and active zemtsy, led by I. I. Petrunkevich, demanded a constitution that would guarantee civil liberties and top off the zemstvo structure with a roof, i.e., extend zemstvo representation to the national level. Alexander III (1881–94) and Nicholas II not only rejected these demands out of hand but also attempted to tighten control over the zemstvos' activities through a series of legislative reforms, budgetary restrictions, administrative sanctions, and police measures—without succeeding in quelling zemstvo activism, however.

A particular target of official suspicions and persecution was the zemstvo staff, the agronomists, statisticians, teachers, veterinarians, and other professionals employed by the zemstvo boards and known as the Third Element in contradistinction with the elected zemstvo members (the Second Element) and state bureaucrats (the First). The Third Element constituted the link between the zemstvo institutions and the rural population. Imbued with democratic and populist ideals and committed to improving the well-being of the peasantry, these predominantly non-noble zemstvo employees had come to discover kindred souls in and

[1] *Dnevnik Imperatora*, January 27 and 30, 1904, pp. 130–31.

hence make common political cause with the elected zemstvo leaders and activists, the so-called gentry intelligentsia.

The latter had taken advantage of their status as noble landowners to participate in zemstvo affairs, yet unlike many of their fellow noble zemtsy they belonged to Russia's intelligentsia by virtue of their university education, urban professions (academia, journalism, jurisprudence, medicine), and, above all, the supraestate, supraclass outlook typical of Russian intelligentsia members. It was these gentry intelligenty who were the driving force behind the zemstvo activism and indeed behind most of the liberation movement up to 1904 and beyond. Defying the repressive policies of Interior Minister Pleve and his predecessor Sipiagin, who had been assassinated in 1902, they organized informal congresses of zemstvo activists to get around the official ban on national gatherings with a political agenda; they availed themselves of their professional and intelligentsia contacts to establish professional societies, unions, and meetings; they founded front organizations, published a newspaper, *Osvobozhdenie* (Liberation), sponsored publications, Sunday schools, and banquets; and they prodded those more moderate and wooed those more radical than themselves, all in order to forge an all-nation coalition against autocracy from the disparate interests of peasants, nobles, workers, professionals, ethnic minorities, and others. The replacement of the hated autocracy by a more democratic regime was proclaimed to be in everyone's interest, regardless of particular grievances and irrespective of each group's ultimate goals.[2]

The lull occasioned by the Japanese attack did not last long, as the old antagonisms were far from dead. Indeed, the very concerns and objectives that had given birth to the liberation movement in the first place continued to be reinforced by the government's enduring distrust, to say nothing of its ineptitude in the conduct of the war. Pleve insisted on living up to his public reputation, one earned during his two-year tenure as interior minister through brutal police persecution, the encouragement of anti-Semitic excesses, and the vigorous defense of bureaucratic omnipotence and the status quo. He not only attached unacceptable conditions to the all-zemstvo war-relief effort but also underlined his refusal to cooperate with the zemstvo in April 1904 by voiding the election of several zemstvo board chairmen, including the widely respected, long-time chairman of the Moscow provincial zemstvo board, D. N. Shipov, a relative moderate. Similarly, he refused to make any amends in the harsh Russification policies directed against the non-Russian border areas of

[2] Much of the preceding summary is indebted to the far more extensive treatments by Roberta Manning, *The Crisis of the Old Order in Russia* (Princeton, N.J., 1981) and Jonathan E. Sanders, "The Union Of Unions" (Ph.D. diss., Columbia University, 1985).

Finland, Poland, the Jewish Pale, and the Caucasus, whose native sons were at that very moment laying down their lives for Tsar and Empire. As the government's inability to counter Japan's surprising naval superiority with victories on land became clearer with every passing day, the liberal opposition began to renew its efforts with ever-increasing determination. More ominously, in the course of six weeks revolutionary terrorists struck twice at the very heart of Russia's autocratic government, assassinating the Finnish governor-general, Bobrikov, on June 3 and the hated Pleve on July 15, 1904.

THE APPOINTMENT OF SVIATOPOLK-MIRSKII

As much as he mourned the sudden loss of his "two devoted and helpful servants,"[3] there is no indication that those daring raids filled the tsar with apprehension and a sense of urgency, or that they made him any more aware of the need for thorough political reforms. Nicholas was too preoccupied with the war effort and the impending birth of his fifth child to contemplate the prophetic implications of these assassinations or the growing unrest and clamor for change among his subjects. Most likely, he was not even conscious of these social stirrings.

Society and even some official circles reacted with unconcealed glee to Pleve's demise. As his old nemesis Witte, now chairman of the Committee of Ministers, put it: "To Mr. von Pleve happened what had to happen, and it is frightening that this crime was not greeted with condolences anywhere. All you could hear was a sigh of relief and cursing of his memory."[4] Although Witte doubted that any one person could turn matters around, the appointment of Pleve's successor was eagerly awaited. In the eyes of society, as represented here by the zemstvo leader Shipov whom Pleve had ousted earlier in the year, "the selection of a person by the Sovereign had to forecast the direction in which the state power's internal policy could be expected to develop in the near future."[5] Hence the announcement of Prince P. D. Sviatopolk-Mirskii's appointment as minister of internal affairs on August 26, 1904, while a surprise to the public, was received favorably.[6] The contrast between the forty-six-year-old Mirskii, who had a reputation for moderate, humane, and sympathetic policies from his previous gubernatorial assignments,

---

[3] *Dnevnik Imperatora*, June 4 and July 15, 1904, pp. 152, 161.

[4] "Perepiska S. Iu. Vitte i A. N. Kuropatkina v 1904–1905 gg.," *KA* 19 (1926): 71–72, August 19, 1904.

[5] D. N. Shipov, *Vospominaniia i dumy o perezhitom* (Moscow, 1918), p. 239.

[6] D. N. Liubimov, "Russkaia smuta," 137; E. A. Sviatopolk-Mirskaia, "Dnevnik kn. Ekateriny Alekseevny Sviatopolk-Mirskoi za 1904–1905 gg.," *Istoricheskie zapiski* 77 (1965): 242.

and the late Pleve and his dismal record could scarcely have been greater.

For Nicholas, however, no programmatic or political considerations appeared to have entered his decision. Instead, given his personality and his lack of awareness, his choice of Pleve's replacement was determined by personal factors, such as trust and the candidate's previous service. Like many of his predecessors and successors at the helm of the ministry of internal affairs, Mirskii had a long record of serving this institution, first as governor of Ekaterinoslav, then as assistant minister and chief of gendarmes, and finally as governor-general of Kovno, Grodno, and Vilno. Mirskii's service record, to say nothing of his military background and his rank of adjutant-general in the tsar's military suite, immediately recommended him for this important position. As a prominent member of the government and the court hierarchy who had already served Nicholas's father as aide-de-camp the prince certainly enjoyed the tsar's trust. Indeed, so obvious was his eligibility for the vacant ministerial chair that only two days after Pleve's death Mirskii had been rumored to be a possible successor.[7]

The new minister, who unlike Nicholas was very much aware of the programmatic implications of his selection, suspected that the tsar did not know him well enough. When Nicholas beseeched Mirskii on August 25, 1904, as a military man, adjutant-general, and loyal subject not to turn down the proffered portfolio, the prince felt compelled to confront him with his deeply held beliefs. Contrary to what Nicholas might have assumed, Mirskii explained, his own views were diametrically opposed to those of his immediate two predecessors; had he not resigned his post as assistant minister over a disagreement on Sipiagin's policies?[8] He then outlined his diagnosis of the ills plaguing Russia and indicated his prescription for a cure. While he had no right to refuse his emperor's wish, he let it be known at the end of his emotional confession that he was already looking forward to the day he would be relieved of his responsibilities. The tsar kissed him, said that he was very glad, and added: "Go see Mama and make her happy!" The dowager empress, whose support of Mirskii's candidacy had carried considerable weight with Nicholas, also kissed the new minister and said: "You see, I am keeping my promise." Three weeks earlier she had promised to embrace him if he agreed to her son's wishes.[9]

There can be little doubt that the new minister came away from this

---

[7] Letter by A. M. Abaza to his wife, "Bezobrazovskii kruzhok," KA 27 (1927): 79–80. Together with Bezobrazov Abaza was the main advocate of Russia's expansionism in the Far East and a participant in the Korean adventure.

[8] TsGAOR, f. 601 Nikolai II, op. 1, d. 247, August 25, 1904; Sv.-Mirskaia, "Dnevnik," p. 240.

[9] Sv.-Mirskaia, "Dnevnik," pp. 241–42, 252.

meeting with the impression that his appointment constituted an endorsement of the program he had just laid out for the tsar. Mirskii had made a point of stressing his profound differences with Sipiagin and Pleve and of airing his own convictions. His analysis added up to a stinging indictment of past and present policies, all of which had been sanctioned by Nicholas. "The condition of things has become so aggravated that one may consider the government to be in a state of enmity with Russia," Mirskii warned, "it is necessary to make peace." To this end, he called for expanded self-government and greater civil liberties, such as freedom of conscience, speech, and press. He recommended that elected representatives be consulted in St. Petersburg and that policies vis-à-vis the borderlands be changed. Instead of taking umbrage, the tsar expressed his complete agreement. Nor did he object when his choice as minister of internal affairs described himself as a zemstvo man who wished to continue attending district assemblies and whose sympathies and loyalties belonged to the land and to the very institutions that had been provoking the tsar's ire. How was that statement to be reconciled with Mirskii's service record as a member of the central bureaucracy? Finally, Mirskii had warned of his poor health and oratorical shortcomings, all to no avail. The tsar simply refused to reconsider his decision. Nothing, it appears, could dissuade Nicholas, for he had already made up his mind. In return for Mirskii's assent, the emperor was ready to go along with anything his candidate might say. His personal trust in Mirskii was all that seemed to matter.

If his responses are any indication, the tsar listened but did not understand. For one thing, he did not seem to share Mirskii's sense of urgency and therefore did not attach as much importance to the need for reform. For another, Nicholas was known for his tendency to agree with whatever person happened to have an audience with him at the moment. Most importantly, the tsar betrayed his own remoteness from the business of government, his very estrangement from the institutionalized and depersonalized notion of rulership. Russia was not alone in being estranged from government, as Mirskii had argued; so was the tsar. Hence Nicholas expressed no reservations about Mirskii's suggestions for improvements. From Nicholas's point of view, such reforms promised to curb the government and regulate its relationship with the Russian people, without infringing, however, on the tsar's personal role. It was only when Nicholas became convinced or was persuaded by others that such changes might forever limit and transform the autocrat's personal power and prerogatives that he indicated his disapproval.

In his first interviews and in a speech to the ranking officials of his ministry upon officially assuming his duties on September 16, 1904, Mirskii extended the olive branch of tolerance and cooperation to society:

Administrative experience has led me to the deep conviction that the fruitfulness of government work is rooted in a sincerely well-meaning and truly trusting attitude toward the societal and estate institutions and toward the population in general. Only under these conditions of work can there be the mutual trust without which speedy success in the building of the state cannot be expected.[10]

As news of these remarks spread like wildfire, reaction was enthusiastic and expectant. More than one thousand telegrams of greetings and support poured in from individuals, associations, town dumas, and zemstvo assemblies all over Russia. Even the conservative *Novoe Vremia* heralded "the coming of spring."[11] The long winter of lawlessness and repression finally appeared to be drawing to an end. As if on command, the forces of society began to stir, eager to escape the enforced quiescence and stifling stagnation of the past, to cast off the shame of an onerous and humiliating war, and to take part in the building of a just and democratic state system.

So high were the expectations raised by Sviatopolk-Mirskii's appointment and first pronouncements that disappointment was bound to follow—on the part of both society and the tsar. Mirskii's wife was worried that they were "expecting so much," while he would be able to do little. Echoing Witte's earlier warning, she continued: "In Russia's present condition, under such a Sovereign, no minister can do anything; besides, all the Petersburg petty squabbles can ruin the reputation of a saint, not to mention an ordinary mortal."[12] During their first official audience on September 22, Nicholas told his new minister that he had liked his speech very much and professed himself gladdened by the response of societal institutions. Yet he reportedly disapproved of Mirskii's recent interviews.[13]

Two weeks later the tsar complained to Mirskii that his appointment had unleashed too many rumors and expectations among society. He therefore intended to issue an official rescript to the minister of internal affairs ruling out once and for all the possibility of any changes. Mirskii protested: "How is it, Your Majesty, that I said what kind of reforms I considered necessary and you agreed?" The tsar backed off and instructed Mirskii to draft a circular to the governors instead. When Mir-

---

[10] Ibid., p. 240; Liubimov, "Russkaia smuta," pp. 140–41. Liubimov speaks of "*durable* success."

[11] Liubimov, "Russkaia smuta," pp. 140–41.

[12] In fact, it had been these apprehensions and her desire to preserve the truth that had prompted her to begin her unusual diary some six weeks earlier, when the prince's selection for the ministerial post was first rumored; Sv.-Mirskaia, "Dnevnik," pp. 240, 243, September 22, 1904.

[13] Ibid., p. 243.

skii apologized for disputing Nicholas, the tsar urged him on: "On the contrary, please, always talk like that."[14] Caught between the tsar's reservations and society's expectations, it did not take Mirskii long to grow tired of contending with Nicholas's contradictory and vacillating statements and of having to argue his position over and over again. By early October, the new minister already felt overburdened and "rather depressed by the mass of business." As his wife put it, "it is becoming clearer each time that nothing worthwhile can be done."[15]

Above all, it was the tsar's apparent indifference, or, worse, his complete lack of understanding, that greatly disturbed Mirskii. Ostensibly preoccupied with the conduct of the war, Nicholas still did not share his minister's alarm about the seriousness of the current situation and hence could not appreciate the need to make concessions to society. Yet even in military matters he remained curiously unconcerned. Despite Mirskii's repeated warnings and presentations about mounting public agitation and growing resistance among newly mobilized reservists, "all these disorders and pogroms along the reservists' lines of movement," his wife wrote in obvious exasperation on October 19, 1904, "leave the Sovereign absolutely cold."[16] His lack of involvement was illustrated during the Dogger Bank crisis, which derived its name from the fog-shrouded waters of the North Sea just off the English coast. Here Admiral Rozhdestvenskii's Baltic squadron, on its way to join the battered remnants of Russia's once proud First and Second Fleets, had opened fire on harmless English fishing-trawlers after mistaking them for Japanese interceptors; the English government and public were naturally incensed, English newspapers demanded revenge, and accusations passed back and forth before calmer heads finally prevailed.[17] At the very height of this crisis, the tsar had still found time for a full day of hunting.[18]

THE NOVEMBER 1904 ZEMSTVO CONGRESS

It was the so-called zemstvo issue, of course, that dominated Mirskii's dealings with Nicholas and exposed their differences. As the central problem of Sviatopolk-Mirskii's four-month stewardship, this issue went

[14] Ibid., pp. 247–48.

[15] Ibid., pp. 245, 247.

[16] Ibid., p. 248.

[17] Minister of Finance Kokovtsev warned the tsar that war with England was out of the question: Sv.-Mirskaia, "Dnevnik," p. 248. After huddling with his foreign and naval ministers and the lord of the admiralty to discuss England's "impertinent behavior," Nicholas offered to submit the dispute to the world court in The Hague. "Our mangy enemies immediately gave up their arrogance and agreed," the tsar gloated; TsGAOR, f. 601, op. 1, d. 248, October 15–16, 1904.

[18] TsGAOR, f. 601, op. 1, d. 248, October 14, 1904.

beyond the question of national representation and the zemstvo's role in the political process. Nothing less than the definition of autocracy was here at stake, i.e., the role of society and the implications of this role for autocratic government. From the very beginning, both in his private talks with the tsar and in his public pronouncements, Mirskii had left little doubt that he was committed to broadening local self-government and giving the zemstvos a voice in national affairs. Nicholas's occasional favorable, though always vague, comments in turn suggested that he was prepared to go along with his minister. Yet as Mirskii's views evolved and crystallized into legislative form, they encountered increasing controversy and resistance on the tsar's part.

Their verbal exchanges were marked by a strange circularity. More than once, Nicholas would agree with his ministerial interlocutor, only to contradict himself the next moment as pet prejudices and obsessive simplifications would assert themselves again. Small wonder that Mirskii described Nicholas's attitude towards the zemstvo as reserved and devoid of clear understanding. Thus, the tsar would affirm his complete confidence in the zemstvos and in the same breath express his fears of the Third Element—the zemstvo employees: "I fully trust the zemstvo. They are all good except for those of Tver, Moscow, and Ekaterinoslav, and that is because there is a lot of the Third Element, the zemstvo must be protected from it." In response Mirskii would insist that the zemstvo itself be allowed to guard against or get rid of any "undesirable elements." It would do so on its own when it felt independent and unconstrained; the very reason for the large presence of such politically unreliable persons lay in past governmental constraints on zemstvo activities. Since the existence of the Third Element could not be denied, it, too, had to find a place and outlet where it could be useful, not dangerous, but first more normal conditions had to be established.[19]

To promote such a normalization the minister raised the touchy subject of the Tver zemstvo on October 1, 1904. Only a few months earlier Pleve had banned the provincial assembly and replaced the elected board with an appointed one, exiling the most objectionable members, such as Petrunkevich, from Tver. The justice minister's request for a restoration of their rights had already met with Nicholas's disapproval, and Mirskii's overture appeared to fare no better. The tsar bluntly reminded his neophyte minister: "I must tell you that everything that was done concerning the Tver zemstvo was done at my personal wish; they are constitutionalists and I do not want to pardon them." Still, Mirskii persisted. Assuring Nicholas that the constitutionalists were not at all dangerous, he appealed

---

[19] Sv.-Mirskaia, "Dnevnik," p. 243, September 22, 1904; p. 247, October 9, 1904; *Dnevnik Suvorina*, p. 321, October 7, 1904.

to Nicholas's sense of mercy and autocratic prerogative: "Permit me, Your Majesty, to tell you that you must not only grant the favors anticipated by law—even we can do that—but also those which may astonish us. Gild the iron scepter of autocracy with your generosity." In Mirskii's plea, the personal nature of autocratic government took precedence over any fears of constitutionalism and its institutional implications. At least partially persuaded of the need to tone down the forbidding image of autocratic "ironhandedness," Nicholas finally yielded to his minister's entreaties and agreed to pardon the exiled Tver constitutionalists on the occasion of his name day, December 6.[20] A week later, he also lifted the ban on the provincial zemstvo assembly, notwithstanding the strong remonstrances and ultimate resignation of the Tver governor.[21]

Temporarily emboldened by his success, Mirskii sought to convince the tsar of the need for national representation, which would help determine the wishes and needs of the population. Different opinions had to be heard out; even Petrunkeviches en masse might prove more useful than dangerous. The sovereign's answer—in French—was oracular and noncommittally vague: "Yes, from the conflict of ideas the truth is born." Such representation was compatible with autocracy, Mirskii stressed, as the zemskie sobory had proven in the seventeenth century and as the very idea of autocracy implied. Alone devoted to the common weal, only the autocrat stood above partisan or estate interests. Still, he had to hear out everyone so that he might balance the interests of all.[22]

Mirskii's description of autocracy elicited a remarkable confession from the tsar: "Precisely: I adhere to autocracy not for my own pleasure, I act in this spirit only because I am convinced that this is necessary for Russia, but if it were for myself I would get rid of it all with pleasure." So sincerely felt were these words, so distraught and even bitter did Nicholas appear at this moment, that Mirskii could not help but feel sorry for him. A few days earlier Goremykin, one of Mirskii's predecessors, had warned him about Nicholas: "Remember one thing: never trust him, he is the most insincere person in the world," but Mirskii's wife demurred: "That is comforting, but I think not completely true: he is weak and equivocating."[23] Somebody, it seemed, was urging him on. Sviatopolk-Mirskaia strove for sympathetic understanding:

Unfortunate man! I hated him before, but now I feel sorry for him. A type of feeble degeneration, it was beaten into his head that he must be firm, and

---

[20] Sv.-Mirskaia, "Dnevnik," p. 245, October 1, 1904.

[21] Ibid., p. 247, October 9, 1904; *KFZ* and TsGAOR, f. 601, op. 1, d. 248, October 8 and 10, 1904.

[22] Sv.-Mirskaia, "Dnevnik," p. 247.

[23] Ibid., p. 249.

there is nothing worse than a weak person wanting to be firm. And who has such a bad influence? Apparently Aleksandra Fedorovna considers it necessary. Maria Fedorovna is of a different opinion, she told Pepka [Mirskii]: "These swine make my son do God knows what and say that this is what my husband wanted." But who are the "swine"?[24]

Nicholas's confession may well have come from the heart, but it revealed a conception of his role that was indeed external to him and hence subject to outside influences and vulnerable to manipulation. Only a formal sense of duty compelled him to abide by the role which he had so obviously failed to internalize. Tsar and minister made an odd pair. Mirskii's unhappiness with his position was surpassed only by Nicholas's dissatisfaction with his own role. Whereas Mirskii was already looking forward to the day of his release, however, the tsar was clinging stubbornly to all of his prerogatives. While the minister was prepared to use his unwelcome office to a higher purpose, the tsar appeared unwilling to execute his at all.

Mirskii's sympathetic attitude and gestures gave hope and encouragement to zemstvo activists who were playing a central role in the growing All-Nation Struggle Against Absolutism. On September 8, 1904, a zemstvo organizing bureau had decided to convene a national congress in Moscow for November 6–7, ostensibly in order to discuss war needs and zemstvo matters. In the wake of the new minister's conciliatory speech, the bureau broadened the congress agenda to include the "problem of the general conditions of our state life and desirable changes in it."[25] Apparently unaware of this ambitious program and the openly political character of the planned meeting, Mirskii followed the advice of one of his department heads, a zemstvo member himself, and requested the tsar's permission for the congress. The minister reminded Nicholas of the government's inconsistent attitude in the past. Provincial nobility marshals had been allowed regular congresses, while provincial zemstvo board chairmen had not. Such discriminatory concern was unfounded, Mirskii assured the tsar, for the periodic zemstvo meetings would confine themselves to the exclusively practical problems of local zemstvo life as stipulated by law. Therefore the zemstvo board chairmen should be granted the same rights as the nobility marshals in holding their congress in St. Petersburg. During the audience of October 1, Nicholas agreed.[26]

When Mirskii learned about the real composition and agenda of the impending congress, however, he was surprised and embarrassed. He immediately asked to meet with Shipov, the former Moscow zemstvo

[24] Ibid., pp. 247–48.
[25] Shipov, *Vospominaniia*, pp. 241–42.
[26] Ibid., p. 244.

chairman. On October 25, the prince explained to Shipov that the anticipated attendance and draft program of the congress bore little relationship to the kind of gathering that he had envisioned and for which he had secured the tsar's approval. In effect, he was guilty of misleading the sovereign. Unless the congress organizers agreed to postpone the meeting until late January or early February, he had no choice but to tender his resignation or face dismissal. While he did not care for his position, such an outcome would be a victory for the enemies of his policy, which in its essentials shared the zemtsy's objectives.[27]

Indeed, in matters of substance, the minister of internal affairs and his interlocutor did not appear to be far apart. Mirskii repeatedly professed his sympathy for the zemtsy's goals and, when asked by Shipov, listed four main problems to be discussed and resolved either by a special committee under the tsar's chairmanship or by the Committee of Ministers then headed by Witte: the peasant question; freedom of the press; zemstvo reform and administrative decentralization with the participation of locally elected zemstvo representatives; and "the involvement of popular representation in one form or another in legislative activity." Shipov saw no contradiction between this program and that of the zemstvo bureau, but, true to his intelligentsia outlook, he added that all estate distinctions had to be abandoned by the state in order to overcome existing social antagonisms and "rally all the available forces of society."[28]

Instead, Sviatopolk-Mirskii's differences with the zemtsy of Shipov's persuasion were of a tactical nature. Cautious and mild-mannered himself, Mirskii was mindful of political realities and the tsar's personal idiosyncrasies. Nicholas was inclined to react negatively to any public criticism or to societal pressures and demands, which lacked all legitimacy in his eyes. For this reason the first three points of the zemstvo draft program, which only contained criticisms of the present state, were superfluous and not constructive, Mirskii argued.[29] Although he, too, considered the status quo intolerable, to declare so publicly and immediately was to invite resistance and retaliation; in Mirskaia's words, "the Sovereign will be frightened and it will be impossible to accomplish anything."[30] Only constant and private suasion would convince Nicholas of the need for reform. As the deputy minister of the court confided to Mirskii, one had "to take the Sovereign by the hand; if one is very persistent, one can influence him, even right against his will, but he is also very suspicious, and there are always secret advisors opposed to the minis-

[27] Ibid., pp. 245–50; Sv.-Mirskaia, "Dnevnik," pp. 249–50.
[28] Shipov, *Vospominaniia*, p. 252.
[29] Ibid.
[30] Sv.-Mirskaia, "Dnevnik," p. 249.

ters."[31] The initiative for reform, Mirskii cautioned Shipov, had to come from above, and problems could only be resolved gradually. With more time perhaps, he could persuade the sovereign to summon elected representatives of the provincial zemstvo assemblies to present their proposals.[32]

The minister's predicament was great. He obviously felt a close kinship with the zemtsy and their objectives. Yet their very actions were a threat to his position and the policies he favored, for they provoked the hostility of influential and well-connected conservatives and jeopardized his relationship with the sovereign. The tsar's uncle, the Grand Duke Sergei, was reported to be in a rage at the interior minister. Mirskii found himself attacked and slandered for his alleged constitutionalist and Polish sympathies and for being Witte's unwitting tool. One of many defamatory rumors then circulating in the capital alleged that as a youth Mirskii had shot Drentel'n, the head of the secret police—early proof of his radical leanings. Joining in the deepening pessimism about the country's external and internal state of affairs, one rightist critic of Mirskii's went so far as to compare the impending congress with the Estates General just before the French Revolution.[33]

While Shipov was sympathetic to Mirskii's plight, he demanded firm assurances in return for a postponement. The announcement of the congress had given rise to great expectations which, if disappointed or frustrated by dilatory tactics, would only heighten popular unrest and agitation.[34] Since Mirskii could not guarantee that the tsar would consent to convene elected zemtsy at a fixed date, however, the congress organizers stuck to their original timetable. With the tsar's blessing so clearly out of the question, they reaffirmed their intention of meeting privately in members' houses. Unwilling to resort to the repressive measures of his predecessor, Mirskii told them that the law did not prohibit such meetings, and he ordered the police not to interfere with the zemstvo proceedings.[35]

From Mirskii's point of view, the zemstvo's actions were ill-advised and rash, and he was deeply disappointed. For many years, the zemtsy had remained silent while repressive policies held them in fear and check. Now, "when a man appears who seriously wants to satisfy all reasonable demands," they were proving unreasonable and determined to

[31] Ibid., p. 250.

[32] Sv.-Mirskaia, "Dnevnik," pp. 249–50; Shipov, *Vospominaniia*, pp. 245–50.

[33] Sv.-Mirskaia, "Dnevnik," p. 250; A. V. Bogdanovich, *Tri poslednikh samoderzhtsa* (Moscow-Leningrad, 1924), p. 299.

[34] Shipov, *Vospominaniia*, pp. 250–52.

[35] Ibid., pp. 256–58; Sv.-Mirskaia., "Dnevnik," pp. 251–52; Liubimov, "Russkaia smuta," p. 147.

create a scandal. How could they expect to correct in two months what had taken ten, even forty years, to corrupt?[36]

Hoping perhaps to anticipate and defuse the zemtsy's demands, the minister nevertheless sought to solicit the tsar's approval for serious reforms before the congress even had a chance to assemble and make its opinions known. During a two-hour meeting on November 1, Mirskii warned the sovereign that "the situation was very critical." The prince asked Nicholas to chair a conference that would decide which fundamental reforms were needed. The tsar would have a chance to hear out others besides his interior minister. While representation was too serious a matter to be approved without first weighing all arguments, in Mirskii's opinion elected people should participate in legislative affairs, a sentiment shared by 99 percent of thinking Russia. Nicholas's response completely missed Mirskii's point: "Yes, it is necessary, then they will be able to look into the veterinary problem." An exasperated minister reminded his imperial master:

"Your Majesty, I am not talking about that, but about the right of permanent participation in legislation. I would not be so insistent if the throne were secure, but now think: with the terrorist direction of the revolutionaries, in what kind of condition can Russia be?"

This time the tsar did not respond. Mirskii later described for his wife Nicholas's lack of reaction: There was "none, you don't understand him, he lets everything unpleasant run off [him]." As if to confirm the parallels with the French Revolution mentioned earlier, the indifference and impenetrability shown by the emperor during their audiences was a continuing source of frustration and despair for Sviatopolk-Mirskii. In a cloaked warning, he finally told Nicholas that he did not feel strong enough to manage. Again no reaction is recorded.[37]

The tsar indeed appeared remarkably unconcerned with the growing restiveness in society: the pressing need and consensus for reform was only a distant murmur to him. When Mirskii reported to Nicholas shortly after the zemtsy had adjourned, he was puzzled to find him "very happy . . . the congress had made no impression whatsoever on him."[38] This was also the picture drawn by the tsar's uncle, the Grand Duke Sergei: "He is an unfortunate man! Painful and pitiful! He is in a blissful state of . . . fatalism! Lord, Lord, have mercy on us!"[39] From Sergei's point of view, Nicholas was not alert enough to the dangers of the current domes-

---

[36] Sv.-Mirskaia, "Dnevnik," p. 251.
[37] Ibid., pp. 251–52.
[38] Ibid., p. 253.
[39] Sergei's diary, November 15, 1904, TsGAOR, f. 648, op. 1, d. 40, l. 324.

tic unrest and too resigned to the unfortunate course of military events and the reformist policies of his interior minister.

THE DRAFTING OF MIRSKII'S REPORT

Sviatopolk-Mirskii, on the other hand, was convinced that the time for some form of popular representation had finally come, and he was determined to see it through or resign. Nicholas had neither encouraged nor endorsed his minister's plans at their November 1 meeting; yet Mirskii pressed ahead. On November 4, with the zemstvo congress still two days away, he had asked one of the senior officials in his ministry, S. E. Kryzhanovskii, to draft a report to the tsar containing a program for domestic reform.

According to Kryzhanovskii, the minister stressed the need for appeasing the moderate segments of society with concessions that would leave the basic government structure intact, but would divorce the liberals from the revolutionaries. The program was to include measures to strengthen the legal system and establish legal accountability, give the population a voice in legislative decisions, curtail declarations of emergency, alleviate religious restrictions, and review existing peasant, zemstvo, and town duma legislation in an effort to enlist the support of broader strata of the population. Sviatopolk-Mirskii was opposed, however, to any acts that might further strengthen the powerful government apparatus. The report also was to emphasize the precariousness of the existing state of affairs. As for form, he wanted Kryzhanovskii to avoid words like "intelligentsia" that might engender conflicting opinions as to the minister's intentions or arouse the tsar's dislike.[40]

This outline was curious, if not perplexing. Small wonder that Kryzhanovskii was none too sure or happy about his assignment; as he would write later, he found Mirskii's instructions confusing and their underlying thought clouded. Most importantly, he came away highly uncertain about whether the sovereign had in fact given Mirskii definite orders to compile such a report. It was as though Kryzhanovskii were being asked to square the proverbial circle by drawing up far-reaching reforms, such as popular participation in legislative affairs and guarantees for legality and civil liberties, without violating the existing government structure. Mirskii's warnings against buzzwords suggested that his proposed reforms might indeed give rise to widely divergent interpretations. In order to minimize that possibility, at least the rhetoric had to be beyond suspicion.

Far from making any claims of originality for his draft, Kryzhanovskii

---

[40] S. E. Kryzhanovskii, *Vospominaniia*, pp. 15–18.

merely sought to give some systematic order to Mirskii's ideas, aided by a forty-six-page memorandum that the minister had brought to Kryzhanovskii's attention. The memo had originally been written for Nicholas, supposedly "with the knowledge and 'blessing' " of the late Pleve, according to its author, one Glinka-Ianchevskii.[41] Glinka's objective was a legal autocracy in which the wall of bureaucratic arbitrariness, ignorance, and disunity that separated the tsar from the narod would be eliminated through some form of popular consultation and through legal checks on the workings of the government bureaucracy. This, too, was the goal of Mirskii, who wanted to preserve the essence of autocracy while altering some of its nonessential forms; hence his insistence on keeping the basic government structure intact. In harking back to the ideals and aborted reform projects of Speranskii under Alexander I and Loris-Melikov under Alexander II, Glinka's criticisms were certainly not original. Nor were they unique; they were but one manifestation of a rapidly deepening anxiety and dissatisfaction on the part of even the most devoted adherents of autocracy, just one example of the ideas that, according to Kryzhanovskii, "lately have been hanging in the air, so to speak."[42]

The "senseless dreams" denounced by Nicholas a decade ago were very much in evidence. Mirskii's wife described the intoxicating hothouse atmosphere of reformist sentiment and the growing sense of possibility:

> In general life here proceeds at a forced pace, now representation, constitution, autocracy, bureaucratism are on everybody's lips. Only two months ago representation would have seemed a "senseless dream," but now they are talking about it as a matter of the near future. May God grant it! In my opinion, it is already better that all came back to life, that passions even flared up, it all is better than deadly apathy. . . . In general all this time there has been too much unrest. I am beginning to realize that my ideas are getting confused, I have lost my bearings, I feel the need to get closer to nature, nature always leads to the truth.[43]

The regime's critics on the right and the left all agreed on the utter unsatisfactoriness of the current state of affairs. Their fragile consensus even extended to some of the necessary remedies: the need for some form of popular representation in the central government, strict limits on the arbitrary power and prerogatives of the bureaucracy, and, to a lesser de-

[41] Glinka's memorandum is dated April 6, 1904, and entitled "The Basic Principles of the Russian State Order, in Conjunction with a Reorganization of the Powers of Supreme Power," TsGAOR, f. 543, op. 1, d. 11, ll. 6–27; Glinka's letter to Nicholas, n.d., after Alexis's birth, ibid., ll. 1–5.

[42] Kryzhanovskii, Vospominaniia, p. 19.

[43] Sv.-Mirskaia, "Dnevnik," p. 254, November 14, 1904.

gree, a safeguarding of the population's most basic interests and rights. These reform proposals were attracting an increasing number of supporters and hence presented a growing challenge to Nicholas's regime. Matters simply could and would not continue as before; reforms were needed and expected.

The fact that many would-be reformers held conflicting opinions about the precise nature and implications of their proposals and pursued radically different goals of either preserving or overthrowing autocracy was often ignored. Ideas like constitution or democracy were anathema to the adherents of autocracy, yet many avowed opponents of autocracy were content with nothing less. This dichotomy was reflected, for instance, in the eleven-point program of the November 1904 zemstvo congress. While the participants agreed in their demands for full civic and political equality without service estate distinctions, for civil liberties, administrative legality, and expanded self-government, they disagreed over the issue of national representation. Serious conceptual differences separated the majority, which backed a legislative popular assembly, from the minority, which preferred a consultative arrangement instead. Blinded by the radical aspects of the congress platform, however, Mirskii and other observers tended to overlook this fundamental split.[44]

Despite his misgivings about the zemstvo congress, for which he assumed full responsibility, Mirskii gave the tsar a memorandum by one of the congress organizers, F. A. Golovin. The author had succeeded Shipov as chairman of the Moscow province zemstvo board and was a member of the Union of Liberation, which was the driving force behind the national opposition against autocracy. Golovin's memorandum dealt with the inclusion of elected representatives of society in the State Council, a lawmaking body to which members of the imperial family and senior bureaucrats, many of them former ministers or their deputies, were appointed as a reward for long or meritorious service. This idea had the minister's full support.[45] Since his own report was just then being drafted by Kryzhanovskii along similar lines and would be presented to Nicholas two weeks later, Mirskii might have used Golovin's recommendations as a trial balloon. If he did, the tsar's reaction must have been encouraging. He kept the memorandum and "generally was very leniently disposed toward the idea of elected people," which he characterized somewhat ambiguously as "very interesting."[46]

When he received Mirskii on November 18, Nicholas raised the idea of a zemskii sobor, which had guided the decisions of Russia's rulers in

[44] Cf. Shipov, *Vospominaniia*, pp. 261–65 (program), 279–81.
[45] Sv.-Mirskaia, "Dnevnik," p. 253.
[46] Ibid., pp. 253–54.

the sixteenth and seventeenth centuries. Mirskii favored the notion in principle, but insisted that the general direction of state policy first be fixed and made known. Given the uncertainty of the moment, the eventual outcome could not be foreseen yet. Unlike those who saw in the zemskii sobor a consultative assembly that was the answer to Russia's current needs, Mirskii appears to have regarded it as a quasi-legislature whose binding opinions threatened the initiative and primacy of autocratic policy-making. If an Assembly of the Land were to be convened, he warned, there had to be a firm commitment to accept its decisions. Such an institution would immediately take up the problem of the war, for example, something the sovereign could not possibly permit.[47]

In a more ominous vein, Nicholas announced—for the second time—that he wanted to put down some of his own thoughts in a rescript to his interior minister. He obliquely referred to the crosscurrents of contradictory and rapidly shifting opinions in which he found himself: "A surprising thing, a couple of months ago everyone was displeased that everybody was being exiled, and now they are displeased that everybody is being allowed to come back." Mirskii was understandably horrified. The tsar might publicly compromise his minister's conciliatory reform course or otherwise embarrass him. Mirskii's concern grew when he received a note from Nicholas within minutes after returning from this audience. Mirskii was about to inform the governors that the recent zemstvo congress had taken place without government permission and that it was their task to remind the zemstvo chairmen explicitly of the ban on all political discussions, i.e., of those matters outside the purview of their institutions; the tsar wanted to review this circular. By the next evening, Nicholas still had not returned the draft circular, and Mirskii's fears deepened. Any changes in the draft would be an indication of complete distrust, Mirskii reasoned, and he would resign on the spot.[48]

The prince immediately suspected his nemesis, the tsar's uncle, behind this matter. Reportedly, the Grand Duke Sergei called Mirskii "Sviatopolk the Cursed," and there was every reason to assume that he communicated his highly unflattering opinions about the minister's policies to the tsar.[49] The fact that Sergei had been in town for almost a week and had walked, dined, and talked with Nicholas every day only fueled such suspicions. Indeed, it was immediately after such an engagement that Nicholas dispatched his note to Mirskii.[50] Sergei evidently had the tsar's ear. When the circular arrived the next morning with a disapprov-

[47] Ibid., pp. 256–57.
[48] Ibid.; Bogdanovich, *Tri samoderzhtsa*, pp. 310–11, November 22, 1904.
[49] Sv.-Mirskaia, "Dnevnik," pp. 250, 254–57.
[50] Sergei's diary, November 18, 1904, TsGAOR, f. 648, Sergei Aleksandrovich, op. 1, d. 40.

ing remark, Mirskii immediately wrote to Nicholas requesting permission to resign and take an eleven-month leave from St. Petersburg.[51]

This resignation request caught Nicholas by surprise and made him "very angry," as he would confide to his diary in one of his rare notes on such an official government matter.[52] He summoned the renegade minister to Tsarskoe Selo for the next day and "had it out" with him.[53] Nicholas told Mirskii that he had been thunderstruck by his resignation-letter: "I even got angry, you cannot leave, I even order you to stay on; why can't I give you instructions?" Mirskii replied that he had to resign: "The Sovereign cannot order me to bake pastries if I am not a pastry chef." How else was he to take Nicholas's disapproval, without any further comment, of the circular? He was in an impossible position, if he was not even trusted to write to the governors. The tsar explained that he did not regard this incident as a sign of distrust, adding: "For example, to Sipiagin, whom I considered my friend—and you, too, they [sic] consider a friend—I nevertheless wrote much worse things." Mirskii could not leave, especially as there was nobody to take his place.[54] In Mirskii's opinion, there would always be misunderstandings between him and the sovereign. St. Petersburg high society was so displeased with Mirskii's actions that it would constantly offer Nicholas its own slanted views of them. Although Nicholas reaffirmed his full confidence in Mirskii and made it clear that he did not think well of such intrigues, he also appeared to give credence to some of those insinuations by suggesting that Mirskii was indeed conducting his own policies. Mirskii was quick to defend himself. He asked rhetorically how a minister could pursue a policy of his own in Russia. By appointing a person of a known persuasion the sovereign signaled his support for such views; if he did not approve of them he could always replace him.[55]

Mirskii warned the tsar that unless reforms were implemented and the natural desires of the people were satisfied, change would come through revolution:

> As I see it, the aspirations of the huge majority of well-intentioned people are as follows: without touching autocracy, to establish in Russia legality, broad tolerance of beliefs, and participation in legislative work in order to prevent the issuing of laws that are totally unsuitable or issued at some minister's whim. Do we really have legality now? If a minister does not like something, he runs to you and finagles a supreme command without worrying whether this is good

[51] Sv.-Mirskaia, "Dnevnik," p. 257.
[52] TsGAOR, f. 601, op. 1, d. 248, November 21,1904.
[53] Ibid., November 22, 1904.
[54] Sv.-Mirskaia, "Dnevnik," pp. 257–58.
[55] Ibid., p. 258.

or bad, but simply because he likes it. . . . Moreover, every person must feel certain that some governor cannot seize him and send him to Perm or Siberia. In general, steadfastness and legality are required; to this end, the arbitrariness of the administration must be curtailed. Whether you summon an Assembly of the Land or a conference of elected people, they will all tell you the same thing; in fact, even at the congress of marshals of the nobility in Moscow the majority would not agree to sign an address that said nothing about the current situation, but merely expressed the feelings of loyal subjects.

Nicholas appeared to miss Mirskii's point: "Yes, they too have fallen under the influence of this zemstvo congress." Mirskii was growing exasperated: "Your Majesty, if you won't even trust the marshals of the nobility, on whom will you rely? Look, they certainly cannot be suspected of a lack of conservatism." The tsar backed off: "Yes, of course, I fully trust the nobles." The tsar's suspicions, however, rendered that trust more rhetorical than real. When his minister brought up the issue of representation again, Nicholas stressed the importance of appointing good people. "What does 'good person' mean?" Mirskii wanted to know. "One must not divide people into good and bad according to their political convictions." A good or bad person was defined by his moral qualities instead; the only way to pick a good person was to let the people vote. Only the intelligentsia wanted changes, Nicholas insisted, not the narod. Mirskii allowed that the narod was primarily interested in land but also desired reforms in order to get out of the existing morass. The people were without rights whatsoever and subject to separate laws of their own, unable to benefit from other laws made for the remaining one-ninth of the population.[56]

Nicholas waxed indignant when their conversation turned to a memorandum claiming that liberal and reactionary reigns had always alternated, that everybody had expected a liberal regime after Alexander III, and that the disappointment of these expectations had helped aggravate the current situation. "How could they think I would be a liberal? I cannot stand this word." "It is not a matter of a word," Mirskii lectured the tsar, "they did not invent a better one, but still everybody expected this and you must be liberal. I say furthermore, I am convinced that you are at heart liberal, that you are adopting all these measures against your conviction at somebody else's suggestion." Nicholas's answer was noncommittal.[57]

Although there had been no meeting of the minds, the minister was at least satisfied that he had had a chance to talk openly with the tsar. Their conversation is said to have been heated, yet in the end Mirskii relented.

[56] Ibid., pp. 258–59.
[57] Ibid. p. 259.

As he later told his family: "There were tears, and I kissed his hand, and I am staying, I couldn't [resign]." The tsarina, too, asked to see Mirskii, but disclaimed any intention of interfering. He essentially repeated to her what he had told her husband, emphasizing the universal desire for legality and representation. "Yes, but that is very frightening," she warned in French, "it must be done little by little." Mirskii's response was the same as before: "If the Emperor does not carry out a liberal reform, you will get a constitution all the same, but one much more severe than you would like."[58]

PLANS FOR REFORM

Ironically, the latest row might have had the effect of strengthening Mirskii's position and enhancing the prospects for his reform program. For lack of a suitable replacement or for fear of public displeasure, the tsar had found it impossible to part with his minister. Mirskii had spoken very candidly to Nicholas and had left no doubt as to where he stood and what policies he favored; the fact that the tsar had insisted on retaining him implied agreement or at least sympathy, or could be interpreted as such. Finally, the resignation of the Grand Duke Sergei as Moscow governor-general—who had symbolized reaction, rule by emergency decree, philistinism, "antizemstvoism," and anti-Semitism, all of which Mirskii had relentlessly criticized and pointed out to Nicholas—could be construed as a moral victory for the minister. He wasted no time in taking advantage of this auspicious conjunction of circumstances. No sooner had he met with the tsar, and no sooner had Sergei and his wife, the tsarina's elder sister, departed for Moscow, than Mirskii sent Nicholas his long-delayed reform program drafted by Kryzhanovskii.[59] Mirskii had made his views known to Nicholas only two days before; now his report served as a written restatement and amplification of those oral arguments.

This document was remarkable both for its broad historical argumentation and the spirit of legality that suffused its more than one hundred pages. Its central thesis held that the government had no choice but to promulgate far-reaching reforms, for these were the logical and inevitable consequence of past measures and of Russia's historical development. The government could not hope to stem, much less reverse, the course of history set half a century ago. The changes proposed were not the alien ideas of some wild-eyed radicals but bore the legitimizing stamp of Russia's own history. The rapid development of Russia's social and economic life, including the transition from a natural to a money economy and the

[58] Ibid., pp. 258–59.
[59] Two copies, dated November 23 and 24, respectively: TsGAOR, f. 543, op. 1, d. 513, and TsGAOR, f. 601, op. 1, d. 872.

destruction of the old patrimonial order (*votchina*), while beginning in
the 1840s, had really gotten under way with the reforms of Alexander II.
The administrative organs by themselves could no longer safeguard local
needs but had decided to share this task with "representatives of the best
forces of the population," i.e., the zemstvos and their urban equivalents,
the town dumas:

> These statutes summoned all inhabitants, without [*sic*] service class distinction,
> to manage local services and improvements for a well-appointed life and [thus]
> established the notion of a public interest—in the broad sense of this word—
> which before had been restricted to the narrow and confined meaning of estate
> benefits and needs, belonging to a man by the accident of his birth.

At the same time, Alexander's judicial and educational reforms "could not
but elevate in society the importance of the individual and the feelings of
self-respect." One of the results of these reforms, aside from the increase
in the general level of societal well-being, "was the growth of its intellectual classes—the inevitable outcome of the development and the necessary condition for further success of the state system [*gosudarstvennost'*]." The report also traced the growing interest in political questions
and the emergence of "public opinion, which is acquiring the significance
of a strong and conscious force that the government has to take into account one way or another in all questions of practical politics."

Mirskii's report contradicted key assertions of the traditional, personalized variant of autocratic ideology. In this respect it differed markedly
from Glinka's memorandum, which had supposedly served as the basis
for Kryzhanovskii's draft. If Russia's historical development was inevitably following that of other countries, it was no longer unique. Although
the word "capitalism" was conspicuous by its absence, Mirskii's report
welcomed the development of a money economy, the evolution of a society based on universalistic rather than particularistic distinctions, and
the new emphasis on the integrity and rights of the individual. The Great
Reforms marked the end of the old votchina order and with it the personalized notions of rulership. Russia was no longer the property and fief-
dom of a ruler who was personally tied to his subjects and who determined their needs. Instead, the report spoke of "public interest" and
"public opinion." The very concept of *obshchestvo*, i.e., a common, public sphere or civil society, was not only irreconcilable with votchina but
also foreign to Nicholas, who thought in terms of narod, not *obshchestvo*.
In fact, narod, that amorphous agglomoration of people mystically united
with their tsar, excluded obshchestvo. By contrast, the conceptual re-
alignment implicit in Mirskii's report was based on the emergence of the
impersonal state and of "stateness" (gosudarstvennost'), with its own
body politic separate from the person of the ruler.

The means and methods of realizing the objectives of domestic policy were hopelessly antiquated, the report continued: "The societal development of the country has outgrown the administrative forms and modes employed till now, and society no longer submits to their influence to a sufficient degree." Only one conclusion was possible: "The time has come to change these methods and to adapt them to the changed conditions." Experience had already proven that police measures could not quash the societal movement. Instead of using such repressive methods, the government had to "take [the movement] firmly in its hands," place it within a framework of law, and direct it towards aiding the growth of the state and commonweal—advice very reminiscent of a similar proposal made by another interior minister, Loris-Melikov, on the eve of Alexander II's assassination a scant quarter of a century before. To this end, the wishes of Russia's intellectual circles had to be considered and satisfied insofar as they were reconcilable with the interests of the state.

In an effort to determine these wishes, the report went on to describe the different strands of public political opinion. Excluding the extreme left, Mirskii saw a small minority espousing constitutionalist principles along Western lines, while a large majority supposedly wanted the main tenets of the Russian state preserved. Within this majority only a small group, however, favored the retention of the existing bureaucratic system with but a few meliorative changes; the overwhelming remainder wished to return to the autocracy of old, under which the population was both consulted by the tsar and in direct contact with him, without bureaucratic interference and with its personal freedoms protected. The last condition was an essential ingredient of Mirskii's program, which declared "that the foundation of the real strength of every state, no matter what the form of its government, is the mature individual who grows stronger through personal initiative." The more developed and autonomous the individual, the stronger the state.

Not only did the report find the desires of the majority to be consonant with governmental policy, but legality (zakonnost') and autocracy were deemed to be compatible. The observance of legality in the bureaucratic and social realm, Mirskii would have us believe, was not necessarily synonymous with a Western-style political constitution that would curtail the rights and powers of the autocratic ruler. To guarantee each person the right to develop talents and personality, to observe the inviolability of the law, to eliminate administrative arbitrariness, and to allow the population to make its needs known directly to the tsar had nothing to do with the issue of a constitution, Mirskii claimed. For example, neither the equality of all before the law nor an end to capital punishment limited the autocrat's prerogative:

Even with zakonnost', the autocrat does not share the fullness of his political power with anybody; they are not in conflict, if for no other reason than that the Autocratic Monarch, in establishing this or that order in the area of administration, is not bound by anything in his right to change it, when he finds this necessary.

It was this freedom to determine the administrative order that constituted the unlimited power of the Russian ruler and distinguished him from his Western European counterparts, in the opinion of the report's authors, Mirskii and Kryzhanovskii. Therefore, the actual form of government, even if it entailed the participation of elected representatives in legislative affairs, was of no consequence for the survival of autocracy, as long as the autocrat remained the sole sovereign source of power and hence retained his freedom to alter this order at any given time. Presumably, such changes would reflect new social and economic realities and would seek to satisfy the population's needs and wishes, which the tsar held dear. Still, the requirement of legality was absolute, transcending any particular administrative structure.

Contradictions abound. The tsar's power would continue to be unlimited in that he would retain the right to change the existing form of government at any time, yet the rule of law was to prevail. Would the ruler not be bound by the law, too, and thus cease to be autocratic? Although all historical signs pointed to the ineluctable victory of the impersonal state principle and the institutionalization of authority through the bureaucracy, Mirskii continued to profess his faith in the autocrat's personal and unlimited rule. The notions of legality and popular consultation were to bridge the gap between the two irreconcilables.

Several reasons suggest themselves to account for this paradoxical conclusion. A certain amount of wishful thinking and practical timidity which made the proposed cure less radical than the diagnosis cannot be altogether discounted. Another explanation might be that of expediency. No matter how fervently Mirskii believed in the supremacy of legality, as on previous occasions his pragmatism forbade him to point to the inevitable consequences for the tsar's power. To admit that the tsar's prerogatives would henceforth be limited of his own free will was to risk an immediate and categorical rejection of Mirskii's program. Another clue is to be found in the authors' understanding of history. The proposed changes, in their eyes, were required and sanctioned by historical development, which no human being, not even the tsar, could resist. Indeed, there would be still further changes in the future, reflecting the forward march of history and making the present little more than a passing moment, a transition toward yet another change. As Mirskii was about to tell Nicholas, there might even be a constitution in some ten to twenty years. On the one hand then, this emphasis on history was a rhetorical device to persuade Nicholas to submit to the designs of history; on the other, it bespoke the writers' belief that the tsar, as the agent of history, should be free to introduce further changes in conformance with historical development. Hence the notion of a *legal* autocracy in which even the tsar was subject to the law, yet free to reform in concert with historical progress.

For the time being the problem was that the government lacked a precise program enunciating the rules and principles of administration or its stand with regard to individual problems. Publication of such a program, Mirskii counselled, would serve to calm public opinion and enlist its support. In addition to codifying these rules, the government had to adhere to them and thus put an end to its almost daily violations of legality. The report urged the decentralization of administration in the sense that local authorities be allowed to act autonomously, subject only to the law and accountable for legal infractions instead of depending solely on ad hoc directions from the center. The watchwords of government had to be *zakonnost'* and *zakonomernost'*: legality, conformity with the law, regularity, and predictability.

To this end Mirskii proposed a comprehensive ten-point program that became the basis for the various projects and reforms of the next years, long after his own departure from power. The five key provisions of this agenda were the restoration of the Senate's independence as administrative and judicial watchdog; unification and coordination of government policy through a reform of the Committee of Ministers; zemstvo reform; the legal integration of the peasantry; and an expansion of civil liberties. A reformed Committee of Ministers, relieved of many of its purely administrative functions, was to become a clearinghouse and quasi-cabinet, though unlike his counterparts in the West the autocrat "not only reigns, but directly governs." As for the zemstvo and peasant issues, the report repudiated the Counter-Reforms and instead picked up on some of the recommendations of the Kakhanov Commission that had been doomed by the accession of Alexander III. The document's authors hoped not only to broaden the zemstvo franchise, but also to distribute financial obligations more equitably between the zemstvos and the state, investing the zemstvos with all responsibility for local property and economic matters and making them independent of local administrative control, subject only to the letter of the law. Moreover, a local zemstvo unit was to be established below the uezd level, and the introduction of zemstvos and town dumas, where not yet extant, was to be considered. Intimately linked to zemstvo matters were the peasant problem and volost' affairs. Given communal land ownership, ill-defined property rights within the family, and a lack of understanding of the guidelines that determined the decisions of the volost', i.e., purely peasant, courts, was it any wonder that the peasantry could not develop clear notions of private property and of legality, the report asked. Clearly, the civil rights of peasants had to be brought closer to those of the other "classes." Describing it as the pre-eminent and unique feature of the report he had helped to draft, Kryzhanovskii later saw behind this provision a call for full private land-ownership that would put an end to communal ownership as a source of unrest and rebellion.[60] And on the subject of civil liberties, the report urged the complete emancipation of the Old Believers, a review and partial lifting of restrictions on Jews, the suspension of prepublication censorship, and a curtailment of internal passports, administrative punishments, and emergency decrees.[61]

Finally and most importantly, Mirskii recommended that these pro-posals be worked out and implemented with the participation of popular representatives. After reviewing in great detail the various methods of consulting local opinion in the past, the report proposed that provincial zemstvos and major city dumas elect those representatives. As for the provinces without zemstvos, representatives could be appointed until a new statute extending the zemstvos had been passed. To ensure that the representatives' opinions would be heard, they would either be included in the State Council directly as regular members or form a separate entity which then would pass its recommendations on to the Council. Of those two options, the report favored the first in order to avoid rivalry and a potential conflict between two institutions composed, respectively, of elected representatives and appointed bureaucrats. Such a consultative voice for Russia's population was certain to restore domestic order and tranquility and steer Russia through its current trials.[62]

THE DECEMBER 1904 CONFERENCE

Despite the fact that Mirskii foresaw the need for additional concessions and even held out the possibility of a constitutional structure in a decade or two, Nicholas gave the impression of being in full agreement with his minister's proposal during their November 30 meeting.[63] Indeed, so con-fident was Mirskii of the tsar's backing that he renewed his request for an immediate convocation of a conference under Nicholas's chairmanship in order to discuss means of implementing his program. This suggestion was a curious one. Nicholas had repeatedly expressed reservations about the usefulness of such occasions, though for strangely contradictory rea-

---

[60] Kryzhanovskii, *Vospominaniia*, p. 19.

[61] TsGAOR, f. 543, op. 1, d. 513, and f. 601, op. 1, d. 872.

[62] Ibid.

[63] Sv.-Mirskaia, "Dnevnik," p. 261; Shipov, *Vospominaniia*, pp. 286–87.

sons: the participants had either failed to support the tsar, merely restated their well-known positions, or simply agreed with the tsar.[64] Nicholas clearly disliked such a direct forum for resolving political issues, with
the likelihood of face-to-face confrontations that would compel him to
take an independent stand or to side with one faction against another in
their very presence. Moreover, Mirskii's proposal for a conference, if carried out, would subject his reform plans to the hostile scrutiny of his
opponents and hence jeopardize approval and implementation of his
project. Was it not more advisable to seek the tsar's endorsement privately, out of earshot of any advisors who might influence him adversely?
Mirskii was hopeful, as he had confided to his wife, that the agenda of
such a conference would be "not in the sense of a discussion of principles,
but as a means of implementation."[65] He evidently expected the tsar to
approve his reform project before soliciting the other ministers' views on
the best ways to carry it out.

In the end, Nicholas overcame his skepticism and agreed to a conference. He suggested that the ministers of agriculture and justice, A. E.
Ermolov and N. V. Murav'ev, State Council members D. M. Sol'skii,
E. V. Frish, and O. B. Rikhter, his trusted Court Commandant Gesse,
and Count Vorontsov-Dashkov be invited. Mirskii inquired about Procurator-General Pobedonostsev and Witte. He must have been relieved
to hear Nicholas object that Pobedonostsev, whose opposition to any reform project was a foregone conclusion, would merely repeat what he
always said and what everybody already knew. As for Witte, the tsar opposed his presence, for he was a Freemason and never said anything definite. To exclude the chairman of the Committee of Ministers, one of the
brightest minds in Russia, Mirskii insisted, was inconceivable, and Nicholas relented. Evidently, the minister saw in Witte a sure ally from
whose influence and persuasive rhetoric he would benefit. Later Mirskii
remembered Minister of Finance V. N. Kokovtsev and received the tsar's
permission to invite him as well.[66]

Mirskii's confidence in Nicholas, Witte, and Kokovtsev turned out to
be misplaced, and his joy over Pobedonostsev's exclusion premature.
Unbeknownst to the minister of internal affairs, Russia's guardian of Orthodoxy had already anticipated Mirskii's initiative and fired his first
salvo. On November 29 Pobedonostsev sent the tsar a memorandum criticizing the annual report of the governor-general of Vilno, Kovno, and
Grodno, who happened to be none other than Sviatopolk-Mirskii himself, who had held this position before his ministerial appointment. Po-

---

[64] Sv.-Mirskaia, "Dnevnik," pp. 251–52; Shipov, *Vospominaniia*, p. 287.

[65] Sv.-Mirskaia, "Dnevnik," p. 256.

[66] Shipov, *Vospominaniia*, p. 287; Sv.-Mirskaia, "Dnevnik," p. 261; Kryzhanovskii, *Vospominaniia*, pp. 24–25.

bedonostsev's memorandum vehemently and vociferously rejected Mirskii's criticism of the government's religious and nationality policies in Russia's northwestern provinces. In Mirskii's eyes, these policies automatically identified Catholicism with Polish nationalism and discriminated against all non-Russian and non-Orthodox people. Such a conclusion, Pobedonostsev claimed, was utterly unfounded, yet he went on to defend it. Given his responsibility for those religious and nationalist policies, he obviously considered Mirskii's report a direct attack on his stewardship of the Holy Synod and on his rabidly anti-Catholic and anti-Polish sentiments.[67]

Ostensibly, the old procurator-general's move was unrelated to the impending conference about Mirskii's reform program, but it was timed too perfectly to be totally coincidental. It was highly unusual for a minister to communicate his views of such an annual report directly to the tsar before they could even be considered by the Committee of Ministers. Furthermore, both the tone and the substance of Pobedonostsev's memorandum demonstrated that he was not content to defend himself against the allegations made in the report. He also sought to discredit the political reliability and wisdom of Sviatopolk-Mirskii, whose disconcertingly progressive views had of late been in ascendance and were in imminent danger of becoming government policy. Pobedonostsev's initiative may well have had the effect of undermining the minister's proposals and of earning its author a belated invitation to the conference. Imagine Sviatopolk-Mirskii's surprise when he found the procurator-general among those journeying to Tsarskoe Selo on the morning of December 2, 1904. "Come help sort out the chaos," Nicholas had written in his last-minute invitation.[68]

The meeting, in the tsar's own words, was to discuss measures "to put an end to the sedition of the last months,"[69] but the participants were evidently confused as to what these measures should be. Should the government crack down on dissenters and demonstrators, or satisfy the demands of moderate society? There seemed to be general agreement that a return to the draconian policies of Pleve was unthinkable, if for no other reason than the fact, mentioned by Kokovtsev, that they had seriously undermined investor confidence abroad.[70] At the same time, however, the conferees denounced the recent violations of order and society's

---

[67] Handwritten cover letter to Nicholas, November 29, 1904, TsGIA, f. 1574, op. 1, d. 16, l. 83, and ob.; typed memorandum, ll. 84–95.

[68] Shipov, *Vospominaniia*, pp. 287–88; Kryzhanovskii, *Vospominaniia*, p. 25; Sv.-Mirskaia, "Dnevnik," p. 261.

[69] TsGAOR, f. 601, op. 1, d. 248, December 2, 1904. There are no extant minutes of this conference, and the published diary and memoir sources are not easily reconciled.

[70] Witte, *Vospominaniia*, 2:331.

clamor for a constitution; those responsible should be severely prose-cuted. Sviatopolk-Mirskii pointed out that this would mean a revival of the very practices, such as administrative exile, that had just been roundly criticized. Nicholas insisted that authority remain firm; as Mir-skii's wife would recount, "in all the talk of the zemtsy he sees only an egotistical desire to obtain rights, and a contempt for the needs of the narod." The minister of internal affairs begged to differ. To the contrary, he asserted, nine-tenths of all zemstvo materials and all their talk were in fact concerned with the narod and its "right-less" position. Nor did he want to see the zemstvo congress lumped together with the banquets and other meetings that had been taking place recently. Still, Mirskii had no choice but to go along with the decision to make public the government's displeasure with the escalating protests. He hoped that society would ignore such an announcement if it was accompanied by an invitation to elect representatives for participation in legislative affairs.[71]

It was this last proposal that provoked the sharpest debate. Sol'skii, Frish, Ermolov, Gesse, and Rikhter spoke out in support of convening elected representatives, Pobedonostsev, to nobody's surprise, squarely against. He denied the tsar's right to limit his God-given power, and gen-erally left the distinct impression that the best action was no action.[72] Mirskii's main antagonist, however, turned out to be Witte, not Pobedo-nostsev. Most of the conferees were apparently unfamiliar with Mirskii's report and therefore unprepared for the discussion. Mirskii may have assumed that the tsar approved of his program and thus saw no need to submit it for discussion by his colleagues, who were merely to address themselves to the best means of implementing it. Witte was quick to exploit their confusion.[73] While refraining from open criticism and giving the impression of personal detachment and objectivity, his comments were the most damaging and incensing to Mirskii. If Mirskii is to be be-lieved, Witte, together with Kokovtsev, simply wore down Nicholas with the argument that autocracy was incompatible with representation.[74] This was, of course, the same thesis that Witte had first advanced anony-mously in 1898; since then his authorship of *Samoderzhavie i zemstvo* (Autocracy and the Zemstvo) had long ceased to be a secret. On the one hand, Witte now declared, he shared "the opinion of those who speak in favor of the need for this measure." On the other hand he could not pos-sibly endorse their assertion that this reform would not shake the existing government system. "Any correct, organized, and permanent participa-tion of elected people in legislation inevitably leads to what is called a

[71] Sv.-Mirskaia, "Dnevnik," pp. 260–61; Shipov, *Vospominaniia*, p. 288.

[72] Witte, *Vospominaniia*, 2:331; Shipov, *Vospominaniia*, p. 288.

[73] Kryzhanovskii, *Vospominaniia*, pp. 24–26; Witte, *Vospominaniia*, 2:328, 332.

[74] Sv.-Mirskaia, "Dnevnik," p. 260.

constitution," and he warned of imminent danger and eventual disaster if such a plan were to be enacted.[75] Mirskii vehemently denied the incompatibility of autocracy and representation. Why was it inconceivable, he asked rhetorically, "that Russia work out such a form of government without falling into a constitution?"[76]

The word "constitution," of course, was anathema to Nicholas. The tsar would never consent to a constitution or a measure hastening its advent. Witte must have known that as well as Mirskii. If Witte really agreed with his colleagues on the need for electoral representation, why did he argue against it by raising the specter of a constitution? Whatever his motives, such contradictions could only serve to scuttle the proposed scheme. Was Witte currying favor with Nicholas by presenting himself as an honest broker who was prepared to subordinate his own convictions to the good of tsar and country? Or was he merely hedging his bets, unsure of the final outcome, foreshadowing similar behavior in the conferences of 1905 and early 1906? The fate of Mirskii's project certainly suggests that Witte would oppose any reforms as long as he was not in charge of them, but would make them his vehicle once he had climbed from the passenger's into the driver's seat. Mirskii himself told Kryzhanovskii that Witte was seeking to have the whole matter referred to the Committee of Ministers, which he chaired.[77] Elaborating on this charge, Mirskii's wife voiced the suspicion that Witte was cunningly jockeying for position, duping and discrediting her husband and sowing general confusion in order to seize control of the reform process: "Only one feeling governs him—personal ambition and a passion for power." Sincere and selfless, Mirskii was no match for such unprincipled behavior, she felt.[78]

The document that was approved by the conference on December 5 in Nicholas's absence bore some resemblance to the program outlined in Mirskii's report, yet placed the elaboration and implementation of those proposals in the hands of Witte's Committee of Ministers. Since the conference did not have a project of the government's program on the table, Witte had disingenuously suggested that Baron E. Iu. Nol'de, who as director of the Committee chancellery was a subordinate of his, be entrusted with the drafting of a ukase on reforms. As it turned out, both Witte and Mirskii went ahead with their projects, relying on Nol'de and Kryzhanovskii respectively.[79] These versions in turn served as the basis for the final draft, which, obliquely or outright, addressed all of Mirskii's

[75] Witte, *Vospominaniia*, 2:331–32; Kryzhanovskii, *Vospominaniia*, p. 26.

[76] Sv.-Mirskaia, "Dnevnik," p. 261.

[77] Kryzhanovskii, *Vospominaniia*, pp. 26–27.

[78] Sv.-Mirskaia, "Dnevnik," pp. 260–61.

[79] The principals disagree as to which of these drafts was officially authorized; cf. ibid., p. 261; Witte, *Vospominaniia*, 2:332; Shipov, *Vospominaniia*, p. 289.

134 · Chapter IV

suggestions except for his recommendations that the Senate and Committee of Ministers be reformed and that the Orthodox parish be revived. The only new item in the ukase was the fifth point on workers' insurance; it most surely reflected Witte's thinking, as did, of course, the provision that placed his Committee of Ministers in control of the reform process.[80] While the spirit of legality and many clauses of the ukase draft can be traced to Mirskii's influence, its wording and the procedure for implementing it point to Witte. There can be no doubt that Witte simply wrested the whole project out of Mirskii's hands and that the final draft of the ukase differed significantly from Mirskii's version.

We no longer have Witte's and Mirskii's drafts, but the following criticism by A. D. Obolenskii, who had close ties to both men, reveals the discrepancy between Mirskii's proposals and the eventual compromise. In an undated letter to Witte, Obolenskii complained about the "inadequacy of the whole project. . . . The proposed ukase is a half-measure from which one can only expect even greater misfortunes for the Sovereign and Russia. The time when such a ukase could pacify society has passed." Obolenskii urged Witte to throw his support behind Mirskii, who was on the sovereign's side and whose draft "contains the minimum of what can serve to calm the stormy seas." He called for concrete measures instead of vague promises: "Something has to be done directly and decisively instead of talking about giving instructions to deliberate about what to do. You cannot talk about legality, for example, without having established this legality already." Everything should be prepared in advance and then announced as a grant from the throne, not the other way around. In particular, Obolenskii wanted Mirskii's proposals for Senate reorganization and for elected representatives in the State Council restored: "It must be said clearly that the Autocracy not only rests upon service by appointment, but on service by election." Witte's book about the irreconcilability of autocracy and zemstvo self-government had been a fatal mistake, as Obolenskii had warned him at the time, since it provided ammunition for reactionaries as well as the zemtsy and the left. The time had arrived to disavow this thesis, to show "that even united zemstvo representation cannot encroach on autocracy, that autocracy can and must seek and find in it a corrective against bureaucratic absolutism. You may think that you will succeed in achieving something through force? Dreams!"[81]

Obolenskii was right. Exhortations had taken the place of tangible measures. The proposed ukase contained no immediate reforms and for

---

[80] This last surmise is confirmed by Sv.-Mirskaia, "Dnevnik," p. 262.

[81] A. D. Obolenskii's letter to Witte, handwritten original, n.d., Witte Collection, REEACU.

the most part lacked the specificity of Mirskii's program; instead, it offered the uncertain prospect of general relief in the near or distant future and relied on the discredited bureaucracy to work out the all-important details. Many of the proposals were hedged and entirely subject to interpretation, as Mirskii, too, had noted.[82] Although the government would be committed, at least on paper, to carrying out these goals, the provisions calling for the full legal integration of the separate peasant estate into society, for a local zemstvo unit and a broadening of the zemstvo franchise, for workers' insurance, and for some form of local participation in legislative proceedings had yet to assume concrete form.

The autocratic rationale for change was expressed in the opening paragraph of the compromise draft: "When the need for this or that change becomes ripe, We then consider it necessary to set out toward its realization, even if the intended reform calls forth the legislative codification of essential innovations."[83] The autocrat was acting in concert with historical development. Conditions had reached the point where he had to introduce important reforms. The tsar's primary concern, the ukase declared, was to improve the existence of the peasant estate. He now ordered that the lengthy preparations and investigations of the Ministry of Internal Affairs, the Local Committees and Special Conference on the Needs of Agricultural Industry produce reforms that would put the peasantry within the province of Russia's general laws and enable it to enjoy "the full rights of free rural inhabitants," as promised by the Emancipation edict. In addition, the ukase called for the observance of legality and legal equality, greater zemstvo autonomy, and a review of emergency laws and various legal restrictions on the press and on religious and ethnic minorities.

The draft ukase outlined two different means of consulting the local population about new legislation before its introduction into the State Council: Witte's and Sol'skii's. Whereas Witte foresaw a *preliminary* consultative role for the presumably appointed *representatives of local institutions*, such as zemstvos, town dumas, and perhaps even noble assemblies and commercial groups, Sol'skii, less ambiguously, had in mind an assembly of *popularly elected representatives*. When Witte informed the tsar on December 6 of the conferees' disagreement, Nicholas reportedly favored dropping the whole idea of the ukase. Witte protested and the final session was fixed for two days later.[84]

Evidently still not persuaded of its necessity, Nicholas was having second thoughts about going ahead with the program. As long as his advisors

[82] Sv.-Mirskaia, "Dnevnik," p. 261.

[83] TsGAOR, f. 652, op. 1, d. 301, ll. 2–4: draft copy of the Grand Duke Vladimir.

[84] *KFZ*; Sv.-Mirskaia, "Dnevnik," p. 262.

could not agree on the extent and nature of the reforms, the tsar preferred to uphold the status quo. Only a new consensus in favor of reform could convince him to take that road. Any misgivings about the need for or advisability of the contemplated reforms are sure to have been deepened by his ministers' lack of unanimity and by the counsel of the Grand Duke Sergei, who was in town for the tsar's saint's day celebrations. Tsar and uncle talked about various topics, including the government's impending denunciation of recent unrest and political demands, and Nicholas asked Sergei to attend the December 8 session of the conference.[85]

Public criticisms only served to reinforce the tsar's doubts. Thus Nicholas was incensed by a telegram from the Chernigov provincial zemstvo assembly. Received on his saint's day, this message criticized bureaucratic arbitrariness, irresponsibility, and lawlessness; the absence of fundamental civil rights, such as freedom of conscience, assembly, and the press; the widespread abuses of laws and emergency decrees; and the lack of judicial independence. The Chernigov zemstvo called on Nicholas to restore the close union between tsar and people by summoning "freely elected representatives of the zemstvo" and allowing them to work out on their own a reform project that would meet the fundamental needs of the Russian population.[86] Although this telegram seemed to anticipate the contents of the proposed ukase, Nicholas indicated his disapproval at the top and ordered Mirskii to publish his resolution: "I consider the action of the chairman of the Chernigov provincial zemstvo assembly impudent and tactless. To concern themselves with the problems of state administration is in no way the business of zemstvo assemblies, whose area of activity and rights is clearly circumscribed by laws." When Mirskii received the address with Nicholas's response the next day, he immediately feared its adverse impact on the conference. Such public demands were likely to make the tsar less conciliatory and agreeable to reform. At the same time, a sharp repudiation would cancel out any positive effect that the ukase was expected to have on public opinion. Yet to dissuade the tsar from publishing his resolution was impossible, Mirskii thought; there was no way to stop him continuously without precipitating "a very strong reaction."[87]

Not surprisingly, the final reading and discussion of the ukase draft on December 8 centered on its third point about popular representation,

[85] Sergei's and Nicholas's diaries, December 5–7, 1904, TsGAOR, f. 648, op. 1, d. 40, and f. 601, op. 1, d. 248.

[86] TsGIA, f. 1284, op. 241, d. 169, ll. 183–85.

[87] Sv.-Mirskaia, "Dnevnik," p. 262; The tsar's rebuke appeared in the official *Pravitel'-stvennyi Vestnik* on December 9, one day after the concluding session of the conference; E. D. Chermenskii, *Burzhuaziia i tsarizm v Pervoi Russkoi Revoliutsii*, 2d ed. (Moscow, 1970), p. 44.

which alone provoked heated arguments. In view of the importance and dynastic implications of the proposed reforms, the conference had been expanded to include the tsar's three uncles, the Grand Dukes Vladimir, Aleksei, and Sergei, his brother Michael, and the court minister, Baron Frederiks. Among those favoring *elected* representatives, only Mirskii, Ermolov, and Frish wanted them included in the State Council, while Sol'skii and several unnamed others opted for a separate chamber. Witte and Kokovtsev, on the other hand, spoke in favor of *appointed* representatives. Once again, Witte insisted that representation and autocracy were in fact incompatible and would eventually lead to a constitution. Mirskii conceded that this might happen in time, but argued that under the current circumstances "involving society in legislation" was the only way to save Russia.[88] The Grand Duke Sergei and Justice Minister Murav'ev reportedly opposed the project altogether. "I *very much* dislike a certain project about elections," Sergei wrote in his diary that day.[89] According to Murav'ev, the Fundamental Laws did not permit the tsar to alter the state order.[90] In the end, the Grand Duke Vladimir threw his support behind Sol'skii's proposal, and Nicholas, unmoved by the various objections, approved it.[91]

THE REJECTION OF MIRSKII AND HIS PROGRAM

As it turned out, however, the matter was far from settled. Although Mirskii considered his mission accomplished after submitting the revised ukase to Nicholas the next day, he began to fret when by December 10 the tsar had not yet signed it. Mirskii knew that Nicholas had been to Gatchina the day before to visit his mother and that the Grand Duke Sergei had been there, too. The fact that Maria Fedorovna also had asked to see him on December 11 only heightened Mirskii's suspicions.[92] He had cause to be concerned. According to Sergei, Nicholas did discuss the ukase with him and Maria Fedorovna, and Sergei was encouraged. During their afternoon walk the following day, December 10, Sergei "worked [on] him concerning the 3rd point of the ukase."[93] If the Grand Duke

[88] Sv.-Mirskaia, "Dnevnik," p. 262.

[89] Sergei's diary, TsGAOR, f. 648, d. 40, l. 347.

[90] Shipov, *Vospominaniia*, p. 289.

[91] M. Szeftel's statement in "Reform of August 6, 1905 (The 'Bulygin Duma')," *A. Marongiu. Mélanges* (Palermo, 1967), p. 138, that "this recommendation did not go beyond General Loris-Melikov's idea of 1881 to introduce into the bureaucratic State Council a certain number of members elected by the organs of self-government" is inaccurate. This had been one of the original proposals, but certainly not Sol'skii's, which was the one approved at this meeting.

[92] Sv.-Mirskaia, "Dnevnik," p. 263.

[93] Sergei's diary, December 9–10, 1904, TsGAOR, f. 648, op. 1, d. 40.

could not derail the entire project, he at least hoped to sidetrack its most objectionable concession, which offered popularly elected representatives a voice in legislative affairs. It was this point that also alarmed the dowager empress, as Mirskii learned during their hour-long conversation. Even though she liked the remaining provisions, it became clear to Mirskii that she did not understand the issues involved and was afraid of innovations. "These gentlemen" should be shut up, she suggested in an apparent reference to zemtsy and other malcontents. Not all of Russia could be silenced, the minister explained. There was nothing dangerous in the ukase; if there was any danger, it came from the reactionaries. Mirskii reminded Alexander III's widow that her late husband himself, were he still alive, would have found it necessary to take some action. Somewhat ambiguously, Maria Fedorovna sought to reassure Mirskii that only now had her son grasped the full difficulty of the situation.[94]

Evidence had begun to mount that both chief architect and key clause of the government's reform program were losing imperial favor. After learning of the resignation of the Grand Duke Sergei, the Moscow governor-general, and D. F. Trepov, his chief of police, Mirskii demanded: "What's going on, are you all running away from me?" Trepov's answer was brutally candid: "Yes, but we better not talk about this; I have been wanting to [leave] for a long time, and you know you will not remain for long." It was obvious to Mirskii's wife that they were all disassociating themselves from Mirskii in anticipation of his imminent dismissal or departure. Moreover, Nicholas's behavior in Mirskii's case typified a pattern: "The Sovereign never lets go on request, but then he drives [them] away." No sooner had Mirskii returned from Gatchina than Nicholas summoned Witte to Tsarskoe Selo that same evening in order to discuss the final editing of the ukase.[95]

The tsar received Witte in the presence of the Grand Duke Sergei. Although the final ukase draft had endorsed Sol'skii's recommendation for representatives elected *by the populace*, Nicholas now told Witte of his reservations about electing rather than appointing representatives *of societal institutions*. It was Witte who had suggested this last solution in the first place, still the tsar asked for Witte's advice. As the person responsible for the drafting of the ukase, Witte pretended to agree in principle with its provisions and their timeliness. Yet there was no doubt in his mind, Witte went on to say, that the disputed point was the first, albeit limited and modest, step towards a constitutional form of government. If the sovereign had truly and irrevocably decided that Russia

[94] Sv.-Mirskaia, "Dnevnik," p. 264.

[95] Ibid., pp. 264–65; Nicholas's handwritten note to Witte, December 11, 1904, Witte Collection, REEACU.

could not go against this universal historical trend, the concession should remain intact. If he objected to such a form of government, however, the clause was better dropped.[96] After straddling the fence for so long, in the end Witte left little doubt as to where he stood. When the Grand Duke Sergei inquired about the particular benefit of elected representatives, Witte replied: "I myself do not foresee any special benefit from this, but the minister of internal affairs thinks that it will appease society."[97]

There could be only one answer, as Witte knew too well: "Yes, never, under no circumstances, will I agree to a representative form of government, for I consider it harmful for the narod entrusted to me by God, and therefore I am following your advice and will strike out this point."[98] Sergei was relieved: "And so the elected [representatives] are buried. God be praised! Witte acted properly!"[99] Witte had merely repeated his performance and arguments of the conference. In fact, one wonders why the tsar even bothered to solicit Witte's advice at this time, when he had just heard it a few days earlier. Surely he did not expect Witte to change his mind so fast. Instead, haunted by his own conservative instincts and the dire warnings of his mother, uncle, and probably others, Nicholas had already resolved not to abandon the status quo. In Witte he was merely looking for confirmation. He deliberately refrained from asking Mirskii or Sol'skii, who most certainly would have disagreed.

When Mirskii learned from Witte later that same night that the tsar had ordered the crucial third point about elected representatives deleted from the ukase, he was understandably shaken. Just when it finally appeared that the whole matter had been resolved, even if not entirely to Mirskii's liking, that the first step toward a better future was about to be taken, his fondest hopes and dreams had suddenly collapsed around him. Everything, he felt, would remain as of old—until a revolution. To make things worse, the tsar had acted "underhandedly, without warning" the minister who had sponsored the project. Mirskii's mind was made up once and for all. He would leave immediately, or, if the tsar insisted, wait another month or two to avoid creating a scandal.[100]

In response to Mirskii's request, Nicholas agreed to receive him on December 13, one day after the signing of the emasculated ukase. Prophetically, Mirskii took issue with the tsar's most recent action: "God grant that I was wrong, but I am convinced that within six months you

---

[96] Witte, *Vospominaniia*, 2:333–35.

[97] Sv.-Mirskaia, "Dnevnik," p. 265.

[98] Witte, *Vospominaniia*, 2:335; Nol'de's memorandum, TsGIA, f. 727, op. 1, d. 1, l. 1, constitutes documentary proof that the third point was in fact struck out during this audience.

[99] Sergei's diary, TsGAOR, f. 648, d. 40, l. 350, December 11, 1904.

[100] Sv.-Mirskaia, "Dnevnik," p. 265.

will regret that you eliminated the clause about the elected people." "I hope not," Nicholas replied, "but if I do regret it, be assured that I will let you know." Mirskii had not yet finished speaking his mind: "In my opinion, it is inconceivable to run the country without the support of societal forces; others hold a different opinion, they must be summoned now. Here Witte says that one can get along without them." "I would appoint him immediately," Nicholas declared, "if I were sure that he is not a Mason." Mirskii denied this and informed the tsar that he could not stay on any longer. This time, he did not meet with any real objections. Since he did not know yet whom to appoint in Mirskii's stead, Nicholas asked him to remain for as much as another month, after which he could take an eleven-month leave. In parting, the tsar sought to appease his fallen minister; reaffirming his own confidence in him, he dangled the prospect of the Caucasian viceroyship before Mirskii.[101]

Mirskii was in a moral quandary. After the defeat of much of his program, his intellectual honesty and integrity did not permit him to remain at his post. At the same time, a powerful sense of duty commanded him to stay on until the sovereign released him. Mirskii had obviously lost the tsar's confidence, and he was eager to disassociate himself from policies that he could not condone; yet he was willing to shoulder the blame for them, if this is what the tsar wanted. When his brother-in-law urged him to leave immediately so as to avoid the blame and to protect his standing in society, Mirskii declined:

> You forget that I took an oath to the Sovereign, I cannot put the Sovereign in such a position for the sake of preserving my prestige. In good conscience, I cannot remain as minister, I explained that and if the Sovereign had not relieved me, I would have fallen ill. I cannot stay on, but since the Sovereign agreed to let me go and only asked that I wait 2 or 3 weeks, I do not feel I have the right not to fulfill this request. You . . . want to make a people's tribune out of me, I am unable to assume such a role.[102]

Sviatopolk-Mirskii no longer considered himself the tsar's minister; he was merely going through the motions of his official responsibilities, anxiously awaiting the promised day of his liberation. Before that would happen, however, a cruel twist of history ordained that he play a key role in and shoulder much of the blame for the events leading up to Bloody Sunday. The epilogue of Mirskii's ministerial career coincided with the opening act of Russia's First Revolution, which he had fought so hard to forestall.

[101] Ibid., p. 266. Despite Mirskii's favorable response, the appointment was never made.
[102] Ibid., p. 267.

CHAPTER V

Bloody Sunday

THE EMASCULATION of the December 12 ukase marked the defeat of Mirskii's conception of Legal Autocracy. A consultative popular presence and measures to establish legality had been designed to restore the unity of tsar and people by checking the abuses and irresponsibility of a tyrannical bureaucracy. It is no coincidence that Mirskii, upon assuming control of this bureaucracy, had insisted on describing himself as a zemstvo man and would discover kindred spirits in the zemtsy of Shipov's persuasion. Witte, by contrast, was still hopeful that some of the contemplated restrictions on the bureaucracy could be avoided. Much like its Prussian model a scant century before, the bureaucracy itself, preferably with Witte as its head, was to become a force for reform and renewal. To achieve this end, Witte had not even been averse to playing on the tsar's anticonstitutionalist biases. From Mirskii's point of view, Witte's notion of "Sovereign and people and between them—beneficent bureaucrats" was fatally flawed. Without some kind of catastrophe first, there would be no liberal reforms: "They do not want to understand that what is now called liberalism is really conservatism, but what is considered conservatism by the highest circles, is anarchy."[1] That catastrophe, as it turned out, was less than a month away.

Mirskii was not alone, of course, in his disappointment with the watered-down ukase and in his gloomy anticipation of the future. Except for Witte and Kokovtsev, all the members of the Committee of Ministers who were present for the reading of the ukase on December 14, 1904, were said to have been filled with anger. Imperial Secretary Baron Iu. A. Iksul' von Gildebrandt, the director of the State Council chancellery who was sitting next to Mirskii, stared at Witte and the ukase the whole time and whispered that "the empire of the two Sergeis"—of Witte and the Grand Duke—had begun.[2] The very incongruity of this suggestion bespoke the pervasive unease among the tsar's most senior servitors. During dinner with Nicholas and Sergei the day before, the tsar's brother, the Grand Duke Michael, apparently spoke his mind and even argued in favor of restoring the deleted third point.[3] Reportedly both he and his

---

[1] Sv.-Mirskaia, "Dnevnik," pp. 266–67.

[2] Ibid., p. 267.

[3] Sergei's diary, December 13, 1904, TsGAOR, f. 648, d. 40, l. 352; and Sv.-Mirskaia, "Dnevnik," p. 267.

cousin and brother-in-law, the Grand Duke Alexander, firmly believed in the need for popular representation and hoped to exert influence in this direction. Several members of the Committee of Ministers, including Sol'skii, vowed to make sure that the reforms announced in the ukase were in fact carried out, but Mirskii remained skeptical. The promised measures would come to naught, as the same bureaucrats were in charge and the people's voice could not be heard.[4]

Even such a committed adherent of autocracy as crusty old General A. A. Kireev, who did not belong to the government and thus had no vested interest in the ukase, echoed Mirskii's criticisms. Sharing some of the minister's Slavophile sentiments, Kireev wrote to Nicholas on December 24, 1904: "your people, who believe in you but not your ministers, see that the precious matter of the reforms envisioned by you has fallen into the hands of those very people who are principally opposed to these good reforms—into the hands of the bureaucracy." Instead of inviting representatives of Russian society to participate, the tsar had entrusted the project to, of all groups, the Committee of Ministers headed by the "all-powerful" Witte. These bureaucrats were not telling Nicholas the truth when they claimed that all people who did not sympathize "with our current bureaucratic 'regime' are either 'empty dreamers' or 'dangerous constitutionalists,' that they are all *enemies* of autocracy." In fact there were "*many, many* people reliable and loyal to Your Majesty who do not desire even the slightest diminution of Your autocratic power, but whose attitude also is unconditionally negative towards our existing bureaucratic system, our police state [*Polizei-Staat*]." Indeed, the only supporters of this system were those with material ties to the current régime and those seeking to "fish in murky waters" by sowing dissension between Tsar and people. The people were opposed to any wall between them and their tsar, whether in the form of a constitutional chamber or bureaucracy; their lack of confidence in the bureaucracy was the fruit of "bitter experience."

If the constitutionalist movement was growing by the hour, Kireev continued, it was because many people saw no other way out of the current morass. Still, it was not too late to consult with the people by summoning nobility marshals, town mayors, zemstvo chairmen, and elected representatives of the peasantry for advice. Freely, without being forced to do so by worsening circumstances, the tsar had to take immediate and decisive action to break the bureaucratic stranglehold and to restore autocracy as of old according to the historical adage: "It is for the people to counsel, for the tsar to decide." To this end, Nicholas should personally address thinking, well-meaning Russia, as represented by the St. Peters-

[4] Sv.-Mirskaia, "Dnevnik," pp. 266–67.

burg, or, better yet, the Moscow nobility and zemstvo: "We want to *see,
hear our Tsar, not read about him.*"[5]

Whatever the merit of his suggestions, Kireev correctly gauged public
opinion. Russian society exhibited a profound skepticism about the prospects of voluntary fundamental reforms on the part of the despised bureaucracy. A long history of repression, shattered hopes, broken promises, and administrative incompetence inspired little confidence in the
government's latest announcement, all the more so since it was immediately followed by a stinging rebuke of society's recent demands and actions: within twenty-four hours after the publication of the ukase, the
government released a statement charging that the wishes for domestic
reform expressed by the St. Petersburg congresses and various provincial
zemstvos in the fall had served as an unacceptable pretext for lively discussions of reforms in the press, among Russian youth, and in zemstvo
and nobility assemblies, and had even led to antigovernment demonstrations. "Any violation of order and calm and any gatherings with an anti-
governmental character," this statement threatened, "must be and will
be stopped by all means at the disposal of the authorities."[6] This warning,
coming on the heels of a similar censure for the Chernigov zemstvo, only
reinforced the public impression that the government was reverting to
its old policies. Once again its true identity had been revealed behind
the façade of reformist pieties. Hence the ukase met with public silence,
skepticism, and, of course, derision, but with very little gratitude or anticipation.[7]

"The Sovereign Does Not Understand Anything"

As if to disprove the widespread doubts, the Committee of Ministers
displayed unbureaucratic haste in drafting proposals for the implementation of the edict. By January 17, the tsar was able to confirm the first
set of recommendations, with more to come throughout the spring and
summer of 1905.[8] While this unexpected reformist direction, which even
included his Senate reorganization plan (which had been ignored in the
December 12 ukase), came as a pleasant surprise to Mirskii, he could not
but help suspect Witte of having purely personal motives and calcula-
tions. By seizing control of the reforms, Witte was hoping to return from
the political wilderness. Mirskii's wife observed with evident sarcasm:

[5] GBL OR, f. 126 Kireevy, 21(2), d. 1, ll. 1–2: Kireev's draft.

[6] This was the announcement that had been proposed in the conference session of December 2; TsGIA, f. 1574, op. 2, d. 51, ll. 2–3 ob.

[7] Cf. Sv.-Mirskaia, "Dnevnik," p. 267.

[8] *Gosudarstvennye Akty osvoboditel'noi epokhi*, comp. M. Mironov (St. Petersburg,
1906), pp. 6–21; Witte, *Vospominaniia*, 2:354–55.

"An assembly of people elected from the population under the State Council is incompatible with autocracy, but the limitation of an imperial command is compatible with autocracy. One can prove anything if one wants to."[9]

Whatever his personal ambitions, underlying these plans was Witte's belief in legal order and regularity, in a state run by a modern bureaucracy without—as yet—popular participation in the legislative process. Witte's Committee proposed to make the State Council, comprised for the most part of former ministers and their assistants, the sole quasi-legislature by reserving the force of law for imperially approved Council opinions and by limiting the legislative functions of the Committee of Ministers to isolated instances of the tsar's own choosing. Individual ministers also would have to obtain State Council and imperial sanction if they made extended use of their emergency powers. Although these recommendations had to survive several more bureaucratic rounds before being crowned with success, they represented an unmistakable innovation.

Witte's faith in the transformative abilities and creative initiative of the bureaucracy not only set him apart from Mirskii, as we have seen, but brought him into conflict with Pobedonostsev. Where Mirskii subscribed to the myth of tsar and people and hence optimistically regarded popular consultation as a check on an arbitrary bureaucracy, Pobedonostsev's cynical worship of power ruled out all such Slavophile illusions. In a remarkable series of exchanges with Witte at Christmas, Pobedonostsev gave vent to his despair: "The crowd which has lost its senses is carrying me with it into the abyss, which I see before me, and there is no salvation." In response to Witte's apprehensions about the immediate future, he asked why, if he really was afraid, he was helping this mob charge ahead without looking back.[10] Pobedonostsev also decried the absence of firm authority that knew what it wanted. This authority at present was "powerless, without awareness and without support, represented by ministers sitting wordlessly and motionlessly in the Committee of Ministers." At least "the very notion and principle of this power" had to be preserved, for without it Russia could not be saved.[11]

Somewhat lamely, Witte denied any personal interest in and responsibility for the reforms being discussed. As chairman of the Committee of Ministers, he had no right to raise questions reflecting his own per-

[9] Sv.-Mirskaia, "Dnevnik," p. 268.

[10] Witte to Pobedonostsev, December 24, 1904, "Perepiska Vitte i Pobedonostseva (1895–1905)," KA 30 (1928): 106. Pobedonostsev to Witte, December 24, 1904, ibid.; handwritten original in Witte Collection, REEACU.

[11] Pobedonostsev to Witte, December 25, 1904, "Perepiska," KA 30 (1928): 107–8; handwritten original in Witte Collection, REEACU.

sonal beliefs, he explained; instead, he had to see to it that the proposed measures conformed to the spirit of the December 12 ukase. Yet in the frank and harsh analysis that followed Witte left little doubt as to where he personally stood. It was necessary to determine *why* the crowd was charging forward and how it could be stopped. Arrests and repression were out of the question. Had the government not relied on such an approach for so many years, the current problems would never have presented themselves.[12] Downplaying the dangers augured by Pobedonostsev, Witte blamed Russia's current malaise on the war, which had put all other problems in its shadow. Above all, the government had to satisfy the most urgent needs of its subjects in order to win over the sensible elements of society and keep them from allying themselves with the extreme elements. To this end, the ukase and previous promises had to be carried out, and all reasonable desires of society had to be met, as long as they did not undermine the regime. At the same time, the limits of any new concessions and freedoms had to be made clear, so as to assure the public that the government knew what it wanted, that it possessed will and power. Government had to lead the public, not submit to the mob. At the moment the government was incapable of doing so, Witte lamented; therefore, he was not very optimistic about any real pacification of the country in the near future.[13]

Out of these three obviously irreconcilable notions of autocracy—Mirskii's, Pobedonostsev's, and Witte's—the tsar appeared to have endorsed Witte's, but how aware and committed was he? Nicholas's decision to entrust the cause of reform to the discredited bureaucracy was not easily reconciled with his own low opinions of his bureaucrats. It also made a mockery of the constantly invoked unity of tsar and narod. Perhaps he preferred the safer bureaucratic solution to the constitutional implications of popular consultation, or simply speculated that nothing much would come of the efforts and that the status quo would be maintained in the absence of any more pressing considerations.

Both Mirskiis, husband and wife, subscribed to the latter interpretation; in their opinion Nicholas had signed the December ukase "unconsciously," without wanting to see the reforms implemented. Disturbed by the tsar's evasive and slippery ways, Mirskii's wife was at a loss to explain his behavior in rational terms:

> He is a perfect sphinx. Those who know him best of all admit that it is impossible to understand him, whether he is intelligent or stupid, good or evil. I think that he is not normal and that the Japanese injury [during the tsarevich's

[12] Witte to Pobedonostsev, December 25, 1904, "Perepiska," *KA* 30 (1928): 107.

[13] Witte to Pobedonostsev, 26 [December 1904], "Perepiska," *KA* 30 (1928): 108–9; the context suggests that this letter, incompletely dated, was part of the Christmas flurry.

world tour] brought us much more harm than the current war. And then there is the worship of autocracy which has become a fetish with him. When it has to do with autocracy, he puts the opinion of people whom he positively does not trust [Witte?] higher than the opinion of people whom he trusts most, if they only mention in passing the inviolability of autocracy or "the fundamental principles of Russia" or something of that sort.

After Nicholas reportedly complimented Finance Minister Kokovtsev for firm convictions that belied his young age, Sviatopolk-Mirskaia commented sarcastically: "Evidently, in the opinion of the Sovereign himself, one has to be 'senile' in order to be for autocracy."[14]

Unlike Witte, Mirskii, and the others, the tsar still did not comprehend the dimming prospects for domestic peace. Not only had the December 12 ukase failed to appease the public, but its implementation was too far off and too much in doubt to assuage society's mounting restiveness. With increasing frequency, the police reports from the Interior Ministry testified to these stirrings, presenting Nicholas with disturbing details about terrorist bombings and assassination attempts, demonstrations, armed clashes between crowds and security forces, and the paralyzing strike in the Baku oil fields.[15] Although the tsar read all the alarming reports, he did not discuss them with anyone; he neither asked questions, solicited advice, nor gave instructions. Rydzevskii, Mirskii's deputy, concluded in obvious exasperation: "The Sovereign does not understand anything."[16]

Even when Port Arthur was forced to surrender to the Japanese on December 19, 1904, Nicholas's religious fatalism and the pathetically devout exhortations of his wife helped him face the "stunning news" calmly. Reacting to the fall of the besieged fortress after tremendous losses, a high sick-rate among the garrison, and the total exhaustion of ammunition, the tsar wrote: "Grave and painful, even though it had been foreseen, but one wanted to believe that the army would relieve the fortress. The defenders are all heroes and did more than could have been suggested. But such is God's will![17] Alexandra's reaction was equally fatalistic, as she sought to reassure her husband in her idiosyncratic style and spelling:

I felt as tho' a knife were dug into me when I read it; some how I cannot grasp it—the horror would be so intense. But if it is God's will, we must bow our heads and bear this burden wh. is overwhelming. Don't loose your faith in

[14] Sv.-Mirskaia, "Dnevnik," pp. 271–72.
[15] E.g., TsGIA, f. 1328, op. 2, d. 1, ll. 71–76; d. 2, ll. 1–3.
[16] Bogdanovich, *Tri samoderzhtsa*, p. 321.
[17] TsGAOR, f. 601, op. 1, d. 248, December 20, 1904.

God, tho' He tries you beyond measure—hope on—in the end victory must be ours—tho' how bitterly gained! God be merciful and have pitty on them.

Only hours before she still had refused to give up hope, even though Port Arthur's fall had been expected for months[18]:

> A miracle *must* happen, pray for it, lovy, pray for it, "il faut exiger avec vehemence," did he [Père Jean?] not say so—that God likes when one calls it out loud, that one insists—you, the Father of yr. people have the right to *insist* in your prayers, and He must, must hear you. I cant and wont believe their succombing. Oh for wings to fly to their succor.[19]

Aleksandra, too, was full of praise for the defenders' heroism, which would be rewarded "only in yonder life." At the same time, she ominously referred to " 'grande deception' No. 2—tho' you had feared it might end thus."[20] Apparently Nicholas had considered surrendering Port Arthur a few weeks before, but then let events run their divinely ordained course. Mirskii came away disturbed and depressed from his next audience on December 26. It seemed as though the fall of Port Arthur had made no impression whatsoever on the tsar; "he was cheerful and mentioned Port Arthur only in passing while referring to some appointment."[21] The dowager empress, too, was reported to be puzzled by Nicholas's tranquility at times of turmoil: "Sometimes I cannot understand this in my son, he is completely calm and content.[22]

If Nicholas's feckless equanimity was punctuated by infrequent outbursts, it was precisely because he still refused to take society's aspirations seriously and hence saw no need to make genuine concessions. Presumably an occasional admonition or show of strength were all that was needed to bring the malcontents to their senses and to restore order. The Grand Duke Sergei did his utmost to encourage this attitude: "I *implore* you not to yield to liberal influences by summoning people indiscriminately from the side for a conference." Referring to the zemstvo chairman and nobility marshall of Moscow province, he continued: "Forgive me, but it's time to show both Golovin and Trubetskoi in their un-

---

[18] As early as August 5, 1904, the Main Administration on the Press had summoned newspaper editors and asked them to prepare the public for the fall of Port Arthur; *Dnevnik A. S. Suvorina*, p. 315.

[19] Alexandra to Nicholas, December 19–20, 1904, TsGAOR, f. 601, op. 1, d. 1148, ll. 161–64: N 207.

[20] Alexandra to Nicholas, December 21, 1904, ibid., ll. 165–67: N 208. Indeed, before receiving their rewards in the hereafter, the defenders had to face a court martial.

[21] Sv.-Mirskaia, "Dnevnik," p. 270; reported, too, in Bogdanovich, *Tri samoderzhtsa*, p. 321.

[22] Sv.-Mirskaia, "Dnevnik," p. 279.

precedented escapades that nothing will be free any longer."[23] When the conservative Russian Assembly of St. Petersburg presented an address to the tsar a few days later, "resolutely reject[ing] even any thought of changing the principles of autocracy," Nicholas promised to stand firm: "I thank you for your honorable, truly Russian thoughts. As for what you said, nothing must be added to nor subtracted from it."[24] Sergei, in town for only a few hours, talked and walked with Nicholas and described him as "again energetically disposed," at least for the time being.[25] That same day Nicholas wrote a "stern" letter to Mirskii, denouncing as an outrage the popular gatherings demanding representation. Repeating Sergei's very word, Nicholas charged that those disorders were "unprecedented"; "the present inaction [on the part of the authorities] is fully tantamount to criminal connivance."[26]

Everything permitted by law to suppress unrest and to restore order had been done, Mirskii personally assured Nicholas the next day. Though he claimed to have read all the agency telegrams concerning the disorders, a cheerful tsar, acting as if nothing had happened and surprised that his minister did not like his letter, called Mirskii's explanation a revelation. He also insisted that any gatherings be prohibited. In that case, Mirskii replied, everyone would have to be locked up and a state of siege declared. Nicholas refused to recognize the absurdity of such a suggestion: "Well, so what, maybe it will have to be declared." Despite his expressed displeasure with Mirskii's actions, however, he still wanted to put off the minister's release. He told Mirskii that it would be dishonorable to leave without awaiting the appointment of a successor. Only after repeated forceful entreaties by Mirskii did Nicholas promise to let him go—in a week "or maybe in two."[27] "I had a firm talk with him," Nicholas wrote in his diary.[28]

Notwithstanding the tsar's New Year's wish for "a lasting peace and a quiet silent existence,"[29] those last two weeks of Mirskii's tenure turned out to be the most tumultuous of Nicholas's reign up to this point. As yet unbeknown to the emperor, more than ten thousand workers at the giant Putilov metal works in St. Petersburg were preparing to strike and to carry their appeals for support into the other factories. The authorities had hoped to avoid such militant actions by establishing the St. Peters-

[23] The Grand Duke Sergei to Nicholas, December 25, 1904, TsGAOR, f. 601, op. 1, d. 1341, ll. 151–52.

[24] D. N. Liubimov, "Russkaia smuta," pp. 161–62, although he is mistaken in the date.

[25] Sergei's diary, January 3, 1905, TsGAOR, f. 648, op. 1. d. 40.

[26] Sv.-Mirskaia, "Dnevnik," pp. 270–71.

[27] Ibid., pp. 271–72; A. A. Kireev's Dnevnik, GBL OR, f. 126, d. 14, ll. 1–2, January 3, 1905.

[28] January 4, 1905, TsGAOR, f. 601, op. 1, d. 248.

[29] Ibid., January 1, 1905.

burg Assembly of Russian Factory and Mill Workers early in 1904 and by putting Father Gapon, a priest working in the prison administration, in charge. In the past few months, membership in the Assembly had increased dramatically, as workers took their cue from the growing opposition within census society and flocked to the tea houses and meeting halls of the local Assembly branches for companionship and discussion, while Gapon indulged his monarchist fantasies of improving the lot of the working masses in concert with their tsar and over the objections of an indifferent bureaucracy. Buoyed by the success of the Baku oil workers, who had wrested a guarantee from their employers of a nine-hour week and significant wage increases, and, in response to the rumor that four of their comrades had been fired because of their membership in the Assembly, workers at the Putilov plant went on the offensive in late December 1904. Within a short time, this strike movement engulfed most of the major industries in St. Petersburg and began to assume political overtones.[30]

"BLOOD WILL BE SPILLED"

In the face of such mounting militancy among the capital's industrial work force, one can scarcely imagine a more unfavorable constellation of circumstances than the all-pervasive presence of a police apparatus that had fallen victim to its own paternalist, pseudo-socialist illusions; a lame-duck minister of internal affairs who was so eager to shed the burdens of office that he ceased being minister in all but name; a minister of finance who was quick to side with the employers against their striking workers; an ambitious, power-hungry chairman of the Committee of Ministers who was bent on promoting reforms while seeking to discredit his colleagues; military forces and their commanders whose only answer to peaceful and unarmed demonstrators was the use of deadly force and who were more adept a shooting and beating their own compatriots than their country's enemies; and, finally, a tsar, informed but divorced from reality, passive yet unyielding, and constantly confounding his own advisors.

No one among this group, to say nothing of Nicholas himself, understood accurately the nature and implications of the escalating strike wave, nor did they foresee, even in their grimmest scenarios, the bloody dénouement of January 9. Three of the five police reports on domestic unrest that had been submitted to Nicholas by the Interior Ministry during the first eight days of January dealt with an assassination attempt on the

[30] For a detailed description of the so-called *Gaponovshchina* and the events leading up to Bloody Sunday, see the works of V. I. Nevskii and, in English, Walter Sablinsky, *The Road to Bloody Sunday* (Princeton, N.J., 1976), with a comprehensive bibliography of published sources, pp. 351–404.

Moscow chief of police Trepov; none mentioned Gapon's Assembly or the strikes.[31]

Apparently, the tsar first learned of the spreading labor unrest on January 5 from his finance minister, V. N. Kokovtsev. By that time, Kokovtsev reported 23,200 workers on strike and detailed their illegal and unacceptable demands: "Voicing serious apprehensions about the outcome of the strike, particularly in view of the results that the workers in Baku had attained," the minister recommended "active measures" to protect those workers willing to work and safeguard the property of the factory owners, lest St. Petersburg witness a repeat of Baku. He also warned of the character of Gapon's Assembly. Its charter, Kokovtsev reminded Nicholas in a swipe at an institutional rival, had been approved by the Interior Ministry without first consulting the Ministry of Finance. Kokovtsev indicated that he would meet with the industrialists the next day "to give them appropriate instructions for the prudent, calm, and impartial consideration of all demands presented by the workers."[32]

The next day was Epiphany, and Nicholas journeyed to town for the traditional blessing of the waters and a reception for the diplomatic corps in the Winter Palace. Meanwhile, in less fashionable quarters of the capital preparations for a general strike and a Sunday petitionary procession to that same palace were afoot. Evidently, the tsar and his government were as yet unconcerned with these ominous stirrings, which were overshadowed instead by the accidental firing of live ammunition from one of the salute cannons during the ceremony on the banks of the Neva river. Aside from a few broken palace windows and the frightened onlookers behind them, however, the only casualty was a man named—by strange coincidence—Romanov, who lost an eye.[33]

When the number of striking workers jumped to 82,000 on January 7, Mirskii "began to worry about the strike and requested calling out more troops for the protection of property."[34] General Fulon, the city governor, posted troops at key points across the city and coordinated plans with General Vasil'chikov, the commander of the Guard Corps. Fulon also issued a proclamation prohibiting all public gatherings and processions and urging members of the public to stay away from any demon-

[31] Cf. TsGIA, f. 1328, op. 2, d. 2, ll. 1–5 ob.

[32] "Doklady V. N. Kokovtseva Nikolaiu II," *KA* 11–12 (1925): 3–4. In light of this report, Kokovtsev's subsequent claim—*Iz moego proshlago* (Paris, 1933), 1:52—that he knew nothing about the person of Gapon and his agitation among the workers until the evening of January 8 is obviously suspect, as are many of his other recollections. At times, these recollections will be cited in their English variant, as Kokovtsov, *Out of My Past* (Stanford, 1935).

[33] TsGAOR, f. 601, op. 1, d. 248, January 6, 1905; Sv.-Mirskaia, "Dnevnik," p. 272.

[34] Sv.-Mirskaia, "Dnevnik," p. 273.

strations, lest they become the casualties of armed force. Simultaneously, Justice Minister Murav'ev summoned Gapon, his nominal subordinate, and demanded that he cease his agitation among the workers and cancel the planned march. A similar summons from the Metropolitan of St. Petersburg went unheeded.[35]

By January 8 the strike had spread to the electrical power station, shutting down street cars, theaters, and restaurants, and plunging the city into an eerie darkness that suggested that something momentous was about to happen.[36] Sviatopolk-Mirskaia was alarmed:

> Today the strikes took on threatening proportions (already 120,000 on strike) and assumed a revolutionary character. Troops are patrolling the city. . . . [Gapon], it appears, is a fanatically convinced socialist. . . . They say that he is inciting the workers to go to the Winter Palace and to smash the factories. So far they are all calm, but they say that tomorrow there will be demonstrations.[37]

Not until the evening, however, only hours before the first workers were to set out for Palace Square from their distant assembly points, did all the officials involved in the preparations for the planned demonstration meet at Sviatopolk-Mirskii's to review their actions and to consider the tsar's order, proposed and conveyed by Court Minister Baron Frederiks, that martial law be declared in St. Petersburg.[38] At Murav'ev's urging, the conference weighed and apparently approved orders to arrest Gapon and his assistants, despite the fact that both Fulon and Mirskii opposed this for fear of further stirring up the workers and delivering them into more radical hands. Both men continued to believe in the efficacy of their preventive measures and in Gapon's ability to keep the movement peaceful. Obviously such a large crowd should not be permitted to congregate on Palace Square, Fulon warned, lest there be a repetition of the 1896 catastrophe at Khodynka, when dozens of people attending the coronation festivities had been crushed to death by a stampeding mob. It would not come to that, Fulon asserted, for he had already informed Gapon that the sovereign would not be in town, and the troops were under orders to turn back any demonstrators at the outskirts of the city. Fulon saw no need for martial law, for the situation was under control and such a proclamation could only make things worse. The conferees appeared calm and confident, with not even the slightest hint of alarm among the representatives of the Interior Ministry and the chief of staff. As Kokovtsev remembered, "it did not even occur to any of

---

[35] Sablinsky, *Bloody Sunday*, pp. 203–6.
[36] Liubimov, "Russkaia smuta," p. 178.
[37] Sv.-Mirskaia, "Dnevnik," p. 273.
[38] Kireev Dnevnik, GBL OR, f. 126, d. 14, l. 6; Sv.-Mirskaia, "Dnevnik," p. 273.

the conference participants that the workers would have to be stopped by force, to say nothing of bloodshed."[39]

The optimism and tranquility of the conference participants was shared by the tsar. He looked "radiant," according to his minister of education, who delivered his weekly report before lunch.[40] When Mirskii reported to Nicholas in Tsarskoe Selo late that night about the conference's conclusions, he found the tsar "completely unworried." Nicholas treated his minister very kindly and seemed more concerned about Mirskii's cold than the situation back in the capital. Though he had dispatched Frederiks only hours before to invoke marital law, he now agreed with Mirskii and his fellow-conferees that this was unnecessary.[41] In his diary, Nicholas recorded his reaction to the ministerial assurances:

> Since yesterday all factories and plants in St. Petersburg are on strike. To reinforce the garrison, troops were ordered from the surrounding areas. The workers are behaving peacefully so far. Their number is estimated at 120,000. At the head of the workers' union is some kind of priest-socialist, Gapon. Mirskii came tonight with a report about the measures taken.[42]

Even after returning from Tsarskoe Selo and encountering a large crowd at the station in St. Petersburg awaiting the tsar's rumored arrival during the night, Mirskii was still confident. As he had done with the tsar, he now reassured his staff that the military authorities were in complete control, that the workers would not be admitted to the center of town, and that everything would turn out well. Until the very end, he clung tenaciously to the belief that Gapon, the priest and police agent, and his loyal workers would call off their march when asked to and when confronted by the threat of force.[43]

As it turned out, Mirskii, together with Nicholas, Fulon, Rydzevskii, Lopukhin, and the others, proved to be grossly misinformed and sadly mistaken. An onlooker described the events as follows. Many of those crowding in the vicinity of the Winter Palace were curious onlookers, among them many women, children, and retired officers, who merely wanted to see the procession and hear what the tsar would say to his people. They were peaceful, unarmed, and had no suspicion that the

[39] Kokovtsev, *Iz proshlago*, 1:53; the preceding account is based on D. N. Liubimov, "Gapon i 9 ianvaria," *Voprosy istorii*, no. 8 (August 1965): 127; Sv.-Mirskaia, "Dnevnik," p. 273; and Sablinsky, *Bloody Sunday*, pp. 206–8.

[40] Glazov's Diary, *TsGIA*, f. 922, op. 1, d. 10, l. 8; TsGIA, f. 516, op. 1, Sdatochnaia op. 219/2718, d.20, *KFZ*: January 8, 1905.

[41] Sv.-Mirskaia, "Dnevnik," p. 273.

[42] TsGAOR, f. 601, op. 1, d. 248, January 8, 1905.

[43] Liubimov, "Russkaia smuta," pp. 183–84, 217, and Liubimov, "Gapon i 9 ianvaria," p. 129.

troops might use force against them as they were reported to have done elsewhere: "Here it won't happen. We are not doing anything. . . . We are not Japanese. [The military] does not bother peaceful people." Even if the tsar did not appear in person, at least he would send somebody to receive the deputies and the petition before announcing his decision.

The crowd standing around the Aleksandrovskii Garden in front of the Admiralty was quiet when the clock struck two. A mysterious trumpet signal sounded. For two minutes nothing happened. Suddenly, a volley sent a screaming human avalanche of four or five thousand people scurrying for cover down Admiralty Prospect. A second volley followed, then a third, as people in vain sought safety close to the garden's iron fence. It was like a

> second Khodynka, but under the shots of the soldiers who like wolves were killing peaceful, unarmed, inoffensive people. Many women were killed. I saw as they carried off three. . . . They killed a child . . . a horrible sight. And all this without warning. . . . Not one voice shouted: "Disperse! They will shoot!" After the first salvo they did not wait a little, so that the crowd might clear the place, but they began to shoot at the panic-stricken, running herd.[44]

Sviatopolk-Mirskii, in writing to Nicholas on January 9 about the bloody events of the past hours, left the clear impression that the troops had had no choice but to fire on the unyielding crowds.[45] Even with the benefit of hindsight, he concluded that he could not have permitted 150,000 demonstrators, no matter how peaceful, to assemble in one spot.[46] The tsar's reaction, aside from requesting more information, mirrored Mirskii's explanation:

> A grave day! In Petersburg serious disorders took place as a result of the workers' desire to reach the Winter Palace. The troops were forced to fire in various parts of the city; there were many killed and injured. God, how painful and distressing! Mama came from town straight for the service. We had lunch with all. I went for a walk with Misha. Mama stayed overnight.[47]

Reality had briefly, if painfully, intruded into his idyllic Sunday routine. Nicholas's comments seemed strangely detached and—as usual—devoid of any insight into the larger implications of the day's happenings, utterly unaware of the prophetic significance of that last desperate letter that Gapon had sent to him on the previous day, together with a copy of the workers' petition: "If Thou will waver and will not appear before the

[44] Leon Zhdanov's telegram to Nicholas, January 11, 1905, TsGAOR, f. 595, ed. 45, ll. 16–22.
[45] TsGIA, f. 1328, op. 2, d. 2, ll. 9–10.
[46] Sv.-Mirskaia, "Dnevnik," p. 277.
[47] TsGAOR, f. 601, op. 1, d. 248, January 9, 1905.

people, Thou will have broken the moral bond between Thyself and Thy people. Their faith in Thee will have been destroyed. Blood will be spilled, and it will lie between Thyself and the people."[48] Unbeknownst to Nicholas, the opening salvos for the first revolution had been fired.

THE APPOINTMENT OF TREPOV AND BULYGIN

Naturally, Nicholas's foremost concern in the wake of Bloody Sunday was the restoration of order that had been so rudely and unexpectedly shattered. Since the existing authorities—including the city governor, the commander of the St. Petersburg military district, the head of the police department, and the minister of the interior—had proven unequal to the task of preserving public order, the tsar resolved to concentrate all authority in the hands of one man, the former police chief of Moscow, D. F. Trepov. "In order to unify measures for putting an end to the disorders in Petersburg, I decided to appoint Major-General Trepov governor-general of the capital and the province," Nicholas wrote in his diary the day after Bloody Sunday. He also noted that there had been "no special occurrences in town today."[49] Although Trepov's appointment has been variously attributed to the influence of the Grand Duke Sergei, his Moscow sponsor and former master, and to Baron Frederiks, the minister of the court, and his associates, who like Trepov at one time all had served in the horse guards,[50] he had previously caught the tsar's eye. At least twice Nicholas had considered Trepov for some new position, only to yield to Sergei's entreaties.[51] This time, however, the Grand Duke wrote to his nephew, convinced that Trepov "will be at the top of his difficult calling" and pleased by his appointment.[52]

The naming of a governor-general who reported directly to the emperor and who was in fact his personal emissary was the time-honored method of Russian tsars for coping with social unrest and sudden problems that exceeded the capabilities of local administrators, commanders, and their superiors on the provincial and national levels. A governor-general enjoyed wide powers over the population, bureaucrats, and troops within his assigned area; Trepov certainly was no exception. Trepov's selection not only reflected Nicholas's belief in the efficacy of force and the pressing need for order, but it bespoke the tsar's lack of confi-

[48] Sablinsky, *Bloody Sunday*, pp. 220–21.

[49] TsGAOR, f. 601, op. 1, d. 248, January 10, 1905.

[50] Witte, *Vospominaniia*, 2:347, 349. Mosolov, the director of the Court Ministry's chancellery, was not only a horse grenadier but also married to Trepov's sister.

[51] Sergei's letter to Nicholas, September 19, 1904, TsGAOR, f. 601, op. 1, d. 1341, ll. 147–48.

[52] Sergei's letter to Nicholas, January 16, 1905, ibid., ll. 155–58.

dence in existing bureaucratic authority. The appointment of a governor-general was a typical ad hoc measure to deal with the failings of the regularly constituted authorities. With his antibureaucratic step Nicholas opted for the personalized conception of rulership, even if only temporarily or halfheartedly. At the same time, he raised the likelihood of conflicts and complications between his personal agent and the established bureaucracy.

Sviatopolk-Mirskaia considered the replacement of City Governor Fulon by Governor-General Trepov a declaration of no-confidence in the minister of the interior, perhaps even a slap in her husband's face. Had Trepov not resigned his post in Moscow back in December because of his objections to Mirskii's policies?[53] The message was unmistakable: Mirskii's role had ended. As he told Liubimov: "In reality, I am no longer minister."[54] During the last days of his ministerial tenure, Mirskii was reduced to executing orders received through Trepov.[55] When a workers' delegation came to see him on January 12, Mirskii sent them on to Trepov, explaining that he was no longer responsible. Twice, the minister renewed his request to be released. A stronger and defter man with greater authority, like Witte, was required now, Mirskii told the tsar; such an appointment also would make a good impression at home and abroad. Nicholas claimed that he had not yet settled on a successor.[56] In the meantime, there was little for Mirskii to do but wait, remain at his post like a sentry about to be relieved, all the while enduring the taunts of his critics.[57] With obvious justification, he felt shabbily treated. Even the dowager empress, his admirer, had to admit that he could no longer remain; she apologized for having put him in such a difficult position through her previous insistence that he stay on, and she promised to ask her son to expedite Mirskii's release.[58]

Finally, to Mirskii's great relief, Nicholas returned his resignation letter with a note of approval, but without any sign of appreciation. Mirskii was the first minister in the one-hundred-year history of the Ministry of Internal Affairs not to receive a State Council appointment, another post, or even a gratuity or medal.[59] The tsar blamed him for the growing domestic unrest of the past months which had reached its climax on Bloody

---

[53] Sv.-Mirskaia, "Dnevnik," p. 275.

[54] Liubimov, "Russkaia smuta," p. 201.

[55] Cf. Mirskii's report of January 14, 1905, TsGIA, f. 1284, op. 241, d. 120, l. 18.

[56] Sv.-Mirskaia, "Dnevnik," pp. 275–76.

[57] Among them Witte, who held Mirskii responsible for the "unnecessary" shootings. Murav'ev and Vorontsov were the only sympathetic exceptions; ibid., pp. 277, 279.

[58] Ibid., pp. 275–79.

[59] Others held responsible, such as Assistant Minister Rydzevskii or Lopukhin, the head of the police department, at least were given new assignments, Rydzevskii as senator, Lopukhin as governor; Liubimov, "Russkaia smuta," p. 216.

Sunday and in the strikes that followed. Indeed, so resentful was Nicholas of Mirskii's ministerial service that even more than a year later, when Mirskii called to pay his respects after returning from abroad, the tsar refused to receive him and did so only after Mirskii threatened to resign his honorific post as adjutant-general.[60]

Sviatopolk-Mirskii's successor as minister of internal affairs turned out to be A. G. Bulygin, a member of the State Council since January 1, former governor of Kaluga and then of Moscow where he had been the Grand Duke Sergei's second-in-command. Bulygin had been Nicholas's immediate choice to succeed Mirskii, and only Sergei's objections appear to have delayed his selection. Bulygin certainly did not hunger after the postition; in fact, he twice resisted the tsar's offer during their two meetings on January 19. Bulygin told his predecessor and perhaps Nicholas, too, that he had never served in St. Petersburg, knew neither the procedures nor the people, and had never even attended sessions of the State Council or Committee of Ministers. As with Mirskii five months before, Nicholas insisted that he accept.[61]

Opinions as to Bulygin's qualifications for his new position very much depended on the speaker's vantage point, though no one seemed to doubt the new minister's integrity and good will. Shipov, who had observed Bulygin in his work with the Moscow zemstvo, described him as one of the best governors of his time, with a "great capacity for work . . . conscientious and attentive . . . always well-prepared and thoroughly informed about matters to be discussed . . . objective and dispassionate" in conducting debates. "In his relations with societal self-government, Aleksandr Grigorievich was correct, did not seek to restrict the rights and autonomy granted it by law," and strove to satisfy zemstvo declarations or to find common ground for compromise.[62] While these would appear to have been ideal attributes from society's point of view, they were unsatisfactory from a bureaucratic perspective. Liubimov, who as head of the ministry's chancellery came to know Bulygin closely, conceded that he made an ideal provincial marshal of the nobility or even a good governor in a quiet province; when it came to political infighting and maneuvering, however, he was utterly unsuitable. Bulygin, in his subordinate's sympathetic, yet unfavorable estimation, was a typical, old-fashioned noble landlord, Goncharev's Oblomov in new dress, who yearned only for his own peace and quiet. Witte described Bulygin as "highly decent, honest, well-bred, very bright, a man with a rather broad knowledge of government affairs, but by character and nature a placid person" who

[60] Witte, *Vospominaniia*, 2:346.

[61] *KFZ*, January 19, 1905; Sv.-Mirskaia, "Dnevnik," pp. 280–81.

[62] Shipov, *Vospominaniia*, p. 110.

disliked difficult situations, political hagglings, and struggles.[63] Sviato-polk-Mirskaia felt sorry for Bulygin: "He is a good and decent person, but limited, and his convictions, inasmuch as I know him, are of the too stereotypical, autocratic sort, but totally sincere."[64]

Bulygin, unlike Mirskii, had never, prior to his appointment, con-fronted Nicholas with his personal political views, nor did the tsar solicit them. Once again, considerations of trust based on possible character references by the Grand Duke Sergei or Trepov, not programmatic affin-ities, appear to have determined Nicholas's decision. Indeed, the placid-ity criticized by Witte and Liubimov might have been an asset in the tsar's eyes. Bulygin was not likely to push for his own reform program, nor would he object to Trepov's extrabureaucratic attempts at restoring order. On the other hand, there certainly was very little in the new min-ister's personal makeup and background to suggest that he might break radically with the course of his predecessor. Devoid of any political am-bitions, Bulygin undoubtedly would have preferred not to become em-broiled in the treacherous quicksands of the politics of the capital. It is equally certain, however, that he brought good will and conscientious-ness to the particular task with which he was about to be charged—the creation of a consultative assembly.

The Response to Bloody Sunday

In the wake of Bloody Sunday a wave of protest demonstrations and sym-pathy strikes by workers, students, and professors swept the major ur-ban-industrial and border regions of the Empire. While daily reports from the Interior Ministry kept Nicholas apprised of the strike movement and of armed incidents in Moscow, Saratov, Kiev, Odessa, Riga, Vilnius, Warsaw, and other places,[65] he and his ministers wrestled with the ques-tion of how to respond to the latest events. Some sort of official an-nouncement was indicated, but who would issue it and what would it say? If there was to be an investigation into the disorders, would it limit itself to discovering the culprits or would it explore the broader causes of workers' discontent and take steps to eliminate them? Finally, should there be reforms beyond those promised in the December 12 ukase?

On January 11 the tsar received a long telegram from a forty-year-old, penniless playwright, Leon Zhdanov, who claimed to have been an eye-witness to the "horrors" in front of the Winter Palace two days before and who now felt duty-bound to tell "Russia's supreme leader how his servants conducted themselves." Zhdanov's vivid and moving account,

---

[63] Witte, *Vospominaniia*, 2:346.

[64] Sv.-Mirskaia, "Dnevnik," p. 279.

[65] TsGIA, f. 1328, op. 2, d. 2, ll. 13–18, 24–25, 27–30, 37–39.

from which we have already quoted, testified to the simple people's naive belief in the goodness of their tsar; indeed, the telegram itself was an expression of this faith. "Maybe some heartless or mercenary servants who surround Thee will not let these lines through," Zhdanov wrote, but that would not stop him from exposing the so-called clashes between troops and demonstrators. Fate had spared Zhdanov to tell the tsar what really happened and to remind him of the loyalty of his people:

> The narod loves Thee. It was so hopeful yesterday. It would have prostrated itself before Thee and beseeched Thee for help. . . . "But for what did they kill us at the palace? We were working peacefully. They let us through to gather. Or did they want to gather more people and then kill them all?" . . . this is what the narod is saying. . . . The heart aches. I say what I saw. And that was awful.[66]

The tsar was sufficiently disturbed or moved by this message to send it immediately to the newly appointed governor-general of St. Petersburg, D. F. Trepov. Even before hearing from Zhdanov, Nicholas explained, he had wondered whether "all necessary measures, i.e., admonitions, warnings, etc.," had been taken before the troops opened fire. Trepov was to investigate this question. The tsar then put forth his own views on how the government should react to the recent events:

> As I already told you yesterday, it appears extremely necessary to me now, together with measures of strictness, to let the good and peaceful mass of working folk feel the fair and concerned attitude of the Government and to separate it from the small groups of scoundrels. If a few factories started to work under the protection of troops, that would be a good omen.

In particular, the tsar endorsed the idea of an official declaration which Sviatopolk-Mirskii, Kokovtsev, and others first had suggested to him: "I think that the publication of a clear categorical announcement would significantly pacify the simple minds which are completely confused." Not only were disorders and strikes criminal in general, but at a time of war, such as this, when the full unity of all Russian people was needed more than ever, they were a genuine betrayal of the motherland: "Even worse is the conduct of educated circles who exploit any disturbances in order to stir up passions and produce insubordination and violence in the streets; all crimes and misdemeanors will be punished immediately, and everyone must honestly carry out his duty and his business, no matter how small, thereby helping the government." In closing, Nicholas invoked God's blessings for Trepov's heavy responsibilities. "I am firmly

---

[66] Leon Zhdanov's telegram to Nicholas, January 11, 1905, TsGAOR, f. 595, ed. 45, ll. 16–22.

relying on you."[67] The next day he noted with evident satisfaction that the day had "passed relatively quitely" and that there had even been attempts at several factories to resume work.[68]

Nicholas's diagnosis of the root causes of the recent troubles was very much in keeping with the myth of the benevolent tsar, mystically and personally united with his loyal people. He faulted Mirskii and his subordinates in the Ministry of Internal Affairs for their insufficiently forceful conduct in preventing a small number of revolutionary agitators, encouraged by Russia's foreign enemies, from stirring up the loyal masses. As he would soon tell a workers' delegation without any sign of remorse, "you let yourselves be drawn into delusion and deception by traitors and enemies of our Motherland." It was these elements that had incited the workers to rebel and that had lured them away from their peaceful work during a time of war. The result was disorders "that always have compelled and always will compel the authorities to resort to armed force, and this inevitably produces innocent victims, too."[69] By the same token, if the simple-minded, gullible narod had been confused and mislead by a "small group of scoundrels" and by "educated circles," then a word from the Little Father Tsar would suffice to bring it back to its senses.

Although Nicholas's ministers, too, invoked the myth of tsar and narod and shared his faith in the magical spell of the autocrat's personal words, they sharply disagreed with his analysis of the sources of the recent disorders. Whereas the tsar blamed the troubles only on the subversive efforts of a few revolutionaries or on the fact that the authorities had neglected to take more forceful measures, his ministers put the main onus on past policies and bureaucratic disorganization. Precisely in order to distance him from that record of failure, they favored a personal appeal to the narod by the tsar, announcing an investigation into the recent events and promising satisfaction of the workers' and the people's justified grievances.

Within hours after the shootings, Mirskii had drafted and sent to Nicholas "an appeal to the narod, calling it to order and promising in the name of the Sovereign to appoint a conference to investigate its situation."[70] During his regular Monday morning audience, Minister of Agriculture Ermolov also urged the tsar to address the narod.[71] On Tuesday, a similar plea arrived from Finance Minister Kokovtsev. More than 100,000 people were out of work in St. Petersburg, he warned Nicholas; together with their families they were "on the path to destitution, which inevita-

---

[67] Nicholas's letter to Trepov, January 11, 1905, TsGAOR, f. 595, ed. 45, ll. 1–2.
[68] TsGAOR, f. 601, op. 1, d. 248, January 12, 1905.
[69] *Pravitel'stvennyi Vestnik*, January 20, 1905.
[70] Sv.-Mirskaia, "Dnevnik," pp. 274–75.
[71] "Zapiski A. S. Ermolova," *KA* 8 (1925): 53.

bly leads to crime." Even more ominously, "beyond the borders of our fatherland complete distrust in us has begun to reign, and Russian credit, which stood so high not long ago, even in the moments of military reverses, has suddenly been shaken." While he did not want to alarm Nicholas more than necessary by describing in detail the consequences of such a development—presumably the certain failure of Russia's efforts to negotiate two large foreign loans—the current disorders had to be stopped immediately. The use of armed force alone would be as ineffective and even counterproductive as the government's policy of "police socialism." The police had proven unable to prevent the eruption of unrest in the first place, when it countenanced, with Pleve's initial approval, the growth of the workers' "criminal organization." Force only provoked new dissatisfaction in society as well as irritation among the lower strata and among those victimized by chance. The only way to restore peace to the capital and to keep the disturbances from spreading to other areas was the "sovereign word of Your Imperial Majesty."

A communication to the narod, announcing that the needs of the working class were close to the tsar's heart and would receive his attention to the extent that they were justified, was to contain the spreading disorders and persuade the workers to return to work, Kokovtsev argued. Others had exploited the workers' ignorance and weakness for their own selfish purposes, deceiving them with promises of quick improvements and with assurances that the government was on their side, Kokovtsev observed, alluding to Gapon and his handlers in the Interior Ministry. The workers would repent of their delusions once they realized that they were the blind tools of others' wills and designs. Only the tsar could convince them, however:

> At this minute, when the streets of the capital are stained with blood, the voice of a minister or even of all ministers together will not be heard by the narod. . . . The workers will believe your word that the working folk shall find the source of all good and care not in the tempting promises of their leaders, but in your kindness.

If Nicholas approved, Kokovtsev would draft such an announcement in agreement with Trepov and have it posted in St. Petersburg and other localities that had concentrations of workers. "I share your thoughts," Nicholas wrote.[72] Yet when the appeal went out on January 13, expressing the government's willingness to consider the worker's justified desires once they returned to work, it bore not the tsar's but Kokovtsev's and Trepov's signatures.[73]

[72] Kokovtsev's report of January 11, 1905, "9oe ianvaria 1905," *KA* 11–12 (1925): 4–6.
[73] *Pravitel'stvennyi Vestnik*, January 13, 1905.

Although his ministers wanted the appeal to come directly from the tsar, he had evidently preferred not to be identified with it personally. When Mirskii had first broached the idea of such an announcement, Nicholas had wondered aloud why it should be issued in his name,[74] and by January 16 he had decided to drop the idea of an imperial announcement or manifesto altogether. In a letter to Trepov, Nicholas urged that instead a delegation of workers with Trepov at its head come to see him and listen to his words which then should be made public. Speed was of essence, the tsar explained, "so as to weaken and halt the course of the strikes in the South."[75] A direct word to the workers, Nicholas hoped, would calm them and persuade their striking colleagues to return to work.[76] While the tsar was willing and indeed eager to remind the workers of their proper place and responsibilities, he clearly did not want to be associated with a public promise to satisfy their grievances. Such a statement implied an admission of previous neglect or wrongdoing and thus was best left to his bureaucrats. That approach also left Nicholas free to disavow any promise of reform at a later date when order had returned.

Ever mindful of these implications, the tsar's senior bureaucratic servitors continued to promote the idea of an imperial manifesto. Prominent officials gathered privately at Sol'skii's to draft such an appeal.[77] On January 17, A. S. Ermolov, the tsar's most senior minister and one of the few bureaucrats whom he trusted personally, renewed his plea for a public proclamation by the tsar. Nicholas asked for Ermolov's opinion about the current state of affairs. This very question, unusual in itself, was proof of the tsar's personal confidence in his minister, and Ermolov answered with his customary frankness. The situation was grave and unprecedented, Ermolov explained. Agitation was continuing in various forms, and nobody, including Nicholas himself, was safe from assassination attempts. Autocratic government could not rest on armed force alone. If the disorders spread to the countryside and engulfed the peasantry, would there be sufficient troops to put down a new *Pugachevshchina*?

[74] Sv.-Mirskaia, "Dnevnik," pp. 274–75.

[75] Nicholas's letter to Trepov of January 16, 1905, TsGAOR, f. 595, ed. 45, l. 3.

[76] There is no evidence, as later charged, that Trepov was responsible for this harebrained scheme. Witte, *Vospominaniia*, 2:348, blamed Trepov and claimed that the workers' appearance before the tsar was totally unexpected—which was obviously not true. The account in Kokovtsov, *Out of My Past*, pp. 38–39, has strong fictional overtones. Sablinsky, *Bloody Sunday*, p. 280, evidently follows Kokovtsev. Belying his strong protestations to the contrary, it is Kokovtsev who might have had a hand in suggesting the idea to the tsar. Cf. *KFZ* and TsGAOR, f. 601, op. 1, d. 248, January 12, 14 and 17, 1905.

[77] The only indications of this private meeting are contained in Glazov's personal protocol of the January 18, 1905, committee session, "Proekt manifesta o sobytiakh 9 ianvaria," *KA* 11–12 (1925): 35, and in Nicholas's letter to Trepov, TsGAOR, f. 595, ed. 45, l. 3.

Nor was there any assurance that the soldiers would continue to obey their officers when asked to shoot on the narod whence they came. "I understand that the position of the government is impossible if it relies only on the military," Nicholas conceded.

Ermolov invoked the narod's belief in a benevolent tsar: "You can rely only on the narod, but for this it is necessary that the narod can believe in you and continue to see in you its defender." The thousands of workers who had marched to the Winter Palace on January 9 had come not to present demands or to overthrow the government, but simply to make their views known and to explain their miserable conditions. They expected to be received by their tsar, not by a hail of bullets which would leave hundreds in the defenseless crowd unaware of what they were dying for. A delegation of the workers should have been received, and Nicholas could have promised to carry out their legal requests. Ermolov made it clear that the recent proclamation by Kokovtsev and Trepov was no substitute for the tsar's own word: "The narod doesn't know us, the ministers, but it knows you, Your Majesty, and it must hear your voice." The sovereign now personally had to make known to the people his regret over what had happened as well as his willingness to satisfy their legal desires and help the innocent victims. Contradicting his letter to Trepov of the previous day, Nicholas told Ermolov that he had already decided to issue an address or manifesto and that several projects were being considered. Finally Nicholas announced that he would receive a workers' delegation as soon as order was restored.[78]

When the ministers met on January 18 to take up the imperial manifesto that Nicholas first had rejected and now had revived, the discussion illustrated the two-edged nature of the myth about the bureaucratic barrier between the tsar and his people.[79] While a majority of the speakers favored a manifesto, they disagreed on its contents and justification. Controller Lobko wanted the document to go beyond the workers' movement and the events of January 9 and address itself to Russia's current wartime difficulties as well as society's demands. The most common argument, however, was that the narod expected and needed an explanation of the events surrounding Bloody Sunday. This explanation could come only from the tsar himself. Such an announcement, moreover, was the sole means of disassociating Nicholas from the actions of his government. Kokovtsev, Assistant Minister of Internal Affairs Durnovo, Murav'ev, and above all, Witte stressed the need for putting distance between the merciful tsar and his wrathful servants. The simple narod had to be shown

[78] "Zapiski Ermolova," KA 8 (1925): 53.

[79] The only record of this meeting is a private protocol hurriedly jotted down on the back of his invitation by the minister of education, V. G. Glazov, KA 11–12 (1925): 28–37; see, too, his diary, TsGIA, f. 922, op. 1, d. 10, l. 18.

that the tsar was not their enemy, that he was chagrined by the course of events and bore no personal responsibility for them. Sol'skii, on the other hand, found it inconceivable that the troops might have acted, as Witte insisted, without the sovereign's orders. He was joined in his opposition by State Council member Chikhachev, who argued that such a manifesto was certain to incite the narod against the troops.

The meeting voted 14 to 9 in favor of a manifesto, yet forty-eight hours later the idea was dead. According to Education Minister Glazov, the tsar's address to a hand-picked delegation of St. Petersburg workers and the subsequent publication of his remarks in the government press had rendered a manifesto "superfluous."[80] Unlike all but two of the speakers at the meeting, Nicholas had retained his faith in the salutary impact of his fatherly admonitions to the workers. Undaunted by predictions that the workers would react scornfully, Nicholas had insisted on the planned reception. Plans called for every one thousand workers to elect one loyal deputy who would then be received by the tsar. When Kokovtsev warned him of the workers' hostility or indifference toward the project, the tsar is said to have replied in a huff: "If this is so, no one can reproach me for being indifferent to the needs of the workers; they are to blame for having refused to come to me with confidence."[81] Nicholas was more interested in assuaging his conscience and erasing possible misrepresentations of his motives than in soothing the workers' wounds.

The thirty-four hand-picked and intimidated workers, who had been escorted to Tsarskoe Selo by police officials and were now lined up against the wall of the reception hall after repeatedly being warned, undressed, searched, and dressed, heard themselves chastised by their tsar. In remarks drawn up by Trepov and published in the official government bulletin the next day, Nicholas told the workers that he had summoned them so they could personally listen to his words and pass them on to their colleagues. After blaming the workers for letting themselves be deceived and incited, Nicholas assured them of his sympathy, but counseled patience and fairness:

> I know that a worker's life is not easy. Much must be improved and straightened out, but have patience. You yourself understand in your consciences that one must be fair to your masters as well as take into account the considerations of our industry. . . . In My cares for the working people I shall see to it that everything possible is done to improve their existence and to guarantee them in advance legal avenues for expressing their most pressing needs.

[80] Glazov's diary, January 20, 1905, TsGIA, f. 922, op. 1, d. 10, l. 20. This decision was made during Nicholas's meeting with Witte shortly after the workers' reception (TsGAOR, f. 601, op. 1, d. 248; and *KFZ*, January 19, 1905—6 P.M.) or the next day.

[81] Kokovtsov, *Out of My Past*, p. 39.

Before sending the delegates back to their jobs with his blessings, Nicholas reaffirmed his faith in the narod in a condescending and ill-advised gesture of intended magnanimity that provoked consternation and derision among moderate and revolutionary circles alike: "I believe in the honorable feelings of the working people and in their unshakeable devotion to Me, and therefore I forgive them their guilt."[82] In his diary, Nicholas called the day "tiring"; "from all this my head became completely weak."[83]

While Nicholas's speech to the so-called workers' deputies rendered moot the imperial manifesto, the question of some sort of official investigation remained. The ministers were still debating the need for an investigative commission when St. Petersburg Governor-General Trepov bypassed them and recommended the establishment of just such a body to the emperor. The recent workers' disorders, Trepov wrote to Nicholas on January 18, had highlighted the need for better government regulation of relations between factory owners and workers and for "managing the existence of the working people." To this end, a special commission was to investigate the reasons for worker dissatisfaction and find measures for preventing it in the future. To assure the fast and successful completion of its tasks and create public confidence in the new organization, its chairman had to be a competent, independent person and its members drawn from all interested agencies, with representatives of the owners and workers included as well. By letting the work of the commission proceed independent of and parallel to the preparations of the Ministry of Finance, the problems at hand could be examined from all angles, and the eventual solution could be thorough.[84]

Trepov's proposal for a new body outside the Ministry of Finance ran counter to the opinion that Finance Minister Kokovtsev had expressed in his January 16 report to the tsar and during the ministerial discussions two days later. Kokovtsev had criticized the absence of clearly delineated bureaucratic responsibilities, which allowed one agency to interfere in the affairs of another without clear direction from the tsar. Bemoaning the proliferation of innumerable ad hoc councils and conferences, Kokovtsev had objected specifically to the "establishment of any kind of exceptional and specialized institution for the resolution" of the workers question. It was his agency, the Finance Ministry's Factory Inspectorate, that had been charged by law with attending to the needs of workers and

---

[82] *Pravitel'stvennyi Vestnik*, January 20, 1905; Trepov's original draft, more sharply worded but identical in content, is printed in "Trepovskii proekt rechi Nikolaia II k rabochim posle 9 ianvaria 1905 g.," *KA* 20 (1927): 240–42.

[83] TsGAOR, f. 601, op. 1, d. 248, January 19, 1905.

[84] Trepov's report of January 18, 1905, TsGAOR, f. 543, op. 1, d. 510, l. 3.

industry, and preparations for reform were nearing completion.[85] The governor-general was certainly familiar with Kokovtsev's position, but was evidently prepared to risk an open struggle with him for the tsar's support.

The next day, January 19, Kokovtsev countered with a long memorandum of his own that explored the roots of the current unrest among the workers and proposed a detailed program to meet their needs. After surveying the government's attempts to regulate the mutual relations of workers and industrialists over the past two decades, Kokovtsev addressed himself to the difficulties brought on by the rivalry between his ministry and the Ministry of Internal Affairs under Sipiagin and Pleve. In 1898, Kokovtsev charged, the Moscow police, which was under the jurisdiction of the Interior Ministry, had begun to interfere in all aspects of factory life, extracting concessions from the employers, founding the first working-class organizations in 1901, and even playing a role in organizing the 1902 strikes. Trepov, though unnamed, had been involved in the so-called *Zubatovshchina*, the experiment in "police socialism," which had gradually spread to other areas, Odessa in particular. In St. Petersburg Gapon's Assembly had been founded in February 1904 without considering the objections of the Ministry of Finance. Kokovtsev also described, in considerable detail, how the Interior Ministry had repeatedly attempted to seize control of the Factory Inspectorate from the Finance Ministry. As a result of such bureaucratic rivalries and this flagrant interference, the Factory Inspectorate had ceased to function effectively, and the ministry's long-standing plans for a shorter workday, medical assistance, workers' organizations, strike regulations, etc., had been held up.

While conceding shortcomings within his own agency, Kokovtsev urged once again that his ministry's Factory Inspectorate be granted exclusive responsibility for the workers' question in the future and that a series of reforms be implemented through legislation, not by administrative fiat. Among the reforms proposed by Kokovtsev was a review of what he characterized as the contradictory and unfair laws and penalties governing strikes. The police's tendency to treat any strike as a violation of the social order, not an economic issue, made it impossible to distinguish between legal and illegal causes, Kokovtsev explained. In fact, every strike, as long as it remained peaceful, was strictly an economic issue and no threat to social order and peace, if certain conditions were met. Russian laws should be revised to conform with foreign laws everywhere, which made no mention of a citizen's obligation to work and which pun-

[85] Kokovtsev's report of January 16, 1905, "9oe ianvaria 1905," *KA* 11–12 (1925): 7–10; "Proekt manifesta o sobytiakh 9 ianvaria," ibid., pp. 28–37.

ished only the use of force.[86] Nicholas agreed. In his struggle with Trepov, it would appear, Kokovtsev had emerged victorious.

Trepov, however, was not inclined to yield. As governor-general, he was not answerable to the Committee of Ministers nor bound by any of its opinions or those of its members. Instead, he was the tsar's personal emissary and confidant, who stood outside the established government hierarchy. On January 27, the night before the Committee of Ministers was slated to take up Kokovtsev's memorandum, Trepov reported to Nicholas that he had learned of the document by chance. In his view, the finance minister had given "a onesided critical evaluation of the activity of the organs of the Ministry of Internal Affairs" and had unjustly condemned Pleve's actions. Moreover, the proposals for future legislation were so vague, Trepov charged, that publication of the report, instead of bringing peace to the workers' ranks, would further agitate them and the masses. For this reason, Trepov asked the tsar not to make public Kokovtsev's memorandum and to appoint as soon as possible a special commission. Trepov then went on to repeat verbatim his recommendations of January 18 concerning the purpose, makeup, and work of the proposed body.[87]

This time the tsar agreed with Trepov. The very next day, Nicholas informed Witte of his decision to establish a special commission, to be chaired by a member of the State Council, Senator N. V. Shidlovskii, and to consist of representatives from all agencies concerned with the workers' question as well as factory owners and elected workers. Echoing Trepov's exact words, Nicholas explained that the commission was to examine the reasons for the workers' dissatisfaction and suggest means of preventing it in the future. At the same time, he ordered that Kokovtsev's memorandum not be published. The Committee of Ministers, which was about to consider Kokovtsev's report that day, was also to take up the new commission.[88]

Trepov, it would appear, had won out in the end over the minister of finance; yet Nicholas had not shelved Kokovtsev's "vague" proposals altogether. Instead, the Committee of Ministers would still discuss Kokovtsev's plans after developing guidelines for Trepov's new commission. The tsar had found it more convenient to approve Trepov's as well as Kokovtsev's recommendations than to choose between them. Henceforth the government's policy with regard to the workers would move along

---

[86] Kokovtsev's memorandum of January 19, 1905, "9oe ianvaria," *KA* 11–12 (1925): 10–23; also reprinted in *Rabochii vopros v komissii V. N. Kokovtsova*, ed. B. A. Romanov (Moscow, 1926), pp. 1–18.

[87] Trepov's report of January 27, 1905, TsGAOR, f. 543, op. 1, d. 510, ll. 4–5.

[88] Nicholas's letter to Witte, January 28, 1905, d. 11, item 35 of Witte Collection, REEACU.

two separate, independent tracks, without any guarantee that these would in fact run parallel to each other. The contradictions and potential for conflict were evident.

In its deliberations of January 28 and 31 the Committee of Ministers reacted to Trepov's interference by endorsing, for the most part, the criticisms and conclusions of Kokovtsev's memorandum. Taking note of the limited geographical purview of the new Shidlovskii Commission, which was confined to the workers of St. Petersburg, the Committee recommended that another commission, chaired by Kokovtsev and without the representation of industrialists and elected workers, study and draft the necessary bills before submitting them to the State Council. To elect workers' deputies on a national basis was impractical and inadvisable, the Committee declared. The Committee left the clear impression that the Shidlovskii Commission would have to await the nationwide findings and recommendations of the Kokovtsev Commission.[89]

Nicholas did not confirm the recommendations of the Committee of Ministers until February 20, 1905, the same day that he had to dissolve the stillborn Shidlovskii Commission on its chairman's advice. The unacceptable preconditions and demands of the proletarian electors sealed the fate of Trepov's brainchild a mere three weeks after Nicholas had assisted in its birth. In the face of the workers' boycott, the door was opened instead for Kokovtsev's bureaucratic commission, which recorded a few, very modest accomplishments during the months that followed.

"THERE IS NO GOVERNMENT"

The tsar's reaction to Bloody Sunday, be it the appointment of Trepov, the high-handed and patronizing reception of the workers' delegation, or the naming of the Shidlovskii Commission, did nothing to assuage popular feelings—quite the contrary. When striking students used university property for political demonstrations and 342 professors submitted a letter of protest, endorsed by some 1,200 prominent scholars, against the government's school policies and in favor of political liberalization, the government closed all institutions of higher learning for an indefinite period of time. In St. Petersburg merchants and industrialists offered financial relief to the victims of official force, while professional organizations everywhere erupted in protest. Appalled by the authorities' behavior, many of the winter meetings of district and provincial zemstvo assemblies endorsed the program of the November zemstvo congress. The number of strikers nationwide reached half a million, more than the combined

---

[89] "Osobyi zhurnal komiteta ministrov 28 i 31 ianvaria 1905 g.," *Rabochii vopros v komissii V. N. Kokovtsova*, pp. 18–34.

totals for the entire previous decade. While protests were peaceful for the most part, armed clashes did break out in the Baltic, Poland, Saratov, and the Caucasus.

Nicholas's inability to direct his bureaucracy to formulate and implement a coherent policy that would defuse growing public unrest and promote a dialogue between society and a united government prompted Minister of Agriculture Ermolov to confront the tsar twice within the space of two weeks. At their January 17 meeting Ermolov criticized the absence of a unified government capable of speaking and acting with one voice: "In reality there is no government, only individual ministers," who appeared to represent different governments and whose expertise and responsibility was confined to their own areas of concern. Generally, the ministers of His Majesty's government did not know any more about impending events than did the ordinary inhabitants of St. Petersburg, Ermolov charged. Thus, the fateful deliberations at Mirskii's house on the eve of January 9 had failed to include several important ministers. Henceforth, any matter of importance to the whole government should be discussed by all ministers assembled. Since it was burdened with so many different tasks, the Committee of Ministers had not lived up to this requirement. Even the Special Conferences under the tsar's personal chairmanship had not produced the expected results. Participants were usually unprepared and ignorant of what was to be deliberated. The fact that they had no prior opportunity for preliminary discussions among themselves often gave rise to disagreements that Nicholas had found difficult to resolve. While a conference of ministers might not always achieve agreement, at least it could present two thoroughly reviewed and well-founded opinions to the tsar.[90]

"But I already decided to found a conference of ministers," Nicholas blurted out. If so, this decision must have been a very recent one, for Nicholas then asked Ermolov to ask Witte, the chairman of the Committee of Ministers, immediately to convene a conference of all ministers and of the State Council department heads in order to discuss the government's response to the recent events and to pacify the country. Absolutely identical with Witte's Committee of Ministers in its makeup, this conference was to assemble at the behest of its chairman or any minister. For some time now, Nicholas explained, he had planned to change the procedures for convening the *Council* of Ministers, the long-dormant forum summoned and chaired by the emperor; he now wanted it merged with the *Committee* of Ministers. Since such a reform required new legislation, however, it remained to be worked out in the near future. In the meanwhile, the new conference could carry out the role of the Coun-

[90] "Zapiski Ermolova," *KA* 8 (1925): 54–55.

cil, especially since he would soon convene another conference under his own chairmanship.[91]

Nicholas's reasoning on this issue was utterly confused. On the spur of the moment in response to Ermolov's pleas, he had established a new ministerial conference, also to be chaired by Witte, which would duplicate the existing Committee of Ministers. Whereas the Committee was preoccupied mostly with day-to-day government business, the new conference, like the now defunct Council of Ministers, was to address the larger issues of state reform—until the functions of the Committee and old Council could be combined. At the same time, the tsar declared his intention of summoning a special conference that would be chaired by him personally; moments before, in apparent agreement with Ermolov, he had voiced unhappiness with such assemblages.

Nothing better confirmed the complaints of Ermolov, Kokovtsev, and others than Nicholas's erratic behavior. There was no unified government, no consistency in government policies, because the tsar was refusing to assert control and resolve disagreements. Instead, he tried to be all things to all people. According to Witte, it was typical of the tsar to lurch constantly from one end of the political spectrum to the other. When confronted with Ermolov's criticisms, for example, Nicholas sought to accommodate him, though without real conviction or readiness to change his ways. After only just criticizing special conferences, he added yet another ad hoc agency to the impenetrable bureaucratic maze. The tsar sadly lacked an overarching design or willingness to direct the different parts of this cumbersome machinery which usually worked at cross-purposes, if at all. Ermolov and Kokovtsev were not the only ones to arrive at this conclusion. This was also the impression that was communicated to society. As an exasperated Kireev concluded on January 22: "There is no government. There is a Tsar, but no general direction, no leading idea."[92]

Not satisfied with the tsar's impromptu concession, Ermolov urged that the government seek support within society. Since the nobility had been considered a firm pillar of support, the government had seen to it that noble influence in the localities was strengthened and that noble predominance in the zemstvos was ensured, Ermolov continued in a reference to the Counter-Reforms of the late 1880s and early 1890s. Times had changed, however. The differences of opinion at the November zemstvo congress had revealed a schism within the nobility and placed in question its reliability as a conservative bulwark. Every day new zemstvo and noble assemblies, by no means extremist and criminal, beseeched

[91] Ibid., pp. 55–56.
[92] GBL OR, f. 126, d. 14, l. 9, January 22, 1905.

Nicholas to hear out representatives of the Russian narod. According to general opinion, not entirely unjustified, a wall of ministers stood in the way of direct communication between narod and tsar. Kept in the dark about the deliberations of the Committee of Ministers, the people had yet to see any evidence that the promises of the December 12, 1904, ukase were being carried out.[93] Ermolov repeated his recommendation of early December that Nicholas summon popular representatives to participate in legislative work. What might have sufficed six weeks earlier, however, did not suffice now. Instead of the "weak form" of popular participation in preparatory legislative work, there had to be "direct immediate contact between Tsar and narod." While he declined to specify what form this representation should take, Ermolov advised Nicholas to act immediately in order to find support for the throne, a task made even more urgent by the war. The new ministerial conference should consider measures going beyond the December 12 ukase. Nicholas did not put up any resistance and agreed.[94]

Was the tsar ready to grant his people some participatory role in legislative matters after rejecting it only a month before? His instructions to Witte echoed Ermolov, ordering the new conference to consider "measures of state importance, called forth by the latest events, in connection with further measures for the pacification of the country and with reforms . . . beyond those announced in the supreme ukase of December 12, 1904." Fleshed out by Witte, these instructions translated into an ambitious agenda. In addition to the commission on the workers' problem and the moot imperial manifesto discussed before, this agenda included the need to heed the nobility and zemstvo addresses in order to rally support around the throne "in the form of representatives from the population," as well as the "problem of state administration" and its "fundamental shortcoming: the lack of coordination among the ministers, the lack of opportunity for the ministers to exchange thoughts, the absence of solidarity."[95] In fact, if Ermolov is to be believed, Nicholas was already planning to convene a Special Conference under his personal chairmanship— presumably to ratify some of those reform proposals. Ermolov himself had left little doubt that these plans should embrace popular represen-

[93] Although Ermolov obviously had in mind even further-reaching measures, Nicholas at least agreed that the newspapers be apprised of the results of those deliberations; "Zapiski Ermolova," *KA* 8 (1925): 56–57. On January 19, two days after Ermolov's complaint, *Pravitel'stvennyi Vestnik* explained the procedures adopted by the Committee of Ministers for discussing and implementing the provisions of the December 12 ukase.

[94] Ibid., pp. 57–58.

[95] Witte's letter to V. G. Glazov, January 17, 1905, "Proekt manifesta o sobytiakh 9 ianvaria," *KA* 11–12 (1925): 28; and Ermolov's communication to Witte, January 17, *KA* 8 (1925): 58.

tation; yet he had spared the tsar the all-important details, speaking instead of "direct immediate contact between Tsar and narod" and of finding support for the throne within the narod.

Although the reform process that had been set in motion by the December 12 ukase appeared to have gained momentum as a result of Ermolov's initiative, the minister of agriculture must have felt that his lecture had not had the desired effect. Exactly two weeks later, on January 31, 1905, he spoke to the tsar with equal frankness, but with a heightened sense of urgency. Repeating much of what he had said earlier, albeit at greater length and in a more organized fashion, Ermolov warned of the danger of further delays. The disorders among Russia's factory workers were threatening to infect the countryside. Agitation was finding fertile ground in the peasants' land hunger and could easily create a situation one hundred times more dangerous than the current one. A reopening of the universities was simply inconceivable for the foreseeable future. Indeed, the unrest, reflecting society's mood, was spilling over into the country's high schools. Even among the nobility many were ready to join extremist parties. Finally, the ministers were still going their own ways, Ermolov complained. While they were legally responsible to the tsar, it was he who bore the responsibility for their actions before the narod. The new ministerial conference was only a partial solution; government unity and coordination did not yet exist. In fact, the establishment of the governorship-general for St. Petersburg had been a step backwards and had further undermined ministerial accountability, as Trepov was now free to act on his own, without consulting other ministers or agencies.[96]

Naturally, the dark masses were bewildered and confused, unable to distinguish friend from foe. They were distrustful of all authorities behind which they did not see the tsar. At the same time, the narod often found itself deceived by agitators whom

> it takes to be tsarist messengers, and it receives from their hands various golden charters that promise it the realization of its secret dreams about the land. In the eyes of the narod, the government and the landlords are one and the same, a hostile force standing between it and the Tsar, preventing the Tsar from pouring out his favors in the form of an additional allotment of manorial lands. It is easy for any agitators to play on this string, and it is a dangerous game, for a grateful soil is always ready. In the Tsar's name one may move the narod to the greatest sacrifices, but also to the most frightful crimes.[97]

Represssive measures would only aggravate an already dire situation. The tsar could not afford to treat the narod, even if it had been misled,

---

[96] Ermolov's report of January 31, 1905, "Zapiski Ermolova," *KA* 8 (1925): 58–60, 63.
[97] Ibid., pp. 62–63.

as an enemy to be persecuted and repressed, Ermolov asserted; "to the contrary, on it, on the Russian narod in its totality, without distinction of social status, convictions, faiths, and language, and on it alone must and can tsarist power lean." Many of the recent zemstvo and nobility addresses, though formally illegal, deserved close attention as loyal expressions of popular concerns and needs that indicated a readiness to rally around the throne as soon as the proper legal framework would give people a voice of their own. Only by meeting general popular interests, and not by force or the satisfaction of narrow estate interests, could the government expect to draw the disenchanted nobles to its side, for the very best of them had risen above such narrow concerns long ago. The zemstvos in their present composition were clearly unrepresentative, especially of the peasantry, which on issues other than the land question was even more conservative than the clergy and merchants. If workers were given the right to elect representatives, as in the case of the Shidlovskii Commission, so should the peasantry. The only way to pacify all but the isolated minority of extremists was "a tsarist summons to common peaceful work for the people's well-being, to serving truth and justice, to expressing before the throne the true, long-pressing needs and requirements of the narod."[98]

Although the tsar had rejected the idea in December, Ermolov stressed the need for a "landed council of freely elected representatives from all classes and walks of life." How else could the people address "the Russian Tsar, in which the narod sees the bearer of truth, justice, and peace in the land, the focus of the Russian state, the source of its might, the preserver of its unity." Nicholas had no choice but to lend his ear to his people's voice. "This must be done before it is too late," Ermolov warned, "before *Rus'* loses faith in its God-given Tsar, in his force and might. If this faith, if this spiritual salt of the Russian earth loses its strength, with what will be salted then?" Ermolov acknowledged the fears that had led many advisors to oppose the convening of a landed assembly—the possibility that the assembly might clamor for fundamental changes in the age-old state structure, a limitation of the tsar's power, a constitution, a black partition (i.e., a forcible redistribution of nonpeasant lands among the peasantry), or a dissolution of the empire—but inaction would be infinitely more dangerous. "When the time is ripe," Ermolov prophesied daringly, "the Russian Tsar will grant his narod a constitution." Since the feelings and voices of the narod required an immediate outlet, Nicholas himself should announce his irrevocable decision to hear out the Russian narod by summoning the freely elected representatives "from all estates of the Russian Land" to an "all-people's

[98] Ibid., pp. 61–62.

landed council." Senior servitors and outstanding "activists of the Russian land were to draw up such a project. Nicholas would also have to decide whether to make this assembly a permanent institution or to find another means of letting popular representatives participate in the preliminary drafting of legislation.[99]

Many of Ermolov's terms harked back to *Rus'*, the Russia of pre-Petrine times, in particular to the Time of Troubles (*smutnoe vremia*, or *smuta*) of the early seventeenth century when *zemlia*, the Land, was the only tangible evidence of Russia's very existence after the death of the Rurikid dynasty. Hence Ermolov's insistence on a *zemskii sobor* or *zemskaia duma* (Assembly or Council of the Land) through which "all estates of the Russian Land," including the peasants, could inform the tsar, the God-given incarnation of *pravda*, i.e., of truth and justice, of their true needs. While the tsar was the source of Russian state might and the preserver of its unity, he depended on the faith of Rus'. So steeped was Ermolov's report in this pre-Petrine rhetoric, that it alternately identified the narod with the peasantry and with society in general. Here Ermolov invoked the mythical union between the narod and its tsar, but not without pointing out the darker underside of this myth: a peasantry hostile to bureaucrats and landlords alike, whom they saw as depriving them of their rightful gifts from the tsar; this naive monarchist faith in the autocrat could be exploited to bring down the very system of autocracy. Ermolov's ideal of a united government, however, had little to do with the reality of the seventeenth-century administrative structure or prikaz system. On the contrary, it was Nicholas's blurring of institutional boundaries and his readiness to create new bodies on the spur of the moment that brought back memories of that system. More importantly still, Ermolov held out the possibility of a constitution. Evidently, he was able to reconcile such inconsistencies in his own mind. The result was a language and imagery so traditional that it allayed Nicholas's wariness and prodded him to take a more enlightened stand.

Ermolov was not alone in viewing the political landscape in terms of the seventeenth century and Russia's original Time of Troubles, nor was his appeal the only one to reach the tsar at this time. Indeed, much of the political discourse was conducted in similar terms, as both proponents and opponents of reform vied for Nicholas's attention. It is reported that in the immediate aftermath of Bloody Sunday, both of Nicholas's brothers-in-law, the Grand Dukes Peter and Alexandr, who were married to his sisters Olga and Xenia, respectively, appealed to him for a zemskii sobor or representation of some kind lest there be a revolution. "What am I to do if that is against my conscience?" the tsar is said to have

---

[99] Ibid., pp. 65–66.

objected. There were moments, he has told, when one should not be guided by one's conscience alone.[100] Addresses by Shipov, Prince Dolgorukov,[101] and the Kharkov provincial zemstvo[102] called for the immediate convocation of popular representatives, similar to the assemblies that had rescued Russia from the smuta three hundred years before. On the other hand, State Council members General O. B. Rikhter and Prince A. Shirinskii-Shikhmatov raised the specter of a zemskii sobor turning into a constitutional assembly and instead favored the inclusion of zemstvo and town duma representatives in the State Council.[103]

In making their language his own, Ermolov aimed at overcoming such objections to a popular assembly. As a result, Ermolov's analysis reinforced and put into words the realization now dawning on both the tsar and those within his environment—that social unrest would continue, even spread, if the government did not undertake reforms beyond those promised in the December 12 ukase. Two weeks before, when Ermolov had first broached the subject, Nicholas had already indicated his willingness to consider further reforms, to be discussed soon by a conference of ministers under his own chairmanship. Since then the daily police reports sent to the tsar, while noting some weakening of the strike movement, had observed continued work stoppages and new flare-ups in the capital, Caucasus, Siberia, and the western borderlands.[104] Evidently, the emperor was prepared to make additional concessions.

THE BULYGIN RESCRIPT

On February 3, 1905, a mere three days after Ermolov's latest plea, the emperor presided over a rare meeting of the Council of Ministers at Tsarskoe Selo. For almost four hours the Council of Ministers discussed, in Nicholas's words, "the timeliness of issuing a manifesto on the war and smuta and the convening of locally elected representatives."[105] Written

[100] KFZ, January 13, 1905; TsGAOR, f. 601, op. 1, d. 248, January 14, 1905; Sv.-Mirskaia, "Dnevnik," pp. 278–79, January 17, 1905.

[101] Contained in the dispatches of the Russian Telegraphic Agency, January 22, 1905, TsGIA, f. 1276, op. 1, d. 49, ll. 5–6.

[102] [January 1905], TsGAOR, f. 601, op. 1, d. 873, ll. 1–2.

[103] O. B. Rikhter's memorandum, TsGAOR, f. 543, op. 1, d. 514(1), ll. 18–19, is dated January 1905 and unsigned, but the handwriting strongly suggests the author's identity. Shirinskii-Shikhmatov's memorandum is dated January 17, 1905, and entitled "Ob"edinenie vlasti s narodom," TsGAOR, f. 543, op. 1, ed. 14, ll. 1–6.

[104] Vsepoddanneishie doklady MVD, January 20 and February 1, 1905, TsGIA, f. 1328, op. 2, d. 2, ll. 51–90.

[105] TsGAOR, f. 601, op. 1, d. 248, February 3, 1905; TsGIA, f. 516 KFZ, op. 219/2728, d. 20, l. 109.

proceedings of the meeting do not exist. According to Witte,[106] who claims to have remained silent himself, the notion of summoning elected representatives to participate in legislative affairs received particularly strong support from Ermolov, Manukhin, the new minister of justice, and Bulygin, the new minister of internal affairs. Kokovtsev, too, considered this necessary in order to improve the climate for his international loan negotiations. No final conclusions were reached. Instead of the manifesto first contemplated, Nicholas ordered Nol'de to draft a rescript[107] instructing Bulygin to compile a project for convening popularly elected representatives and to thank the noble assemblies, though not the zemstvos, for their loyal addresses on the occasion of the heir-apparent Alexis's birth. The rescript was also to announce that Nicholas intended to take up the nobility on its offer to assist the throne with their expertise and knowledge of local conditions. In addition, Nicholas ordered that Witte's special ministerial conference discuss ways of implementing these intentions and submit its conclusions to the Council of Ministers chaired by the emperor.[108]

There is no indication that the assassination on February 4 of the tsar's uncle, the Grand Duke Sergei, directly affected these deliberations. Nicholas's own reaction was surprisingly matter-of-fact: "A terrible evil deed was committed today in Moscow. Uncle Sergei was killed by a bomb when he passed the Nikolskii Gate in a closed carriage. The driver was fatally injured. Poor Ella, may God bless and help her!" Except for the daily requiems and the large memorial service on the day of Sergei's burial, we find no further mention in the tsar's diary of Sergei and his violent end.[109] Although the decisions to consider further reforms and to issue an imperial rescript predated Sergei's death, his demise and a concern for the emperor's safety, instead of cutting short such reforms, may actually have dramatized the need for them.

The original version of the rescript, which Nol'de sent to the tsar on February 6, called for popular representation along estate lines: "I consider it beneficial to summon people elected by the estates so that they may participate in drafting legislative proposals prior to their consideration by the State Council."[110] Four days later Nol'de forwarded to Nich-

---

[106] Witte, *Vospominaniia*, 2:375–76.

[107] Confirmed by the Tsar: "Decided to substitute rescript to MIA," TsGAOR, f. 601, op. 1, d. 248, February 3, 1905.

[108] TsGIA, f. 1276, op. 1, d. 195, l. 5.

[109] TsGAOR, f. 601, op. 1, d. 248, February 4, 5, 6, 7, 8, 9, 10, and 12, 1905. Nicholas does not say so, but security considerations prevented him from personally attending his uncle's funeral.

[110] Actually there were two drafts, virtually identical except for three additional sentences in one of them that referred obliquely to the smuta of the seventeenth century and to the

olas a revised version that presumably incorporated the editorial suggestions and criticisms submitted by various Council members in the interim. This revision deviated from the original when it came to the convocation of elected representatives: "I . . . consider it good, in order that they express before the Throne the voice of the narod about its true needs, to summon people elected by the population [*prizvat' vybornykh naseleniem*] to participate permanently in the preliminary drafting of legislative measures of state importance corresponding to those needs."[111] *Estate* elections had given way to *more universal popular* elections in this version, though it said nothing about their exact form. Moreover, popular representation was to be a *permanent* feature of state life, granting the people a voice in all important state matters and helping to satisfy their true needs.

Contrary to Nicholas's expectation, the second session of the Council of Ministers on February 11 did not produce a final decision on the rescript. There may well have been some dissenting voices who warned of undue haste and concessions in the face of continuing unrest. The new draft that grew out of this meeting announced the tsar's intention, for the sake of improving his contact with the narod and making its needs better known, "to convene people elected from the population [*sozyvat' vybornykh ot naseleniia*] of the Empire so that they may participate in the preliminary drafting and discussion of legislative proposals." The new wording, suggesting repeated acts of convening, and the absence of the word "permanently" left some doubts as to the permanence of the projected forum, while the election of people "from the population" as opposed to "by the population" betrayed misgivings about outright popular elections.

Obviously, this new version represented a compromise between its two predecessors. More cautious minds evidently had prevailed. For the first time the rescript draft warned of various obstacles that might delay the implementation of the new reform: "But because of the special conditions of our fatherland, its broad expanse, the multitribal composition of the population, and the weak development of a civic sense in some of its parts, the realization of My will presents many difficult problems which require time for their well-deliberated resolution."[112] Not only did such a warning seek to discourage excessive expectations, it also cloaked the eventual outcome of the reform in a veil of uncertainty. Clearly, the Council members were not prepared to commit themselves to a particu-

---

unity of tsar and people which had always been Russia's salvation; TsGIA, f. 1276, op. 1, d. 195, ll. 9 (longer version) and 10.

[111] Again there were two drafts, but only one is extant, which was either Ermolov's copy or in fact drafted by him; TsGIA, f. 1276, op. 1, d. 195, l. 16.

[112] TsGIA, f. 1276, op. 1, d. 195, l. 19.

lar franchise, whether the estate-based one of the first version or the more universal one of the second. Two dissenters even went so far as to present an alternative proposal that was still more traditionally worded and far less specific and accommodating.[113]

Two days before the Council was to resolve the final wording of the rescript, however, the whole project drew fire from a prominent nonparticipant, the governor-general of St. Petersburg. The rapid pace of events, Trepov wrote to Nicholas on February 16, made it difficult to comprehend their full significance and to gather one's thoughts. Great care had to be exercised when issuing new acts of state importance. Unless new principles were certain to be helpful and could be implemented, they were best avoided, all the more so since public pronouncements from the throne could not be revoked and since delays in carrying them out would harm government authority. Pointing to the vacillations in domestic policy and the lack of unanimity among the tsar's closest advisors on how to pacify the country, Trepov commented: "Those people are recommending contradictory measures." He had in mind the rescript and a manifesto, apparently one being prepared without the Council's knowledge. New concessions on top of those announced on December 12 "will completely shatter power and satisfy nobody." On the other hand, a manifesto calling the people and authorities to order and to duty, while pleasing some, would invariably be exploited as reactionary by ill-meaning people in order to prove the insincerity of the December ukase. "I am deeply convinced," Trepov continued, "that neither today nor in the near future will it be possible to pacify minds through any promises; you cannot satisfy the so-called Third Element with any kind of concessions."

Only "a silent demonstration of firm power," both in St. Petersburg and in the provinces, would yield positive results. To this end, the tsar had to compel the ministers and his other servitors to carry out their duties under the threat of punishment. Nicholas's wrath, not the mob and street, should make those surrounding his throne tremble. Unwilling ministers had to be replaced by more reliable servants; "there are still enough of them." Order would be gradually restored if the tsar's demands and orders were simply passed on to all of his subordinates. Reform had to await the restoration of order and the end of the war, at which time special attention should be paid to the peasantry, the cornerstone of the entire state edifice. Any immediate concessions could only lead to new demands, while confusing those servants who had remained loyal. In the end, power would slip out of Nicholas' hands. Instead of issuing a new state act, the tsar had to force his servants to discharge their duties conscientiously before their sovereign and the country. The

[113] Ibid., l. 18: Nol'de's cover letter to Nicholas of February 15, 1905, and l. 20.

minister of education, for example, had yet to demonstrate authority ten days after the disturbances at the St. Petersburg university, Trepov charged. Witte, too, had aroused his ire; Trepov stated: "Your Majesty, bring yourself to broaden the competence and increase the membership of the Council of Ministers, this institution will ease Your royal labors and paralyze to a significant degree the activity of the Committee of Ministers and the perniciousness of its chairman, from whom you absolutely must part, and it will curb Your Ministers."[114]

Trepov's letter was an extraordinary attack on the entire government, its workings and institutional integrity, as well as on the loyalty and qualifications of its members, of whom two were singled out for special criticism. As governor-general with a personal mandate from the emperor, he obviously did not consider himself a part of this government and therefore felt free to criticize it. As a military man, moreover, he believed in a clear chain of command that would relay and execute orders and punish any failure to do so. Any retreat was treasonous, any appearance of weakness fatal. The tsar had simply to give his commands, and the country would obey. Without having been asked for his advice or apologizing for its bluntness, Trepov exceeded his responsibilities and in effect told Nicholas how to run the country and whom to purge from his government. He urged the removal of Witte or, at a minimum, the paralysis of Witte and the committee he chaired. Nicholas did not heed Trepov's warnings against any new government edicts, yet did not rebuke him for unwarranted interferences either. Not only did the personal, extrainstitutional nature of Trepov's position seem to justify, even invite, his anti-institutional, antibureaucratic views, but his hostility was shared to a significant degree by Nicholas himself.

On the morning of February 18 Witte and his colleagues were en route to Tsarskoe Selo to discuss the final wording of the rescript, when much to their consternation they learned of the publication of an imperial manifesto that reasserted the fundamental principles of autocracy and denounced internal sedition.[115] At a time when many of Russia's best sons were laying down their lives in a war for supremacy in the Pacific, for Russia's future, and for Christianity in general, the manifesto declared that

the malevolent leaders of the insurrectionary movement, blinded by arrogance, are insolently attacking the foundations of the Russian State, sanctified by the Orthodox church and ratified by laws. By severing the natural bond with

---

TsGAOR, f. 543, op. 1, d. 536, ll. 148–50; typed copy: ll. 151–53.

115 At least, this is the claim of Witte, *Vospominaniia*, 2:376; Glazov's diary, TsGIA, f. 922, op. 1, d. 10, l. 49, February 18, 1905, and Liubimov, "Russkaia smuta," p. 229.

the past, they seek to destroy the existing state system and to establish in its place a new government along principles not characteristic of Our Fatherland.

In the face of the recent assassination of the Grand Duke Sergei, the manifesto continued, Nicholas found strength and consolation in the full assurance of God's grace and the age-old loyalty of his narod. While Russia had always emerged from repeated wars and troubles with its strength renewed, the latest disorders and discords now compelled the tsar "to remind the Government Institutions and Authorities of all agencies and on all levels of their service duty and the commands of their oath, and to call for a deepening of vigilance in the preservation of law, order, and safety, in the strict consciousness of their moral and service responsibility before Throne and Fatherland." Nicholas summoned

the well-meaning people of all estates and walks of life, each in his task and at his place, to unite in concertedly assisting Us by word and deed in the sacred and great sacrifice of overcoming the stubborn foreign enemy, in rooting out sedition in our land, and in the judicious opposition to internal discord, mindful that only if the spirit of the whole population is calm and cheerful will it be possible to accomplish the successful realization of Our intentions which are directed toward a renewal of the narod's spiritual life, the strenghtening of its well-being, and the perfection of the state order.

After calling on all Russian people true to the precepts of the past to rally around the throne, the tsar closed by asking God to grant "to the Priests the holy essence, to the Rulers judgment and truth, to the narod peace and quiet, to the laws force, and to faith good health, so that the true Autocracy may be still further strengthened for the good of all Our loyal subjects."[116]

The manifesto was an appeal for popular unity in the face of external and internal threats to Russia's unique mission and character. Though Trepov evidently had gotten wind of its impending release, the preparations for the manifesto took place with such secrecy that its authorship and evolution remain obscure. Notwithstanding rumors to the contrary, the evidence rules out Pobedonostsev as author, but any definitive judgment is impossible.[117] The very idea of some form of public address or manifesto, as we have seen, had first been broached after Bloody Sunday and, though twice rejected since then, may well have received further impetus from the continuing unrest and the murder of Nicholas's uncle.

Despite its denunciation of the "insurrectionary movement" and the

---

[116] *Gosudarstvennye akty*, pp. 213–15.

[117] For a detailed discussion of the evidence, see Verner, "Nicholas II and the Role of the Autocrat during the First Russian Revolution, 1905–7" (Ph.D. diss., Columbia University, 1986), p. 297 n.72.

correspondingly hostile reception in the press and society at large, the manifesto did not mean to signal a return to the inflexible and repressive policies of the past. The exhortation of all government agencies and officials to uphold law and order was directed as much against administrative arbitrariness and illegality as against the legal infractions of rebellious subjects. The manifesto also acknowledged the need for further reforms, though not before the external and internal enemy had been defeated. In signing this manifesto, to say nothing of the ukase and rescript that followed in short order, Nicholas chose not to heed Trepov's recommendations for a military crackdown. Instead, he deliberately eschewed repression in favor of a more moderate course.

Moreover, in an unprecedented and far-reaching gesture, Nicholas issued a ukase to the Senate at the same time as the manifesto and announced that henceforth the Council of Ministers under the tsar's chairmanship, in order to make it easier for all subjects to be heard by him, was to consider "the views and proposals from private persons and institutions on questions concerning the perfection of the state's commonweal and the improvement of the people's welfare."[118] The right of individuals and public institutions alike to make known their opinions on state affairs and political issues was recognized for the first time. To be sure, they were granted the right not as free Russian citizens, but as consultants and adjuncts to the administrative machinery. The existence of public opinion, however, was at least acknowledged and endowed with a modicum of legitimacy.

Yet this apparent concession to society could be easily reconciled with, and in fact derived from some of the postulates of autocratic ideology, for it breached the mythical bureaucratic barrier between tsar and narod, thus reaffirming their organic unity. The narod was to inform the tsar of its needs. Nicholas, unlike some of his senior bureaucrats, tended to view the import of the ukase exclusively in these traditional terms, for he personally lacked any conception of society different from the narod, let alone the notion of public opinion. No one would be more shocked than the tsar by the outpouring of political opinion and by the politicization of society as a result of the ukase. When several of the surprised ministers asked Nicholas at the outset of their February 18 meeting about the meaning and implications of the two measures, he flatly denied any contradiction between them and the reforms announced in the December 12 ukase, or, for that matter, the contemplated rescript to the minister of internal affairs.[119] From the tsar's point of view, the reaffirmation of autocracy and the call for unity and order did not preclude—indeed, the

---

[118] *Pravitel'stvennyi Vestnik*, February 18, 1905.
[119] Witte, *Vospominaniia*, 2:377.

two were consistent with—gradual reform and a consultation of the na-rod.

Apparently, Nicholas no longer saw the need for an elected consulta-tive assembly; the new ukase may have seemed a suitable substitute for the rescript which promised much the same. According to Education Minister Glazov, Nicholas "made a stern speech,"[120] and hearsay evi-dence described him as hesitating. The ministers, however, insisted that a rescript be issued. Kokovtsev was anxious to calm Russia's foreign cred-itors, while others, among them Ermolov and Bulygin, regarded a na-tional consultative assembly as the only hope of restoring order and of guaranteeing the safety of government officials threatened by assassina-tion. "One could think that you are afraid of a revolution," the tsar is reported to have said to Bulygin. "Sovereign" he supposedly replied, "the revolution has already begun."[121] After debating the wording of the rescript, the Council members approved it, and Nicholas signed it in the afternoon, moving Prince Khilkov, the minister of communications, to tears and Count Sol'skii to words of thanks.[122] The occasion was suffi-ciently momentous to be recorded in Nicholas's diary. The rescript, he wrote, concerned "the drafting of a means of convening local represen-tatives in order to participate in the consideration of legal projects, to be introduced into the State Council. May God grant that this important measure brings Russia benefit and success." The night before he had also invoked God's blessings on his manifesto.[123]

The final draft of the rescript, which Witte identifies as Bulygin's ver-sion, was considerably longer, more detailed, and more floridly worded than any of its predecessors. Still falling short of the scheme that had been deleted from the December 12 ukase in the last minute, the crucial clause about convening popular representatives combined elements from previous drafts and added new ones. Nicholas introduced the new mea-sure as the logical continuation of his forebears' efforts to gather and or-ganize the Russian land: "I conceived the idea of summoning from now on, with God's help, the most deserving people, vested with the confi-dence of the narod and elected from the population, to participate in the preliminary drafting and discussion of legislative proposals."[124] The pre-

[120] Glazov's diary, TsGIA, f. 922, op. 1, d. 10, l. 49, February 18, 1905.

[121] Chermenskii, *Burzhuaziia i tsarizm*, p. 58, bases this account on a letter by P. Gei-den, the liberal activist, and on Kireev's diary entry of February 24 (actually, February 28), GBL OR, f. 126. d. 14, l. 18. Kokovtsev's concern at this time about foreign financial circles is confirmed by his memoirs, *Iz moego proshlago* (Paris, 1933), 1:64, and *Out of My Past*, pp. 44–45, although much of this is inexact.

[122] Witte, *Vospominaniia*, 2:378.

[123] TsGAOR, f. 601, op. 1, d. 248, February 17–18, 1905.

[124] TsGIA, f. 1276, op. 1, d. 195, l. 21, or *Gosudarstvennye akty*, pp. 215–16.

cise wording suggested repeated summonses, i.e., ad hoc consultation, rather than a permanent institution. Moreover, the representatives were to enjoy the people's trust, yet they would be "the most deserving," a phrase that was reminiscent of "the best" and implied the authorities' confidence and approbation. Conceivably, the government would retain the final say in the selection of representatives, although the precise method of selection remained to be determined. Bulygin was to chair a Special Conference to find ways of realizing the tsar's will.

In view of Russia's special geographic, ethnic, and cultural conditions, Nicholas warned, any reform demanded "consistency" and "circumspection" in order to maintain "the strong historical tie with the past" and to assure its future success:

> And now, undertaking this reform with the assurance that the knowledge of local requirements, the life experience, and the intelligent open word of the best elected people will ensure the fruitfulness of the legislative labors for the true benefit of the narod, I, at the same time, foresee the whole complexity and difficulty of implementing this reform while absolutely preserving the inviolability of the Empire's fundamental laws.[125]

As with the manifesto and ukase that had preceded the rescript by a few hours, Nicholas sought to reaffirm the immutability of the basic autocratic order, without ruling out political reforms. With this last explicit reminder, which had been absent from all previous drafts, the tsar asserted the organic unity and logical continuity of all three measures. He also cautioned against possible obstacles, delays, and misapprehensions ahead. Whatever shape the new popular representation might take, Nicholas was determined to nip in the bud any speculation that it might become a constitutional assembly or legislature along Western lines.

While Nicholas himself was able to rationalize manifesto, ukase, and rescript as complementary expressions of autocratic principles and values, others in his entourage were not. The consensus that Nicholas had "discovered" was in fact a mirage, a fiction of his own mind. Those of his advisors who favored the reform promised in the rescript were shocked by the manifesto, which to them appeared to run counter to the spirit, if not the letter, of the rescript. By the same token, the unidentified proponents of the manifesto obviously wanted to delay concessions such as those contained in the rescript. The ukase, in turn, allowed for differing, diametrically opposed interpretations embracing personal as well as impersonal conceptions of autocratic government. Nicholas, instead of selecting one of those proposed solutions or actively fashioning a new consensual one, had chosen once again the path of least resistance. He

[125] Ibid.

had passively agreed to all of them without noticing the inherent contradictions that troubled his ministers and had prompted them to speak out in the first place about the lack of government unity, consistency, and direction. Precariously and unconvincingly, the tsar continued to balance the two hats of Tsar' Batiushka (Little Father Tsar) and Gosudar' Imperator (Sovereign Emperor) on his head, until events and an overwhelming consensus would leave him no choice. As long as he was able to reconcile in his own mind the disparate recommendations of his advisors, he could avoid the personally discomfiting choice between them. The February 18 acts contained something for everyone—from Pobedonostsev to Ermolov—though they failed to satisfy anyone completely. Ironically, the public, too, treated the government acts of February 18 as a coherent whole, interpreting the rescript in the light of the manifesto, to be welcomed or, more probably, to be deplored as an affirmation of autocratic rule and principles.

CHAPTER VI

The Bulygin Duma

AT THE URGING of several key advisors, the tsar had ordered the drafting of various reforms; now it would be up to the bureaucracy to formulate the exact proposals. Of all the reforms contemplated so far, Nicholas's promise of February 18, 1905, to convene a popularly elected, consultative assembly was certainly the most important. Aside from a few general principles and vague conditions, however, the Bulygin rescript could be of little guidance to those charged with the task of working out the precise form of the new popular representation or the method by which it was to be selected. The rescript itself merely stipulated that the representatives exercise a consultative and preliminary role in the legislative process and that this reform not contradict Russia's historical traditions and political system; it did not specify how and by whom "the most deserving" would be chosen and whether the representatives would constitute a separate body, join the departments of the State Council, or even be assigned to various government agencies in an advisory capacity.

If there were any clues, they were to be found instead in the drafting process of the rescript and in the very evolution of the proposal for popular representation. This notion had gained sufficient currency and momentum to be included already in Sviatopolk-Mirskii's program and draft ukase of late 1904, only to be dropped at the very last minute, as we have seen. Mirskii's plan had called for a separate consultative assembly below the State Council, an idea that Minister of Agriculture Ermolov had revived and reintroduced into bureaucratic circulation with his two reports in January. Thus it was only natural, in the absence of any contrary instructions, for Bulygin and his intraministerial conference to take up where his predecessor and Ermolov had left off.[1] As for the method of selecting popular representatives, the Bulygin committee would take its cue from the prehistory of the February 18 rescript. This document in its final variant had deliberately eschewed the two extreme suggestions of

[1] Part of the bureaucratic tradition consulted at least nominally by the Bulygin commission were the old reform projects of Speranskii, Novosil'tsev, Valuev, the Grand Duke Konstantin Nikolaevich, and Loris-Melikov; these were collected under the heading "Predpolozheniia vysshago pravitel'stva o privlechenii izbrannykh ot naseleniia lits k zakonodatel'noi deiatel'nosti." They can be found in TsGAOR, f. 543, op. 1, d. 514(2), ll. 81–128, International Law Library, Harvard University (*ILLHU*) and, in excerpted form, in Marc Raeff, ed., *Plans for Political Reform* (Englewood Cliffs, N.J., 1966).

an estate-based and a universal franchise in favor of a yet-to-be-defined compromise, thereby serving notice on any would-be reformers.

As will become clear shortly, the actual discussion and drafting of the legislation for the new assembly and electoral system excluded nonbureaucratic viewpoints and seemed immune to all external impulses. Neither the secret influence of court connections nor the publicity of society's opinions appears to have impinged measurably on the pace and results of this work. The reasons for this autonomous reform process are to be found in the tsar's aversion to all manifestations of public opinion, his reluctance to intervene, his tendency to conform to bureaucratic rules that were at once external to and resented by him, as well as in the bureaucracy's superordinate pretensions and its respect for precedent and continuity.

"WITTE SHOULD BE RESISTED"

Before that process would run its course, however, some old scores had to be settled among the tsar's top servitors. Not only were there sure to be disagreements on principle within the bureaucracy, but the very autonomy of the bureaucratic reform process and the personal nature of tsarist politics demanded that it be determined once and for all who would be in charge.

Ever since he was kicked upstairs in 1903 from the Ministry of Finance to the chairmanship of the Committee of Ministers, Witte had been bent upon recovering his former political eminence. He had used the discussions surrounding the December 12 ukase to advance his own cause and by early 1905 had garnered the main responsibility for any current and future reforms, whether political, economic, or social. The Committee of Ministers which Witte chaired had been charged with drawing up guidelines for the implementation of the reforms promised in the December 12 ukase. His look-alike Special Conference, established after Ermolov's intervention, was to address itself to any other egregious government shortcomings, such as the lack of administrative unity and cooperation. Finally, Witte presided over the Special Conference on the Needs of Agricultural Industry, his brainchild, which had sought to enlist representatives of society in formulating proposals to solve the stubborn agrarian problem. With Pleve, his most implacable opponent, and Sviatopolk-Mirskii, his most zealous and sincere reforming rival, out of the way, Witte, it would appear, had rescaled the political pinnacle.

Appearances lied, however. The February 18, 1905, ukase was the first indication that government reform would not remain the exclusive province of Witte and that his star was on the wane. By directing the public's proposals to the hitherto defunct *Council* of Ministers the measure assigned to that body a permanent role in the reform process and thereby denigrated the importance of Witte's work in the *Committee* of Ministers, just as Trepov had advocated.[2] Much to Witte's vexation, not he but the venerable Count Sol'skii was put in control of the resurrected Council. So taken aback was Witte that he later equated the act with the abolition of the Committee of Ministers.[3] Within six weeks Witte received another blow. On March 30 the tsar suddenly closed down the Special Conference on the Needs of Agricultural Industry and put in its very place a Special Conference on Measures to Strengthen Peasant Landholding, to be chaired by the former minister of the interior and current State Council member, I. L. Goremykin. A fortnight later, on April 16, 1905, Nicholas added insult to injury by doing away with Witte's Special Conference on state reform. Although Witte remained at the head of the Committee of Ministers, his role in the reform process had ended—at least for the time being.[4]

Subversive assistance from rival bureaucrats played a considerable role in Witte's sudden fall from imperial grace. Continuing his vendetta against Witte, Governor-General Trepov had written to Nicholas on February 19, 1905, to present him with a draft proposal for amending the charter of the Council of Ministers so it could carry out its new obligations as outlined in the ukase the day before. He had stressed the supremacy of the Council over the Committee of Ministers and had sought for it the greatest possible powers independent of Committee tutelage. His own project was briefer and less restrictive than the rules worked out by the Committee of Ministers, Trepov claimed. With feigned casualness he also reminded Nicholas that if he decided to do away with the Committee altogether, he would have to issue a separate order transferring its functions to the Council.[5] Far from being alone in seeking to have Witte stripped of his power, Trepov in turn was part of a conspiracy that included, by Witte's and others' accounts, Trepov's brother Vladimir, the senator; Goremykin, Witte's successor; and A. V. Krivoshein, the head of the Migration Administration in the Interior Ministry.[6] And in a tan-

[2] For this reason perhaps, Chermenskii, *Burzhuaziia i tsarizm*, p. 56, credits Trepov with the initiative for the ukase.

[3] The fact that he placed this episode exactly one month earlier confirms his evident bewilderment; Witte, *Vospominaniia*, 2:370–71.

[4] This did not prevent Witte, however, from making a futile stab at having a continued voice in the reforms; see draft of Witte's report, [April 1905], TsGIA, f. 1276, op. 1, d. 1, l. 308. The report went to Nicholas on April 20, 1905.

[5] TsGAOR, f. 543, op. 1,d. 514(1), ll. 103–4, and TsGIA, f. 1276, op. 1, d. 4, l. 3. Cf., too, Chermenskii, *Burzhuaziia i tsarizm*, pp. 56–58.

[6] Witte, *Vospominaniia*, 2:536–37; K. A. Krivoshein, *A. V. Krivoshein (1857–1921 g.)* (Paris, 1973), pp. 25, 27, 51–52; D. A. J. Macey, "The Russian Bureaucracy and the 'Peas-

talizing glimpse behind the court scenes, Minister of Education Glazov quotes a close confidant of the dowager empress as saying to him on March 26 that "V[itte] should be resisted and [that] the Sovereign is so inclined."[7]

No matter how self-serving these arguments may have been, it is clear that Nicholas shared the urge of Witte's opponents to clip Witte's wings. The tsar's reservations about Witte's trustworthiness, never far from the surface, had come to the fore again, precipitated perhaps by Witte's oracular pronouncements and calculatedly ambiguous conduct during the discussions preceding the December 12 ukase and during the events surrounding Bloody Sunday. The fact that the discredited Sviatopolk-Mirskii had recommended Witte as his successor and that Witte had asked not to be considered for the post unless given full powers could not have endeared the chairman of the Committee of Ministers to Nicholas. Indeed, in looking at the array of responsibilities Witte had accumulated, the tsar must have become convinced that the man had already taken complete control of the reform process, if not of the entire government.[8] This enormous concentration of responsibility and reforming zeal, when combined with Witte's well-known ambition, scornful bluntness, and cynical political maneuvering, was bound to provoke jealousy, suspicion—and retaliation.

In addition to the careerist opportunism and envious insinuations of his rivals, Witte himself later blamed the demise of his peasant conference on fears that the reforms contemplated might threaten the existing order.[9] Witte's contention has been variously interpreted as pinning the primary responsibility for the sudden closing of his conference on profound conceptual differences concerning the future of peasant landholding and the peasant estate; yet the evidence adduced is far from convincing.[10] Nor does this argument account for the shutdown of Witte's conference on government reform two weeks later or the eclipse of Witte and his Committee of Ministers by the long-dormant Council of Ministers under Sol'skii, which had signalled the beginning of Witte's decline some six weeks before. Instead, the real reason has to be sought in Witte's understanding of bureaucratic government. For Witte it existed,

---

ant Problem.' The Pre-History of the Stolypin Reforms, 1861–1907." (Ph.D. diss., Columbia University, 1976), p. 364n.2.

[7] Glazov's diary, TsGIA, f. 922, op. 1, d. 10, March 26, 1905.

[8] Indeed, Witte later boasted of having made every effort imaginable to see through, as speedily and completely as possible, the reforms envisioned in the December 12 ukase, not to mention, of course, the projects of his two conferences; Witte, *Vospominaniia*, 2:354–55.

[9] Witte, *Vospominaniia*, 2:536–38. It is this last factor which is singled out by Macey, "Russian Bureaucracy," pp. 364–65, 423–24.

[10] For a detailed discussion of the evidence, see Verner, "Nicholas II and the Role of the Autocrat," pp. 305–8.

independent of the person of the autocrat and, in effect, excluded him. Nicholas, while he stopped short of firmly embracing the personalized alternative, had never been comfortable with the impersonal and bureaucratic dimensions of autocracy, and Witte's notions were even less palatable. By exceeding both in form and substance the traditional confines of the bureaucratic servitor's role, Witte only managed to heighten the tsar's discomfort and thus provoke his own eventual demotion.

Most objectionable of all, from Nicholas's point of view, was Witte's growing realization that the government had no choice but to enlist support for its policies within society. There was not another tsarist bureaucrat who was more attuned to public opinion and cognizant of its importance than Witte. During the Russo-Japanese peace negotiations in Portsmouth, N.H., later that year he proved himself a master at wooing and manipulating the American press and public, and when he assumed the premiership in October he sought to do the same with the Russian press and public, though with far less success. In its efforts to engineer social assent, Witte believed, the government in effect had to assume a mediating role between ruler and ruled. As he told Pobedonostsev, whose cynical contempt for so-called public opinion was boundless and well-known, the government, while satisfying "the justified demands and desires" of society, had to take charge of its "flow of thoughts. . . . Unfortunately, the government still does not understand this or appears impotent."[11] Unfortunately for Witte, public opinion still lacked autonomy and standing in autocratic ideology. No one was more suspicious of public manifestations and their alleged sympathizers than Nicholas II.

It is this very suspicion that helps account for the sudden closing of the Conference on the Needs of Agricultural Industry and the decline in its chairman's political fortunes. Through his reports and recommendations for reform Witte appeared to be secretly identifying with public elements and their aspirations. Thus he may well have been playing with fire when he warned Nicholas on March 14, 1905, of "a special kind of movement among [the peasants], which, if it organizes itself and attracts the masses, may present a huge danger."[12] Whether or not Witte sought to improve the chances of his own program by impressing on the tsar the ominous escalation of peasant demands in the absence of such reforms, this warning would only have reinforced Nicholas's antipathies to societal aspirations and, by implication, to the makeup and course of Witte's agrarian conference.

Both the local committees and the general assembly of the Conference

[11] Witte's letter to Pobedonostsev, March 25, 1905, "Perepiska Vitte i Pobedonostseva (1895–1905)," *KA* 30 (1928): 111–12.

[12] Witte's report of March 14, 1905, TsGAOR, f. 102, op. 166, d. 19, ll. 49–51. Nicholas asked Bulygin to report about this matter.

on the Needs of Agricultural Industry included representatives of society, especially from the zemstvo and academic worlds—the very spheres whose recent pronouncements and actions had raised the tsar's hackles. Neither the zemstvo congress of November 1904 nor the banquet campaign nor the individual zemstvo addresses of the fall and winter had done much to endear such specimens of public opinion to Nicholas. Still more unsettling, from the tsar's point of view and that of many of his bureaucratic servitors, was the torrent of public and private petitions, proposals, and recommendations on the subject of state reform unleashed by the invitational ukase of February 18. Although most of the schemes and demands for political reform solicited by the ukase did not reach the tsar's desk, several of his senior advisors occasionally apprised him of their existence and content. As early as March 11 Bulygin warned Nicholas that society was widely abusing its new right to petition on political matters.

At the tsar's behest, the Council of Ministers looked into the problem ten days later and reported back its conclusions on the last day of March. The Council painted a disturbing picture. Private individuals were clearly overstepping the bounds of their new privilege by forming circles for the public discussion of state reform. Private societies, too, were exceeding the explicit purview of their charters, while town dumas and zemstvo assemblies were ignoring the law that confined their deliberations and petitions to local affairs and needs. They even had gone so far as to plan another national zemstvo congress. With the local authorities evidently interpreting the February 18 statute in differing ways, the enemies of the existing order were exploiting this ambiguity to promote their own ideas and to conduct agitation against the government.

Finance Minister Kokovtsev wanted to issue a second ukase that would expressly restrict the discussions of private groups and societies to their legally permitted, i.e., nonpolitical, activities, but his colleagues disagreed. The February 18 measure, the ministers explained, had granted all subjects and all legal organizations the unconditional right to present to Nicholas directly any kind of suggestion concerning the general national welfare and state needs. This unprecedented privilege had been received with joy and gratitude; to limit it now would make a terrible impression. On the other hand, the ukase had said nothing about public discussions and congresses, criminal speeches, or meetings that endangered the public order. Whenever the ukase became a mere pretext for criminal attacks on the government in word and print, local authorities were not only entitled but indeed obligated to take all legal measures to prevent and prosecute acts against the state and public order. This agitation had begun even before February 18. The ministers of internal affairs and justice were to issue circulars spelling out such measures. They also should determine whether existing legislation needed to be amended. Nicholas agreed, demanding "the *most energetic and unanimous action* by local administrative and judicial officials."[13]

Following up his warning about society's politicization with a second report to Nicholas, Bulygin in the meantime had sought the emperor's consent for a "compilation of initial proposals" without considering public opinion—ostensibly to speed up and safeguard the course of reform. The materials that the public had submitted to his Special Conference, Bulygin claimed, were often sketchy and, coming from diverse sources, differed widely in their conclusions. If his conference were to take up these diverse proposals, moreover, it would have to include, in addition to senior bureaucrats and representatives of various government agencies, local people familiar with local conditions. Though Bulygin did not say so directly, many of the petitions in fact were demanding that public spokesmen be consulted in the preparation of the reforms. Not only had Nicholas already indicated his skepticism toward these demands,[14] but a conference with such a varied membership, Bulygin explained, would have "significant and perhaps fundamental differences of views." To avoid the complications and delays that would inevitably result, it was best if Bulygin's conference drafted its own recommendations for submission to the Council of Ministers and to another Special Conference, to be chaired by Nicholas. Thus the reform preparations could be concluded within two to three months, and they would be based on "definite proposals which have been reconciled in advance with the general state interests in all their diversity, according to the localities and conditions of various regions of the Empire."[15]

While time might indeed have entered into Bulygin's considerations, his real concern was the protection of state interests as defined by the central bureaucracy. Though aware of the "fundamental differences" between the views of bureaucracy and those of society, Bulygin and the tsar, through his approval of his minister's report, were still not inclined to hear out the public spokesmen. Their recommendations and proposals, Bulygin appeared to suggest, reflected only unrepresentative, parochial, selfish interests, and not the general interests of the state and the country at large, which remained the exclusive province of the tsarist

[13] "Memoriia Soveta Ministrov," 31 March 1905, approved by Nicholas April 1, TsGIA, f. 1276, op. 1, d. 5, ll. 34–36.

[14] TsGAOR, f. 601, op. 1, ed. 882, ll. 1–6, March 3, 1905.

[15] Bulygin's report of March 12, 1905, approved by Nicholas on March 16, TsGAOR, f. 601, op. 1, ed. 881, ll. 1–3, and in "Materialy, zapiski i memorii Soveta Ministrov po delu o primenenii ukaza 18 Fevralia 1905 goda. Uchrezhdenie Gosudarstvennoi dumy i Polozhenie o vyborakh," *ILLHU*. An announcement to this effect was made in *Pravitel'stvennyi Vestnik* on March 18, 1905.

bureaucracy and the emperor himself. According to Bulygin, only the bureaucracy, while intimately familiar with and mindful of local conditions and needs, had the absolute, superordinate vantage point and broad vision to reconcile these with the national needs.

There was as yet no recognition that compromise is the stuff of politics, that from the clash of differing, yet equally justifiable opinions a higher truth emerges. For Bulygin and the tsar, such disagreement was impermissible, for it threatened loss of control and made the bureaucratic standpoint a relative instead of an absolute one. Lest the disagreeable sentiments and plans of society adulterate the government's own pure intentions, Bulygin preferred to exclude them altogether from the reform process. Notwithstanding the February 18 ukase, which seemed to recognize its existence at least, in the eyes of Nicholas and some of his associates public opinion continued to lack any real legitimacy.

Thus, to return one last time to the sudden dissolution of Witte's Special Conference on the Needs of Agricultural Industry with its contingent of public representatives, it is precisely this attitude of statist exclusivity and superiority and the openly expressed anxiety about society's interference that may have prejudiced Nicholas's decision. The closing of Witte's Special Conference followed by only two weeks the exclusion of society's proposals and spokesmen from Bulygin's bureaucratic body of reformers, and it happened at the very moment when the Council of Ministers was considering measures to curb the public's dangerous enthusiasm. By no mere coincidence, the immediate successor to Witte's Conference, Goremykin's Special Conference on Measures to Strengthen Peasant Landholding, was a strictly bureaucratic affair that shunned non-bureaucratic spokesmen.

NICHOLAS AND SOCIETY

Society was all too painfully aware of having been excluded. The government's refusal to consider society's proposals in working out the reforms, as the zemstvo leader Shipov later recalled, merely fuelled public distrust in the work of the Bulygin commission and confirmed the public's sense of confronting a hostile and insensitive bureaucracy. Public appeals to Nicholas were of no avail.[16] Consequently, the same groups, taking advantage of the legal twilight created by the February 18 ukase, would feel compelled to restate their views even more emphatically.[17] Such a

[16] E.g., V. I. Kovalevskii's memorandum of April 7, 1905, *KA* 11–12 (1925): 109–14; the address of twenty-six marshals of the nobility who met in St. Petersburg from June 12–16, 1905, TsGAOR, f. 543, op. 1, d. 516, ll. 6–11; and by Kireev, GBL OR, f. 126, d. 14, l. 24, March 21, 1905.

[17] Shipov, *Vospominaniia*, p. 297.

radicalization of methods—and goals, one might add—in turn both exacerbated and justified the government's initial disregard, thus creating a vicious circle and rapidly reducing the likelihood of an eventual peaceful accommodation.

The news from the front only fanned the flames of public discontent. After sustaining ninety thousand casualties at the Battle of Mukden in late February, Russian land forces were forced into a slow but ignominious retreat. Still more devastating was the engagement in the Straits of Tsushima on May 14, 1905, which wiped out the better part of what remained of Russia's once-proud fleet. Indeed, the military situation had become so hopeless that by May 24 the emperor had decided to initiate secret peace negotiations, while adhering publicly to the continuation of Russia's troop buildup in Manchuria.

Faced with the country's steadily deteriorating military fortunes and with the government's failure to live up to the spirit of the February 18 ukase, the Union of Liberation convened its Third Congress in March. It called for a constituent assembly based on universal suffrage which was to implement a broad program of far-reaching political and social reforms. In April the Second Zemstvo Congress, although not as radical as the Liberationists, went beyond the eleven-point program adopted by its predecessor in November 1904. The public debates triggered by the February ukase also gave new impetus to the movement of professional unions. By May, nine of these unions, representing lawyers, professors, pharmacists, veterinarians, doctors, teachers, journalists, engineers, and agronomists—joined two workers' unions—the clerks and bookkeepers, and the railroad workers—the Zemstvo-Constitutionalists, and two unions devoted to the emancipation of Jews and women in forming an umbrella organization. This group was known as the Union of Unions and was chaired by Pavel Miliukov. The cherished goal of a common front devoted to the overthrow of autocracy appeared to be nearing fruition. The strikes which had abated somewhat in February flared anew in various parts of the Empire; the number of strikers reached 80,000 in April and 220,000 in May. Even more ominously, unrest was spreading in the hitherto peaceful countryside. Rural disturbances erupted in several provinces of the Central Agricultural Region—Ekaterinoslav, Saratov, Kursk, Orlov, and Chernigov—as well as in the border regions of Georgia and Latvia. Almost every day Nicholas received new and disturbing evidence of these events from Bulygin.[18] At the same time, the tsar's chan-

---

[18] Between February 18 and March 31, 1905, alone, there were at least forty such summaries of police reports; TsGIA, f. 1328, op. 2, d. 2, ll. 119–89 ob; TsGAOR, f. 102, op. 166, d. 20, l. 167, and d. 19, l. 30.

cellery was being inundated by hundreds of peasant petitions every week clamoring for more land and other concessions.[19]

Instead of persuading the tsar and his officials to heed the public's wishes, however, the mounting protests and petitions merely reinforced superordinate bureaucratic pretensions and Nicholas's own determination to insulate the reform process from what he regarded as the vagaries and nonrepresentative radical tendencies of society's views. When informed, for example, of the latest session of the Moscow Pedagogical Society and the "childish nature" of their proceedings, he angrily demanded: "*It is high time* to put an end to such nuisances."[20] Similarly, the announcement of another zemstvo congress scheduled for May 24, 1905, provoked the following reaction from Nicholas: "I hope that this congress will not be permitted. They have talked enough nonsense already."[21] Lacking the very conception of society—as opposed to the more amorphous notion of narod—the tsar could not possibly appreciate the nature and legitimacy of its interests. As for the narod, he blamed their petitions on "some kind of pen-pusher"[22]—scribes, renegade priests, and literate outsiders—and hence could reject them out of hand with the myth of Tsar and People preserved intact. Nicholas's understanding of the crisis troubling the Russian body politic was limited to impotent exclamations of "nonsense" or "nuisance" (*bezobrazie*—literally: "without form"), i.e., diagnostic findings of senselessness and formlessness, of chaos, that reflected Nicholas's inability to accommodate in his own universe what he observed around him. Order and chaos were simply irreconcilable.

While Nicholas's refusal to entertain the advice and demands of moderate and liberal elements within society may come as no great surprise, his unwillingness to listen to more conservative circles and devoted autocratic loyalists is perhaps less understandable. To be sure, the tsar often expressed his gratitude for any public affirmations of loyalty, but he gave no indication that their ideas would be heeded in formulating the reform proposals. Nor did he make any effort to avail himself of the active support offered by adherents of autocracy. These loyalists had always taken their cues, as well as derived their identity and legitimacy, from the autocracy and therefore were slow to descend into the partisan political arena hitherto monopolized so successfully by the enemies of the existing

[19] Chermenskii, *Burzhuaziia i tsarizm*, p. 57, claims to have counted some sixty thousand petitions in the spring of 1905 alone.

[20] Telegraphic news summary, March 28, 1905, TsGAOR, f. 543, op. 1, d. 562, l. 9.

[21] Dated 21 [May] 1905, TsGAOR, f. 543, op. 1, d. 562, ll. 10–11.

[22] For example, a petition by a village in Riazan province, dated June 29, 1905; TsGIA, f. 1284, op. 241, d. 224, ll. 71–73 (handwritten original with many signatures), l. 70 (typed copy with the tsar's resolution).

state order. When conservative political organizations finally did form, prepared to do battle with the opponents of autocracy, they encountered a noticeable lack of enthusiasm on the part of the very institution and its incumbent that they had rallied to defend. Imagining themselves as the new shock troops of autocracy, they found the autocrat reticent to lead them into battle.

Nowhere is the resulting frustration and disappointment revealed more pointedly than in the diary of General A. A. Kireev. In early April Kireev noted that the government was doing nothing to encourage the newly rising conservative organizations[23]; three weeks later he sought to impress on Nicholas by letter the need to rely on the conservative party.[24] Responding to the political mobilization of society around them, Kireev and three of his associates informed the tsar on June 5, 1905, that they had decided to organize the St. Petersburg Patriotic Union, which would endeavor to preserve and strengthen the principles of the Russian state. Believing in the autocratic power and the union between the tsar and his people, they were sworn to fight all tendencies hostile to those principles and to the state order.[25] In mid-June a delegation from the Patriotic Union sought out Nicholas. In addition, Kireev repeatedly wrote to and even visited Empress Alexandra Fedorovna in the hope that she might influence her husband in the desired direction.[26]

In the eyes of Nicholas, such manifestations of conservative sentiments were indeed commendable for their loyalty and their traditional values, but as contributions to a political dialogue, as independent political alternatives, they possessed no more legitimacy than their counterparts to the left. The very concept of such a dialogue was missing. The role of autocracy was to stand above and aloof from partisan interests and factional struggle; it alone was capable of determining the objective needs of the country and its mixed population and was under no obligation whatsoever to satisfy inherently selfish concerns and desires. Nor was there as yet any sense that the government rested on the approval of the people, that it required the active support of at least some social segments to ward off attacks and rival claims to power by others. Society was still perceived as passive, an amorphous collection of loyal—or disloyal—subjects, as opposed to a body of active citizens. Its name and rhetoric notwithstanding, the very idea of a conservative party departed from the traditional understanding of autocracy, which eschewed stepping into the fray and al-

[23] GBL OR, f. 126, d. 14, l. 32, April 9, 1905.

[24] Ibid., l. 38: May 1, 1905.

[25] TsGAOR, f. 543, op. 1, d. 514(2), ll. 55–56.

[26] Cf. GBL OR, f. 126, d. 14, l. 38, April 30; l. 40, May 16; ll. 44–45, May 28; l. 59, July 8; l. 61, July 13; ll. 62–63, July 18, 1905. See, too, Kireev's letter of June 4, 1905, f. 126, 21(2), d. 19, ll. 42–43.

lying itself with political parties, no matter how loyal or supportive. As a result, conservative overtures on behalf of an estate-based, consultative Assembly of the Land and for tokens of imperial approval were no more productive than the initiatives of their political opponents.

Moreover, even those proposals purporting to express loyalist sentiments usually contained implicit or explicit criticisms of current practices and the existing order. Whether they assailed the bureaucratic wall between the tsar and his narod or advocated the convocation of an Assembly of the Land along estate lines, by seeking to restore autocracy "as in olden times," these ideas challenged the status quo and its principal defender, Nicholas II. On the other hand, a statement by autocratic partisans affirming the inviolability of this order was often meant or certainly could be construed as a veiled attack on even the most modest concessions by the tsar and his servitors. For one reason or the other, and regardless of political affinity or content, such appeals were almost equally unacceptable.

Finally, in turning a deaf ear to the pleas of autocratic apologists, Nicholas betrayed his reluctance to embrace in a wholehearted and convincing way the role they expected of him: that of direct arbiter between corporate interests and personal guarantor of truth and justice. He might have felt sentimentally drawn to that role, yet was incapable of exercising it. At the same time, he was no more inclined to adhere firmly and consistently to alternative conceptions put forth by moderate and liberal elements of society—or, for that matter, by his reform-minded bureaucrats.

When the tsar did meet with representatives of the public, as happened several times in June, it was not to solicit their opinions, but to restore order by calming their fears and assuring them of his determination to see the promised reforms through to a successful conclusion. That such meetings did take place at all may seem surprising in view of Nicholas's aversion to any political declarations by the public, but then an imperial audience, unlike a public congress, demonstration, or newspaper editorial, was a very traditional forum that preserved the illusion of individual subjects personally presenting their wishes and grievances to their tsar.

The first of these encounters involved the delegation of the May 1905 zemstvo congress and took place almost against Nicholas's will.[27] When he finally received the fourteen-member delegation headed by Prince S. N. Trubetskoi at his summer residence in Peterhof on June 6, the tsar sought to dispel the growing public doubts about the implementation of

---

[27] "Zapiski F. A. Golovina," KA 19 (1926): 115. Golovin described the preliminaries as real bargaining "unworthy of the Sovereign."

the February 18 Bulygin Rescript. Responding in kind to Trubetskoi's pre-Petrine terminology and antibureaucratic sentiments, he tried to reassure the delegates that the reforms would proceed, yet he insisted that the new order would not constitute a break with Russia's unique historical past and traditions:

> Relinquish your doubts. My will, the tsar's will, to summon popular electors is unswerving. . . . I look after this matter every day. Of this you may inform everyone. . . . Let the union between the tsar and all of Russia be established, as it was in olden times, the contact between Me and the *zemskie liudi* [people of the land], that will underlie the order in comformance with original Russian principles. I hope you will assist Me in this work.[28]

Although Nicholas's choice of verbs indicated a repeated summons rather than a permanent institution of popular representatives, there was nothing evasive or duplicitous about this statement, despite assertions by an eyewitness to the contrary.[29] The tsar was indeed determined to live up to his word, but he was equally committed to the preservation of the autocratic order. He had not perceived any contradiction in this policy in February and still did not. If he was vague as to the all-important details of the reform, it was because he himself did not yet know.

This is exactly the position he took when he received two other delegations on June 20 and 21. The first was from the nobility of Kursk province, the second from the Moscow Union of Russian People and the St. Petersburg Patriotic Union. Serving, in Nicholas's own revealing description, as "a counterbalance to the zemstvo and town [activists],"[30] both groups came to plead for an estate-based consultative assembly that would truly be a voice of the Russian land, i.e., of the nobility and peasantry.[31] Although participants, public circles, and latter-day observers interpreted the tsar's words of appreciation as contradicting his earlier remarks,[32] the carefully worded replies he gave at both audiences were in keeping with his previous position and with the promise he had made to the zemstvo delegation. Without committing himself to the estate-based system advocated by the Kursk nobles, the tsar assured them: "I fully recognize the benefit that the presence of the two basic landed estates of

---

[28] *Pravitel'stvennyi Vestnik*, June 8, 1905; Liubimov, "Russkaia smuta," pp. 274–76; "Zapiski Golovina," pp. 115–16; Chermenskii, *Burzhuaziia i tsarizm*, pp. 70–71. Nicholas's remarks were much more conciliatory than a draft speech prepared by Trepov, the St. Petersburg governor-general and new assistant minister of internal affairs in charge of police and the corps of gendarmes; TsGIA, f. 1276, op. 1, d. 49, ll. 4, 8–11.

[29] "Zapiski Golovina," p. 115.

[30] TsGAOR, f. 601, op. 1, d. 248, June 21, 1905.

[31] TsGIA, f. 1276, op. 1, d. 38, ll. 587–92; TsGAOR, f. 543, op. 1, d. 516, ll. 1–3.

[32] Liubimov, "Russkaia smuta," pp. 278–80; Chermenskii, *Burzhuaziia i tsarizm*, p. 71.

the nobility and the peasantry, who from time immemorial have shared happiness and grief with their TSARS, can impart to the future legal-consultative institution."[33] This bland statement contained nary a clue as to how these two estates would be represented.

In advance, Nicholas rejected any criticism of the contemplated reforms; time and experience alone would tell:

> Only that state is powerful and sound that keeps sacred the precepts of the past. We ourselves have sinned against this and God may be punishing us for that. Concerning the fears expressed by you, I can say that life itself will show us the way to eliminate those imperfections and errors that may turn up in such a new and great matter as the one I conceived for the good of all MY subjects. I am convinced that you all and each in his sphere will help ME restore peace and quiet in our land and thereby will render ME the service that I expect from all MY loyal subjects. May God help you.[34]

While Nicholas conceded the possibility of "imperfections and errors" in his reform efforts, this did not give anybody the right to suggest changes beforehand. On the contrary, the tsar wanted everybody to obey and serve faithfully as charged till such time that further adjustments might be required. In the meantime, the reform process would go forward as he had promised.

AUTOCRACY IN TRANSITION

If Nicholas did not divulge the precise terms of the promised reforms, it was because at the time he was speaking they remained to be worked out. Once his bureaucrats had completed their preliminary proposals, the tsar, in turn, would react to these drafts, refer them onward for further consideration, and then render his final verdict. For example, the proceedings and recommendations of the Committee of Ministers concerning the implementation of the December 12, 1904, ukase had all been confirmed by Nicholas as of June 25, 1905. These proceedings were remarkable for their enlightened reformist spirit and for the candor with which they criticized past government practices and existing regulations. Some of the proposed changes, such as stricter procedures for the issuing of laws, greater religious freedoms for Old Believers and non-Orthodox Christians, the easing of restrictions on land rentals and sales by Poles, the elimination of several legal provisions directed against Jews, and the abrogation of certain limitations on the published word, were put into law either immediately or after State Council action. Others were re-

[33] TsGAOR, f. 543, op. 1, d. 519, ll. 1–2.
[34] Ibid., l. 1.

ferred, as suggested by the Committee, to specially constituted conferences and other government agencies for further review and elaboration.[35]

Once the signal had been given, Nicholas's reactive role, when joined
with the superordinate pretensions and suspicions that excluded nonbureaucratic societal impulses, made for considerable bureaucratic autonomy in shaping the terms of reform. Not only was this autonomous reform process set and kept in motion at crucial conjunctures by imperial
fiat and independent of several important personnel changes, such as the
resignation of Sviatopolk-Mirskii, the eclipse of Witte, or the recent departure of Ermolov, but it remained largely immune to the intrigues of
ranking autocratic servitors. Since bureaucratic government was external
to and hence distant from him, Nicholas for the most part declined to be
goaded by dissenters into interfering with the course of preparations. The
suggestions and criticisms of people well-connected at court fell on the
same deaf ears that had ignored similar efforts by spokesmen of society.[36]

On May 17, 1905, a mere nine weeks after the tsar had approved Bulygin's recommendation that the drafting proceed without considering
outside proposals, the minister of internal affairs presented the completed draft to Nicholas. Included in the project were various explanations and a request that it be referred to the Council of Ministers for
further discussion.[37] The new consultative assembly, elected for five
years and known as the State Duma, would be separate from the existing
State Council, which was comprised of imperial appointees. The Duma's
role would be to take up draft legislation and appropriation requests from
the government before they went to the State Council and then to the
tsar. In addition, the new institution would have limited rights to initiate
legal changes and to investigate alleged legal infractions by members of
the executive agencies. Measures rejected by the Duma were still to undergo State Council scrutiny and could be approved by the tsar; only if
they were turned down by both houses would they have to go back to
the minister who had first proposed them.

The electoral law envisioned by Bulygin's commission came out against
estate principles and embraced a modified property franchise instead.

[35] *Gosudarstvennye akty*, pp. 6–235, contains the Committee's proceedings as well as the
applicable ukases and orders by Nicholas.

[36] See, for example, the initiatives of Prince Mikhail Putiatin, a man reportedly close to
the dowager empress (TsGAOR, f. 543, op. 1, d. 515, ll. 7–10, February 22; ll. 3–6, [early
March]); Governor-General Trepov (TsGAOR, f. 543, op. 1, d. 514[1], ll. 116–25, March
8; and "Iz bumag D. F. Trepova," *KA* 11–12 [1925]: 452–54, May 8); and State Council
member Boris Shtiurmer (TsGAOR, f. 543, op. 1, d. 515, ll. 11–12, May 25, 1905).

[37] Bulygin's report of May 17, 1905; TsGAOR, f. 601, op. 1, d. 881, l. 4. The draft Duma
charter is in f. 543, op. 1, d. 514(2), ll. 57–80.

The accompanying explanation was noteworthy for admitting the anachronism and dissolution of the traditional service estate structure based on juridical definitions:

> Although according to law [Russia] rests on principles of estate organization, the economic process common to all peoples, together with a whole series of state reforms enacted in recent decades, has already long shaken and to a great extent even destroyed the estate divisions outlined in the law.[38]

By invoking the universal laws of economic development this statement not only denied the uniqueness of Russia's history but also put in doubt the tsar's ability to organize Russia's social structure in a peremptory way. Socioeconomic change was autonomous, producing a large number of landless nobles and a peasantry that was leaving the countryside for industry in ever growing numbers, Bulygin claimed. The so-called estates of merchants and townspeople had less of a corporate character than ever before, to say nothing, of course, of large stretches of the empire that were altogether without estate organizations of any kind. Purely practical considerations, too, made estate elections inadvisable in Bulygin's opinion. With a population of 96 million peasants and a mere 1.2 million nobles, there would have to be eighty peasant representatives for each gentry deputy. Any adjustment of voting strength to correct this imbalance would be widely resented as artificial. Therefore, the estate principle, which past reforms had already cast to the winds, had to make way for a more universal franchise based on property qualifications.[39]

Underlying these proposals was a conceptual revision that acknowledged the emergence of a cohesive society with a sense of shared interests:

> The evolution of social life is gradually advancing to the fore a series of interests that are binding people together as through a strong chain, without distinction of status and origin, replacing the notion of estate virtues and needs with the notion of the public [obshchestvennyi] interest.[40]

This acknowledgment of the public interest conferred a first semblance of legitimacy on the collective strivings of society. So far this notion had been unacceptable from the superordinate view of autocratic government. Indeed, only a few weeks earlier, as we have seen, Bulygin had insisted on excluding society's opinions from the drafting process. Yet

---

[38] "Soobrazheniia ministra vnutrennikh del o poriadke osushchestvleniia Vysochaishikh Ego Imperatorskago Velichestva predukazanii vozreshchennykh v Reskripte ot 17 fevralia 1905 goda," *Materialy po uchrezhdeniiu gosudarstvennoi dumy* (St. Petersburg, 1905), p. 129.

[39] Ibid., pp. 129–33.

[40] Ibid., p. 129.

now he appeared ready to recognize public interest as a force in its own right that was no longer to be denied and that was freed from all selfish or illegitimate connotations.

This conceptual transition was also expressed in Bulygin's memorandum on the press at about the same time. The press, the minister explained to Nicholas on May 30, 1905, reflected the extreme mood of Russia's population. Noting the ineffectiveness of the government's traditional means of control, Bulygin called for new approaches. Until now the government had displayed an exclusively negative attitude toward the press and, except for a few feeble and half-baked attempts, had not sought to use it as a means of influencing public opinion. This failure stemmed from the "unique conditions" of Russian government organization and the peculiar features of the Russian press, i.e., its evolution under a "strict proscriptive system" that did not depend on the use of the press against any oppositional currents. Conditions had changed. Judicial accountability had to replace heavy-handed administrative sanctions. Censorship was powerless to prevent a hostile press. In fact, it was impossible to find any paper, even among the most conservative, that sided unconditionally with the government. Therefore the only way to pacify the majority of the population still loyal to the government, to assuage their doubts and preserve their faith in the future, was for the government to publicize by means of the press its views on all problems exciting the public. Bulygin recommended that the government publish its own official organs and that it emulate the French and Central European system of patronage for the loyal press, through outright financial subsidies if necessary.[41] Autocratic government not only had to consider and contend with the divergent manifestations of public opinion, Bulygin seemed to imply, but it also depended on the support of society.

Before passing on the proposed Duma charter to the Council of Ministers on May 23, the tsar read it carefully. His notations indicate that he felt uncomfortable about some of the authority envisioned for the new institution and that he preferred to restrict its purview. As far as Nicholas was concerned, the Duma's voice was to be purely consultative, i.e., nonbinding, confined to giving advice on newly contemplated legislation. Any hint of Duma involvement or interference in administrative affairs, any suggestion of legislative initiative or interpellant powers, aroused the tsar's suspicion and was red-penciled by him. When Bulygin's commission recommended that legislative proposals rejected by a majority in both the Duma and the State Council should be returned to the ministers instead of being submitted to the tsar for final consideration, Nicholas

---

[41] Bulygin's memorandum of May 30, 1905, TsGAOR, f. 543, op. 1, d. 228, ll. 49–51.

disagreed.[42] In his eyes these points were objectionable because they put in question the tsar's traditional role as arbiter, which had allowed him to choose between different opinions and proposals.

In the ensuing discussions of the Council of Ministers, none of the participants appears to have been prejudiced by Nicholas's criticisms. Except for the language giving the Duma a voice in executive matters, virtually all of the objectionable passages survived the deliberations. Before these could be concluded, however, a controversy erupted as to the next step.

If general practice and the original timetable could serve as guides, the proposal would now be taken up by the State Council. Yet on June 7 Sol'skii, the chairman of the Council of Ministers, informed Nicholas that he and his colleagues were unanimously opposed to any State Council review. Such a review constituted normal legislative procedure, Sol'skii conceded, but it would mean a further delay of two to three months and might give rise to all sorts of disputes, quite irrelevant in themselves as the matter had already been predecided by the tsar. In the past, too, such fundamental reforms had received imperial approval without the involvement of the State Council. Speed was of the essence in quieting public unrest. In fact, State Council consideration of the proposed bill was outright dangerous, since it would only play into the hands of the agitators by reinforcing the widespread demands for the participation of elected representatives or at least local consultants in the drafting of the project.[43]

Reports that the Council of Ministers favored bypassing the State Council stirred up those circles on the right who winced at the direction and the pace of the reforms. As early as June 4 the editor of *Grazhdanin* had urged a delay that would permit the State Council to scrutinize the Bulygin project. Kireev and his confrères in the St. Petersburg Patriotic Union were hopeful that the State Council would alter the draft proposal "in our direction." To this same end, a prominent official in the Interior Ministry, who was familiar with the progress and status of the reform bill, advised his fellow members in the Union to write directly to Tsarina Alexandra Fedorovna.[44] Three State Council members joined other officials in sending Nicholas a detailed criticism of the Bulygin project that revealed considerable knowledge of the bill and of the changes made by the Council of Ministers. The undersigned expressed their preference for mixed estate and population group elections that would ensure a larger peasant representation and a more reliable assembly. In a transparently

[42] TsGAOR, f. 543, op. 1, d. 514(2), ll. 57–80.
[43] Sol'skii's report of June 7, 1905 (copy), TsGIA, f. 1276, op. 1, d. 38, ll. 352–53.
[44] GBL OR, f. 126, d. 14, l. 57, June 27, 1905.

self-serving argument, they claimed that all criticisms of the project would be directed at the tsar personally, if it were directly submitted to a Special Conference under his chairmanship. Why not let the members of the State Council take the blame instead for any shortcomings? They would be happy to effect the changes necessary in order to make the planned reform accord with the Fundamental Laws.[45]

In view of such determined opposition, Sol'skii was understandably apprehensive when he reported on the conclusions of the Council of Ministers during his audience with the tsar on July 4, 1905. Expanding on the Council's written record, he felt conscience-bound to present "with complete candor" even those considerations that "for reasons fully understood and not requiring explanations could not be included in the printed materials."

The key issue was, of course, the compatibility of the new institution with autocracy, which Nicholas had repeatedly pledged to uphold. According to Sol'skii, the Council had adhered strictly to the tsar's instructions that the Bulygin project not result in a constitutional form of government. After considering the country's agitated state of mind as well as its current and future needs, however, the members had arrived at some conclusions that "the enemies of reform" might misinterpret as "resembling a constitutional order." Such a similarity, Sol'skii contended, was "to a certain degree inevitable," for the main tasks of state administration and the paths leading to "the benefit of the state and the good of the people" were the same or at least similar everywhere. Yet the proposed system "differs vitally from a constitution, in that constitutional charters represent in themselves nothing other than contracts between the Monarchs and the peoples, as if between two sides having their own interests." In those cases, a piece of paper defined the rights of one side and limited those of the other. No such limitation of autocracy was part of the Council draft. Instead, "the Autocratic form of government is so elastic that all the highest good that the subjects seek can be granted to them by the Monarch's free will and without the introduction of a representative form of government."[46]

The spread of education and the constant contacts between Russia and the West had helped to acquaint the people with Western political ideas and systems:

[45] The three State Council members were A. S. Stishinskii, Boris Shtiurmer, and Senator Prince Shirinskii-Shikhmatov; TsGAOR, f. 543, op. 1, d. 514(2), ll. 150–54, undated; and ll. 57–58, June 27, 1905. Prince Mikhail Putiatin, too, sent a memorandum and letter; ll. 57–58, 61–62, June 30, 1905.

[46] TsGIA, f. 1544, op. dop. k 16 t., d. 1, ll. 565a–566a.

Like a youth entering adulthood and seeking to begin to live a fully independent life, our society, considering itself completely mature and trying to free
itself from superfluous supervision [*opeka*], expresses the passionate desire to
take part in state affairs through freely, popularly elected people, seeing in this
right, which the people in the majority of states already possess, the guarantee
for the further prosperity of our fatherland.

In the opinion of the Council of Ministers and some parts of society, this
right could be granted and safeguarded "without such a radical change of
the basic principles of our state order" as a constitutional system.[47]

Sol'skii and the Council of Ministers had sought to hew a fine line between preserving the essence of autocracy, as stipulated by the tsar, and
reforming it so as to meet the constitutional-democratic aspirations of an
increasingly restive society. This delicate balancing act was fraught with
contradictions. On the one hand, Sol'skii claimed, Russian society and
the body politic were following the examples of Western Europe, which
confronted Russia with identical problems demanding the same or similar
solutions. Russia's maturing citizens, he argued, like their Western peers
before them, chafed under government tutelage and were entitled to the
same political rights. On the other hand, the unique flexibility of Russian
autocracy rendered a representative form of government unnecessary.
Representative government, or constitutionalism, Sol'skii would have us
believe, had its origins in antagonism and coercion, with one side com-
pelling the other to make concessions that could be redeemed contrac-
tually. Such conflict, compulsion, or contractual limitation was alien to
autocracy, which permitted the holder of autocratic power to bestow, of
his own volition, political favors on his people. Autocratic power, in effect, was unlimited in the sense that it was free to limit itself, i.e., it
could not be compelled to do so. The essential difference between the
respective systems, Sol'skii seemed to suggest, lay in their roots rather
than in their actual forms which could well resemble each other.

By the Council's own written admission, there was no guarantee that
the planned consultative assembly might not one day become a legislative chamber. In the final analysis, any projection as to Russia's future
destination depended entirely on one's own personal beliefs about the
uniqueness or derivative nature of its historical development. Although
Sol'skii and his colleagues were quick to affirm their faith in the originality of this path,[48] these assurances failed to convince Kryzhanovskii, who

[47] Ibid., l. 567.

[48] "Memoriia Soveta Ministrov po delu o poriadke osushchestvleniia Vysochaishikh predukazanii vozreshchennykh v reskripte 18 Fevralia 1905 goda," *Materialy po uchrezhdeniiu
gosudarstvennoi Dumy*, p. 3.

had helped draft the Bulygin project and was part of the Council's technical staff. As he remembered events three decades later, "all understood that the matter would lead to the de facto limitation of autocracy, but they acted as if they did not notice that."[49]

While denying any limitation of autocracy, Sol'skii admitted that the government's modus operandi "must change." Until now, for instance, the legislative conclusions of the State Council had not been binding on the emperor because the State Council members, usually selected for their administrative experience, had been isolated from the people and therefore had not always been cognizant of popular needs. With the convocation of five hundred people's representatives, Sol'skii explained, the tsar could no longer disagree with their opinions by claiming that these new legislators, too, were ignorant of the needs of the people whence they came. Sol'skii cited another example: Some of the expenditures authorized by Nicholas had not always conformed with existing state laws or had not even been justified by real state needs. From now on, the existence of the new chamber would rule out such highhanded behavior. Readjustments and conflict were inevitable, Sol'skii warned, before the Duma would become "a real pillar of government and organ of unity between the throne and the people." If the planned reform was watered down, however, it would not pacify the country and might only lead to dangerous concessions in the future.[50]

"I am getting ready for this," the tsar declared to Sol'skii's immense joy and relief. The count admitted to having been very anxious before the audience, for the emperor's views on the proposed Bulygin Duma were not known, and information, "apparently from well-informed sources," had given reason to believe that Nicholas was not sympathetic to reform. As those rumors had it, the project would go to the State Council where the tsar would eventually affirm the opinions of its avowed opponents, thus "reducing the reform to naught." Such information was utterly without foundation, Nicholas protested, and he authorized Sol'skii to issue an unprecedented official denial in the tsar's name.[51]

With the audience drawing to a close, Nicholas announced that he had not yet familarized himself with all the details of the proposed legislation. Hence he intended to preside personally over a final review of the project by the Council of Ministers which also was to be attended by a few members of the State Council who had not left the capital environs for the summer recess. As this gesture makes clear, the tsar, while yielding to his ministers' arguments against a separate and invariably protracted

[49] Kryzhanovskii, *Vospominaniia*, p. 41.
[50] TsGIA, f. 1544, op. dop. k 16 t., d. 1, ll. 567–68, 570.
[51] Ibid., ll. 569–70.

State Council review, evidently was unwilling to exclude the State Council altogether. That this institution and its continued importance must have been very much on his mind became clear when Nicholas, in parting and apparently on his own initiative, ordered Sol'skii and the Council of Ministers to take up the matter of State Council reform, with a view toward coordinating the activities of the two "legal-consultative" bodies.[52]

THE PETERHOF CONFERENCE

The question whether the proposed assembly was really compatible with autocracy dominated, both explicitly and implicitly, the deliberations of the Special Conference that convened in the Great Palace of the imperial summer residence at Peterhof between July 19 and July 26, 1905. As Nicholas made clear in his opening remarks, only if the meeting could demonstrate that the new law "is in beneficial agreement and correct accord with our Fundamental Laws," would there be any point in examining the details.[53] A carefully orchestrated debate between proponents and well-known opponents of the planned consultative assembly was to shed light on this all-important question from all sides.

There is no reason to suspect that the tsar tried to pack the conference, either to help one side prevail or to bring about a stalemate. In true autocratic fashion, numerical constellations were of little concern; instead, Nicholas sought to assure the representation of all opinions from which he would then make his choice. In addition to the members of the Council of Ministers, virtually all of whom had already gone on record as endorsing the Bulygin project, Nicholas invited Governor-General Trepov and several State Council members. Some of them, such as A. A. Polovtsev, V. V. Verkhovskii, N. N. Gerard, the legal scholar Nikolai Stepanovich Tagantsev, and others, had a reputation for enlightened, moderate views. Others, such as A. S. Stishinskii or Count A. P. Ignat'ev, were known for their conservative leanings and, in the case of Prince A. A. Shirinskii-Shikhmatov, for their opposition to the projected reform. Some of the same people who had previously urged a State Council review in order to amend the project now found themselves invited. Thus the St. Petersburg Patriotic Union was represented by three of its presidium members, the senators A. A. Naryshkin and A. A. Bobrinskii, and the inspector of the cavalry, General A. P. Strukov, all of whom had visited Nicholas a month before. Acting as historical consultants were the liberal V. O. Kliuchevskii, Russia's pre-eminent historian, and his conservative colleague N. M. Pavlov, who was a member of the Moscow

[52] Ibid., ll. 570–71.
[53] *Petergofskoe Soveshchanie o proekte gosudarstvennoi dumy pod lichnym Ego Imperatorskago Velichestva predsedatel'stvom. Sekretnye Protokoly* (Berlin, n.d.), p. 9.

Union of Russian People and of the Imperial Historical Society, over which the tsar presided. Finally, the presence of five members of the imperial family—the Grand Dukes Michael, Vladimir, and Aleksei Aleksandrovich, Alexander Mikhailovich, and Nikolai Nikolaevich—highlighted the conference's potential implications for the dynasty. All five also happened to be members of the Committee of Ministers, together with Sol'skii, Frish, Gerard, Chikhachev, and all the ministers.

Predictably, those members of the Council of Ministers who had approved the Bulygin project denied that the reform contradicted the Fundamental Laws or in any way served to limit the autocrat's power. Sol'skii, the chairman, repeated essentially verbatim the arguments from his audience with Nicholas. Frish, the head of one of the State Council departments, characterized the draft law as the direct and logical consequence of Nicholas's earlier decision to summon elected representatives. If no real change had been intended, Frish argued, it would have sufficed to continue the traditional practice of soliciting the opinions of selected zemstvo or municipal institutions on a particular problem. While the planned reform did not infringe on the empire's basic law, it obviously required that the tsar pay close attention to the opinions and conclusions of the Duma.[54] N. N. Gerard distinguished between the power of the autocrat and the power of its "executive organs in the area of legislation, administration, and jurisprudence." By definition, the autocratic power was not subject to limitation, for it was the source and concentration of all power, and any act originating from it could only apply to subordinate authorities.[55]

Unswayed by such generalities, opponents directed their fire at one key provision of the Duma project, Article 42. According to this clause, bills rejected by majorities in *both* the State Duma and the State Council would be returned to the respective minister for further consideration instead of being submitted to the tsar. The tsar's traditional right to hear and confirm minority opinions was at stake here. The Council of Ministers had already split over this and a closely related issue when State Controller Lobko objected to the majority-vote rule as a Western-style, quasi-constitutional limitation of the tsar's legislative powers; his eighteen colleagues, on the other hand, had claimed that the new principle, aside from holding ministers more accountable for any new legislative projects, would actually enhance popular respect for any bills that reached the tsar's desk and thus would preserve his power in the public's eyes.[56]

[54] Ibid., pp. 9–12.

[55] Ibid., pp. 21–22.

[56] "Memoriia Soveta Ministrov," *Materialy po uchrezhdeniiu gosudarstvennoi dumy*, pp. 21–23.

Now Lobko's dissenting opinion became the right's rallying cry. Article 42 went beyond the intentions of the February 18 rescript and was irreconcilable with the Fundamental Laws, charged A. S. Stishinskii; if only those bills approved by a majority in either the Duma or State Council could be signed into law, then the role of the elected representatives would be elevated from a strictly consultative to a legislative one. Not only would this dangerous provision be interpreted as a step toward a legislative system along Western lines, but through it further concessions, such as—God forbid—ministerial accountability, could be extracted.[57] On much the same grounds, A. A. Naryshkin criticized article 42 as tying the hands of the sovereign and as being alien to Russian popular consciousness and political tradition:

> The resolution of matters according to a majority of votes is a principle borrowed from Western Europe. . . . This or that opinion must be evaluated not according to the number of members siding with it, but according to its intrinsic essence, i.e., according to the degree of understanding for the real state requirements and the best ways of realizing them.[58]

A perfectly sincere Count A. P. Ignat'ev rounded out the picture of autocratic ideology that served to justify the right's opposition to key aspects of the Bulygin project:

> In the popular image the charming fascination of Autocracy resides in the very fact that the Monarch stands outside of parties, is not subject to certain combinations of votes, is not carried away by petty and fervent yearnings, but is guided in all his decisions by the true good and happiness of his subjects, attentively listening to the opinions of the majority as well as the minority of advisors summoned by Him.[59]

Given such an outlook—and there is little reason to question its authenticity—conservative dissatisfaction with Article 42 and related clauses is understandable. Compared with previous practice, the tsar would indeed be subject to certain negative restrictions, though under no positive injunction to act in a particular way. While he remained free to reject legislation *approved* by majorities in the new Duma or State Council, he would be barred from approving any bill or opinion that had been *vetoed* by simple majorities in *both* chambers. In this sense, the proposed Duma charter did, indeed, depart from the traditional conception of autocracy, which placed the tsar above all particular interests and made him utterly independent of all segments of society. The contested

---

[57] *Petergofskoe Soveshchanie*, pp. 12–13.
[58] Ibid., pp. 16–19.
[59] Ibid., pp. 22–23.

clauses recognized for the first time some kind of dependent link, however tenuous, between autocratic government and the political support of society.

As far as the right opposition was concerned, the tsar should be under no legal obligation whatsoever to society or its elected spokesmen. For this reason, too, the autocratic loyalists objected to the requirement that the tsar, when dissolving the Duma, immediately fix the time for convening a new assembly.[60] By the same token, they sought to restrict the Duma's rights vis-à-vis autocratic government as much as possible.[61] Lest there be any doubt, men like Lobko, Ignat'ev, Shirinskii-Shikhmatov, and even the Grand Duke Nikolai urged that the inviolability of autocracy be emphasized by expressly reaffirming Article 1 of the Fundamental Laws about the unlimitedness of autocratic power. Although Sol'skii saw no need for such a statement, Nicholas eventually approved a less emphatic reference to the Fundamental Laws. Gerard's suggestion to reserve such a reaffirmation for a separate manifesto drew a rare imperial rejoinder: "No, it's not all the same: A manifesto will be read and forgotten, but the new law about the Duma will be in effect permanently."[62]

As the debate raged back and forth for two sessions, Article 42 and related clauses received unexpected support from the governor-general of St. Petersburg. According to Trepov, the chances were very slim that the State Council might join the Duma in rejecting a legislative proposal that had the tsar's backing. To be sure, any kind of popular assembly contained risks and dangers, no matter what precautions were taken: "The people elected from the population will undoubtedly seek to widen the boundaries of their jurisdiction and rights." Yet to restrict the Duma's activities as Ignat'ev had urged would be counterproductive, Trepov found, for the narrower the Duma's purview and powers, the sooner these strictures would be violated and the more often conflicts would arise between the Duma and the autocratic power. Thus, Article 42 had to be preserved, if for no other reason than to minimize the opportunities for such conflicts.[63] To the extent that the disputed rule constituted a limitation of autocracy, Trepov later had to concede, it was "a limitation issuing from Your Majesty and beneficial for a legislative matter, eliminating the possibility of vacillations in it." Concurring with Trepov, Chief Administrator of Agriculture and Land Management P. A. Shvanebakh saw this self-limitation as actually strengthening the autocrat's power: "After all, even God himself is subject to laws by which His wisdom gov-

[60] Count A. A. Golenishchev-Kutuzov, for example; ibid., p. 30.

[61] Cf. Count A. P. Ignat'ev, ibid., pp. 22–23.

[62] Ibid., pp. 26–30, 34–35. In another telling comment, Nicholas objected to the word *sessiia* (session): "It is desirable to avoid foreign expressions"; p. 37.

[63] Ibid., pp. 24–25.

erns the universe."[64] In other words, *pace* Rousseau, only the tsar was free to obey the law he had prescribed for himself.

The opponents of Article 42 may well have been convinced that they had an ally in Nicholas. Had he himself not taken exception to the controversial clause—before the Council of Ministers took up the project and ignored his criticism? He, too, had expressed doubts about the Duma's compatibility with the autocratic form of government and had sought to restrict the powers and responsibilities of the new assembly. At the end of the second session on July 21, 1905, however, the tsar decided in favor of the majority rule, though not without some modification that betrayed his own misgivings and that also might have been meant as a face-saving concession to the right. According to a compromise formula suggested by Count A. A. Bobrinskii, a bill had to be rejected by a *two-thirds* majority in both the State Duma and the State Council before being returned to a minister.[65]

Still, the conservative opponents of the majority rule refused to take "no"—even an imperial "no"—for an answer and submit. Evidently, the tsar's right to hear minority opinions, to which these men clung so tenaciously, also commanded the minority to make its views known to him at all costs. Although Nicholas had already announced his decision, they prepared to reverse or at least weaken it through continued open attacks as well as subterfuge. Between the second and third session, Naryshkin, Ignat'ev, Stishinskii, and Pavlov met with Kireev at Shirinskii-Shikhmatov's home to discuss strategy. Since Nicholas had not taken votes on any of the issues but simply agreed with one or the other side, they decided to offer a series of amendments during the upcoming session. Regardless of where the other participants stood, if the rightists could get the tsar to side with these conservative corrections, their case would be won.[66] By the next day, the right-wing lobby had submitted an amendment directly to Nicholas, i.e., outside of regular chancellery channels and unbeknownst to the other conference members. The amendment gave the tsar the right to consider a legislative proposal even if two-thirds majorities in both houses turned it down.[67] Other amendments sought to exclude the clause that defined the Duma's official conclusion or opinion as that of the majority.

Quite deliberately, the opponents of reform tried to strike down or alter one provision in order to undermine another. As might well have been intended, the ensuing debate on July 23 left Nicholas so confused

---

[64] Ibid., pp. 85–86.

[65] Ibid., p. 86.

[66] GBL OR, f. 126, d. 14, l. 64, July 22, 1905.

[67] N. S. Tagantsev, *Perezhitoe*, vol. 1: *Uchrezhdenie Gosudarstvennoi Dumy v 1905–1906 gg.* (Petrograd, 1919), p. 23.

that he ended up rejecting and approving successive amendments with similar content, until Sol'skii, Frish, and others pointed out the contradictions and reminded the tsar that he had already decided the issue. In the end, Nicholas confirmed the majority principle as recommended by Bulygin and the Council of Ministers.[68]

Although Stishinskii and Co. would periodically return to these issues, they now launched a well-prepared offensive against the property-based franchise of the Bulygin project. In its stead they hoped to put a detailed plan for estate elections, drawn up and submitted previously by the St. Petersburg Patriotic Union. Its three presidium members, Bobrinskii, Naryshkin, and Strukov, joined by Stishinskii and Ignat'ev, spoke up one after another in favor of an estate-based system that would favor the nobility and the peasantry. Naryshkin in particular extolled the virtues of the nobility, which through its zemstvo work had demonstrated its genuine concern for the peasantry. The Russian peasantry, in turn, was the group most suited to turn the Duma into a true "Council of the Land." Estate (soslovie) elections, moreover, had the advantage of weeding out "unreliable" elements from Russia's towns—Jews, lawyers, and intelligentsia members in general.[69] As another participant had observed at the outset, "the very holding of Duma elections that are not historically Russian, not estate-based but parliamentary, borrowed from Western examples, is foreign to the Russian people."[70]

The adherents of the estate principle made no bones of wanting to exclude undesirable or less than loyal groups, yet even the Council of Ministers project did not pretend to be all-inclusive. While the Council had insisted on extending the right to vote to Jews who could meet the property requirements for the curia of townspeople, it had effectively excluded the workers. Witte had warned of intensifying ferment among the proletariat and of change from below if the government did not accept the labor movement as Germany had done under Bismarck, but the Council left workers only to vote as peasants where applicable.[71]

Prompted by such criticisms, Nicholas asked the conferees, who assembled for the fourth session on July 25, 1905, to state briefly and clearly which of the two alternative electoral systems would ensure Duma representation for *all* strata of the population. As he had promised the Kursk delegation in June, he would see to it that both the nobility and the peasantry were represented appropriately, but the same had to apply to other groups as well.[72]

[68] *Petergofskoe Soveshchanie*, pp. 87–96, 100–103.
[69] Ibid., pp. 103–115.
[70] Ibid., p. 33.
[71] "Memoriia Soveta Ministrov," *Materialy po uchrezhdeniiu gosudarstvennoi dumy*, p. 26; Tagantsev, *Perezhitoe*, 1:29–30.
[72] *Petergofskoe Soveshchanie*, pp. 135–36.

Much of the discussion of the franchise turned on the alleged or perceived qualities of nobility and peasantry, their intrinsic conservatism, loyalty, sense of duty, and historical accomplishments. The defenders of the Council project, among whom Kokovtsev, Sol'skii, Verkhovskii, Kliuchevskii, and Polovtsev were the most articulate and persuasive, found themselves in an awkward position; courtesy and offical myth forbade most of them to express directly what they no doubt thought, namely, that those alleged virtues had been sorely lacking in the conduct of so many nobles. While Kokovtsev did remind his listeners of the recent history of the zemstvo and zemstvo congresses,[73] it took one of the tsar's uncles, the Grand Duke Vladimir, to cast off all restraint. "Permit me to ask," he interrupted Naryshkin, who was making another impassioned plea on behalf of greater noble and peasant representation through estate elections, "to which estate belong the Princes Dolgorukov, Trubetskoi, Golitsyn, the Shakhovskois, the Kuz'min-Karavaevs, the Petrunkeviches? . . . They are nobles. And what are they saying and writing?" By ticking off the names of prominent zemstvo and liberal opposition leaders, all of them nobles, Vladimir pierced the myth of a loyal conservative nobility. Naryshkin tried to defend himself: "There is no doubt—," when the Grand Duke interrupted again: "I am not talking about doubts. They are nobles—I ask you. . . . Well." Naryshkin sought to dismiss these individuals as radical aberrations, but Vladimir would have none of it:

> How can there be talk about the estate mentality and traditions of the noble estate after all that happened? If the noble estate had been the least bit united and firm, then such nobles as Petrunkevich would have been excluded long ago from the ranks of nobles by the verdicts of the noble assemblies and would not have been admitted anywhere. Was this done, I ask you?[74]

This reminder was certain to strike a responsive chord in Nicholas, who not only had taken a dim view of the zemtsy's demands since coming to the throne but also had been scandalized by what he considered to be the impudent and disloyal behavior of many nobles in the recent zemstvo and noble assemblies. The fact that the debate on this point went on as long as it did testifies to its importance—and to the tsar's indecision; with other disputes and amendments he would announce his verdict after only a few, rarely more than two or three, statements for or against. In the end, however, Nicholas sided with the Council of Ministers and its property-based franchise[75]; though he did not divulge his reasons, he evidently considered it more equitable and broadly representative.

Once again, the right did not give in but instead shifted its point of

---

[73] Ibid., pp. 130–34.

[74] Ibid., pp. 149–50. All ellipses are part of the original text.

[75] Ibid., p. 236.

attack to the question of separate or combined elections on the provincial level for the curiae of communal peasants, private landowners, and non-landed taxpayers. Separate curial elections of Duma representatives were tantamount, of course, to estate elections for the peasantry as well as for the nobility, which would dominate the curia of private landowners. In a major departure from the 1864 zemstvo franchise, which had served as the basis for Bulygin's original project,[76] the Council of Ministers had already agreed to separate curial elections at the district level, yet, except for Controller Lobko and Minister of Education Glazov, the Council had refused to do the same for the provincial elections. The two dissenters at least had consistency on their side, for in favoring separate curial elections of Duma deputies on the *provincial* (guberniia) level, too, they used the same argument that they and the rest of the Council had advanced against combining *district* (uezd) curiae: the communal peasantry would be outmaneuvered and hence underrepresented if it had to meet jointly with the other two curiae. This argument the right now made its own as a backhanded way of restoring the estate principle to the franchise.

For this very reason, Pobedonostsev here parted company with the right, proving once more that he should not be mistaken for an exponent of the nobility. While he, too, had favored the tsar's right to hear minority views as a means of safeguarding the autocrat's power, he was opposed to separate estate representation, except for the peasantry, which he considered the only genuine estate and which therefore was to elect its own Duma deputies. The nobility, he argued, had long since lost its estate character and did not merit such favoritism—to say nothing of other groups, such as merchants or urban artisans, whose estate features had always been in doubt.[77]

The tsar had already vetoed estate elections, but he shared the concern as to whether the peasantry would be sufficiently represented in the new consultative assembly. Kokovtsev, Bulygin, Polovtsev, and others sought to allay these fears, pointing to both the number of provinces in which the peasants formed a majority, and the peasants' eagerness to participate, if only to receive the allowance promised to Duma deputies. Moreover, a large number of peasant deputies in the Duma might be too much of a good thing, for they would be unprepared for the complex business awaiting them and might easily succumb to the agitational suggestions and enticements of more sophisticated oppositional Duma members.[78] Drawing on his historical studies, Kliuchevskii attempted to debunk the

[76] Kryzhanovskii, *Vospominaniia*, p. 42.
[77] *Petergofskoe Soveshchanie*, pp. 201–2.
[78] Ibid., pp. 193–94, 205–7.

notion of a uniformly loyal, conservative, and unselfish peasantry by emphasizing the stratification and heterogeneity of the Russian peasantry. Only a collective selection process would produce deputies who, while not necessarily members of the peasant estate itself, would understand the peasants' true needs, be immune to demagoguery, and have the general rather than a particular interest at heart.[79]

Nicholas remained unpersuaded, however, opting instead for yet another compromise formula.[80] The peasants from each province would be permitted to elect one Duma deputy of their own before joining the other two curiae in determining the remaining representatives from their province. As a result, the Duma would include at least fifty-one peasants and probably many more. Those provinces that had been allotted only one Duma deputy under the terms of the original project now were granted a second representative in addition to the obligatory peasant, to be selected by the three curiae combined.

Thus, the right had been at least partially successful in making the franchise conform with their own values and ideas. Despite the underlying property requirements, the electoral law preserved the estate principle for more than four-fifths of Russia's population—the peasantry. It also upheld the political influence of the noble estate through the private landowners' curia, where the gentry in effect controlled thirty-three percent of the total electors. On the other hand, this proportion at least vaguely corresponded to the gentry's contribution to the government budget, and it represented a significant cutback from the 1891 zemstvo statute or even the original 1864 legislation on which the Bulygin franchise was modelled.[81] The new consultative assembly also was opening its doors to Jews and members of the free professions, two groups that were sometimes one and the same and that the right had fought so hard to exclude.

In this sense, the final version of the Bulygin Duma bill, which Nicholas approved at Peterhof and signed into law on August 3, 1905, had all the hallmarks of a compromise, reflecting the transition from traditional conceptions and practices of autocracy to something more modern that was yet to be clearly defined. No new consensus had yet emerged, as the fractious debates of the Peterhof conference proved, leaving the tsar to tread gingerly between the two sides.

To be sure, Nicholas had personally sought to ensure—and came away convinced—that the new consultative assembly did not contradict the fundamental tenets of Russian autocracy. The notion of the people mak-

[79] Ibid., pp. 185–87.
[80] Ibid., pp. 192, 194, 207–8.
[81] Cf. Doctorow, "Introduction of Parliamentary Institutions in Russia," p. 72.

ing their needs known to their most august monarch appeared to flow directly from traditional autocratic ideology. From Nicholas's point of view, the new institution did not signify a departure from autocratic government and a first step toward a constitution, as some of his advisors seemed to hope or fear. This assurance found its expression in the manifesto of August 6, 1905, which accompanied the promulgation of the new State Duma and the Statute on Elections: "Preserving inviolate the Fundamental Law of the Russian Empire about the essence of Autocratic Power, We have deemed it good to establish the State Duma and have confirmed the Statute on elections to the Duma." It was the tsar who in his unlimited power and constant concern for the well-being of his subjects was graciously calling on the best representatives of his people to assist him in part of his governmental labors. He expressed

> the certitude that the people elected by the confidence of the whole population, being now summoned to common legislative work with the Government, will prove worthy before all of Russia of the Tsar's confidence, which called them to this great task, and will, in full agreement with the other state institutions and with the authorities established by Us, render to Us useful and zealous assistance in Our toils for the sake of Our common Mother Russia, to uphold the unity, security, and greatness of the State as well as popular order and prosperity.[82]

The Duma was to convene no later than mid-January 1906.

Yet the establishment of the consultative State Duma did represent a departure of sorts, notwithstanding the tsar's protestations to the contrary. For the first time the voice of the people in matters of national interest and general concern had been officially recognized and given an institutional expression as an integral component of the political system. A national roof had finally been added to the structure of local representation, which hitherto had been confined to parochial and ostensibly nonpolitical affairs. The autocrat and his government had always claimed to be the best and only judges of the people's true interests; but now they were willing at least to consult with the people on a permanent and comprehensive basis where before they had done so only irregularly, haphazardly, and selectively, if at all. The condition for participation, i.e., property ownership, though shot through with exceptions and inconsistencies, was a universal criterion that transcended the traditional barriers of birth and political rank and thus confirmed the breakdown of the old estate order. The very justification for this reform, at least in the eyes of its creators and most ardent defenders, was social and economic change

---

[82] *Gosudarstvennye akty*, pp. 235–37, text of August 6, 1905, manifesto; for similar translation of most of this passage, cf. Szeftel, "Reform of August 6, 1905," pp. 142–43.

and a political maturation process not unlike what Western Europe had experienced earlier, which had rendered the old order obsolete and in need of renewal. Indeed, in the manifesto Nicholas himself held out the possibility of further improvements in the Duma charter, if "the demands of the time and the good of the state" made it necessary,[83] though he scarcely could have had the quasi-constitutional changes of October in mind.

The specter of just such a radical break with autocratic tradition alarmed the right. Even after the Peterhof conference had ended the defeated minority persisted in its efforts to kill or at least water down the proposed measure. On the very next day, July 27, Count A. P. Ignat'ev reiterated his previous objections in a letter to the tsar. The new State Duma was a bureaucratic invention, he charged, that in its essence "does not correspond to the understanding of autocracy." True to the Fundamental Laws only in form, not in spirit, and without historical precedent, the reform measure would satisfy neither the revolutionaries, nor the constitutionalists, nor the faithful majority for whom "the Russian Orthodox Tsar is and will be forever the incarnation of Divine Providence over Orthodox *Rus'*, the Father of the people entrusted to Him by God, God's Anointed and the source of truth/justice [pravda] and mercy." At best, the Duma in general and the peasants in particular would be incapable of discharging the tasks expected of them. More likely, it would turn into a Constituent Assembly which would have to be disbanded.[84] Similar dissenting opinions came from six other conferees. Although they all belonged to the forum that had already given its final approval to the Duma charter and election statute, these gentlemen now proposed a long series of amendments, ostensibly editorial, that aimed at weakening some provisions and at asserting the authority of the autocrat more forcefully.

When these overtures failed to change the tsar's mind,[85] Kireev tried to find the way to his heart. Only "a few hours" before Nicholas would sign the manifesto proclaiming the State Duma, Kireev wrote to the tsarina hoping that "she after all might have influence on her husband." Kireev reminded her of her husband's past promises that all would remain as of old. The new Duma, Kireev maintained, violated that commitment, for, unlike the Assemblies of the Land in the sixteenth and seventeenth centuries, it would be elected and did not accord the church a prominent place. Although not long ago he himself had pleaded for an

[83] He explicitly instructed his minister of the court that words to this effect, recalling his remarks to the June 21 delegation, be incorporated into the manifesto. Baron Frederiks's letter to Pobedonostsev, July 27, 1905, TsGIA, f. 1544, op. dop. k 16 t., d. 3, ll. 255–56.

[84] Opinion of Adj. Gen. Count A. P. Ignat'ev, July 27, 1905, TsGAOR, f. 543, op. 1, d. 515, ll. 13–14.

[85] Ikskul's report of July 29, 1905, TsGIA, f. 1544, op. dop. k 16 t., d. 3, ll. 283–84 ob.

elected, if estate-based, assembly, Kireev now urged the adoption of an alternative contained in a previous memorandum.[86]

Obviously, the rightists' professed faith in the unlimitedness of autocratic power did not keep them from challenging that authority on particular decisions it had made. In this regard, they displayed a glaring lack of respect toward Nicholas, in marked contrast to the moderate reformers who appeared to accept any decision once it had been announced. Their high positions as State Council members and Senators notwithstanding, most of these obstinate critics were without substantive administrative responsibilities and thus saw themselves as outsiders conscience-bound to rescue the well-meaning but impressionable tsar from the clutches of the reformist bureaucratic insiders. By pleading their cause directly and repeatedly with Nicholas, as they did before, during, and after the Peterhof conference, these rightist Cassandras sought to break through the bureaucratic wall which in their eyes isolated the ruler. Kireev, who despite his court connections was just such an outsider, captured this attitude in his diary. According to Kireev, Nicholas had been outmaneuvered by the bureaucrats, even though "he seemed to have been splendidly prepared by us."[87] Commenting on the nobility's failure to be represented as an estate in the Bulygin Duma, Kireev wrote: "Of course, it never even entered the poor Tsar's mind to hurt the Nobility, [rather] they have duped Him like a small child. The bureaucrats have gone over to the side of the constitutionalists. The various Sol'skiis, Verkhovskiis, Kokovtsevs, Kulomzins. . . . They all fear for their own skins."[88]

While it is true that Nicholas for the most part had followed the Council project and the recommendations of Kokovtsev—who was its most intelligent, concise, and skillful defender—as well as those of Sol'skii, Frish, and others, he had not been deliberately misled. Except for those rare instances when the right had succeeded in confusing him, the tsar had been very much on top of things, businesslike, efficient, and mostly content to listen before rendering his verdict, as even Kireev had been forced to admit: "The Tsar presided patiently, calmly."[89]

This is not to deny an element of self-deception on Nicholas's part, however, as he clung stubbornly to the belief that the new consultative assembly was fully compatible with the unlimited exercise of autocratic power. This reform had indeed grown out of traditional autocratic ideology and had, to some extent, remained consistent with it. Yet at the same time, especially when viewed in the context of the reform process that had begun with Sviatopolk-Mirskii and when seen against the back-

[86] GBL OR, f. 126, 21(2), d. 13, ll. 24–25.
[87] GBL OR, f. 126, d. 14, l. 65, July 27, 1905.
[88] Ibid., l. 70, August 13, 1905.
[89] Ibid., l. 65, July 27, 1905.

ground of events within society, this measure signified a turning away from that traditional world view. The dimensions and contradictory implications of this departure in part would be defined by subsequent developments and thus would only become evident later. The conceptual transition marked by the reform, in turn, would help determine the dramatic events yet to come.

CHAPTER VII

The October Manifesto

EVEN WITHOUT the benefit of hindsight, it should have been clear at the time that the proclamation of the consultative Bulygin Duma represented but a major way station on the path of reform, not its final destination. Russian society continued to clamor for further changes in the state order. While persuading some of the regime's moderate critics, including a majority of the September congress of zemstvo and town duma delegates, to adopt a more conciliatory and cooperative stance, the latest concessions only succeeded in heightening the fears and suspicions of its other opponents. In order to dramatize their demands for broad civil liberties and a real legislative voice, the leadership of the Union of Unions called for a boycott of the Bulygin Duma. Most of the socialist parties did the same, but with another ultimate objective: an armed uprising that would usher in a democratic republic. The government restored university autonomy on August 27 and thus put an end to the academic strikes, only to find students and some university personnel taking advantage of the new immunities and organizing mass meetings for outsiders on university premises. In the Baltic and Georgia, peasants were resisting attempts at forcible pacification, and in the agrarian provinces of Southwest, Central, and Southeastern Russia the population displayed a growing restiveness that could not be blamed on the agitation of the newly founded Peasant Union alone. Perhaps most ominous of all, in the large cities and railroad centers there was rising militancy and talk about a general political strike among the Union of Railroaders and newly formed trade unions.

WITTE AND THE NEED FOR A UNIFIED GOVERNMENT

Although they could hardly have envisioned anything as far-reaching as the October Manifesto, the bureaucracy and even the tsar himself were fully aware of the need for additional reforms. Indeed, it was the newly promulgated Duma that made just such revisions necessary. The election statute remained to be worked out in its all-important details, as did the rules and procedures for the Duma. Goremykin's commission on peasant reform still had to come forward with its proposals. Work was continuing on those points of the December 12 ukase that had not yet been implemented. When the British journalist W. T. Snead asked Nicholas in an interview on September 1, 1905, about civil liberties as a prerequisite for Duma convocation, he was told: "Oh, but there will be laws granting all these necessary liberties. Preliminary liberties are being elaborated and they are to be submitted to me very soon."[1] The upcoming election campaign demanded a resolution of such thorny issues as freedom of association, speech, and assembly at electoral meetings, freedom of the press in campaign reporting, and police surveillance of political actors and gatherings. All these matters had to be resolved before the Duma convened; otherwise they might become the subject of debate and agitation by the nation's representatives. In addition, there was the task of State Council reform that the tsar had brought up in his July 4 audience with Sol'skii. The State Council had to be adapted to make room for a second chamber with a consultative voice in legislative affairs.

The promised presence of the State Duma also raised the delicate question of the government's position vis-à-vis that body. To be sure, the tsar and his ministers would hear out but would not be bound by the opinions of the people's representatives. Moreover, the Duma was supposed to be cooperative, thanks to a franchise that had been carefully crafted in order to assure generous representation for the peasantry and the nobility, groups presumed conservative and loyal to autocracy. Yet the debates at Peterhof and the negative reception of the consultative Duma by large segments of society, to say nothing of the continued and growing unrest in the towns and countryside, cast doubt on the accuracy of this assumption. At the very least, the government had to agree on how to deal with the Duma.

On the very day the Duma was announced, Kryzhanovskii, who had helped draft all the reform proposals since Mirskii, sent Bulygin a memorandum in which he stressed the need for a "homogeneous ministry" or "cabinet" with a clearly defined program as a means of coordinating government policy and managing the Duma. Although unable to make exact predictions, Kryzhanovskii expected the new consultative body to add its voice to those calling for changes in the state order. In entering a new stage of political life, "firmness and decisiveness" on the part of a unified government were essential, especially given its long tradition of internal strife and dissent. Invoking the example of Louis XVI, whose government had lacked a program with which to confront the Estates-General in 1789, Kryzhanovskii warned: "If the lessons of history and life teach

---

[1] Joseph O. Boylen, "The Tsar's 'Lecturer-General.' W. T. Snead and the Russian Revolution of 1905 with Two Unpublished Memoranda of Audiences with the Dowager Empress Marie Fedorovna and Nicholas II," *Georgia State College School of Arts and Sciences Research Papers*, no. 23 (July 1969): 64–65. Acting as advocate instead of interviewer, Stead urged the tsar to grant such liberties before Witte's return, lest he and not Nicholas receive all the credit.

anything, then obviously the most pressing, urgent task of the present historical moment must be the unification of the Government into one like-minded whole, with a definite program of action." The ministers, instead of vying for the tsar's confidence and seeking to discredit each other, should be united by a community of interests and convictions. To this end, Kryzhanovskii proposed that the chairman of the Council of Ministers become the "leader" of domestic policy, with the right to report to the tsar on behalf of the entire council and to nominate ministerial candidates who shared his views. The tsar, of course, would retain the power to make the actual appointments. Not to be nominated by the chairman were the ministers of the court, war, navy, foreign affairs, and the state controller. While the first four would continue to report to Nicholas individually, none of the ministers would be permitted to take general measures without prior sanction by the whole Council of Ministers.[2]

As for the autocrat, he was to function as the "Supreme Representative" of executive and legislative power, without participating directly in the administration or being drawn into party conflict: "The Autocratic Power, first and foremost, must be equally raised above all parties and estates, above those who govern and those who are governed; from this situation derives the commonality of its interests with the real state weal and popular good."[3] Despite such traditional wording, Kryzhanovskii appeared to hint at a major break with autocratic ideology, at least with its personal, if not its bureaucratic, variant. Supposedly the tsar had always stood above the selfish factional interests of society as the embodiment of truth-justice. He had resolved these conflicts in conformance with the real state interest with the aid of and through his bureaucratic servitors. Although these officials on occasion distorted his will, on the whole they shared the autocrat's superordinate pretensions and indeed derived their legitimacy from them. Now Kryzhanovskii's phrasing placed "those who govern" on the same level as the "governed," equally far removed from the autocrat, who became the "supreme representative" of executive and legislature. The notion of "the king who reigns, but does not rule" comes to mind. In his memoirs, however, after only just conceding the inevitability of a constitution, Kryzhanovskii refused to see his proposal as a concession to constitutionalism designed to restrict the role of the tsar; he described it instead as a necessary adjustment to the existence of the Duma in order to preserve the system.[4]

The proposal for a united government was not a new one, of course. Kryzhanovskii's criticism of the shortcomings of the existing ministry

---

[2] "Ob"edinenie deiatel'nosti ministrov," ILLHU.

[3] Ibid.

[4] Kryzhanovskii, *Vospominaniia*, pp. 50–51; cf., too, *Padenie tsarskogo rezhima* (Leningrad, 1925), 5:386.

were reminiscent of Ermolov's comments in January 1905 that had finally persuaded Nicholas to charge Witte with working out measures to achieve greater government unity. Although Witte had eagerly seized upon that task, it had lapsed with the closure of his Special Conference in April 1905. Now the impending convocation of the State Duma served to revive the project with an even greater urgency, which only Bulygin failed to appreciate: "Let's leave that for the next generation."[5] Kryzhanovskii's memorandum found its way into Nicholas's hands. After Sol'skii requested the tsar's permission to have his Special Conference look into measures "that could give the activity of the individual agencies unity of direction and thus prevent differing preliminary proposals of a legislative nature from being presented to the Duma," Nicholas passed on the document on August 27 with the following words: "There is much that is true and useful in it."[6] Thus, Sol'skii's conference came to take up yet another reform, in addition to those already promised and others still to be announced.[7]

Almost as soon as the new proposal for government unification had seen the light of day, it became entangled in the politics and conflicts of personalities. For friend and foe alike, behind the issue of a unified ministry loomed the powerful figure of Witte. People's attitudes toward such a reform, whether positive or negative, were bound to be influenced by their feelings about Witte, who inspired hostility, distrust, envy, admiration, sympathy, and hope, but never indifference or equanimity. As chairman of the Committee of Ministers, a largely ceremonial position, he not only had a vested interest in the fate of the suggested government unification, but many suspected him of using this issue deliberately to enhance his power and to reassert control over government affairs. Had Witte not been the prime mover behind the proposal in the early part of the year, until the closing of his Special Conference put an abrupt end to those discussions, though not to his ambitions?

Much had happened since then to repair his political fortunes. His political star, on the wane only a few short months before, had swiftly risen to a new zenith with the successful conclusion of the peace negotiations in late August 1905, which had at least preserved the honor that Russia had been unable to defend on the battlefield. Rightly or wrongly, Witte received major credit for this outcome. His return from Portsmouth, N.H., by way of New York, Paris, and Berlin, was a triumphal procession during which the French president and cabinet as well as the German emperor and chancellor showered him with honors and attention. The

---

[5] Kryzhanovskii, *Vospominaniia*, pp. 50–51.

[6] "Ob"edinenie deiatel'nosti ministrov."

[7] E.g., TsGIA, f. 1544, op. dop. k 16 t., d. 7, ll. 50 and ob., 57.

dowager empress offered her heartfelt congratulations on the brilliant results achieved for the good of the fatherland, and the tsar's brother-in-law, the Grand Duke Alexander, somewhat cryptically added to his message: "I thought about how you had to suffer—now time for domestic peace."[8]

The presumed cause of those sufferings, Nicholas II, was almost alone in showing a notable lack of enthusiasm for Witte's most recent achievements. When he first learned of the agreement from Witte on August 17, he wrote in his diary: "After this I walked around the whole day as if in a trance." After a day's reflection, he continued: "Only today I began to accustom myself to the thought that peace will be concluded and that this is probably good, for that's the way it ought to be." On August 25, after a formal church service to mark the official signing of the peace treaty, the tsar wrote: "Must confess that I was not in a happy mood."[9] According to Witte, the tsar waited more than three days before sending him a "rather dry" telegram, but succeeding messages grew friendlier in tone.[10] Eventually, if grudgingly, Nicholas even invited Witte to his yacht in the Gulf of Finland and bestowed on him the title of count.

Many now expected Witte to turn his deft touch to Russia's vexing internal troubles. His name, Liubimov would later recall not without hyperbole, "was surrounded by a halo." He was hailed as a possible savior, capable of accomplishing anything that he put his mind to; scarcely anybody believed that his luck would ever desert him.[11] Even before the conclusion of the peace negotiations, "the almost diabolic pre-eminence of Witte" had been the subject of Snead's interview with the dowager empress, who was full of praise: "He is wonderful. . . . There is nothing he cannot do. Nothing. . . . Witte is so clever it is almost as if he were a devil, he is so clever."[12] Her son echoed some of those sentiments in his interview with Stead a fortnight later. In commenting on Witte and the Portsmouth settlement the tsar is reported to have said: "Yes, he has

[8] Witte Collection, REEACU, carton 11, item 39, Maria Fedorovna's telegram from Copenhagen, September 18, 1905 (N.S.); item 37, Alexander Mikhailovich's telegram, September 2, 1905 (N.S.). The tsar's brother, the Grand Duke Michael, was another congratulant, August 31, 1905 (N.S.), item 3.

[9] TsGAOR, f. 601, op. 1, d. 249.

[10] "Dnevnik A. A. Polovtseva," *KA* 4 (1923): 63.

[11] Liubimov, "Russkaia smuta," p. 290. Among the more touching, if naive, manifestations of this faith in the miracle-making powers of Witte was a letter from one Aleksandra Kokoreva, dated October 8, 1905, sending Witte fifteen thousand rubles for the relief of students and workers in both capitals who had been adversely affected by recent events. As one who had shown himself able to solve much more complicated and serious problems, Witte was to dispose of the money as he saw fit; Witte Collection, REEACU.

[12] W. T. Snead's interview with Maria Fedorovna, August 15, 1905, in Boylen, "The Tsar's Lecturer-General," p. 43.

done very well. He is a clever man, not very sympathetic, but a clever man." Stead, while faulting Witte for his roughness of manner and lack of geniality, came away with the impression that Nicholas "was intending to accept Witte as the inevitable," though the tsar did not say so outright.[13]

Clearly, Witte's name and the fate of government reform were becoming inseparably linked in everyone's mind, including Witte's own. Within four days of receiving Nicholas's mandate on government unification, i.e., a full two weeks before Witte's return, Sol'skii asked the tsar to invite Witte to participate in the Special Conference's deliberations on this matter.[14] Despite the urgency of the proposed reform, Sol'skii awaited Witte's arrival before taking up the problem. Witte, of course, was a firm believer in the need for a united cabinet with a prime minister at its head, as he reminded Polovtsev during their conversation on September 19, and he gave the definite impression that he was counting on being appointed to such a position.[15]

A consensus on the need for government unification was fast emerging. When Sol'skii's conference held its first informal meeting on September 20, all but one of its members agreed with Witte's remarks about the dangers of the current political situation and the need for a cabinet. According to the draft proposal in front of the participants, the Committee of Ministers would be eliminated and its responsibilities divided among various agencies including the State Council. In its place a reorganized Council of Ministers, no longer chaired by the tsar but by a first minister, was to become the central and unifying organ of government.[16]

Any unhappiness with the arrangement may have had less to do with considerations of principle than with the prospect of seeing the redefined chairmanship occupied by Witte. As the lone dissenter at the September 20 gathering, Finance Minister Kokovtsev insisted that ministers retain their right to report to the tsar on all matters not affecting their colleagues, with copies of these reports to be submitted to the Council. In addition, Kokovtsev wanted to retain the Committee of Ministers for all matters that did not fall within the purview of a reformed State Council, or, as Polovtsev noted sarcastically, "all matters in which the law is violated and this violation is covered up by supreme [i.e., Nicholas's] or-

---

[13] Stead's interview with Nicholas, September 1, 1905, ibid., p. 57. They both spoke English here; presumably, Nicholas used "sympathetic" in the Russian and German sense of the word—"likeable, nice."

[14] Sol'skii's report of August 31, 1905, TsGIA, f. 1544, op. dop. k 16 t., d. 5, ll. 11 and ob. Nicholas indicated his agreement the next day.

[15] "Dnevnik A. A. Polovtseva," KA 4 (1923): 64–70.

[16] "Ob"edinenie deiatel'nosti ministrov."

ders."[17] N. V. Murav'ev, a former minister of justice and a well-known opponent of Witte's, composed a memorandum on "immediate government tasks"; his proposal would have reduced the chairman's role to that of government spokesman before the Duma and State Council, a first among equals invested with the tsar's full confidence, not unlike the Prussian practice. The individual ministers were to present their reports to the Council in the tsar's presence.[18]

One of those attending Sol'skii's conference was Governor-General Trepov, who as Bulygin's deputy was responsible for public security and who enjoyed the tsar's supreme confidence. On September 25 he, too, pleaded with Nicholas on behalf of government unification.[19] In a sweeping report, Trepov laid out for his imperial master the developments since August 6. Liberal circles of Russian society had banded together in professional unions that were holding periodic congresses to discuss and coordinate their plans, Trepov explained. Through the promise of economic and political reforms, these circles, in conjunction with radical zemstvo elements, were trying to elect as many of their sympathizers as possible to the new Duma in order to gain a majority and turn it into a constituent assembly. The more radical constitutionalists, on the other hand, were favoring a boycott of the Duma. Meanwhile, the revolutionary underground, fearful of losing popular support once the Duma convened, was intensifying its activities through armed demonstrations, strikes, and propaganda among the peasantry. The troubles had also affected university youth. To make matters worse, the periodical press was almost entirely in the "hands of the opposition," distributing—free of cost, even in the provinces—its tendentious accounts of the government's attempts to pacify the country. As a result, the moderate forces were utterly demoralized and disoriented. Much, therefore, would depend on the initial actions of the Duma.

Trepov argued in favor of establishing a "firmly united conservative party of order, on which the Government could lean in the Duma," assuming, of course, that it would achieve a majority. To this end, the government had to draw up and publicize widely a clear program of its intentions. The lack of a firm and consistent domestic policy had to be rectified by reorganizing the Council of Ministers in a way that would be "based on the mutual tie of the Ministries in implementing the program worked out by the Government." Guided by clear and identical instruc-

---

[17] Though at first vocally opposed to Kokovtsev's arguments, Witte eventually did a complete about-face, much to Polovtsev's and everyone else's surprise, forcing Sol'skii to scratch the clause that called for the abolition of the Committee of Ministers; "Dnevnik A. A. Polovtseva," *KA* 4 (1923): 64.

[18] "Ob"edinenie deiatel'nosti ministrov."

[19] TsGAOR, f. 601, op. 1, d. 249, September 25, 1905; Trepov's report, TsGAOR, f. 543, op. 1, d. 645, ll. 10–12 (copy, 1a–4).

tions from the top, governors-general, governors, and other officials had to see to the realization of the government's program on the local level. By rallying influential local people around them, they could fight the opposition. Trusted agents, moreover, were to tour the provinces and ascertain that the actions of local officials conformed with the government's intentions. Finally, Trepov called for a "special semiofficial organ," through which the government could make its views known and "thereby discipline the public." Existing conservative papers were too small and uncoordinated to exert any influence. The government also was to subsidize a cheap provincial press to provide the population with "healthy mental food." If these conditions were met, Trepov predicted, the great mass of the population would rally around the throne and give the government its needed majority, ignoring those people "alien to it in spirit and strong only through their party organization."

Trepov's report was remarkable for its frankness as well as its conclusions, which departed considerably from the traditional tenets of autocratic nonpartisanship and superordination. While attaching great significance to the new Duma, Trepov did not believe that the electoral law automatically guaranteed a conservative and pliable Duma. Unless the government took decisive steps to present a united front with a clearly articulated program and to win over public opinion through its policies and through the press, it would find itself confronted with a hostile radical Duma majority. Whether the Duma was limited to a consultative voice or not, Trepov recognized public opinion as a potent force that had to be reckoned with just as in a parliamentary democracy. Indeed, within a few days, Trepov would return to the very issue of influencing and subsidizing the press as a means of rallying the public behind the government. Trepov's analysis contained the premise that the government would have to seek active support within society. Such support would not be forthcoming without the changes he suggested. Quite plainly, the government of autocratic Russia could no longer afford to hover above society, peremptorily determining what it considered to be society's own best interests and ignoring or dismissing the allegedly selfish and hence illegitimate aspirations of society. This did not mean, however, that henceforth society was to decide government policy. Believing that a majority within society existed or could be fashioned to back those policies, Trepov continued to insist that the government retain the initiative and a decisive voice.

AUTOCRACY UNDER SIEGE

After the informal meetings at Sol'skii's in late September, his Special Conference formally took up the matter of government unification on October 3 and 4,[20] yet with each passing hour it must have become more apparent that a reorganization of government alone would do little to stem the revolutionary tide and the steady disintegration of authority. Since September 19, a strike by Moscow printers had spread to the city's bakeries, textile, tobacco and metallurgical factories, and railroad shops. It reached a preliminary climax on October 2 with the formation of a coordinating committee. Just when their limited means and the setbacks inflicted by government force were beginning to sap the strength of the Moscow strikers, sympathy strikes by St. Petersburg printers and metal workers, as well as the popular demonstrations surrounding the funeral of Prince Trubetskoi, the liberal rector of Moscow University who had died suddenly, revived their sagging spirits. On October 6 the Moscow-Kazan railroad was hit by a strike; within two days all the lines operating out of Moscow had been shut down, and shops, businesses, institutes, and factories followed suit. The railroad stoppages rapidly spread to other rail centers, first Kharkov, then St. Petersburg, then Warsaw, the Caucasus, Siberia, and Finland. More importantly, these stoppages provided the signal and impetus for what came to be known as the October General Strike, which by the middle of October had brought virtually all forms of public life to a halt in most of the Empire's urban and industrial centers. More than a million factory workers, seven hundred thousand railroaders, fifty thousand government employees, and tens of thousands of shop clerks, students, and professionals joined in the nationwide condemnation of autocracy and the demand for fundamental reforms.

By October 13, according to one eyewitness, an "ominous silence" had fallen over St. Petersburg. While external order remained largely intact, street life came to a virtual halt, as many stores closed down, streetcars stopped running, and total darkness enveloped the city at night. There was the near-universal expectation that something was about to happen, but nobody was quite sure what. Without instructions from the center, local officials outside of the capital no longer knew how to act, often proceeding at cross-purposes, sometimes energetically, sometimes not. Almost cut off from the outside world, the Ministry of Internal Affairs, which was responsible for the preservation of public order, was swept by wild and often improbably fantastic rumors as bureaucrats passed from office to office. Interior Minister Bulygin appeared strangely untouched by the steadily escalating crisis, satisfied with himself for having accomplished what he had been hired to do, i.e., the establishment of a consultative Duma, and resigned to referring any and all matters on to Trepov for possible action. Trepov, in turn, although in charge of the police, dismissed any alarm about the spectacle of openly tolerated mass meet-

---

[20] "Dnevnik A. A. Polovtseva," *KA* 4 (1923): 72–76.

ings on university property, regarding them instead as an invaluable opportunity to observe the development of the revolutionary movement,
"since all unreliable elements come together there daily."[21]

This air of unreality and blitheness also enveloped the tsar, if his daily
routine and the pages of his diary serve as any indication. After his two-
week cruise among the Finnish isles from September 4 to 18, Nicholas's
life had resumed its usual pattern, replete with ministerial reports, receptions for maimed veterans from the Far East, walks, boat rides,
weekly hunts, family dinners, and social revelry. Nary a hint of revolutionary mass meetings at the recently reopened institutions of higher
learning, of the September zemstvo and town duma congress, of the
Duma boycott, of the growing radicalization of public opinion in general
and of the professional union movement in particular, to say nothing of
the September strikes in Moscow, interrupted Nicholas's record of his
daily doings and musings or altered his routine.

Although Trepov's regular reports had faithfully charted the growth of
the revolutionary movement, the very relentlessness and repetitive detail of these accounts, instead of alerting Nicholas to the gravity of the
steadily worsening situation, may have numbed him. In the idyllic environs of the tsar's summer residence on the Gulf of Finland, the world
and events described in these reports seemed unreal. On October 1 General Kireev observed quite accurately: "The tragic aspect of the situation
is that the tsar lives in an utter *fool's paradise*, thinking that He is strong,
all-powerful as before!"[22] The tsar was indeed living in his own little
world, unwilling or unable to do anything about the world at large. To
the extent that the outside world intruded on him in the form of the
hated ministerial reports, it remained curiously abstract and failed to stir
him to action.

From Nicholas's point of view, these reports attested above all to the
utter incompetence of the authorities in dealing with the relatively few
rabble-rousers and seditionists, who were misleading the good and loyal
narod. Inasmuch as these reports were and always had been part of his
onerous routine, the cross that fate had condemned him to bear, their
contents had to be accepted with equal passivity. Moreover, as long as
these reports continued together with the rest of his daily ritual—the
touching displays of loyalty and affection by those received into the tsar's
presence, the military reviews, services, and his multifold private distractions—all was not lost; life retained its purpose. It is this estrangement from reality, this fatalistic resignation and inability to comprehend
the true nature of Russia's latest and most serious crisis, that also help

---

[21] Liubimov, "Russkaia smuta," pp. 297–305.
[22] GBL OR, f. 126, d. 14, l. 86. The words that are italicized were originally in English.

explain the abrupt retreat on Nicholas's part, when he finally was made aware of the real threat and confronted with a consensus in favor of reform.

Witte, on the other hand, as early as October 1 was described as "extremely gloomy," considering the general situation to be so hopeless as to demand a dictatorship.[23] Witte had every reason to be despondent. He was reportedly afraid that he did not enjoy the tsar's trust[24] and thus might have sensed his own chances of becoming prime minister fading with each additional day. Even if he attained the coveted position, it might be too late, and he might find himself swept away by the social upheaval that seemed imminent, indeed, that had already begun.

Urged on by Sol'skii, on October 6 Witte requested an audience with Nicholas in order to warn him of the grave danger Russia and the dynasty were facing. This meeting had to be put off until the morning of the 8th because of an imperial hunt that had been scheduled for the 7th. When they finally met, the tsar did not react to Witte's remarks. Yet he considered the matter important enough to arrange a second audience which included the tsarina and took place the next day, October 9, despite the fact that Sundays were ordinarily kept free of official business.[25] Although he undertook some revisions and deletions for the second audience, on both occasions Witte essentially restated the contents of a lengthy position-paper prepared by V. D. Kuz'min-Karavaev, a moderate zemstvo leader who enjoyed Witte's confidence.[26] Witte's gambit was an act of desperation, inspired by his concern over what he perceived as a steady drift towards disaster. While offering himself as the man to lead Russia down a new path, he could not possibly have been confident of the outcome of this gamble.

Both in tone and substance the report represented such a dramatic departure from traditional formulations of autocratic ideology that it deserves to be described at length.[27] "The basic motto of the contemporary societal movement in Russia," Witte told Nicholas and Alexandra, "is freedom." While the roots of this movement could be found in Novgorod

[23] "Dnevnik A. A. Polovtseva," KA 4 (1923): 71.

[24] GBL OR, f. 126, l. 82, September 20, 1905.

[25] Witte, Vospominaniia, 3:11. Witte mistakenly dated these audiences October 9 and 10, a mistake that is repeated in all the other accounts I have seen. Both KFZ and TsGAOR, f. 601, op. 1, d. 249, however, leave no doubt as to the correct dates.

[26] Kuz'min-Karavaev's piece was later published under the title "The Eve of October 17. The Tasks of the Government" in a collection of his articles, V. D. Kuz'min-Karavaev, Iz epokhi osvoboditel'nago dvizheniia (St. Petersburg, 1907), 1:184–97.

[27] The following is based on the second of Witte's reports, the shorter and revised version; TsGAOR, f. 543, op. 1, d. 515, ll. 20–25. Since it is dated October 10, it must have been submitted to Nicholas the next day after Witte's oral report; this may account for the confusion surrounding the dates of the actual audiences.

and Pskov, among the Zaporozhe Cossacks, among the runaway serfs along the Volga, in the seventeenth-century church schism and the protests against Peter's reforms, in the Decembrist uprising of 1825, the Petrashevskii affair of 1849, and even in the Emancipation Act of 1861, they went "still deeper—these roots are in the nature of man. The task of a civilized state is to oppose law [pravo] to this natural movement toward individual liberty. But the law that limits personal freedom must at the same time guarantee it. Otherwise it will degenerate into violence and despotism." Civil liberty, i.e., liberty limited but safeguarded by law, could not be a goal in itself; it was the government's means of satisfying the spiritual and physical needs of the population. For this reason, too, the law was not immutable. Instead of clinging to its external form, the government should remain true to its essence and seek to give the law that form which best corresponded to the spirit of the changing times.

The situation was critical, Witte warned. Society's demands could still be met, but with each passing day signs of a "stormy explosion" were mounting. Never mind the radicals, the existence and integrity of the state "rests on the mood of the wide masses of society and on the harmony of government actions with this mood." For the first time, these masses were no longer resisting extreme political passions but exacerbating them. The reform of August 6 had come too late: "The more swiftly the political thought of society, driven on by events and by the eruptions of extreme tendencies, races onward, the less the existing real order corresponds to government promises." Yesterday's extremist ideas, such as universal suffrage, the political equality of women, the nationalization of land, or social transformation, today had become the "catechism" of wide circles of society.

The government's "fundamental error," according to Witte, had been its failure to discriminate between the adherents of peaceful renewal and the anarchists. Unlike the reaction of the 1880s, when the government's policies had evoked a positive echo within the antirevolutionary mood of society, conditions and education had by now prepared the public for constitutionalism. This trend had been reinforced by the impotence, incompetence, inconsistency, ignorance, and division of authority, the unfortunate war being the final blow.

"A government that does not direct, but follows events, leads the state to disaster—such is an axiom of history," Witte proclaimed. There had to be a common political goal, however. "Societal consciousness always looks for authority and leadership," since only the strength of authority could protect civil liberties. That strength, in turn, was directly proportional to the clarity of the government's goals and to the amount of support that the majority of thinking society was prepared to give to those goals. Unfortunately, at the moment not a single positive goal inspired authority, only the negative tasks of "restraining, suppressing, curtailing." "In order to save the authority of power, and with it the state, the physical force of power has to be animated by a positive ideal." The public notion of liberty was such an ideal, which the government had to make its own in order to lead society: "Power must put itself under the banner of liberty. There is no other way out." The victory of civil liberty was inevitable, if not through reform, then through revolution. By placing itself at the head of the liberation movement, as it had done with the peasant reform before, the government would signal a formal departure from the past without rejecting it altogether. Only thus could the split of government and society into two hostile camps, which dated back to the aftermath of 1861, be overcome. The success and gains of the societal movement had to be recognized: "The government must sincerely take upon itself those obligations from which even yesterday it would have shied away with horror." But every day was critical.

The ideals of the liberation movement, according to Witte, were of three distinct types: (1) negative, such as the elimination of arbitrary rule and despotism; (2) positive, such as freedom of speech, assembly, association, person, and equality before the law; and (3) formal, i.e., guarantees for achieving and safeguarding the first two. In essence, the December 1904 ukase had already recognized the negative and positive ideals, though they had yet to become firm guiding principles of government policy, without compromise or concessions to force. As for the formal ideals, they had found their "expression in society's consciousness in the word 'constitution.'" Almost as if he had expected the question mark that Nicholas would later pencil in the margin of the written report, Witte continued: "This word, although it has not been recognized from the heights of the Throne, does not present a threat to the Monarchy. The principle of Monarchical power is preserved even under representation with the so-called decisive voice: not a single decision of the representatives can take effect without the Monarch's sanction." The result might be a unique "political combination" still untried in the West and befitting Russia's uniqueness. In the meantime, however, the government had to announce its sincere readiness to establish full civil liberties and to enter onto the constitutional path. Once convinced "that this path will lead to the popular good, the Autocratic Monarch without doubt will be the first to take it."

Society had already suggested the reforms necessary to reach this goal. The August 6 electoral law was obviously inadequate, "an artificial system of representation based on the accidental fact of meeting the property qualification," which isolated the peasantry and excluded whole classes such as the workers. In conformance with the public's desire, the government's new program therefore might promise a new election statute based on a universal franchise. With other issues, such as worker, agrarian, and border area problems, the enunciation of guiding principles would suffice. As for the worker question, the government could also implement a series of meliorative measures, including limits on the workday, government insurance, and arbitration boards. The agrarian problem, too, could be alleviated through "partial satisfaction of the land hunger in various provinces," with the help of state lands and the peasant bank. The government might even assume some of the peasants' rent payments to their private landlords, a form of expropriation with compensation that would serve to increase the amount of land under direct personal cultivation and one that was not much different from government purchases of land for railroad construction. Since the Russian people were still not sympathetic to separatist and autonomous tendencies in the border regions, the government should strongly reaffirm the unity of the Russian state, without excluding, however, the expansion of local self-government in Poland, Georgia, and other areas of the Caucasus, as long as only local needs were at stake.

Witte cautioned against placing excessive hopes in the Duma, for its future composition was as yet undetermined; even in the best of circumstances it would take several months before the Duma would settle down to productive business. But he ruled out any interference in the election process. Government agents had to be categorically enjoined from infringing on freedom of the press and of campaign meetings. Witte also called for a ministry of people "sincerely committed to the impending reforms," as well as the addition of elected representatives to the State Council until it could be reorganized into a genuine upper legislative chamber. Finally, to establish close links between Duma and government, ministers were to have the right to stand for election in the Duma. Here, too, Nicholas would signal his doubts, probably suspecting behind this seemingly innocent suggestion a ministry accountable to the Duma.

In conclusion Witte readily admitted that this program was strong medicine indeed, but that Russia's crisis demanded such drastic treatment. In the next few days he would repeatedly return to this theme:

> There is no choice: either stand at the head of the movement that has seized the country, or proceed firmly and methodically in the opposite direction. I do not believe in a happy outcome on such a path; I think that it will lead to horrible consequences sooner than the first. But I am a human being and could be mistaken. In any event, at the head of the government can only be a person who believes in the expediency of his opinions and who will be given the means to implement them.

According to Witte, neither the tsar nor the tsarina expressed any opinions during his presentation, except for Nicholas's remark that "it might be better to publish the basis of the memorandum as a manifesto."[28] The audacity of Witte's report must have left Nicholas speechless; rarely if ever had the imperial ears been treated to such radical, not to say, sacrilegious ideas by one of the senior autocratic servitors.

With one bold stroke Witte had cut through official rhetoric and brushed aside cherished tenets of autocratic ideology. Man's natural striving for personal liberty had become the motive force of historical change; in this sense Russia and the Russian people were no different than their European neighbors. In the place of the imagined harmony of tsar and people that reflected the unique spiritual qualities of the Russian narod and its desire to submit to power, Witte posited the conflict of opposites. Russia's development was the history of a dialectic between individual freedom and the civilizing force of law: freedom without law was anarchy; law without freedom was despotism. *Pravo*, the term used by Witte, embodied this dialectic—the tension between state and individual—for it meant both "law" and "right." Law was necessary to mold individualistic drives into a coherent society; hence the importance of a modern bureaucracy as the source of, yet under, the law. Where autocratic ideology had exclusively identified Russia's historical evolution with the personal accomplishments of its rulers and with autocracy, Witte saw historical significance also in the reactions *against* those rulers and their system. Not only Ivan the Terrible, Alexis, Peter the Great, Catherine, and Nicholas I populated Witte's historical pantheon, but so did their victims—the freedom-loving people of Novgorod and Pskov, Zaporozhe Cossacks and runaway serfs, Old Believers, Decembrists, *Petrashevtsy*—an intelligentsia circle led by the Fourierist M. V. Petrashevskii—and peasants. Russian history according to Witte included outsiders, dissenters, and liberationists—the very people implicated in Russia's latest and gravest crisis. They determined the course of the country's development as much as did Russia's nominal rulers. Unless the monarchy accommodated itself and accepted the inevitable, it would be swept away by this irresistible historical force.

To this end, the government had to ally itself with the moderate and peaceful majority of society, quickly, without reservations or preconditions, lest this majority in turn be superseded by one even more radical and less pacific. Most pressing was the grant of a constitution, this word of foreign origin that acted on Nicholas like a red flag and that Witte in his first audience had defined as "the contact of the tsar and the people on the grounds of shared legislative authority, budget rights, and control over the administration."[29] Society and government, in fact, were inter-

[28] Witte, *Vospominaniia*, 3:12.
[29] Doctorow, "Introduction of Parliamentary Institutions in Russia," p. 169.

dependent; the former required the stability, protection, control, and direction of authority, while the latter could not continue without the support that came with the representation and recognition of society's legitimate interests. Ideally, as the last part of Witte's proposal seemed to imply, members of government should be the elected representatives of the people and should be accountable to them. Witte's was an all-or-nothing proposition ruling out any half-measures. Either Nicholas accepted his scheme and gave him the authority to carry it out, or he could choose the road of dictatorship and repression.

"RUSSIA IS BEING GRANTED A CONSTITUTION"

For three days, just as the Moscow strikes were infecting the rest of the Empire, Witte did not hear from the tsar. During this time Nicholas received not only the ministers and officials who were part of his regular weekly schedule, but others as well, including the minister of communications who was in charge of Russia's striking railroads.[30] Without a doubt they discussed the current situation, the prospects for improvement—and Witte's program.[31] Witte, meanwhile, chaired an interagency discussion of the railroad strikes at the tsar's behest. As Witte wrote to the tsar on October 12, Governor-General Trepov and the five participating ministers had concluded that the rail strikes were part of the general revolutionary movement. Therefore, measures to end this movement would also mean the end of the strikes, especially if a homogeneous government was established with a definite program. While action should be taken to protect railroad equipment and those workers willing to work in the capitals and at key junctions, military forces did not suffice to secure all lines, let alone other industries affected by the spreading disorders.[32] Not everyone shared these conclusions, however. At a session of Sol'skii's conference on government unification that same day, two State Council members, Adjutant-General Chikhachev and Count Palen, the venerable former minister of justice, argued for the use of force,[33] reportedly prompting Witte to suggest to Nicholas that he consider Chikhachev as a radical alternative.[34]

By the evening of October 12 the extreme gravity of the situation had finally begun to dawn on Nicholas. His diary, usually silent on matters of substance, read that day:

[30] TsGAOR, f. 601, op. 1, d. 249; and *KFZ*, October 10–12, 1905.
[31] Witte, *Vospominaniia*, 3:12.
[32] Witte's report of October 12, 1905, "Manifest 17 Oktiabria," *KA* 11–12 (1925): 61.
[33] Witte, *Vospominaniia*, 3:12.
[34] "Dnevnik A. A. Polovtseva," *KA* 4 (1923): 76, October 13, 1905.

The railroad strikes which began around Moscow reached Petersburg, and to-day the Baltic [Railroad] struck. [Minister of Justice] Manukhin and the people who were to present themselves barely got to Peterhof. To communicate with Petersburg, the "Dozornyi" and "Razvedchik" have started sailing twice a day. Nice times. Because of the delayed receptions we sat down to lunch at 2 o'clock.[35]

The existence of the strikes was nothing new by this time. What was new was the fact that the events for the first time had directly intruded into the tsar's idyll at Peterhof. With the rail-link between the capital and the imperial seaside residence closed down, ships had to convey messages and transport visitors. The inevitable delays interfered with his prized routine, which until now had been the guarantee of normalcy for Nicholas as well as tangible proof that he was properly discharging his responsibilities as tsar.

Clearly, some form of drastic action was in order, but its precise nature was still very much in doubt. Would Nicholas grant a constitution, or would he appoint a dictator with sweeping powers of repression? As early as October 9 Kireev's contacts at court were claiming that "matters are leading to a constitution." Despite his intensified efforts to dissuade the tsar from taking such a disastrous step, three days later Kireev had to acknowledge the persistent rumors that a constitution was imminent and that Witte would be the first minister.[36] According to Chikhachev, who had been summoned to Peterhof on October 13, Nicholas had signaled his readiness to grant a constitution.[37] Notwithstanding such rumors, however, no firm decision had yet been made.

Nicholas's own recollections of the events several days later, when the full dimensions of the crisis had of course become obvious to all, revealed a ruler content to wait helplessly:

In Moscow various congresses took place which Governor-General Durnovo permitted, I do not know why. There they prepared everything for the railroad strikes, which began around Moscow, and then immediately engulfed all Russia. . . . In the universities God knows what happened! All kind of folk walked in from the streets, every kind of abomination was expressed there—and all this was tolerated. . . . It made me sick to read the telegraphic dispatches. Nothing but strikes in educational institutions, pharmacies, etc., killings of towns people, Cossacks, and soldiers, various disorders, riots, and mutinies. And the Messrs. Ministers, like chicken-hearts, assemble and discuss how to achieve unity of all ministers instead of acting decisively.

[35] TsGAOR, f. 601, op. 1, d. 249, October 12, 1905.
[36] GBL OR, f. 126, d. 14, ll. 91–92.
[37] "Dnevnik A. A. Polovtseva," KA 4 (1923): 76.

Nicholas claimed to have taken firm steps with Trepov's aid to prevent any armed uprising, yet "the terrible quiet days began, quiet indeed, because there was complete order in the streets, but everybody knew that something was being prepared—the troops were awaiting the signal, but the others did not begin. It was the same feeling as in summer before a thunderstorm."[38] The metereological analogy betrayed the tsar's impotence. Although fully informed about the events, he appeared paralyzed. He faulted the authorities for their indecision and inaction, only to concede the futility of opposing a natural force.

When Nicholas finally broke his silence on October 13 with a telegram to Witte, it was to do exactly what he would later fault his ministers for doing—to promote government unity:

> Until confirmation of the law about the cabinet I instruct you to unify the activity of the Ministers, for whom I set the goal of establishing order everywhere. Only if state life flows calmly, will it be possible for the government to work constructively and jointly with the freely elected representatives of my people.[39]

Nicholas had failed to address Witte's proposals for constitutional reform. Instead he went along with the new consensus on the need for ministerial unity. He did so in time-honored autocratic fashion, i.e., not by altering the institutional framework through legal procedure, but in an impromptu way, by entrusting a particular individual with the task. In the absence of any legal-institutional safeguards there was no guarantee, of course, that the change would be effective or that it would not be reversed by yet another ad hoc personnel decision. For the time being, Nicholas had simply deferred his decision on how ministerial unity could be realized or how society was to be appeased.

It appeared as though the tsar hoped to enlist Witte's services without granting him the broad authority and the concessions that Witte had stipulated three days earlier. Sensing these reservations and unwilling to undertake the proffered assignment without such assurances, Witte journeyed to Peterhof on the 14th to press Nicholas for further concessions. As Nicholas noted in his diary, he and Witte talked for a long time—before lunch and throughout the afternoon—about a "program of future measures."[40] Unification alone without other decisive measures, Witte told the emperor, would do little to calm the troubled nation. Instead of the manifesto draft suggested by Nicholas, Witte submitted a report that

[38] Nicholas's letter to Maria Fedorovna, October 19, 1905, TsGAOR, f. 642, op. 1, d. 2328, ll. 11–14; or "Perepiska Nikolaia II i Marii Fedorovny," KA 22 (1927): 166–69.

[39] Witte Collection, REEACU, carton 20, item 10 (original) and 1 (copy); see, too, Witte, Vospominaniia, 3:12.

[40] TsGAOR, f. 601, op. 1, d. 249; and KFZ, October 14, 1905.

he described as a summary of his memorandum and that the tsar was to confirm. A manifesto, Witte objected, could not go into the necessary details. By the same token, publication of an imperially sanctioned report merely signified Nicholas's acceptance of the program contained therein, but put the responsibility for the proposed measures on the writer, Witte, without tying the tsar's hands.[41]

Witte's stance was odd, to say the least. On the one hand, he was promoting far-reaching constitutional reforms and civil liberties, the details of which were not appropriate for or could not be compressed into a manifesto. On the other hand, he insinuated that such a manifesto would publicly commit the tsar to such reforms once and for all, thus making it impossible for him to disavow these concessions later.

The tsar remained to be persuaded. Later that night Witte learned by telephone from Prince Orlov, the acting head of the emperor's personal chancellery, that he was to return to Peterhof the following day with the draft of a manifesto. Such a manifesto was necessary, Witte was told, "so that everything would issue personally from the Sovereign, and [in order to] elevate the measures mentioned in his report from the province of promises to the realm of facts granted by the Sovereign."[42] Nicholas wanted both the facts and the credit. Two of Witte's associates drafted a manifesto during the night and on their way to Peterhof, where they accompanied Witte the next morning.[43] There the tsar and Witte continued their discussions for some four hours in the presence of the Grand Duke Nikolai, Nicholas's cousin and the new commander of the St. Petersburg military district, as well as Minister of Court Frederiks and Adjutant-General O. B. Rikhter, both of them trusted advisors. The very makeup of this conference suggests that the alternative of establishing some form of military rule was still very much on the emperor's mind. Primarily for the benefit of the Grand Duke, Witte essentially restated the contents of his earlier memorandum and submitted to detailed questioning. In the afternoon, Witte produced the revised manifesto draft, but once again he expressed his preference for an imperially sanctioned report.[44] The conference ended without resolving the matter.

That same night Nicholas not only consulted with Frederiks, Goremykin, and Budberg, the head of the Imperial Chancellery on Petitions,[45] but also solicited Trepov's advice. Through Frederiks the tsar asked his trusted governor-general to respond with complete candor after

[41] Witte, *Vospominaniia*, 3:13.

[42] Ibid., p. 14.

[43] Ibid., pp. 14, 20–22, 27–28.

[44] TsGAOR, f. 601, op. 1, d. 249; and *KFZ*, October 15, 1905; Witte, *Vospominaniia*, 3:14, 20–22, 27–28.

[45] TsGAOR, f. 601, op. 1, d. 249; and *KFZ*, October 15, 1905—10:15 P.M.

reading Witte's memorandum and manifesto draft. He also wanted to know how much longer order could be preserved without the shedding of blood and, somewhat contradictorily, whether order could be restored without excessive losses. Despite the advanced hour an officer was standing by to take back Trepov's answer, for Nicholas wanted to reach a decision the next morning.[46] At the same time, Prince Orlov, the acting chancellery head, apparently took it upon himself to write Trepov a "Dear Mitia" letter that not only urged haste but seemed to suggest how Trepov should respond:

> My personal opinion is that there are unnecessary phrases in the Manifesto concerning sedition, that it is useless to talk like that about force, that it would be possible to mention it only in passing, and better to show force in deeds than to refer to it again in writing. Reforms have to be granted, indisputably, and by the Sovereign personally, but not by the future government. Witte must be *finished* on these grounds.[47]

In his answer, Trepov responded point for point to the Witte program and to the tsar's questions. While endorsing freedom of the press, conscience, assembly, and association in principle, he warned that if Nicholas was serious about taking the road to freedom, he would have to continue to put up with injustice and unfairness until new laws could be implemented and court personnel could be retrained to prevent abuses. As for equality under the law, Trepov maintained, it applied mainly to Jews. Although inevitable in the long run, it would be a political mistake to emancipate them completely and suddenly, before the "consciousness of the indigenous Russian population" had developed sufficiently to "protect" themselves from the Jews. Turning to Witte's draft manifesto, Trepov followed Orlov's advice and ruled out any threats. It was to contain only what Nicholas wanted to grant his subjects, "and I do not believe that you want to grant a universal, direct, equal, and direct franchise." Such an electoral law should be worked out carefully and completely before being announced, with "the Prussian constitution (there is no need to be afraid of this word)" and its three-tier franchise as a possible moderate precedent. Even before the Duma convened, however, elected elements should be included in the State Council. Article 3 had to be redrafted so that laws would take effect not only with the Duma's but with the State Council's and the tsar's approval as well. Trepov also urged that the article on the inviolability of person be excluded for lack of time, money, and adequately trained personnel. Finally, Trepov confessed

---

[46] Frederiks's letter to Trepov, marked "Highly Secret"; "K istorii manifesta 17 oktiabria 1905 goda," *Byloe* 14 (1919): 109.

[47] Prince Orlov's letter to Trepov, October 15, 1905, ibid: 109–10.

openly that he could not guarantee the avoidance of bloodshed, since sedition had spread too far. In the last analysis, however, Nicholas was the best judge: "I believe that the Tsar's heart is in God's hand. Pray to the Lord and He will strengthen and not desert you." As an afterthought, Trepov also suggested that Nicholas establish his own personal cabinet "to consider and represent you on all questions of both military and civil administration" under the new constitutional arrangement.[48]

Now that even Trepov had joined the ranks of the "constitutionalists," there was little for Nicholas to do but bow to the inevitable. Within hours after receiving Trepov's letter, the tsar had made up his mind. He wrote to Trepov:

> You are the only one of my servants on whom I can rely *completely*. I thank you with all my heart for your devotion to me, for zealous service to the motherland, and for rare honesty and straightforwardness. I was touched by your letter . . . written during the night despite your exhaustion . . . so clear and systematic. It *significantly* eased the difficulty of making a final decision on the question of entering onto the path of very broad reforms. I recognize the whole solemnity and significance of the moment Russia is living through and implore the merciful Lord to bless with His Providence all of us and the great deed completed by my own hand. Yes, Russia is being granted a constitution. There were not many of us who fought against it. But support in this struggle was to be found nowhere, every day an ever-larger number of people turned away from us, and in the end the inevitable happened! Nonetheless, in my conscience I prefer to grant *everything at once* than to be compelled in the near future to yield bit by bit and still arrive at the same result. Once again I thank you heartily. Your sincere friend Nikolai.[49]

This autocratic swan song left no doubt that Nicholas was yielding to the superiority of numbers and the consensus that had evolved in favor of constitutional concessions.

At this point only the precise wording of these reforms remained to be resolved. In the course of that same day, October 16, Nicholas resumed his discussions with Goremykin, Frederiks, and Budberg "about the editing of the manifesto."[50] Witte heard of these talks from Frederiks and his assistant, General Mosolov, who together came after midnight to see him. When shown the two manifesto drafts proposed by Budberg and Goremykin, Witte labeled them unacceptable. Whereas his own draft simply instructed the government to carry out the tsar's immutable will to grant liberties, Witte claimed, the new drafts contained an outright

[48] Trepov's letter to Nicholas, October 16, 1905, TsGAOR, f. 543, op. 1, d. 232, ll. 1–4; see, too, *Byloe* 14 (1919): 110–11.
[49] Nicholas's letter to Trepov, October 16, 1905, TsGAOR, f. 595, d. 45, ll. 6–7.
[50] TsGAOR, f. 601, op. 1, d. 249; and *KFZ*, October 16, 1905.

grant of all liberties by the sovereign. At the same time, the proposed manifesto omitted several important measures contained in Witte's report and would therefore cast doubt on the sincerity and firmness of the principles put forth in the report. Once again, Witte argued that publication of his report would make a manifesto unnecessary. The decision to announce the reform in an imperial manifesto, Frederiks informed him, had already been irrevocably made. In that case, replied Witte, since Nicholas evidently doubted the correctness of his views, it might be best to appoint someone who possessed the tsar's confidence and whose program enjoyed complete imperial support. Either Budberg or Goremykin would fit the bill. With feigned humility, Witte indicated his willingness to serve in whatever capacity the tsar might deem appropriate, if only as governor in some province.[51]

Why was Witte so adamant in his opposition to a manifesto, especially to the versions drafted by Goremykin and Budberg? Was Witte equivocating in his support of civil liberties, which the manifesto in its alternate variant was to grant outright? A manifesto, he had told Nicholas, would unnecessarily tie the tsar's hand and put the burden of responsibility for success or failure squarely on his shoulders. By its very nature, moreover, a manifesto was not suited to define with precision the extent and limitations of the new freedoms, nor could such a document express the spirit and the principles that infused these concessions. Those tasks, Witte argued, were best left to a longer, more nuanced programmatic position paper and to the drafting apparatus of the government.

The real issue, however, was the source of these constitutional reforms, i.e., the role of the autocrat in the reform process and his position vis-à-vis his government. Nicholas and his advisors—witness the pronouncements of Prince Orlov—insisted on the manifesto for the same reason that Witte opposed it. They wanted these liberties to issue directly from the autocrat, as favors granted by the sovereign in his infinite wisdom and his untiring concern for the welfare of his people, rather than as rights that were properly theirs and had only to be spelled out by the government. Such favors had always been announced from the heights of the throne in the form of an imperial manifesto, which was read aloud in the churches and posted in every government office; there was no reason why it should be any different this time. Just such a break is what Witte had in mind, however. He deliberately wanted to make a distinction between the person of the sovereign and his government, between personal and institutionalized authority. The government, with the consent of the sovereign, was to propose a set of principles and reforms that had the implied approval of the people, or, as Witte was to write somewhat

[51] Witte, *Vospominaniia*, 3:17.

lamely in his memoirs, would even be submitted for legislative sanction.[52] Not coincidentally, of course, such a procedure would also have served to strengthen the position of the government and its chairman vis-à-vis the monarch, as Nicholas and his associates were quick to perceive.

The conflict ended in compromise. Summoned to Peterhof once again, Witte learned from Frederiks upon his arrival in the afternoon of October 17 that the tsar, after consulting with the Grand Duke Nikolai once more, had decided to sign Witte's version of the manifesto *and* to confirm his report. The ceremony took place at five o'clock in the presence of the Grand Duke, Witte, and Frederiks. It was, as Nicholas recorded in his diary, the anniversary of the railroad wreck at Borki,[53] from which, as by a miracle, Alexander III and his family had escaped unharmed. The Grand Duke, too, reportedly commented on the coincidence: "Today is the seventeenth—that's an important date. Twice on this day the imperial family has been saved."[54] Reacting to the signing of the manifesto— he failed to mention the report—the tsar wrote: "After such a day my head became heavy, and my thoughts began to get confused. Lord help us, save and pacify Russia."[55]

In an attempt to rationalize and defend his momentous decision before himself, his mother, and the sacred memory of his father, Nicholas reconstructed the events and the wrenching emotional turmoil of the past few days for the benefit of Maria Fedorovna:

> The choice of one of two paths was presented: to appoint an energetic military man and try to crush the rebellion with all available force; then there would be a breathing spell and after several months we would again be compelled to apply force; but that would have cost rivers of blood and in the end would inevitably have led to the same situation as now; i.e., the authority of the government would have been demonstrated, but the result would have remained the same and reforms could not have been carried out. The other path was to grant the population civil rights—freedom of speech, press, assembly, and association, and the inviolability of person; furthermore, the obligation to guide every legislative project through the State Duma—that, in essence, is a constitution.[56]

The choice was an illusory one; in reality, there was none. As Nicholas went on to explain, for lack of a viable alternative he had to overcome his own personal misgivings and enter the constitutional path:

---

[52] Ibid., p. 33.

[53] TsGAOR, f. 601, op. 1, d. 249, October 17, 1905.

[54] Witte, *Vospominaniia*, 3:53, and for a slightly different version, p. 31.

[55] TsGAOR, f. 601, op. 1, d. 249, October 17, 1905.

[56] TsGAOR, f. 642, op. 1, d. 2328, ll. 13–14, October 19, 1905; or "Perepiska Nikolaia II i Marii Fedorovny," *KA* 22 (1927): 166–69.

Witte hotly insisted on this path, claiming that while it is risky, it is neverthe-less the only one at the present moment. Almost all to whom I put this ques-tion gave the same answer as Witte and said that there was no other way out. He declared bluntly that if I wanted to appoint him chairman of the Council of Ministers, I would have to consent to his program and not interfere with his actions. The Manifesto was drawn up by him and Aleksei Obolenskii. We dis-cussed it for two days and, finally, after praying, I signed it. My dear Mama, you can't imagine how much I suffered until then. I could not explain to you by telegram all the circumstances which led me to this frightful decision, which nevertheless I made completely consciously. This was what they screamed for, wrote for, begged for from all over Russia. Around me I heard the same from many, very many people, there wasn't anyone I could rely on except for honest Trepov—there was no other way out left than to cross myself and to grant what everybody was asking for. My only consolation is the hope that such is God's will, that this grave decision will lead my dear Russia out of the intolerable chaos in which she has found herself for almost a year.[57]

From her safe haven in Denmark, Alexander III's widow showed un-derstanding for her son's predicament and bestowed her blessings:

It is difficult to believe that all this has been happening in Russia! In the end you could not act otherwise, God helped you out of this terrible and more than agonizing situation, and I am convinced that with your deep faith He will fur-ther help you and support you in your good intentions. He reads in the hearts and sees with what patience and humility you bear the heavy cross He has placed on you.[58]

Nicholas's account left no doubt where his true sympathies lay; he had finally consented to a "constitution" against his own better judgment and with immense pain. Though his attitudes had not necessarily changed, his own isolation, public clamor, and the panic of his entourage had ruled out any other path. Everyone had abandoned him except for loyal Tre-pov, and even he by the very end had recommended constitutional re-form. Nicholas's own mother had strongly urged her son to seek out Witte's advice and aid, "the only man who can help you and be of use . . . because now he surely is well-disposed, a man of genius, energetic, and clear-sighted."[59] And Witte in turn had made his appointment con-ditional on the acceptance of his constitutional program and on complete freedom of action.

Nicholas's entire description reveals how little events were structured

[57] Ibid.

[58] "Perepiska Nikolaia II i Marii Fedorovny," *KA* 22: 171–72, November 1, 1905.

[59] Ibid: 165–66, October 16, 1905. Nicholas's letter suggests, however, that his mother's letter arrived only on the 19th.

ı his own mind. He comes across as a passive object enveloped by form-
ıess chaos, carried along by an unfathomable fate to which he has no
choice but to submit. While claiming to have granted his people civil
rights and a legislative voice—"in essence . . . a constitution"—in a fully
conscious way, the tsar made it clear that he had bowed to the unanimous
consensus and expectations of his entourage, to say nothing of Witte's
virtual ultimatum or of God's will, of course. Circumstances had forced
this decision upon Nicholas. The dangers of this justification are obvious:
if those circumstances or external expectations changed once again, he
might well reconsider. He would also nurture resentment and distrust
toward those whom he blamed for extracting the October Manifesto from
him, in particular toward Witte. Having swallowed the bitter constitutional pill, the tsar expected order to return virtually overnight. If order
failed to materialize or, conversely, if the original need disappeared and
order was restored, he might even feel free to take back what he had
granted so unwillingly in the first place.

Although Nicholas's rhetoric suggested the role of the Sovereign Emperor (Gosudar' Imperator) and the institutionalization of authority that
had entrusted the fate of the country to a unified cabinet with its own
program for restoring domestic tranquility, the very remoteness prescribed by such an arrangement masked his lack of personal conviction
and fealty to that role. On the face of things, he could play the constitutional monarch, yet in reality be distant and divorced. In his own eyes at
least, Nicholas still remained free to embrace other models. By the same
token, in the absence of any real commitment and internalized content
on Nicholas's part, Witte and others could invest the monarch's role with
whatever meaning they preferred. Thus, differing conceptions of the October acts vied with each other, influencing and in turn influenced by the
reality they sought to define.

The wording of the manifesto's three main articles had not been
changed, Trepov's criticisms notwithstanding; these articles stated:

We impose upon the Government the obligation to carry out Our inflexible
will:

1. To grant the population the unshakeable foundations of civil liberty based
   on real personal inviolability, freedom of conscience, speech, assembly,
   and association.
2. Without halting the scheduled elections to the State Duma, to admit now
   to participation in the Duma, as far as is possible in the short time remaining before its convocation, those classes of the population who at
   present are totally deprived of the franchise, leaving the further development of the principle of a universal electoral law to the newly established legislative order.

3. To establish as an unbreakable rule that no law can become effective without the approval of the State Duma, and that the elected representatives of the people be guaranteed the opportunity for actual participation in supervising the legality of the actions of the authorities established by Us.[60]

Not only did Nicholas promise a considerably expanded electoral law in time for the Duma elections, but he seemed to hold out the possibility of a universal franchise in the not-so-distant future. While granting the Duma at least a veto right in all legislation, the manifesto did not define what constituted a law—a major problem both in the past and in the future. Moreover, the third article remained conspicuously silent concerning both the roles of the tsar and State Council in the legislative process and the Duma's powers to initiate bills. Yet the grant of such a veto right meant that the government would be dependent on the support of the Duma and hence of society, or at least parts thereof. The guiding thought behind the constitutional reforms announced in October 1905, Kryzhanovskii would later argue, was for the government to divest itself of part of its responsibilities and to strike a new balance of responsibilities with parts of society.[61] This did not mean, however, that the government had abandoned its claim to direct events and society—quite to the contrary, if Witte's memorandum and report are to be believed.

Witte's imperially sanctioned report represented a much tamer and briefer version of his original memorandum. It had been shorn of its harsh criticisms, its dire predictions, and, significantly, of some of its all-important details, but many of the underlying ideas were left intact. Witte reaffirmed his belief that the people's needs and ideas must determine their form of government, which was neither sacrosanct nor immutable: "Russia has outgrown the form of its existing order. She is striving for a legal order based on civil liberty. Therefore the external forms of Russian life must be raised to that level of ideas animating the moderate majority of society." The offensive word "constitution" had been replaced by the more innocuous "legal order." Civil liberties, the basic elements of this legal order, were to be established immediately, without awaiting legislative approval. The strengthening of these freedoms and the implementation of equality before the law was to take place by regular legislative procedure: "The next task of the Government is to establish those institutions and those legislative norms that correspond to the emerging political ideal of the majority of Russian society and that pro-

---

[60] N. I. Lazarevskii, *Zakonodatel'nye akty perekhodnago vremeni (1904–1908 gg.)*, 3d ed. (St. Petersburg, 1909), pp. 152–56.

[61] *Padenie tsarskago rezhima*, 5:380.

vide a positive guarantee for the inalienability of the granted blessings of civil liberty. This task will lead to the construction of a legal order."

In its actions the government would be bound by the following general principles:

1. Frankness and sincerity in the establishment of all the newly granted blessings of civil liberty and guarantees for this liberty.
2. A desire to eliminate extraordinary regulations.
3. Coordination of the activities of all Government organs.
4. Avoidance of repressive measures against actions that do not threaten society and the State.
5. Opposition to all actions clearly threatening society and state, in conformance with the law and in spiritual union with the moderate majority of society.

As he had in his original memorandum, Witte urged the implementation of the December 12, 1904, ukase, as well as total noninterference in the impending Duma elections. All government actions had to uphold the prestige of the Duma and refrain from opposing its decisions "as long as these decisions will not, as is likely, radically diverge from Russia's greatness achieved in her thousand-year history." What precisely constituted this greatness, Witte did not say. Since the apostles of autocratic government equated Russia's grandeur with the autocracy, this clause might conceivably be used to defend the inviolability of this tradition, even though such an interpretation would not necessarily be in keeping with the rest of Witte's report.[62] Witte also reminded Nicholas of his pledge of August 6 to adapt the Duma to the demands of the times, with the sentiments of a majority in society to act as guide. Similarly, the State Council was to be reorganized to include elected elements.

As far as Witte was concerned, Russia had irrevocably entered the path toward a constitution; he then went on to caution against exaggerated expectations of immediate results:

The foundations of government activity outlined here in brief require significant legislative work and systematic administrative management for their full implementation. Some time is bound to elapse between the most sincere enunciation of a principle and its realization in legislative norms, and in particular between the introduction of these norms into the customs of society and the practices of governmental agents. The principles of a legal order are realized only to the degree that the population becomes accustomed to them—civic experience. No government is able at once to prepare a country, with a het-

---

[62] Interestingly enough, in his penultimate draft Witte had written, "diverge from the tasks and obligations of authority," a wording that was more in keeping with government tutelage.

erogeneous population of 135 million and an extensive administration brought up on different principles, to accept and assimilate the norms of a legal order. For this reason, it is far from sufficient for authority to come forward with the motto of civil liberty. Effort and untiring firmness are needed to restore order in the country.

Pleading for time and patience, Witte appeared to acknowledge that government servitors and parts of society might be slow to adjust to the newly proclaimed Rechtsstaat tenets. In conclusion, Witte appealed for "the broad and active cooperation of society" and for public peace: "One must believe in the political tact of Russian society. It cannot be that Russian society should desire anarchy, which in addition to all the horrors of war threatens the dismemberment of the state."[63] From Witte's point of view, the manifesto and the report accompanying it did not signify the beginning of a constitutional order, merely the government's intentions to establish such an order. In this sense, Witte was far more realistic than Nicholas in regarding the acts of October 17 as a first step on a long and arduous road ahead, though not even he would be prepared for the events that followed.

In retrospect, Witte's heated objections to the issuance of the manifesto are perfectly understandable. Not only did the cautious wording, the repeated warnings and qualifiers, of Witte's report contrast with the sweeping statements of the tsar's manifesto, but, more importantly, behind their simultaneous publication loomed two divergent understandings of autocratic government. On the one hand, the manifesto embodied the myth of the unlimited autocrat who granted a quasi-zemskii sobor to his people. Here personal, patriarchal authority was identified with and indistinguishable from state and administration. Witte's concern, on the other hand, had been to establish himself and the government he now headed as an intermediary between the autocrat and society, an effort that was bound to be regarded with suspicion by both. His imperially sanctioned report represented the ideal of a "legal order," in which depersonalized, institutionalized bureaucratic authority was separate from that of the sovereign. This was the notion of a modern bureaucratic state headed by someone other than the ruler. While excluding the person of the monarch, this state laid claim to his unlimited power in order to shape and refashion actively the institutions of social and political life as it saw fit. Consciously or not, October 17 thus marked a superficial compromise between conflicting conceptions, which was to be sorely tested in the days and months to come—with far-reaching political and personal consequences.

[63] TsGIA, f. 1276, op. 1, d. 36, ll. 1–2 ob.; ll. 34–38 (penultimate draft, with editorial changes pencilled in by Witte); see, too, Lazarevskii, *Zakonodatel'nye akty*, pp. 152–56.

CHAPTER VIII

The Restoration of Order

THE PROCLAMATION of the October Manifesto and the simultaneous confirmation of Witte's report, as everyone from Nicholas on down agreed,
was truly a historic occasion. In a telegram congratulating the tsar for
"this act of statesmanly wisdom, inspired by your selfless love for the
Russian people," Count Sol'skii spoke of a "new era of Russian history.
. . . [M]illions will forever bless your name."[1] After reading the manifesto
to the assembled members of the State Council, which he chaired,
Sol'skii declared that the document "gives Russia the state structure
adopted by all civilized peoples, and grants the whole multimillion population of the Empire the fundamentals of civil liberty." Sol'skii's brief
remarks were also significant for what they did not say: the word "autocrat" never once crossed his lips.[2] An era had ended and with it Russia's
uniqueness. The dawning of the constitutional age would bring Russia
the forms and benefits of Western government and thus confirm its place
among the advanced nations on earth.

Or so it appeared. The fact is that the new acts meant different things
to different people, with nary a hint of agreement. As long as the all-
important details and wording of the announced reforms and even some
of the general principles underlying them had yet to be worked out, their
precise meaning and implications remained very much in dispute. Considerable time would elapse between October 17 and the publication of
the amended franchise on December 12, 1905, of the State Council and
Duma charters on February 20, 1906, and of the Fundamental Laws on
April 23, 1906. These delays raised doubts in the minds of those favoring
the advent of a new order, and hopes among those still unreconciled to
the demise of the old. The ensuing void left people of all persuasions free
to speculate and to express their demands and frustrations, while members of society and the government alike sought the answers to important
questions: Had the autocrat's power been limited once and for all, had
Russia really been granted a constitution, or would the old regime endure behind the new façade of October 17?[3]

Likened by one observer to "the goddess Athena springing in full ar-
mor from the head of Zeus," the October Manifesto had come as an utter

---

[1] TsGAOR, f. 601, op. 1, d. 1431, l. 120, October 18, 1905.

[2] TsGIA, f. 1276, op. 1, d. 36, l. 23, October 21, 1905.

[3] Cf. the reaction of Naumov, *Iz utselevshikh vospominanii*, 2:17.

surprise to everyone. With most of the country's railroads, postal and telegraphic services, and newspapers laid low by strikes, rumors took the place of hard facts. Total confusion reigned as some officials chose to play it safe by doing nothing, while others, wittingly or not, acted in flagrant violation of the newly enunciated principles. Even when communications of one kind or another were restored, the information transmitted was often incomplete and contradictory. Telegraphic inquiries from provincial and local authorities asked the Interior Ministry for confirmation of the manifesto's authenticity and wording. Less conscientious governors ordered that posters and newspapers with the text of the manifesto be confiscated. Until the belated arrival of Witte's report and clarifying instructions from the center, there was no clue at all as to whether existing laws and statutes remained in force or had been superseded by new ones.[4]

The very confusion surrounding the new acts in official circles only served to heighten public suspicions, as government agents were accused either of attempting to suppress or distort the tsar's act of charity toward his people or of ignoring its provisions. Dissatisfied and distrustful protestors vied and frequently clashed with loyal crowds who were demonstrating their gratitude for the newly granted liberties, while loyalists of another sort, the so-called Black Hundreds, sought to hunt down all enemies of autocracy: "Jews," "socialists," "liberals," "revolutionaries," "traitors," "foreigners," "professionals," or whatever they chose to call their prey. The major cities of the Empire—Moscow, Kiev, Odessa, Warsaw, and others—were rocked by disorders on October 18 and 19 and in the days that followed; the situation was still more confused and worrisome in many remote localities without rail or postal services.[5] Even when Witte's report, together with official confirmations and clarifications, finally reached the outlying areas, public agitation did not subside—quite the contrary.

So pervasive were the doubts regarding the government's sincerity, so contradictory its signals, that none other than Count Vorontsov-Dashkov, the enlightened Caucasian viceroy who had always enjoyed the emperor's trust, felt compelled to intervene. He warned Nicholas that only a victory of the "sensible party" in Russia could guarantee the pacification of his region and presumably of other areas as well:

[4] Liubimov, "Russkaia smuta," pp. 326–28; Witte, *Vospominaniia* 3:72–73. Fear of just such confusion had been his reason for opposing the issuance of a manifesto, Witte would later claim. By announcing the main tenets of reform without providing any details, the manifesto also supposedly forced the pace of all subsequent government measures, which therefore often bore the stamp of haste and imperfection. Yet he defended the act as historically necessary surgery; ibid., pp. 46–47.

[5] Liubimov, "Russkaia smuta," pp. 327–28; Witte, *Vospominaniia*, 3:137.

The essential condition for this pacification is the strict observance of the principles proclaimed by Your Majesty's manifesto of October 17. Any hint of a violation of these principles stirs up the minds and inclines people toward new manifestations of force in the form of strikes, street disorders, and political assassinations. All our hope rests on the State Duma and the representatives of the [central government] . . . but if a repressive reaction begins in Russia, and measures are taken that do not correspond to the words of the manifesto, then there is no doubt that this will provoke large disorders in the Caucasus.[6]

How could the government possibly hope to allay popular fears and apprehensions when even one of its most eminent representatives had not remained immune to them?

The constitutional elixir had proven far less potent than either the emperor or Witte had expected. Far from soothing the public, it only aggravated the revolutionary condition. Trepov reported to Witte on October 20 that the government's most recent concessions were being interpreted as a sign of weakness and exploited by those with more radical ambitions.[7] In fact, the disorganization and disintegration of authority was felt from metropolitan areas to isolated rural hamlets, drawing into question the legitimacy of all superordinate authority and creating a palpable sense of possibility for challenging the established order and improving one's own fortunes.[8]

At the center of this confusion stood the tsar and his new first minister, Witte. Their relationship, problematic even before October, was made still more difficult by the fact that it did not exist in a vacuum, but was subject to the ties and pulls of reality around them. Although he had promised Witte a free hand, Nicholas would scrutinize Witte's every move and react to his statements and actions. These reactions depended on the tsar's own reading of the situation, his personal preferences, and the opinions of others. Witte, in turn, had to contend with widely diverging and changing expectations, be they those of Nicholas, those of the tsarist entourage, or those of society, in implementing his program. His plans, Witte would learn to his chagrin, did not accord with the political realities; as a result, he found himself torn between his own conception of bureaucratic order and the exigencies of the moment, confounding his admirers and swelling the ranks and voices of his detractors.

Given Nicholas's failure either to develop a consistent and coherent conception of his most recent announcement or to agree with Witte's underlying rationale, the contradictions that characterized both his own and Witte's views were bound to communicate themselves to the govern-

[6] "Pis'ma I. I. Vorontsova-Dashkova Nikolaiu Romanovu (1905–1915 gg.)," *KA* 26 (1928): 101–2.

[7] TsGAOR, f. 102: 1905, d. 2540.

[8] While admitting the "complete disorganization of authority," Witte denied somewhat lamely that it was confused or had no plan of action; *Vospominaniia*, 3:73.

ment and to the public. In his letter to his mother, the tsar complained about just this uncertainty and the revolutionary dangers it had created:

> Although I am now receiving lots of very touching declarations of gratitude and sympathy, the situation is still very serious. The people have gone completely mad, many from joy, others from discontent. The local authorities, moreover, do not know how to apply the new rules—nothing has been worked out, everything goes by gentleman's agreement. The very next day Witte realized what a task he had taken upon himself. Many whom he asked to take this or that position are now turning him down. . . . [O]rder must be supported in the cities, where two kinds of demonstrations, loyal and hostile, are taking place with bloody clashes between them. We are in the midst of a full-scale revolution, with the entire administration of the country disorganized; in this lies the main danger.[9]

Standing at the apex of this order, Nicholas was understandably concerned with its all-too-evident disintegration, and he looked to Witte to reverse the descent into chaos. It was in order to bring about domestic peace that the tsar had turned to the international peacemaker Witte as a last resort and had reluctantly consented to his reform program. Now he was waiting warily for the program's author to deliver on his promises. Left with little choice but to give the new chairman of the Council of Ministers a free hand, the tsar found it difficult to overcome his emotional and intellectual aversion to the path chosen by Witte; he would maintain his distance, yet be quick to criticize.

Witte was well aware of Nicholas's misgivings and his longing for an immediate return of domestic tranquility. Without it, both his ministry and his projected reforms were doomed, as Witte understood only too well; but he also must have realized that once peace returned he and his agenda might become expendable. These irreconcilable realizations were the source of much anxiety on Witte's part. Whereas for Nicholas the pacification of Russia was the all-important goal, for Witte it was only a prerequisite and a means to a much greater end—the remaking of Russia. Whether viewed as end or means, however, the restoration of order became the testing ground for Russia's first prime minister and his relationship with the tsar.

THE NEW GOVERNMENT

As the head of the new government and the author of the October program, Witte was the center of attention for everyone, whether the tsar, his entourage, the bureaucracy, or society. A deluge of telegrams from organizations and private citizens at home and abroad greeted his ap-

[9] TsGAOR, f. 642, op. 1, d. 2328, ll. 13–14, October 19, 1905; or "Perepiska Nikolaia II i Marii Fedorovny," *KA* 22 (1927): 166–69.

pointment. They expressed thanks and praise for the October Manifesto, credited Witte personally with inaugurating a new era, and declared their faith in his leadership.[10] He clearly was the man of the hour, "the only person whose name is pronounced on both the right and the left," as Kuz'min-Karavaev, Witte's advisor, would later tell him: "There are no other names in Russia."[11] Witte wasted no time in seeking to implement two key sections of his blueprint: the unification of government under a first minister, with cabinet members of his own choosing, and the manipulation of public opinion in order to build support within society.

Nicholas evidently gave Witte free rein in picking his ministerial colleagues.[12] The only holdovers from the old regime would be the ministers of foreign affairs, war, navy, and the court, areas still considered the tsar's personal responsibility, as well as Minister of Justice Manukhin, whom Witte respected. The rest were to be replaced by other bureaucrats or, as Witte hoped, public men—representatives of society. His attempts to recruit men who represented the public or at least enjoyed its respect began in earnest on October 19 but came to naught a week later.[13] Commenting on Witte's troubles in forming a cabinet, Nicholas wrote to his mother: "All this week I have bid farewell to the ministers and offered new ones their jobs. Witte asked me about these changes before, but not all of his candidates have agreed. Generally, he did not expect his position to present so many difficulties."[14]

The main sticking point in these negotiations appears to have been the reputation of Witte's candidate for the crucial post of minister of internal affairs, Assistant Minister P. N. Durnovo. From the outset, the public men had called Durnovo unacceptable on account of his responsibility for past police practices. His presence, moreover, would concentrate all effective power in the hands of old-time bureaucrats, leaving the public men to be little more than window-dressing, discredited in the eyes of

[10] Represented among the hundreds of senders of telegrams were town dumas, zemstvo boards, noble assemblies, volost' assemblies, bourse committees, merchant organizations, banks, mine and factory owners, homeowners, railway workers, peasants, and, yes, even the Stammtisch of the Altdeutsche Weinkneipe, the regular patrons of a local wine pub in Cologne, Germany; TsGIA, f. 1276, op. 1, d. 32.

[11] Kuz'min-Karavaev's letter to Witte, November 2, 1905, Witte Collection, REEACU.

[12] Nicholas's letter to Maria Fedorovna, October 19, 1905, TsGAOR, f. 642, op. 1, d. 2328, l. 13, or "Perepiska," KA 22 (1927): 168: "The ministers are departing and have to be replaced, but that is Witte's business."

[13] For a more detailed and complete description of this entire curious episode, see V. I. Startsev, Russkaia burzhuaziia i samoderzhavie v 1905–1917 gg. (Leningrad, 1977), pp. 10–22, which in turn is based in its entirety on the published reminiscences of Witte, Shipov, Guchkov, Miliukov, and Petrunkevich. Cf., too, my "Nicholas and the Role of the Autocrat," pp. 435–36.

[14] TsGAOR, f. 642, op. 1, d. 2328, ll. 15–16, October 27, 1905; also in "Perepiska Nikolaia II i Marii Fedorovny," KA 22 (1927): 169–70.

both the public and their more radical confrères. Witte, while acknowledging the objections to Durnovo, in retrospect blamed the public men's rejection of the proffered ministerial portfolios on their fear of terrorist bombs and revolvers which were then threatening all bearers of authority.[15]

Witte's insistence on Durnovo's appointment in the face of vehement objections from his public interlocutors suggests that he considered Durnovo's presence in his cabinet more important than that of the public men. According to Witte, Durnovo was by far the most experienced and qualified candidate. He was a man of independent views who at one time had directed the Department of Police, had been assistant minister since 1900, and whose career, with the exception of two sexual indiscretions, had supposedly been marked by correctness and intelligence, as well as humane and enlightened attitudes.[16] The restoration of order was obviously uppermost in Witte's mind. He was pained by the manifesto's failure to quiet the fractious populace and knew that the promised reforms could be implemented only in a peaceful social environment. Realizing the need for energetic measures to restore order and seeing in Durnovo just the right man for this difficult task, Witte evidently concluded that he could not dispense with his expertise and services. As irony had it, Witte would later regret this decision as one of his main mistakes,[17] whereas the tsar, after first resisting Durnovo's appointment, came to appreciate and reward his services in putting down the revolution by force.

In opting for a bureaucrat to fill this all-important portfolio, Witte remained true to his faith in the idea of a modern bureaucratic state. With the public men out of the picture, Witte selected only experienced bureaucratic administrators and specialists in their respective fields.[18] Except for Durnovo and the new minister of education, all the men chosen owed much of their careers to Witte and had at one time or another served under him, either in the Ministry of Finance or in the Ministry of Communications. For this reason they could be expected to be loyal to Witte and his program and do more than pay lip service to the notion of a united ministry. With the exception of the trade minister—and Durnovo, of course—Witte was not to be disappointed in this regard. The choice of technocrats with considerable bureaucratic expertise bespoke

---

[15] Witte, *Vospominaniia*, 3:68, 110.

[16] *Ibid.*, pp. 73–77, 109–10; Liubimov, "Russkaia smuta," p. 351.

[17] Witte, *Vospominaniia*, 3:77.

[18] I. P. Shipov as minister of finance, N. N. Kutler as chief administrator for agriculture, K. S. Nemeshaev as minister of communications, V. I. Timiriazev as the newly created minister for trade and industry, I. I. Tolstoi as minister of education, and D. A. Filosofov as state controller.

Witte's belief in a modern bureaucracy based on professional achievement and a functional delineation of responsibilities, regulated by law, centralized, united by a common purpose, and accountable to a first minister. Even the selection of Durnovo and the retention of Manukhin as minister of justice were consistent with these principles, at least in Witte's eyes. For the first time in tsarist history someone besides the tsar had single-handedly dictated the identity of most of the ministers; by the same token, their participation in a united ministry and close identification with Witte also proved to be their undoing, for as the tsar's trust in Witte declined, so did his faith in the aides chosen by Witte.[19]

In fact, some of the very personnel changes engineered by Witte contributed directly to the erosion of Nicholas's confidence in him. Thus Finance Minister V. N. Kokovtsev submitted his resignation in the belief that the tsar, under pressure from Witte and aware of the differences between Witte and him, expected it. Reluctant to part with Kokovtsev, Nicholas offered to appoint him chairman of the State Council's Department of Economy, only to encounter vehement opposition from Witte.[20] There was little love lost between the two; Witte had passed up few opportunities to ridicule his successor as minister of finance,[21] and in his memoirs he repeatedly criticized the excessively cautious and unimaginative—i.e., typically bureaucratic—policies pursued by Kokovtsev. Suspecting him of intrigues against the recent reform measures,[22] Witte threatened a ministerial boycott of all meetings chaired or attended by Kokovtsev.[23] Faced with this ultimatum, Nicholas had no choice but to retract Kokovtsev's promised appointment. Witte's heavy-handed tactics had been successful, but at a considerable price. "I shall never forget this insolence," the tsar wrote,[24] and in his farewell address to Kokovtsev he let it be known how much pain this decision had cost him:

> My late father always told me not to change my signature unless I saw that I had acted rashly and without due consideration. As regards your appointment, I was sure that I was acting not only justly but also for the best interests of the

[19] Manukhin, Kutler, and Timiriazev were forced from office even before the end of Witte's six-month tenure, while the others found themselves dismissed into the political wilderness with their mentor, sometimes without as much as a gesture of appreciation or an honorific appointment from the emperor. Three of them returned subsequently for brief stints as ministers of trade and industry.

[20] Kokovtsov, *Out of My Past*, p. 75.

[21] P. P. Mendeleev, "Svet i teni moei zhizni (1864–1933). Obryvki vospominanii" (manuscript, REEACU), pp. 91–92.

[22] Witte, *Vospominaniia*, 3:123, 126.

[23] Witte's report, October 24, 1905, TsGAOR, f. 543, op. 1, d. 536, l. 145.

[24] Ikskul's report, October 24, 1905, "Graf S. Iu. Vitte i Nikolai II v oktiabre 1905 g.," *Byloe* 4 (1925): 107.

state, and yet I have been forced to renounce my decision and to destroy my signature. I shall never forget this, especially since I can see clearly now that there is open hostility toward you and even personal caprice. You must not judge me too severely, and I am sure you understand the state of my feelings.

Instead, Kokovtsev was made an ordinary member of the State Council.[25] Only after Witte's fall was he able to resume his ministerial career.

Similarly, the departure of Assistant Minister of Internal Affairs D. F. Trepov could not but help detract from the tsar's opinion of Witte. Trepov tendered his resignation from his ministerial responsibilities and his position as St. Petersburg governor-general on October 23, 1905, the very day that Durnovo was appointed acting minister of internal affairs.[26] As he told Nicholas, he had remained at his post in the past in the belief that he could be of service to the fatherland and his sovereign, but he no longer felt that way. His disagreement with Witte on how to implement the government's program made it impossible for him to participate in a united ministry: "Since my name and the orientation of my activity are sufficiently defined and known to all of Russia, my continued stay in Count Witte's unified government may even, in several classes of society, earn Your Majesty the reproof of insincerity." According to the government's program, its actions were to be characterized at all times by "sincerity and straightforwardness of its intentions"; unable to renege on the "straightforwardness and sincerity of my own actions," Trepov requested his release.[27] In a separate letter to Witte, Trepov explained that his name had become a red flag for many segments of society, making it impossible for him to remain in service.[28]

Although Trepov had urged its adoption the night of October 16–17, his disagreement with Witte's program was bound to raise second thoughts in the emperor's mind. "To my regret, Trepov is leaving," Nicholas wrote to his mother on October 27, immediately after criticizing Witte for some of his actions. He stated:

He warned me long ago that if Witte were appointed he could not serve with him. Although they got on with each other during the first days and Witte himself was full of praise for Trepov's actions, various kinds of difficulties constantly arose nevertheless. As painful as it may be, I had to yield to Trepov's insistent requests to relieve him; the poor fellow is completely exhausted, for none of the Messrs. Ministers helped him with anything! He acted *magnificently* during these troubled days in St. Petersburg, and it is only thanks to

[25] Kokovtsov, *Out of My Past*, p. 77.
[26] Liubimov, "Russkaia smuta," p. 349.
[27] TsGAOR, f. 543, op. 1, d. 645, ll. 18–19 (copy, ll. 6–7).
[28] Trepov's letter to Witte, October 25, 1905, Witte Collection, REEACU.

him and the amazing self-restraint of the troops that horrible bloodshed did *not* occur.

Nicholas made Trepov the new palace commandant, responsible for the security of the imperial family and the court, a post "where he will be extremely useful and can rest."[29]

Trepov had enjoyed Nicholas's boundless confidence and would continue to do so. His new position gave him daily access to the tsar as imperial confidant, advisor, and secretary. Several months after Trepov's new appointment, Nicholas confirmed how invaluable Trepov was to him: "Trepov is an indispensable secretary, in a way, for me. He is experienced, clever, and cautious in his advice. I give him Witte's bulky memoranda to read, and then he reports on them to me quickly and concisely. This, of course, is a secret to all."[30]

D. F. Trepov played an important, though ambiguous, role. He was honest, sincere, well-meaning, and above all devoted to his imperial master. One associate described him as "not dumb, with the psychology of a good, honest officer, but without any preparation for government affairs," and therefore potentially an unwitting tool for those who had access to him.[31] Upright to a fault, Trepov had little experience with and use for the personal backbiting and devious scheming typical of autocratic politics. He did not seek power for himself; instead, he wanted to protect the person and power of his sovereign. His style befitted his background as a former guards officer: direct, dutiful, and devoid of subtlety or finesse. The whole world to him was a hierarchical chain of command. Trepov would have looked askance at Witte, who had never concealed his political ambitions or his usually uncharitable estimates of others. By the same token, Trepov could well have been taken in by those who were more deferential and diplomatic than their antagonist Witte, though no less unscrupulous or ambitious.

Trepov's very frankness and sincerity recommended him to Nicholas. No matter how much he disliked or disagreed with Witte, for example, it was Trepov who on October 17 had urged the tsar not to carry out his intention of making Goremykin "head" of his own future cabinet as a counterweight to a "first minister" Witte. Such a plan, if true, would have suggested a lack of imperial trust toward Witte from the very outset. Reminding Nicholas that "I will never lie and will only say what I think and feel," Trepov had called on the tsar to display his "full trust" in Witte

[29] TsGAOR, f. 642, op. 1, d. 2328, l. 16, and "Perepiska Nikolaia II i Marii Fedorovny," *KA* 22 (1927): 170, October 27, 1905.

[30] TsGAOR, f. 642, op. 1, d. 2328, ll. 39–40, and "Perepiska," *KA* 22 (1927): 190–91, January 26, 1906.

[31] Mendeleev, "Svet i teni," pp. 95–96.

by appointing somebody "not belonging to the party of his open enemies."[32] Instead of promoting his own views, the new court commandant sought to present for the tsar's consideration the recommendations of others whom he regarded as more knowledgeable and experienced than himself, be they bureaucratic traditionalists or members of the Kadet party. As a result, both Trepov's advisors and his advice appear to have changed repeatedly. The only constants were his untiring loyalty to the emperor, his eagerness both to expose Nicholas to different opinions in good autocratic fashion and to protect the autocrat from being dominated by any one person or group. In this regard, Witte noted, his successor Goremykin would fare no better than he himself had done.[33]

Ultimately, of course, the changeability, to say nothing of the extremes, of Trepov's political advice appears to have doomed him; it also raises serious questions about the nature of his influence on Nicholas. Trepov did not possess a consistent programmatic alternative to Witte's conception nor did he argue for a return to the *status quo ante*. Nothing in his recorded utterances and written reports suggests anything other than the earnest, reasonable, and not unintelligent—by both contemporary and present standards—soldier that he was, least of all the rigid reactionary that he has been made out to be. Nicholas probably trusted and confided in Trepov precisely because he was neither a member of the hated bureaucracy nor an exponent of a particular viewpoint. For this very reason, Trepov's influence in matters of principle was bound to make itself felt only indirectly through personnel decisions. In other words, Trepov might well have affected the ways in which the tsar trusted or related to somebody like Witte or Durnovo.

Witte, in turn, viewed Trepov's mere proximity to Nicholas as a threat and a gesture of no-confidence in his own stewardship. He likened Trepov to an "Asian eunuch" who had his master's ear, was involved in all aspects of government, and was sought out by everybody who wanted to get through to the tsar. According to Witte, Trepov and his staff would draft the resolutions to be recorded by Nicholas on Witte's reports[34]; in fact, many of these resolutions are in Trepov's own handwriting. Whether justified or not, Witte's perceptions naturally colored his actions and his dealings with the tsar. Even more importantly, the precedent of this extrainstitutional, nonbureaucratic, personal relationship between tsar and military aide must have encouraged Nicholas to act out the role of the personal ruler and to feel increasing resentment toward the strictures of that impersonal and routinized rulership role repre-

---

[32] TsGAOR, f. 543, op. 1, d. 645, ll. 13–14 (copy, l. 5).

[33] Witte, *Vospominaniia*, 3:89–91.

[34] For Witte's estimation of Trepov, see *ibid*., pp. 80–83, 88–91.

sented by Witte and his united ministry. Although Witte's later claim that Trepov had been the real head of government was certainly exaggerated, there can be little doubt, in view of Trepov's previously stated beliefs, that Trepov's transfer was a blow to Witte's position.

WITTE AND PUBLIC OPINION

Witte was serious about unifying government under his leadership, the forbidding weight of tradition notwithstanding. His very first act upon assuming office had been to bring Nicholas's instructions on ministerial unification to the attention of all the old ministers, the chair and department heads of the State Council, the St. Petersburg governor-general, the Caucasian viceroy, and others. Witte asked them for information about all "the main events of a political nature" as well as specific data concerning their respective agencies.[35] Such detailed requests might well have stirred resentment among officials who were jealous of their prerogatives and autonomy and who felt accountable only to the emperor. Still, most complied.[36] Witte and his chancellery moved to the more secure and convenient location of a Winter Palace wing and became a virtual clearinghouse for information.[37] They received copies of almost every telegram that governors-general, governors, and various military commanders addressed to the tsar; in addition, many of these same officials sent separate messages directly to Witte.[38] In accordance with his instructions, Witte's ministerial colleagues also forwarded telegrams from local agencies within their jurisdictions, such as prosecutors, military commands, railroads, banks, or bourse committees. On occasion, Witte had copies of such messages sent to other ministers or included in his reports to Nicholas. As a result, Witte at times was better informed—and hence more optimistic or pessimistic—about the state and mood of the country than Nicholas.

Besides staying abreast of events throughout Russia and keeping the tsar and the cabinet advised, Witte sought to use this information to influence public opinion. Having personally edited some of the telegrams addressed to the tsar by deleting all unfavorable information, Witte

[35] TsGIA, f. 1276, op. 1, d. 36, ll. 11, 13–18; "Manifest 17 Oktiabria," *KA* 11–12 (1925): 97–98.

[36] Cf., for example, Trepov's and Durnovo's detailed reports in TsGAOR, f. 102: 1905, d. 2540.

[37] Mendeleev, "Svet i teni," p. 86.

[38] General Linevich, for instance, the commander in chief of the Far Eastern forces, between November 1905 and January 1906 reported almost daily to Witte about the situation in Vladivostok and on the Siberian railroad, even though Witte clearly stood outside of the military chain of command.

would order them to be published by the Russian Telegraphic Agency.[39] In their revised and sanitized form, these telegrams were short and to the point, giving the impression that the government and local authorities were acting firmly and that order was being restored everywhere.

Lest this message be lost on the public, Witte also launched a concerted press campaign to set the record straight and put his government's views before the public. Recognizing the importance of the press, Witte, in the words of one of his subordinates, "sought to use it for his own purposes."[40] He supervised and even had a personal hand in the drafting of articles that took issue with reports published elsewhere and that attempted to persuade the Russian and foreign public of the government's sincere determination to carry out the promised reforms.[41] To assist him in these efforts, Witte even went so far as to employ his own "press secretary," most certainly a first in the annals of tsarist government and an eloquent testimony to Witte's appreciation of public opinion and of the press's role in shaping it. His choice for this post was A. A. Spasskii-Odynets, a twenty-eight-year-old official in the Ministry of Finance with professed liberal sympathies. Hired on November 25, 1905, Spasskii, by his own reckoning, was to compile digests of the Russian press and of foreign press reports about Russia for Witte's diligent perusal; in addition, he was to write "inspirational" articles for secretly subsidized domestic and foreign organs and maintain contacts with "societal and political activists."[42]

Similarly, it had been Witte's desire to shape and steer public opinion rather than any principled belief in the public's right to take part in government affairs that had inspired his negotiations with the public men. More important than their actual participation was the public image of the government's first minister talking to the representatives of society and lending a sympathetic ear to their grievances. As early as October 18 Witte had met with journalists and editors of St. Petersburg newspapers in a bid for their support and cooperation.[43] Other meetings followed with petitioners and delegations of all kinds, including strikers from one St. Petersburg factory. A friendly Witte would shake their hands, offer them cigarettes, and talk to them at length. To a skeptical official of his chancellery he explained that it was necessary to communicate with them

[39] TsGIA, f. 1276, op. 1, d. 82.

[40] Mendeleev, "Svet i teni," pp. 102–3.

[41] E.g., TsGIA, f. 1276, op. 1, d. 36, l. 21; also, "Manifest 17 Oktiabria," KA 11–12 (1925): 99.

[42] A. A. Spasskii-Odynets, "Vospominaniia" (manuscript, REEACU), p. 23.

[43] Witte, Vospominaniia, 3:60–65; stenographic text of meeting in "Manifest 17 Oktiabria," KA 11–12 (1925): 39–106, and Liubimov, "Russkaia smuta," pp. 340–42.

and that he knew how to do it.[44] Witte was determined to repeat in Russia the courtship by which he had ingratiated himself with American public opinion during the Portsmouth peace negotiations. By talking to journalists, workers, peasants, and activists of diverse persuasions, Witte hoped to convince them of his sincerity and trustworthiness and to keep open various channels of communication. In the case of the public men, he would later insist that they parted on friendly terms; as if to assure them of his continued good will, he even asked them to discuss and present proposals for broadening the franchise, as envisioned by the October Manifesto, and for a revision of the Fundamental Laws.[45]

Ominously, Nicholas took a dim view of his first minister's efforts to woo public opinion:

> It is strange that such an intelligent man would be mistaken in his estimates regarding speedy pacification. I do not like his way of talking to various people of an extreme persuasion, especially since all these talks appear in the papers the next day and, of course, are always full of lies. I told him about this and I hope he will cease.[46]

Whether chastened by such warnings or dissatisfied with ad hoc efforts and personal contacts alone, Witte realized that the government also needed an official forum through which to present its views. By mid-December he had approved a plan calling for a new paper to complement the official *Pravitel'stvennyi Vestnik* (The Government Herald). As Witte reported to all ministers and agency heads on January 21, 1906, this paper was to be a government bulletin, appearing in the morning and printing only official acts and announcements, while a separate evening paper called *Russkoe Gosudarstvo* (The Russian State) would illuminate state and public matters from all angles, within limits "compatible with the country's normal development." Two important considerations had led to this plan, according to Witte. First, editorials would permit the government "to explain, in a form intelligible and accessible to all, the motives for this or that action, decision, or plan." It was only reasonable "that in a country with an advancing societal self-consciousness," the government's authority could best be supported through the force of reason, "with arguments acting on the private convictions of every citizen." Secondly, the opportunity to put facts systematically before Russian society would counter their constant distortion and the circulation of untrue rumors, of lies both deliberate and unconscious, which were causing great

---

[44] Mendeleev, "Svet i teni," pp. 84–86.

[45] Witte, *Vospominaniia*, 3:110; Startsev, *Russkaia burzhuaziia*, p. 20.

[46] TsGAOR, f. 642, op. 1, d. 2328, ll. 15–16, October 27, 1905; also in "Perepiska Nikolaia II i Marii Fedorovny," *KA* 22 (1927): 169–70.

harm to the state.[47] The very name chosen for the new organ reflected its backer's modern statist vantage point. *Gosudarstvo* was the depersonalized, institutionalized entity codified by Peter the Great, and *Russkoe* sounded more sober, contemporary and nationalist than the old-fashioned, if more common, *Rossiiskoe*.

The battle for the minds and loyalties of Russia's citizens was to be won by ink rather than force. Witte obviously had faith in the potency of the printed word, as these steps and his October 18 encounter with journalists attest. Although the latter had confronted him with a series of unacceptable demands for constitutional guarantees and immediate additional reforms, he continued to believe in his ability to shape the printed word and thus influence and win over its readers. To the extent that the importance of the printed word had been recognized by previous tsarist administrations, it had been only in negative terms: by repressive censorship, administrative sanctions, and the bribing of journalists. Through such restrictions the government had sought to shield what was believed to be a naive, immature, and essentially loyal readership from both untruths and truths. By contrast, Witte's more activist conception, already anticipated in Bulygin's memorandum of May 1905,[48] was predicated on a notion of society as an independent, sophisticated, mature force to be won over through the power of reason. Even the Russian peasantry, a repository of illiteracy and cultural backwardness, was not considered immune to the suggestive lure of the printed word.[49]

Witte envisioned yet another function for *Russkoe Gosudarstvo*: to acquaint the tsar with the thinking of his prime minister and to elicit his reaction if possible. On several occasions Witte instructed his "press secretary" to write anonymous articles for this purpose. One of these, as usual approved in advance, sought to determine whether Nicholas had changed his views about the implementation of the October Manifesto. Unfortunately, so obscure was the wording that he reportedly had little difficulty endorsing it.[50] Indeed, Spasskii would have us believe that Witte viewed this solicitation as the new organ's main role, though it was also meant for foreign consumption. According to Spasskii, "the decorum of communications between a faithful subject and his Sovereign" was such that even the prime minister could not speak freely in his presence and expect an equally direct answer, especially if there was any disagree-

---

[47] TsGIA, f. 1276, op. 1, d. 152, ll. 43b–44; the plan itself, ll. 4–16, was drawn up by S. S. Tatishchev, head of the Press Administration in the MIA.

[48] See *supra*, p. 200.

[49] Witte wanted the countryside flooded with copies of *Sel'skii Vestnik* (The Rural Herald), which would be made to fit the peasants' needs and appeal to their interests; draft of Witte's report of January 22, 1906, TsGIA, f. 1276, op. 1, d. 152, ll. 53–54.

[50] Spasskii-Odynets, "Vospominaniia," pp. 25–28, 39, 211.

ment to cause unpleasantness or pain to the tsar.[51] Either Witte had concluded that Nicholas could not be relied upon to give an honest answer face-to-face—since he reportedly agreed with every visitor—or Witte was so unsure of the tsar's backing that he was constantly looking for positive or negative signals. In either case, he had to resort to oblique techniques for ascertaining the emperor's true thinking.

Similarly, after reading each of the hundreds of telegrams that had begun to descend on him after October 17, Witte ordered several of them answered and made public. These published messages all emphasized that the October Manifesto represented the tsar's sacred and unbending will and hence was irrevocable. Perhaps Witte was simply hoping to reassure a suspicious public. Yet the constant repetition of such identical signals also had the effect, if not the intention, of reminding the sovereign, his government, or anyone who might entertain hopes to the contrary, that Nicholas could not go back on his word.[52]

THE PRESERVATION OF AUTOCRACY

As Witte understood only too well, it had not taken the tsar long to grow impatient with the delay in restoring order and to have second thoughts about the measures he had approved. As early as October 27, 1905, Nicholas had sent the dowager empress the following description of the most recent events:

> In the first days after the manifesto, the bad elements strongly raised their heads, but then a strong reaction set in, and the whole mass of loyal people came alive. The result was understandable and normal here: the narod was outraged by the impudence and audacity of the revolutionaries and socialists, and, since nine-tenths of them are kikes, the whole fury of the people turned against them—thus pogroms against the Jews. It is startling with what *unanimity and suddenness* this happened in all the cities of Russia and Siberia. In England, of course, they are writing that these disorders were organized by the police, as always this is the old familiar fable! But not only the kikes suffered; so did the Russian agitators, engineers, lawyers and all kinds of other bad people.

While noting some improvement in Russia's situation, he still considered it "very difficult and serious." After referring to events in specific cities, Nicholas continued: "I am receiving many telegrams from everywhere, very touching, grateful for the granting of liberty, but clearly indicating that they would like autocracy to be preserved. Why were they silent

---

[51] Ibid., pp. 207, 213, 302.
[52] TsGIA, f. 1276, op. 1, d. 3 and d. 179 passim.

before, the good people?"[53] Eight days earlier Nicholas had justified his decision to grant concessions by pointing to a vocal consensus: "This was what they screamed for, wrote for, begged for from all over Russia." Those voices, Nicholas now appeared to suggest, belonged to the bad people, "nine-tenths of them kikes," whereas the good and loyal narod, although grateful for the civil liberties, continued to defend the principles of autocracy. The clear implication was that the tsar's own feelings and course of action to a considerable extent would be determined by the reactions of the narod and by his own entourage.

In Nicholas's eyes, the silent majority of autocratic partisans was finally making itself heard after remaining silent for so long. Appeals for a show of power and a reaffirmation of traditional autocratic authority came from people in all walks of life, or at least so Nicholas imagined: from Old Believers, peasants, workers, noble assemblies, and political organizations.[54] No matter how unrepresentative or manipulated—and there is evidence of both—these opinions found a receptive ear in the tsar, who simply wanted to believe them. He paid close attention to these pleas, which confirmed his natural prejudices and inclinations, his skewed view of the causes of revolutionary unrest, and his preference for the traditional variant of autocratic power. From Nicholas's point of view, a relatively small number of revolutionaries, of bad elements, was responsible for spreading terror and insurrection throughout the Empire. As the flood of loyal messages seemed to suggest, the vast majority of Russian people were peaceloving and faithful to the precepts of autocracy, but had fallen prey to the evil designs of a few bad men: "On the railroad out there, the engineers and their assistants are Poles and kikes, the whole strike and then the revolution was organized *by them* with the help of the confused workers."[55] Referring to his own, God-given peace of mind, Nicholas would write: "It is this peace of mind which unfortunately is lacking in many Russian people. That is why the threats and intimidations of a small group of anarchists affect them so strongly." Civil courage, never in great abundance, was now hardly evident at all, Nicholas complained to his mother.[56]

Not only the "loyal narod," but Witte's opponents both within the

---

[53] TsGAOR, f. 642, op. 1, d. 2328, ll. 15–16, October 27, 1905; also in "Perepiska Nikolaia II i Marii Fedorovny," *KA* 22 (1927): 169–70.

[54] E.g., TsGIA, f. 1284, op. 241, d. 135 passim; d. 172 passim; f. 1412, op. 242, d. 179, ll. 1–6; TsGAOR, f. 601, op. 1, d. 1033; V. P. Semennikov, ed., *Revoliutsiia 1905 goda i samoderzhavie* (Moscow, 1928), p. 24.

[55] TsGAOR, f. 642, op. 1, d. 2328, ll. 33–36, or "Perepiska Nikolaia II i Marii Fedorovny," *KA* 22 (1927): 186–87, January 12, 1906.

[56] TsGAOR, f. 642, op. 1, d. 2328, ll. 23–26, or "Perepiska Nikolaia II i Marii Fedorovny," *KA* 22 (1927): 180, December 8, 1905.

court and without were making their voices heard, disparaging his efforts and encouraging the tsar to assert his autocratic powers. A meeting of diverse patriotic groups and unions in Moscow in early November heard its organizer assert the unity and indivisibility of Russia and its autocratic ruler and call for determined opposition to a constituent assembly.[57] One of the participants, the retired General Kireev from the St. Petersburg Patriotic Union, had already warned Nicholas the week before not to expand the pool of eligible voters by including workers and intelligenty. If the franchise had to be altered, then it should be done only in a conservative direction, by weighting it toward the clergy and nobility.[58] Immediately after the Moscow conclave, Kireev accused Witte of manipulating and discrediting the "poor Tsar" and of seeking popularity by favoring democratic and nihilist measures, such as a direct and universal electoral law. "Witte is not at all the strong man on whom they counted," Kireev wrote to Nicholas on November 6, 1905, "he strives for popularity with the revolutionary (and constitutional) party by making concessions to them, but *without any success*." Those who told the tsar that he was weak, that there were not enough troops and too many revolutionaries, and that the situation was hopeless were deceiving him. If only the government had decided to rely on its loyal subjects, it would have received support surpassing its wildest dreams, Kireev asserted.[59]

According to one source, D. F. Trepov served as a conduit for "adroit behind-the-scenes intrigues" launched by Witte's sworn enemies Goremykin, Krivoshein, and V. F. Trepov, the brother of the court commandant.[60] The same individuals had been implicated in Witte's temporary fall from power earlier in the year. Witte's own chancellery staff was reportedly unsympathetic to him and his policies. Without denying his intellect and other talents, they resented what they regarded as his duplicity and lack of scruples, and would have preferred to have a more traditional bureaucrat in charge.[61] Prince Orlov, a member of the tsar's personal chancellery, saw the sovereign at least once, often twice and even three times a day after October 17. Since he had been the one to urge Trepov on the very eve of that event to finish off Witte once and for all, he presumably would not have passed up any chance to make his views known to the tsar.

By the middle of November, Kireev saw Witte's star as fading. It was reported that he was struggling with Durnovo, increasingly deserted by

[57] GBL OR, f. 126, d. 14, l. 104, November 4, 1905.

[58] Ibid., l. 104, October 26, 1905.

[59] Ibid., l. 105, November 6, 1905.

[60] Mendeleev, "Svet i teni," pp. 95–96.

[61] At least this is the claim of one chancellery official, whose very favorable picture of Witte would have made him an exception to the rule; ibid., pp. 62–63, 68–70.

his allies, and disliked by the emperor.[62] On several occasions in late November and in December Kireev even speculated about possible successors to Witte, his hopes buoyed by reports that a number of individuals and delegations had visited the tsar and called upon him to get rid of Witte.[63] By the middle of December 1905 one of Nicholas's regular visitors, the director of the tsar's Chancellery for Petitions, Baron A. Budberg, even claimed to have told Nicholas of his wish to see Witte exiled abroad, or, better yet, arrested. Otherwise a secret society composed of guard officers might have to make good its threat of physically eliminating the hated first minister. The tsar neither approved nor rejected the brazen suggestion outright; instead, his reported answer, "Oh, yes," was distractedly noncommittal.[64]

"Stand up, Sovereign, with your Tsarina before the Russian people in the halo of your sacred greatness. Show yourself to all of *Rus'* in the full force of your might at the head of a government obedient to you." With this emotional appeal, A. N. Naumov, the newly elected marshall of the nobility of Samara, urged Nicholas during their audience on November 23, 1905, to reestablish authority on a firm basis and thus provide a rallying point for the country. If power was not shown, the reforms would be interpreted as a sign of weakness, not grace. At present there was more talk about Witte and a false tsar signing forged manifestos than there was about the real tsar, Naumov claimed. The choice was between Nicholas and "Khrustalev with his Union of Unions," a reference to Iu. S. Nosar'-Khrustalev, the head of the St. Petersburg Soviet of Workers' Deputies, and that soviet's connections to the oppositional umbrella organization. There was no room for compromise. Only firm and strong authority with definite policies could save Nicholas and Russia; otherwise, Russia's enemies "will start with us and finish with you!" Nicholas was apparently so moved by Naumov's plea that he told several people about it and even expressed the wish to have Naumov serve as a regular advisor. To Durnovo the tsar is said to have repeated Naumov's message almost verbatim.[65]

Although October 17 had come as a rude shock to the unreconstructed adherents of autocracy, it had also untied their hands. The new acts and Witte's return to power had given them visible targets on which to vent their spleen. Until this point, any open criticism had smacked of disloyalty toward the very person and principles they were sworn to defend.

[62] GBL OR, f. 126, d. 14, ll. 107–8, November 16–17, 1905.

[63] Ibid., ll. 110, November 26, 1905; l. 112, December 2, 1905; l. 121, December 28, 1905.

[64] Iu. B. Solov'ev, *Samoderzhavie i dvorianstvo v 1902–1907 gg.* (Leningrad, 1981), pp. 188–89.

[65] Naumov, *Iz utselevshikh vospominanii*, 2:43–47.

In the general confusion that followed the promulgation of the manifesto, however, they were free to organize and to go public with their opposition—all in the name of autocratic traditionalism.[66]

Maria Fedorovna sought to stem her son's growing disenchantment with Witte: "Witte, too, deserves great sympathy for all his terrible difficulties, particularly since he did not expect them. You must now show him your confidence and let him act according to his program."[67] This is the very message that the Russian ambassador Izvol'skii, upon his return to Copenhagen, had urged her to send; he feared that the sovereign was becoming increasingly receptive to the insinuations of a reactionary court party which alleged that Witte was aspiring to become president of a Russian republic.[68] Yet in his response Nicholas bemoaned what he diagnosed as a lack of initiative and an unwillingness to shoulder responsibility on part of Witte and his colleagues:

> They talk a lot but do little. All are afraid to act courageously; I constantly have to force them, including Witte himself, to be more decisive. Here nobody is used to assuming responsibility, and everybody expects orders which then they don't like to carry out. You write me, dear Mama, to show confidence in Witte. I can assure you that on my part I am doing everything possible to ease his difficult position. And he feels this. But I cannot hide from you some disappointment in Witte. Everybody thought that he was an awfully energetic and despotic man and that he would turn immediately toward restoring order above all.

Evidently the tsar agreed with Witte's critics that the appearances of strength and energy merely masked weakness and indecisiveness. Witte, Nicholas appeared to suggest, had misled him into expecting the immediate pacification of the country:

> He *himself* told me [while we were] still in Peterhof that as soon as the October 17 manifesto was issued, the government not only could but should vigorously introduce reforms and *not* permit violence and disorders. But almost the opposite happened—everywhere these demonstrations, then the Jewish pogroms, and, finally, the destruction of the landlords' estates. . . . The courage of the authorities is least of all apparent in Petersburg, and this produces a strange impression of fear and indecisiveness, as if the government did not dare say openly what is permitted and what is not. I constantly talk to Witte about this, but I see that he still doesn't believe in himself.[69]

---

[66] Cf., too, Doctorow, "Introduction of Parliamentary Institutions in Russia," p. 176.

[67] "Perepiska Nikolaia II i Marii Fedorovny," *KA* 22 (1927): 172, November 1, 1905.

[68] Iswolsky, *Recollections*, pp. 15–16.

[69] TsGAOR, f. 642, op. 1, d. 2328, ll. 17–18, or "Perepiska Nikolaia II i Marii Fedorovny," *KA* 22 (1927): 173–74, November 10, 1905.

In Nicholas, a personal distrust of Witte was joined with unhappiness over the continuing unrest and with disaffection from the form and substance of Witte's political behavior. For the tsar, the person of Witte and the new order were virtually indistinguishable; any weakening of confidence in one was also a blow to the other.

WITTE IN DESPAIR

The fact that domestic peace failed to materialize immediately, the demonstrations and criticisms of autocratic loyalists, and these loyalists' appeals to the traditional autocratic role not only contributed to Nicholas's disaffection with Witte and with the conceptions he represented, but took their toll on Witte as well. For all his confidence in his own ability to control events and manipulate opinion, Witte betrayed considerable anxiety about the strength of his own position. Such insecurity was, of course, endemic to autocratic politics, and the October Manifesto had done nothing to change this. In the absence of any institutional or social power base, an autocratic servitor remained fully dependent on the sovereign's favor and hence vulnerable to personal intrigue. In Witte's case, the perceived decline in imperial trust and the lack of anticipated support from society only heightened this insecurity. According to his "press secretary," Witte felt that he was surrounded by enemies. Eager to find out "what they breathe in the highest circles," he sought to stay or get into their good graces by receiving and hearing out anyone deemed influential, whenever possible and regardless of what they had to say. These desperate efforts, often based on little more than hearsay, were a measure of Witte's mounting anxieties, now that his strategy had failed to satisfy society and appeared to be alienating the tsar as well, whose backing Witte could not do without.

Notwithstanding his various protestations to the contrary, there can be no doubt that Witte had been taken aback by the vehemence of the public's reactions and by his government's evident inability to restore order with the promise of reforms. The ink on the October 17 acts had barely dried when one member of Witte's chancellery, upon returning to St. Petersburg, already found his superior "pinched and worried."[70] By month's end, the public's congratulatory messages had become more insistent and critical, professing doubts about the government's sincerity and demanding the implementation of the promised "constitutional reforms" and a resolution of the agrarian problem. An uncharacteristically and extremely pessimistic Witte had told Izvol'skii, before the latter returned to his diplomatic post at the Danish court, that the October Man-

[70] Mendeleev, "Svet i teni," p. 83.

ifesto had "prevented an immediate catastrophe," but that the situation was "still fraught with peril" and held the possibility of a new revolutionary explosion. Maligned and derided personally, Witte found himself "the object of violent attacks on the part of extremists of both Right and Left as well as the contempt of the moderate Liberals."[71] After working feverishly and energetically for more than two weeks,[72] he evidently began to despair at the disappointing results. Kuz'min-Karavaev, whose report had formed the basis for Witte's October 17 report, returned from visiting Witte on November 1 "with the most painful impressions." Kuz'-min wrote to Witte that not only was there the very real specter of a descent into "anarchy and a Pugachevshchina," a reference to the eighteenth-century peasant war and a synonym for chaos, in view of the imminent general strike, but "the horror is compounded by your tendency to fatigue and your depressed mood."

Kuz'min-Karavaev's letter permits insight into the state of Witte's mind at the time. Apparently, Witte was at least talking about, if not seriously considering, handing over the reins to a military dictatorship, as he had originally suggested in mid-October. If Witte were to abandon power, Kuz'min-Karavaev warned, an explosion would inevitably follow. A military dictatorship would be condemned to impotence, as associations of the "all-leveling Social Democracy" would spring up and chaos would ensue. Witte's situation, to be sure, was extremely difficult, since he was bearing an "unbelievable burden" by himself, reproached from "above," unsupported from "below." It was easy for people without responsibility to offer advice and make demands. Theirs were mere words, whereas the responsibility belonged to Witte alone. Under no circumstances, however, must he "lay down his arms."

During their conversation the night before, Kuz'min-Karavaev had sensed in Witte's remarks a reproach for having "evaluated the situation incorrectly" and for "stating mistaken conclusions about the tasks and means of the government." Perhaps he, too, seemed an irresponsible advisor to Witte, but after rethinking everything during the past night, he had arrived at the same conclusions: "The only way out is to take the revolutionary movement in hand and therefore to stand at its head. In revolutionary times two weeks are a huge time-span." Instead of using this time to make known its intentions through action, the government had done nothing except to proclaim an amnesty; even that had been needlessly restrictive and four days overdue. "You say: everything cannot be done at once. Normally that's correct, but not in revolutionary times." In the absence of governmental leadership, public sentiments were

---

[71] Iswolsky, *Recollections*, p. 14.
[72] Mendeleev, "Svet i teni," p. 94, confirms this.

bound to grow more radical: "Society's thoughts have to be fed, the formation of absolute demands in the consciousness of the masses must be prevented." To this end, Kuz'min-Karavaev counseled that not another day be wasted in drawing up a new electoral format and in implementing civil liberties. Unless the convocation date for the Duma was fixed presently, demands for a constituent assembly could be expected within ten days.

It would be a grave mistake, Kuz'min-Karavaev warned, to yield to reactionary suggestions that order be restored before any reforms were undertaken. Such a direction would only stoke the revolutionary fires. Kuz'min called on Witte to take advantage of the impending zemstvo congress in Moscow. By letting it proceed and by presenting for its discussion proposals for franchise reform, for instance, its participants could be made to feel the seriousness of the situation and share some of the responsibility. Risky though such a step might appear, these risks could not be avoided at this time, as the very existence of the state and not mere personal interests were at stake. "Take care of yourself!" Kuz'min admonished Witte. Nobody's strength of nerves could bear the workload and pace that Witte had imposed on himself. Others needed to be assigned some of Witte's responsibilities. While the situation was terrible, not everything had been lost yet. If still more time was wasted, however, "the beginning of the end" would be near.[73]

The letter highlights Witte's disheartened mood at a time when he was caught in the cross fire between the opposite extremes of the political spectrum and the tug-of-war between differing conceptions of order and realities. At a meeting on November 20, 1905, Naumov found Witte still worn out.[74] The reality of Russia in revolutionary turmoil did not square with Witte's goal of peacefully transforming the political and social order through bureaucratic initiative. There was no order, much less a peaceful one. Everybody, whether Nicholas or Kuz'min-Karavaev, critic or supporter, was insisting that Witte and his government take charge, but to what end? The pacification of the country as a precondition, perhaps even a substitute, for reform, or reform as a means of restoring domestic tranquility? It was precisely this contradiction between Russia's reality and his own theory that Witte was wrestling with and that prompted him to revive his earlier alternative proposal of a military dictatorship. Uncertain about his political backing from the sovereign, maligned and envied in the netherworld of court and administration, unable to muster sufficient support within society, Witte confronted this acute dilemma in a state of despair.

[73] Kuz'min-Karavaev's letter to Witte, November 2, 1905, Witte Collection, REEACU.
[74] Naumov, *Iz utselevshikh Vospominanii*, 2:34–36.

CRACKDOWN

Although Witte wanted to see order repaired, of course, he could not bring himself to undertake or authorize drastic repressive measures that did not accord with his program and his image of his own role. That task of reasserting order instead fell to the new minister of internal affairs, Durnovo, who was not hamstrung by undue scruples or a crisis of belief. Witte would later blame Durnovo for the unnecessary severity of his actions and his failure to observe ministerial unity. That charge rings hollow, however, in light of Witte's eventual conversion to forcible measures and his apparent willingness to let Durnovo proceed while he himself was still experiencing his crisis of confidence and following the high road of moral suasion.[75]

Even before his appointment as acting minister, with Bulygin still nominally in charge, Durnovo had begun to take energetic actions, summoning departmental directors, issuing instructions, and firing off telegrams to provincial governors about the October 17 acts.[76] As soon as he had been confirmed in office, Durnovo initiated a massive shuffle of personnel within his ministry and its agencies on the provincial level. At least half of all the provincial governors were replaced, either transferred to other governorships or fired and reassigned to the ministry without specific responsibilities. Assistant ministers, departmental directors, their deputies, and members of the minister's council were affected by these changes, as were several town prefects and, surprisingly, a number of governors-general, the tsar's personal emissaries.[77] According to one of his subordinates, Durnovo was determined to replace all officeholders who had revealed their indecisiveness, lack of administrative abilities, or political unreliability during the most recent disorders.[78] This game of musical chairs involved many others as well, who were now beholden to the new minister and thus more likely to comply with his policies. Many of the new governors were military men, presumably in keeping with Durnovo's belief in the need for decisive action in quashing the disorders. To this end, he also sent coded messages to all governors, promising his unqualified support for any measures deemed necessary except inaction.[79] Senators were dispatched to Kiev and Odessa, among other

[75] This is also the point made by Liubimov, "Russkaia smuta," p. 359.

[76] Ibid., pp. 344–45.

[77] Durnovo's reports, October 26–December 30, 1905, TsGIA, f. 1284, op. 241, d. 121, ll. 156–293.

[78] Liubimov, "Russkaia smuta," pp. 352–55, although he underestimates the number of governors replaced.

[79] Ibid., p. 355.

places, to investigate the causes of the disorders and the conduct of local authorities.[80]

In the tsar's mind, however, the results of such investigations were a foregone conclusion. As he wrote to his mother on November 10, "every place with good and honest governors has been calm; but many did nothing, and a few even led the mobs with red flags; those, of course, have been fired already."[81] Order, to Nicholas, was a direct function of resolute action by the authorities. Only a show of strength could hold the revolution at bay. When a new railroad strike fizzled without shutting down communications or provoking a general strike, Nicholas congratulated Witte: "I am glad that the senseless railroad strike is over—this is a great moral success for the government. The main thing now is not to concede anything and to stand firm and to secure order decisively."[82] To Maria Fedorovna, Nicholas somewhat prematurely reported the eclipse of the "notorious 'Union of Unions' which has led all the disorders"; the workers gave in this time because they "had not achieved anything but hunger for themselves and their families." The start of widespread agrarian disorders in Russia's central provinces, on the other hand, sounded an ominous note: "This is a very dangerous phenomenon, due to the ease with which the peasants are incited to take away the landlords' land, but also because there are few troops anywhere."[83]

Belief in the efficacy of force not only prompted the replacement of many governors, often by military men as we have seen, but it also persuaded the tsar to resort to the time-honored practice of sending governors-general to the areas most affected by peasant disturbances: Saratov, Penza, Tambov, Voronezh, Kursk, Chernigov, and Poltava—i.e., the broad band of agrarian provinces extending from the western Ukraine to the Volga.[84] Eventually these firefighters of the revolution were also dispatched to put down rebellions in Moscow and in the Baltic provinces. Other areas, usually border regions such as Poland, Lithuania, Finland, Siberia, and the Caucasus, had been administered by governors-general for some time already. Some of these men, if they had acquitted themselves well during earlier assignments, were repeatedly sent on rescue missions. Their authority derived from their direct, extrainstitutional as-

[80] Cf. Durnovo's reports, November 3 and 8, 1905, TsGIA, f. 1284, op. 241, d. 121, ll. 176, 199.

[81] TsGAOR, f. 642, op. 1, d. 2328, ll. 17–18, or "Perepiska Nikolaia II i Marii Fedorovny," KA 22 (1927): 173–74, November 10, 1905.

[82] Nicholas's note to Witte, November 7, 1905, Witte Collection, REEACU. An approximation of this message is also quoted in Witte, Vospominaniia, 3:139.

[83] TsGAOR, f. 642, op. 1, d. 2328, ll. 17–18, or "Perepiska Nikolaia II i Marii Fedorovny," KA 22 (1927): 173, November 10, 1905.

[84] Liubimov, "Russkaia smuta," pp. 251–52; Witte's report of October 30, 1905, TsGAOR, f. 102, op. 166, d. 20, l. 226.

sociation with the person of the tsar, and it automatically transcended that of the regularly constituted bureaucratic agencies and officials. By appointing these personal emissaries, the tsar sought to bypass his bureaucracy and extend his personal control to those far reaches of the Empire beset by emergencies that regular authorities seemed incapable of resolving. Ironically, by attempting to cut through the mythical bureaucratic barrier between ruler and ruled, the dispatch of governors-general only served to reinforce the myth. More importantly still, it reaffirmed the personal aspects of the autocrat's role, the personalized conception of his authority.

A similar device, the ad hoc dispatch of military commanders to put down mutinies and clear out strikers, found broad and increasing application during this time. To Nicholas, such measures offered the only promise, as hardly a day passed in November without new rural disturbances, military insurrections, assassination attempts, and strikes. Representing tens of thousands of workers and commanding their own sizable detachments of armed workers, the St. Petersburg and Moscow Soviets arrogated to themselves sufficient administrative responsibility to constitute an open challenge to existing authorities and agencies. These two bodies in turn served as examples for and sought to coordinate the activities of numerous other soviets nationwide. Open rebellions among Baltic, Pacific, and Black Sea bases had virtually paralyzed Russia's remaining naval forces, while the reliability of the army was being called into question by dozens of major and minor mutinies. The one-million-strong Manchurian army, which was on the point of returning to European Russia, was hit especially hard, as entire garrisons and cities along the Trans-Siberian railroad passed into the hands of striking civilians and fraternizing soldiers. After Court Commandant Trepov had presented a particularly vivid and detailed picture of all-pervasive insubordination and growing chaos in Poland, Finland, the Baltic, the agrarian provinces, and in the army,[85] Nicholas shared some of the news with the dowager empress: "It is horrible to think that these are all my people." He also announced his intention to begin personal inspections of all regiments in order to counteract revolutionary propaganda and to impress on the officers the need for close supervision of their soldiers and greater attention to their concerns.[86]

The judicial authorities, in particular, came in for harsh criticism from the tsar, who held Justice Minister Manukhin directly responsible for their allegedly dilatory and insufficiently forceful conduct. Nicholas twice

[85] Trepov's report, November 17, 1905, TsGAOR, f. 595, op. 1, d. 24, ll. 1–20.

[86] TsGAOR, f. 642, op. 1, d. 2328, ll. 19–20, or "Perepiska Nikolaia II i Marii Fedorovny," KA 22 (1927): 174–75, November 17, 1905.

summoned the Council of Ministers into his presence in order to listen to Manukhin defend himself against charges that his subordinates had been conspicuous in their failure to support the government. The tsar wanted to know why investigators could not discover the culprits, why prosecutors did not find the evidence necessary to indict, and why the courts often acquitted people who were obviously guilty. Indifference— or worse, open sympathy—greeted political criminals, Nicholas charged. Manukhin reminded the tsar and the others criticizing him that the judicial agencies had been established on the principles of openness, independence, and the notion that it was better to forgive a few guilty ones than to convict one innocent man—but to no avail.[87] Manukhin's courageous defense of his agency's work and of judicial independence only served to seal his fate; by November 23 it had been decided that he relinquish his office.[88]

As Manukhin's replacement Witte proposed Senator Akimov, whose conservative views and rightist reputation supposedly made him preferable to Nicholas's candidate.[89] The tsar received Akimov on December 15: "I talked with him for a long time, liked him. Clear firm views—just what is needed in a judicial agency."[90] His political leanings, advanced age, and family ties to Durnovo notwithstanding, Akimov's actions as minister of justice met with Witte's approval and even prompted him, upon leaving office, to suggest Akimov as one of two possible successors.[91] As for Nicholas, he had finally found a minister of justice who could be counted on to act forcefully in pursuing the regime's enemies, without undue scruples or regard for legal niceties. Within less than a month, Nicholas noted a change for the better: "I very much like Minister of Justice Akimov," he wrote to his mother on January 12, 1906. "Unfortunately, he is not young, but remarkably cheerful and energetic, with honest views, and he has started a strong clean-up of his vile agency." The only other minister to merit such praise was Akimov's brother-in-law Durnovo, presumably for his equally energetic conduct: "Durnovo—Internal Affairs—is doing splendidly; I am very pleased with him, too. The remaining ministers are people *sans importance!*"[92]

In his resolutions, marginal comments, and epistolary observations,

---

[87] Witte, *Vospominaniia*, 3:183–84; "Dnevnik A. A. Polovtseva," *KA* 4 (1923): 86–88; TsGAOR, f. 601, op. 1, d. 249, November 18–19, 1905.

[88] "Iz rezoliutsii Nikolaia II," *Byloe* 9 (June 1918): 145; Witte, *Vospominaniia*, 3:184–85.

[89] Witte, *Vospominaniia*, 3:185.

[90] Mistakenly dated December 18 instead of December 15; "Iz rezoliutsii Nikolaia II," *Byloe* 9 (June 1918): 145.

[91] Witte, *Vospominaniia*, 3:187–88.

[92] TsGAOR, f. 642, op. 1, d. 2328, ll. 33–36, or "Perepiska Nikolaia II i Marii Fedorovny," *KA* 22 (1927): 187, January 12, 1906.

Nicholas praised and encouraged forceful, even brutal action, while condemning any sign of weakness or inaction on the part of the civil and military authorities. Words like "energetic," "firm," "resolute," "decisive," "no negotiations," to say nothing of "vlast' " (power) and his more graphic reactions, all testified to his belief in the efficacy of uncompromising force and in typically military values. When Witte reported the rumored arrival of 162 "instigator-anarchists" on the Chinese-Eastern Railroad, the emperor wrote incredulously: "Are they really letting these 162 anarchists corrupt the army?—They should all be hanged."[93] Or when Durnovo, as part of his daily summary of the latest revolutionary events, terrorist acts, and strikes, mentioned the sacking of several landlords' estates in the southern province of Taurida, the tsar underlined the name of Prince Trubetskoi, the brother of the late Moscow rector and himself a liberal activist, and added in the margin: "It serves him right."[94]

Some reports brought out a cruel and bloodthirsty streak in the otherwise gentle and noncombative autocrat who eschewed any personal confrontations. A breathtakingly graphic account by a governor-general from the Baltic region described the revolutionaries as controlling railroads, telegraph lines, and entire towns. One town surrendered only after several days of gun-battles and after the threat of blanket artillery shelling. At that point the commanding officer called off the bombing, partly for lack of grenades and other ammunition, and sent a detachment into town to receive the townspeople's surrender and arms. Nicholas was not appeased, however: "That's no reason. The town should have been destroyed."[95] The tsar, or Durnovo with the tsar's explicit approval, repeatedly instructed local authorities and commanders not to enter into any agreements with the rebels or to make any concessions.[96] The slightest sign of resistance was to be met sternly and forcefully; immediate retaliation and punishment on the spot were preferable to negotiations or drawn-out judicial proceedings.[97] Individual detachments were encouraged to display greater initiative and autonomy in their actions. The reported arrests of various revolutionary leaders prompted an im-

[93] Witte's report, November 5, 1905, in Semennikov, *Revoliutsiia 1905 goda*, pp. 23–24.

[94] Durnovo's report, December 3, 1905, TsGIA, f. 1328, op. 2, d. 10, ll. 3–8.

[95] Report of Temp. Governor-General B. A. Bekman to Nicholas, December 14, 1905, in *Revoliutsiia 1905–1907 gg. v Rossii. Dokumenty i Materialy: Vysshii Pod"em Revoliutsii 1905–1907gg.* (Moscow, 1957), 4:308–19.

[96] E.g., Durnovo's report, December 16, 1905, about situation in Moscow, TsGIA, f. 1328, op. 2, d. 10, ll. 61b–v.

[97] Letter from Minister of War Rediger to Witte, December 17, 1905, Witte Collection, REEACU; Nicholas's telegram to Governor-General Sollogub in Riga, December 19, 1905, and n.d., Semennikov, *Revoliutsiia 1905 goda*, p. 166; Durnovo's telegrams to Governor-General Freze of Vilno, Kovno, and Grodno, December 18 and 21, 1905, *Dokumenty i Materialy: VPR 1905–07*, 4:238–39.

perial response of "vlast',"[98] while the summary executions of twenty-six insurrectionary railroad workers by a punitive expedition were greeted with a "bravo" from Nicholas.[99] The same exclamation welcomed the news from the Baltic that the leader of one detachment, "Captain Rikhter, not only shot but hanged the main agitators."[100]

At the same time, Nicholas's actions and reactions in the face of near-universal anarchy appear strangely passive or helpless, rarely going beyond idle ravings and exhortations. To the tsar, Witte and his government appeared to be dragging their feet and prevaricating, paralyzed by unnecessary legal scruples and the fear of alienating society. As a result, Nicholas was losing faith in Witte personally and becoming alienated from the impersonal notion of rulership represented by Witte's regime. Yet, while reasserting the personal component of his role through his insistence on vlast', direct action, and the appointment of personal emissaries, he continued to display a peculiar remoteness of his own. During his audience with Naumov on November 23, 1905, the tsar reportedly asked: "What is to be done now?" A disturbed Naumov blamed the emperor's "uninformed isolation and practical helplessness" on his advisors' reticence to tell unpleasant truths,[101] but that was not the case. Nicholas was undoubtedly well informed and fully aware of the gravity of the situation by now, as his letters to his mother attest. Still, the impression of imperial helplessness persists, and justifiably so.

Although Nicholas kept abreast of events, they were so unstructured in his own mind that he was incapable of issuing specific instructions to remedy the situation. He had become the captive of events and of autocratic government. He bemoaned the lack of initiative and the unwillingness to shoulder responsibility that were the natural outgrowth of the autocratic system, yet he waited for his subordinates to put an end to the disorders by displaying just such responsibility, initiative, decisiveness, and strength. Seeing his own role as more passive than active, exhortatory rather than commanding, he would urge on his men with rising impatience like a fiercely involved, yet physically removed spectator, alternately applauding and lashing out verbally—and impotently. Indeed, the tsar's own passivity sharply contradicted the energetic and ruthless activism that he expected from his subordinates. Nicholas II appeared to equate the exercise of autocratic power with the forceful actions of others.

[98] Durnovo's report, January 2, 1906, TsGIA, f. 1328, op. 2, d. 11, ll. 1–4a.
[99] Durnovo's report, December 19, 1905, ibid., d. 10, ll. 79–80.
[100] Telegram from Governor-General Sollogub, included in Witte's report, December 30, 1905, in Semennikov, *Revoliutsiia 1905 goda*, pp. 43–45.
[101] Naumov, *Iz utselevshikh vospominanii*, 2:42–43.

WITTE IN ARMS

On December 1 the tsar informed Maria Fedorovna: "On the whole, the situation is very dangerous in view of the unabating peasant disorders, but on the other hand, voices are beginning to be raised from all sides, getting louder and stronger, to the effect that it is time for the government to begin acting energetically, and this is a very big success!" It was as if the adherents of order first had to give the signal for a show of force before such force could be applied by the government:

> This is just what Witte was waiting for, and now he will begin to put down the revolution decisively—at least, that's what he told me. He realizes that all well-intentioned people are displeased with him and have become impatient with his inaction, and therefore he is prepared to order the arrest of the principal leaders of the insurrection. I told him about this long ago, but he hoped to manage without drastic measures.[102]

The tsar's analysis was not far off the mark. By his own admission, Witte had indeed refrained from any repressive measures in St. Petersburg, hoping for a disintegration of the revolutionary movement and for a gradual return of order under the influence of the October Manifesto and subsequent reform acts. When these hopes were dashed, the government finally ordered the arrest of Nosar'-Khrustalev on November 26 and of the entire St. Petersburg Soviet a week later. Although Witte would later justify this step in terms of the Soviet's weakened authority and the diminished danger of armed resistance,[103] there can be little doubt that the sovereign's mounting impatience with such dilatory tactics and the rising anxieties of the propertied classes had prodded Witte into action.

In his weekly letter to the dowager empress, the tsar acknowledged the government's new activism and the change of sentiment among the more moderate parts of society: "The mood has changed completely. The former frivolous liberals who always criticized every government measure are now clamoring that resolute action is needed. When about 250 of the main leaders of the workers' committee and of other parties were arrested the other day, *everybody* was delighted." The same enthusiasm had supposedly greeted the closing of twelve newspapers and the prosecution of their publishers for printing the St. Petersburg Soviet's declaration of financial warfare against the government: "All of this, of course, gives Witte the moral strength to continue to act as he must."[104]

---

[102] TsGAOR, f. 642, op. 1, d. 2328, ll. 21–22, or "Perepiska Nikolaia II i Marii Fedorovny," *KA* 22 (1927): 178, December 1, 1905.

[103] Witte, *Vospominaniia*, 3:100–101, 140.

[104] TsGAOR, f. 642, op. 1, d. 2328, ll. 23–26, or "Perepiska Nikolaia II i Marii Fedorovny," *KA* 22 (1927): 180, December 8, 1905.

The government's latest measures precipitated a final showdown with its enemies. The Moscow Soviet was joined by the organizations of postal, telegraph, and railroad workers in calling a nationwide general strike as a prelude to an armed uprising. The strike began, impressively enough, in Moscow on December 7 and within a week had spread to most urban areas; yet, comprised mostly of workers, students, and mutinous soldiers, it lacked the broad social support of the October general strike. Unlike the other lines operating out of Moscow, the St. Petersburg railway continued to run, allowing authorities to reinforce the Moscow garrison and begin their counteroffensive on December 15. After two days of brutal street-fighting and thousands of casualties on both sides, the government gained the upper hand, though hostilities continued for two more days in Moscow and still longer elsewhere.

By the end of December Nicholas could report to his mother with evident relief the successful suppression of the rebellion: "As was to be expected, the energetic actions of Governor-General Dubasov and the troops in Moscow produced a most reassuring impression in Russia. Of course, all the bad elements in the Northern Caucasus, the South of Russia, as well as the Siberian towns, have lost heart." While the insurrection in the Baltic provinces was continuing, the lesson was clear: "Terror must be answered by terror. Now Witte himself has realized this."[105]

As late as the beginning of December, Witte had sought to bring the government's persuasive powers to bear on the local population in order to calm troubled minds and discourage false expectations.[106] By mid-December, however, Witte was singing another tune. Adopting his sovereign's prescription for curing Russia's ailments, Witte had finally come to the conclusion that the use of force was in order, and he sought to carry out this sudden insight with all the zeal of a recent convert. Witte's initial moderation and wait-and-see attitude, if not to say paralysis, had given way to a new militancy and ruthlessness that shocked even Nicholas. This change of heart coincided with the defeat of the uprising in Moscow, as the tsar correctly noted:

Witte, after the Moscow events, has changed sharply; now he wants to hang and shoot everyone. I never saw such a chameleon or a man who changed his convictions as he does. Because of this character trait almost *no one* believes

[105] TsGAOR, f. 642, op. 1, d. 2328, ll. 31–32, or "Perepiska Nikolaia II i Marii Fedorovny," *KA* 22 (1927): 185, December 29, 1905.

[106] Cf. December 3, 1905, MIA circular, issued at Witte's insistence and over Durnovo's objections, concerning measures to enlighten the peasantry about the true content and meaning of the October 17 and November 3 manifestos; TsGIA, f. 1276, op. 1, d. 52, ll. 27–28, and Liubimov, "Russkaia smuta," pp. 253–54.

him anymore, he has ruined himself in everyone's [eyes]—perhaps with the exception of the kikes abroad.[107]

One observer, upon returning to Russia, was struck unpleasantly by the changes that had taken place during his six-week absence. Witte "rules," wrote Polovtsev, the one-time high-ranking aide to Nicholas's father and grandfather; ever since Dubasov's Moscow victory, "he has thrown himself from indecisiveness and weakness into drastic measures, though Durnovo is the main culprit for those." When confronted by Polovtsev, Witte claimed that events had proven Russia's fealty to the monarchical principle and the army's complete loyalty.[108]

Witte had been jarred out of his despondency of November by a sense of panic lest the spreading revolt devour the system of which he was part. Once the insurgents in Moscow had been isolated and crushed by superior force, fear in turn gave way to a sense of possibility, that of seizing the opportunity presented by this victory. Whether in his reports to Nicholas, or in his appearances before the Council of Ministers, or in numerous messages to military authorities on the scene, Witte suddenly came to insist on the broad and unrestrained application of military force. On December 17, the day that the back of the Moscow uprising was broken, Witte called on the emperor to send immediately a punitive expedition to the Ekaterinskaia railroad under the command of a "decisive general . . . with the same instructions and powers given to General Rennenkampf with regard to the Siberian railroad." Furthermore, all major railroad junctions were to be secured by troops to prevent constant interruptions. Witte also requested permission to confer with the commander of the St. Petersburg military district, the chief of staff, and the ministers of war and internal affairs in order to decide on the deployment of military forces according to political, i.e., internal security, considerations rather than purely strategic or external security concerns.[109] The very next day Witte telegraphed Governor-General Sollogub in the Baltic provinces, urging "without exception . . . the most decisive and equally severe measures concerning the rebels and their leaders."[110] Within twenty-four hours another exhortation from Witte arrived: "It seems to me that in view of the lack of troops, the troops must act with particular severity. The destruction of a few farms in the most rebellious insurgent regions could have a sobering effect."[111] Two days later Witte

[107] TsGAOR, f. 642, op. 1, d. 2328, ll. 33–36, or "Perepiska Nikolaia II i Marii Fedorovny," KA 22 (1927): 186–87, January 12, 1906.

[108] "Dnevnik A. A. Polovtseva," KA 4 (1923): 90, January 30, 1906.

[109] Witte's letter to Nicholas, December 17, 1905, in Semennikov, Revoliutsiia 1905 goda, p. 27.

[110] Dokumenty i Materialy: VPR 1905–1907, 4:326–28.

[111] Ibid.

in effect gave an order of "No prisoners!" Warning against putting large numbers of people on trial, he reminded Sollogub of the Council's opinion that shooting always be answered by shooting; even the slightest provocation was to be met by armed retaliation. These messages in turn were reinforced by equally ruthless instructions from the minister of war and the chief of staff.[112] Witte's desperate tone of urgency contrasts sharply with Sollogub's much more matter-of-fact response, in which Sollogub pointed out the difference in perceptions between Riga and St. Petersburg. He assured Witte somewhat prematurely that the situation was under control, that force was indeed being used at the slightest provocation, but that people, once arrested, of course could not simply be shot without court proceedings.[113]

In the days leading up to Christmas, Witte showered the tsar with a flurry of reports and messages that seemed to overwhelm their addressee. "You have written me so many letters that I have not been able to cope with them these days," Nicholas responded on December 24.[114] Seized by panic, Witte was firing off one communication after another, hoping to stamp out the revolutionary movement while at the same time trying to convince the sovereign of his new-found diligence and hard line. One report in particular revealed how agitated its author was; in effect, it amounted to one long "I told you so." The main problem, according to Witte, was that troops were always deployed after the fact, rarely to forestall new disturbances. Ever since the middle of October he had been pushing for the immediate return of the Manchurian army, he claimed, bringing the matter to the repeated attention of the ministers of war and the court, all to no avail. Had his plea for "extraordinary measures of dispatching military executionary trains" to clear the return route of the Far Eastern army been heeded a month earlier, "then maybe we would have several divisions more in Russia." A skeptical Nicholas underlined the word "maybe." As if to prove him wrong, two days later Witte ordered the dispatch of two more "executionary trains."[115]

In a similar vein, Witte reminded the tsar that he had long recommended the replacement of old and incompetent generals by outstanding ones. "The Moscow disorders pointed up the whole bankruptcy of the

[112] Ibid.

[113] Telegram contained in Witte's December 25 letter to Nicholas, Semennikov, *Revoliutsiia 1905 goda*, pp. 36–38. Such levelheaded restraint may account for Sollogub's replacement by the far more ruthless and unscrupulous Meller-Zakomel'skii.

[114] Witte's letters to Nicholas, Semennikov, *Revoliutsiia 1905 goda*, pp. 27–30, 34–35; TsGAOR, f. 543, op. 1, d. 557, l. 5, 7; Nicholas's letter to Witte, Witte Collection, REEACU.

[115] Witte's letter to Nicholas, December 23, 1905, Semennikov, *Revoliutsiia 1905 goda*, pp. 34–35.

local high command," he wrote. The St. Petersburg military commander and the ministers of war and the court had all agreed, but Witte claimed not to know what had become of his recommendations. Witte also renewed his complaint about the lack of coordination between civil and military authorities beginning at the highest levels, as neither he nor the minister of internal affairs had any information about the distribution of troops. Their purpose at this time was not strategic, but to suppress disorders and to safeguard the foundations of the state. Therefore those entrusted with domestic policy were entitled to a voice in their deployment; for instance, both Witte and Governor-General Dubasov had pleaded in vain for several days before reinforcements had finally been sent to Moscow. Additional forces were needed in the Baltic area and on the Black Sea.[116]

Witte also recommended an immediate State Council investigation, as provided by law, into the recent events in Moscow. The heavy human and material losses, Witte explained, placed a "heavy moral responsibility on the government," not only on local authorities but, "perhaps rightly so," on the highest echelons of government, including the chairman of the Council of Ministers, officials of the Ministry of Internal Affairs, and former governors-general. Since Witte expected society and the press to blame the authorities for "lack of foresight and preparedness, inactivity, and connivance" in view of the uprising's suddenness, an investigation to examine the circumstances and to assess responsibility was in order.[117] Far from seeking to indict himself, Witte obviously expected such an inquiry to bear out his negative estimation of senior military commanders that he had just conveyed to Nicholas.

Complaints and suggestions poured forth in quick succession. The immediate establishment of militia detachments was to make up for the lack of regular forces. Already several days had passed since he had proposed a high-level conference to coordinate military actions, Witte complained. He was clearly exasperated: "But maybe a radical solution of this problem would be to put a military man at the head of government and entrust to him, with the participation of all the ministers, the coordination of the actions of all branches of the administration, including army-navy affairs."[118] This, of course, was the alternative that Witte had first described in the negotiations leading up to his appointment and during his conversation with Kuz'min-Karavaev. In reviving this proposal for a military dictatorship, Witte was in effect demanding a free hand to pursue the course of action that he had just laid out and deemed best.

[116] Witte's letter to Nicholas, December 21, 1905, ibid., pp. 32–33.
[117] Ibid.
[118] Witte's report, December 21, 1905, ibid., pp. 30–32.

Witte was not given a free hand, however, nor was he replaced by a military man. His urgent tone and host of proposals for the most part failed to persuade the tsar—or his own ministerial colleagues, for that matter. They reacted coolly to the idea of a new militia, recommending the expansion of mounted police instead. As for the need for special measures to protect the military from revolutionary propaganda, even Nicholas did not appreciate it. Similarly, attempts to restore discipline within the ranks of the bureaucracy and to bring to justice provincial officials accused of a dereliction of their duties did not go as far as Witte would have liked.[119]

It was as though Witte were seeking to atone for past sins and omissions, now that the worst of the revolutionary danger appeared to have passed. On January 2, 1906, Durnovo could confidently predict that except for a few isolated terrorist attempts, there would be no mass disturbances on the first anniversary of Bloody Sunday and that the revolutionary movement was being routed. While there still remained problems to be dealt with, Durnovo very much gave the impression of being on top of things. The arrests of revolutionary leaders were continuing, he wrote Nicholas, and had "yielded excellent results to date." "Vlast'!" was the tsar's reaction.[120]

As the imminent danger seemed to recede and order was gradually restored, there was a palpable sense of relief at being rescued from an abyss, coupled with a renewed emphasis on the reassertion of state authority. Even Witte began to breathe more easily, though he would still warn of renewed agrarian unrest. Ironically, the return of domestic peace did little to shore up Witte's sagging personal fortunes or to help his political cause. If his initial reticence to resort to open force had damaged his standing in the eyes of the tsar and others, his belated conversion did nothing to repair the damage, as Nicholas made clear when he criticized Witte for his chameleon-like qualities.[121] In fact, Witte's attempts to in-

[119] Witte's reports to Nicholas, December 16, 1905, TsGIA, f. 1276, op. 1, d. 89, ll. 18–19; December 23, 1905, ibid., d. 93, ll. 18–19; December 23, 1905, Semennikov, *Revoliutsiia 1905 goda*, pp. 33–34; [December 23 or 24, 1905], ibid., pp. 38–39; Nicholas's memo to Witte, December 24, 1905, Witte Collection, REEACU; Witte's report, December 25, 1905, TsGIA, f. 1276, op. 1, d. 93, l. 24; December 31, 1905, ibid., d. 89, l. 67, including Govenor-General Panteleev's telegrams from Poltava, December 29, 1905, ll. 68–70, and December 30, 1905, l. 71; Proceedings of Council of Ministers, January 3, 1906, ll. 105–11; Witte's report, January 11, 1906, Semennikov, *Revoliutsiia 1905 goda*, p. 54; January 14, 1906, ibid., pp. 54–55.

[120] Durnovo's report to Nicholas, January 2, 1906, TsGIA, f. 1328, op. 2, d. 11, ll. 1–4a; January 2, 1906, TsGAOR, f. 102, op. 166, d. 20, l. 202 and ob.; January 12, 1906, TsGIA, f. 1328, op. 2, d. 11, ll. 26–30. Cf., too, Trepov's memo to Nicholas, December 29, 1905, TsGAOR, f. 595, op. 1, d. 24, ll. 22–25.

[121] See supra, p. 275.

terfere in military matters over which he had no jurisdiction may have put the tsar even more on his guard. More important still, the very suppression of the worst features of the revolution appeared to render Witte and his program less essential than before, if not altogether unnecessary, thus allowing the tsar to go back on concessions he had made unwillingly in the first place. The temptation to do so became almost irresistible during the discussion of the political reforms promised in October.

CHAPTER IX

The Meaning of Reform

OF ALL THE REFORMS advertised in October, the main order of business was the convocation of the legislative assembly. Under the provisions of the August 6 electoral law, the consultative Bulygin Duma was to have opened no later than January 15, 1906. While superseding the August 6 edict, the October Manifesto reaffirmed that date. First, the franchise had to be expanded, however, in order to include, "as far as is possible in the short period remaining before the Duma is convened, those classes of the population that at present are completely deprived of electoral rights."[1] To this end, Kryzhanovskii, under Witte's guidance, drafted a new electoral law.[2] Yet seven precious weeks passed before a Special Conference chaired by Nicholas took up the question of electoral reform on December 5, 1905.

In the interval, restoration of order had taken precedence over reform of the system. The delay had only drawn the government's sincerity further into question and thus served to exacerbate public dissatisfaction. Taken aback by the public's mounting impatience as well as the protests of autocratic loyalists, Nicholas and Witte, as we have seen, had begun to entertain serious doubts about the wisdom of the new course. In Nicholas's case, these reservations had translated into growing disenchantment with Witte and the new order that he represented. Witte, on the other hand, had found himself torn—to the point of contradiction, indecision, and paralysis—between the need to assert the state's authority through force and the need to enlist the support of society through further concessions.

THE NEW ELECTORAL LAW

These strains were very much in evidence when Witte personally reported to Nicholas just before the opening of the Special Conference on December 5. According to Kryzhanovskii, who witnessed the audience, Witte was hemming and hawing instead of acting his usual assertive self. Nicholas "clearly realized that the new order would bring him little comfort." Witte's claim that the tsar and his government would find support in popular representation met with imperial incredulity:

[1] Lazarevskii, *Zakonodatel'nye akty*, p. 151.
[2] Doctorow, "Introduction of Parliamentary Institutions in Russia," p. 185.

Don't tell me this, Sergei Iulevich, I understand very well that I am not establishing a helper but an enemy, but I am consoling myself with the thought that
I will succeed in fostering the state strength that will help guarantee Russia's
peaceful development in the future, without a sharp breach of those foundations on which she has existed for so long.

Nicholas also spoke of his dream of passing on a pacified Russia to his
son.[3]

Clearly, the tsar harbored no illusions about the composition and cooperation of the new legislative body. Still, he believed that the new
institution, even if hostile, did not and should not signal the end of autocratic principles and tradition. He had evidently become convinced
over the course of the past seven weeks that he had no right to precipi-
tate "a sharp breach of those foundations," as he had done with the "constitution" of October. The state had not been his to give away. Russia, he
would proclaim a few weeks later, remained an autocracy "as of old."

During the audience, Witte discussed not one but two reform proposals. One was the Kryzhanovskii-Witte version, the other, a project prepared by several public men and providing for universal male suffrage.
Considering that the October Manifesto had ruled out just such a broad
franchise for the time being, the presentation of this second project
comes as a real surprise. Indeed, Witte would later blame some of the
delay in the publication of the new law and in the convocation of the
Duma on the time needed to draft this very proposal. To add to the confusion, during the conference Witte would abandon the plan he and Kryzhanovskii had proposed, and instead endorse that of the public men, yet
he would later deny doing so.[4]

How then is the emergence of this second version to be explained?
Whether for reasons of principle or expediency, Witte was still hopeful
that the moderate elements within society could be accommodated.
Even after the failure of their negotiations on a public ministry, he had
parted amicably with his public interlocutors, or so he imagined, confident of retaining their good will. In mid-November Prince E. Trubetskoi
had complained to Witte that no supporter of a direct (and presumably
universal) franchise had been invited to the impending meeting of the
Council of Ministers that was to discuss the matter.[5] Trubetskoi's intervention evidently led to the drafting of the second project, for on Novem-

---

[3] Kryzhanovskii, *Vospominaniia*, pp. 65–67; during his report on the technical details of
the Duma electoral reform, Kryzhanovskii was struck by the "ease with which the Sovereign, although he had no special preparation, understood the complicated problems of electoral procedures, both as planned in Russia and as adopted in the Western countries, as
well as by his curiosity."

[4] Witte, *Vospominaniia*, 3:127ff.

[5] Prince E. Trubetskoi's letter to Witte, n.d., TsGIA, f. 1276, op. 1, d. 33, l. 7.

ber 30 Witte could report to Nicholas that the discussions in the Council of Ministers had produced two drafts, with a majority favoring the more restrictive franchise. Witte also recommended that four activists from society be included.[6]

Final deliberations on the new suffrage law took place at the imperial winter residence in Tsarskoe Selo on December 5, 7, and 9. In addition to the Council of Ministers, among those attending were several State Council members who had also been present at the July Conference in Peterhof, as well as the Moscow zemstvo leader D. N. Shipov, the Moscow industrialist and town duma activist A. I. Guchkov, Tula nobility marshal Count V. A. Bobrinskii, and Baron P. L. Korf.

Shipov led off by arguing the case of the second project, apparently drafted by him and Guchkov: "Insurrection and demoralization pervade society, which has lost any awareness of not only civic, but moral obligations; the notion of duty has vanished. Under such circumstances, the organized cooperation of government and society is absolutely essential, but in reality a gulf exists between government and society." A new electoral law and a deadline for the opening of the new Duma had to be announced immediately. Only a universal franchise could produce a Duma that enjoyed the confidence of all the tsar's subjects. In response to a question from Nicholas, Shipov assured him that the public men's proposal safeguarded the well-being of the narod, which was paramount.[7] Although Witte had invited Count Bobrinskii and Baron Korf as conservative counterweights to Shipov and Guchkov, they all came out squarely in favor of universal suffrage. Until recently, declared Bobrinskii, he would have favored "elections according to class [klassovye] interests," but the interests of all of Russia were at stake now. In estate-based elections, moreover, the peasants would be influenced by the intelligenty and vote for them.[8]

In his first recorded remark, Witte asked whether elections could be held in those areas where disorders were taking place, the conservative elements had fled, and government was under the influence of revolu-

[6] Witte's report, November 30, 1905, ibid., d. 41, ll. 37–38. Ibid., d. 39, ll. 29–39, contains a summary of the ministerial discussions about the two proposals. Many of the arguments presented at the December conference are anticipated here, albeit more systematically—and coherently.

[7] Soveshchanie dlia razsmotreniia predpolozhenii Soveta Ministrov o sposobakh osushchestvleniia Vysochaishikh predukazanii rozveshchennykh v punkte 2 Manifesta 17 Oktiabria 1905 goda. 5, 7 i 9 dekabria (St. Petersburg, n.d.), pp. 9–12. The official record of the proceedings is woefully incomplete, and is edited haphazardly and incoherently; while Nicholas or Witte are apparently cited in full, others of lesser significance are not. Cf., too, Tagantsev, Perezhitoe, 1:91. As the only extant record, however, the protocols still capture the general direction and flavor of the debates.

[8] Soveshchanie 5, 7 i 9 dekabria, pp. 15–16.

tionaries. Shipov expected the presence of landowners to have a calming and healthy effect on the peasants, all the more so since in most cases they were not considered personal enemies. A more realistic Korf conceded possible problems and resistance on part of the revolutionaries, which would have to be countered by increased police and military protection. Only the convocation of the Duma would end revolution once and for all. Bobrinskii insisted that elections marred by violence would have to be nullified, of course. Witte reminded his listeners that "no army is sufficient to safeguard the elections" but allowed that with only a few exceptions, they probably could take place "almost everywhere"; the revolutionaries, although determined, were few in number.

Such sanguine views provoked Interior Minister Durnovo, who denied that the solution to sedition lay in elections, no matter what the format. Not loyal elements, but the Third Element—the radical zemstvo professionals—would enter the Duma under a universal franchise. In seventeen provinces noble landlords had been killed; how could their peers be expected to rub elbows in the Duma with "medical assistants, zemstvo statisticians, and other such people, who only recently were leading the robber detachments and ruining their holdings?" Universal elections would open the doors to people who were "alien to all traditions" and incapable of discussing state affairs.[9] State Council member Stishinskii, too, opposed the Shipov-Guchkov draft, though for reasons that by his own admission were diametrically opposite to those he had advanced in July. Then he had favored the peasantry as a most reliable and conservative element. Now, presumably after being traumatized by the recent peasant disorders, Stishinskii feared that under universal suffrage the landowners and commercial classes might be drowned in "a sea of peasant votes." Clearly, the peasants were insufficiently developed to manage Duma affairs and thus were easily manipulated by revolutionary parties and unions.

On the other hand, as a landless bureaucrat, Minister of Agriculture Kutler continued to believe in the peasant "as a pillar of the state and throne"; he therefore backed the second project as more democratic, giving predominance to the peasants.[10] This draft also appealed to State Controller Filosofov for very much the same reasons: "The universal franchise is based on those principles which correspond to the world view of the Russian people: before God and the tsar all are equal."[11] Both Kutler and Filosofov thus invoked the belief in peasant monarchism inherent in autocratic ideology in order to justify democratic reforms.

[9] Ibid., p. 19.
[10] Ibid., pp. 22–23.
[11] Ibid., p. 24.

Witte reminded his confused listeners[12] that there was a revolution going on and that the issue should not be discussed in the abstract. "Outside of space and time," he argued, the Bulygin franchise was perfect; indeed, it might be made more conservative still. Given the revolutionary mood of not just the upper classes, but of the whole narod, however, such a solution now was unthinkable and impractical, especially as the troops were still far away and of unknown reliability:

> One must grant the kind of Duma that will not turn into a constituent assembly. The whole question is whether we are able to end the troubles by force or whether it is necessary to enter the path of moral pacification. Can we count on success in the first case? Outside of the large cities this is unthinkable: we do not have a sufficient quantity of troops at our disposal. Therefore we cannot delay the convocation of the Duma and must adopt that principle which best satisfies the whole population, the entire narod, and not this, that, or a third element separately.[13]

Abstract preference had to yield to reality. Witte thought that the narod had to be appeased by a universal franchise so that order might be restored. In referring to the August 6 franchise, which was not even on the conference agenda, Witte must have had in mind the first project, drawn up under his own direction by Kryzhanovskii. This draft was essentially an amended, somewhat broader version of the Bulygin franchise and represented a similar mixture of estate and property principles. Such a hybrid, while perhaps appropriate in another context or in the abstract, would not satisfy current needs, Witte seemed to say.

As the deliberations continued, Witte's opposition to the first project became more explicit. At issue was the representation of workers in the new legislative assembly: "If the workers are excluded, then we return to the situation of August 6, and there will be no lasting Duma. In order for authority to find real support in the Duma, it must be convened in such a way so as not to have to be defended with arms. . . . Such a Duma will not enjoy any authority whatsoever."[14] Witte flatly ruled out a suggestion that Kryzhanovskii's project be amended to provide for workers' representation. The two principles were simply incompatible. In what curia should the workers be included anyhow, and what about the railroad workers outside of the cities, Witte wanted to know. If all who lived by their labor were to be enfranchised, that was "equivalent to recognizing the universal franchise. In no way can you satisfy, according to the property principle, those elements of the population who do not meet

---

[12] Cf. Tagantsev, *Perezhitoe*, 1:93.
[13] *Soveshchanie 5, 7 i 9 dekabria*, p. 25.
[14] Ibid., pp. 26–27.

the property requirements. If we agree to this, then the whole law will be based in general not on principle but on arbitrariness."[15] There was no way of knowing which of the two proposed franchises might yield the best Duma, Witte insisted: "According to project #1, the Third Element will not have a voice, but nobody will prevent it from stirring up the narod. Theoretically at least, this project will supply a Duma contingent more loyal to the Sovereign, but I am not convinced of that."[16]

In fact, Witte eventually came out squarely in support of project #2. To have workers represented separately under the terms of the Kryzhanovskii draft was to recognize them as a state within a state and was therefore dangerous. Still, the workers had to be satisfied; hence the need for a universal franchise. Additional justification for a universal suffrage was to be found in the narod's devotion to their tsar and in the simplicity and naturalness of the project:

> That which is correct is always simple, because there is no artificiality in it. Everything incorrect, not flowing from the nature of things, is always more complicated and more difficult to carry out. In the West, the contemporary state structure was established under the influence of the feudal system, whereas our history took shape completely differently thanks to the narod, which now says about the state: "tsar and narod."[17]

Here Witte, like Kutler and Filosofov before him, sought to defuse objections to his impersonal and rational system by invoking the notions of organicity, simplicity, historical uniqueness, and above all, peasant monarchism, all of which were part of autocratic ideology. Despite the continuing agrarian unrest, a universal franchise was good because it included the entire narod.

Yet Witte could not hide his own apprehensions. Digressing from the subject of electoral reform, Witte had already urged that the State Duma not "be set on a level with the Sovereign." Instead, a revamped State Council was to serve as counterweight and second chamber.[18] Either Witte harbored few illusions about the future composition of the Duma and thus wanted to insulate the monarch from a direct confrontation with it, or he hoped to allay the fears that Nicholas had expressed at their most recent audience. More to the point, just after denying that the Shipov-Guchkov project presented "a particular danger," Witte admitted to

> fears stemming from the current traditions. When I judge with my mind, I am inclined in favor of the second project, but when I act according to my heart,

[15] Ibid., p. 28.
[16] Ibid., p. 26.
[17] Ibid., pp. 30–33.
[18] Ibid., p. 20.

I am afraid of this project. One must keep in mind the troubled mood of the population, which for at least several months already we have been unable to calm. . . . The second project is good in that it corresponds to the Russian consciousness, and this is very soothing medicine. Nevertheless, I am apprehensive under the present circumstances. If I had to decide the question of elections, I would cross myself and decide in favor of the second project. With the first project, all the dangerous elements are concentrated in the cities: they comprise a minority. The project creates divisions that parallel the strata of society and eliminates the possibility of a political threat by one class of the population to another. Under this system the Duma may be weak in its intellect, but not in its conservatism.[19]

Witte was rapidly losing his nerve, perhaps even his bearings. The conference split almost evenly on the question of which franchise to adopt, and Nicholas had as yet given no indication where he stood. Witte did not consciously seek to hedge his bets. Instead, he had become convinced in the course of the deliberations of the need for a universal franchise, only to give free and honest rein to his anxieties and to the possible hidden implications of the proposed legislation. His often rambling and self-contradicting speech mirrored his current state of mind. It was as though Witte was thinking aloud, with confusing results that cannot be blamed on editing alone. Small wonder that someone as educated and perceptive as State Council member Tagantsev would later write that he could not tell where Witte stood with regard to the universal franchise, or that Kryzhanovskii would accuse him of hiding his own opinions in order to put the onus on the tsar, whatever the outcome. Witte's incoherent musings and apparent indecisiveness did nothing to help the fate of universal suffrage, nor did they stem the rapid decline of the emperor's confidence in his first minister or the continued erosion of Witte's reputation in bureaucratic circles.[20]

Still, the general tenor of Witte's comments suggests that he preferred universal elections to the hybrid version, though not without some reservations. For this reason, he jumped at a compromise plan offered by A. D. Obolenskii, procurator-general and until recently Witte's close confidant. According to Witte, Obolenskii's project had the advantage of establishing universal suffrage while grouping the electorate into different "classes," such as landowners, peasants, and townspeople, who would vote separately.[21] Everyone would be enfranchised, yet votes were to be weighted differently. Voting would be "universal, but not equal," Obo-

[19] Ibid., pp. 33–34.
[20] Tagantsev, *Perezhitoe*, 1:93; Kryzhanovskii, *Vospominaniia*, pp. 72–73.
[21] *Soveshchanie 5, 7 i 9 dekabria*, p. 34.

lenskii told the quizzical tsar.[22] The drawback of this plan, in Witte's opinion, was that it would take longer to implement than either the original or the Shipov-Guchkov proposal. Clearly, time was of the essence. On the other hand, the promises of the October Manifesto ruled out a return to the August 6 franchise and presumably any derivatives thereof, whereas the second project might have other consequences, "equally undesirable." Obolenskii's plan thus could be considered an acceptable middle path after all.[23]

Up to this point the tsar had refused to be drawn into the discussions, with the exception of posing a rare query and urging the participants to be concise. To one participant it appeared as though "generally throughout the Conference [the Sovereign] had felt burdened by the sessions and tiredly had pressed forward: 'onward, onward,' as if he were bored by these deliberations, and did not expect any use from our talks."[24] To his mother Nicholas reported: "This week I have very serious and exhausting conferences dealing with the elections to the State Duma. Its future depends on the resolution of this very important problem. A. Obolenskii and a few others proposed universal elections, i.e., universal suffrage, but yesterday I rejected that with conviction. God knows how far these gentlemen's fantasies will go!"[25] After soliciting the opinion of State Council member Frish, who favored the first project, though without a separate workers' curia, Nicholas had broken the suspense:

> This problem was not at all understood by me and even interested me little. I studied it only after the Manifesto of October 17. During both sessions I found myself vacillating. But since this morning it has become clear to me that for Russia the first project is better, safer, and truer. As for the second project, my heart whispers to me that I cannot accept it. One cannot take steps that are too big. Today it is universal voting, and then it is not far to a democratic republic. That would be unthinkable and criminal. The first project gives more guarantees for the implementation of the reforms promised in the October 17 Manifesto.[26]

If the identical wording is any indication, Witte's intuitive or visceral misgivings had struck a responsive chord in Nicholas, despite the emperor's growing disenchantment with his first minister. Yet the tsar had also reaffirmed his determination to see the promises of October 17 carried out. Without ruling out change per se, he considered a universal fran-

---

[22] Ibid., p. 40.

[23] Ibid., pp. 34, 38–39.

[24] Tagantsev, *Perezhitoe*, 1:91.

[25] TsGAOR, f. 642, op. 1, d. 2328, ll. 23–26, or "Perepiska Nikolaia II i Marii Fedorovny," *KA* 22 (1927): 180–81, December 8, 1905.

[26] *Soveshchanie 5, 7 i 9 dekabria*, pp. 42–43.

chise too radical a break with Russia's traditions, for it would inevitably lead to a Western form of government. Although he claimed to have given no thought to the matter at the time, in retrospect Nicholas did not wish to sanction such a departure with the acts of October 17.

Cassandra-like, Witte warned toward the end of the proceedings that the new franchise would pacify neither revolutionary circles nor moderate elements: "The results will be bad, but in what intensity they will appear is, of course, impossible to foresee." Was it his displeasure at seeing the first project approved that provoked Witte's gloomy foreboding, or would he have felt the same way in any event? A picture of puzzlement and contradiction to the end, he now urged that no firm date be set for convening the State Duma; only recently he had pushed for a speedy convocation precisely in order to head off further unrest.

Nicholas either was more optimistic about the outcome or wanted to remain true to his words, for he flatly ruled out any postponement of the Duma.[27] But the task of organizing the first national elections in a country as far-flung, heterogeneous, and administratively inefficient as the Russian Empire would be formidable and time-consuming.[28] Given the earlier delays, the original January 15 deadline was obviously out of the question. On February 12, 1906, a ukase prepared at the tsar's behest finally fixed the opening of the Duma for April 27, 1906.[29]

Officially announced on December 11, 1905, exactly one year after Witte and Nicholas had rejected Mirskii's proposal for a mere consultative assembly, the new electoral law was quite similar to the August 6 franchise, though considerably more generous. It, too, represented a mixture of particularistic and universalistic principles, of estate and property-based requirements. The communal peasantry maintained its separate role in the election process and elected its own Duma deputy in thirty-four of the European provinces before joining the rest of the electors at the provincial level. Two other categories, the curia of private landowners and of townspeople, were defined by property, commercial and apartment taxes and were subdivided according to their places of business or residence, i.e., countryside or city.

A fourth group, the workers of all factories, mines, and railroad depots with at least fifty male employees and located in certain areas, received the right to vote for the first time. Like the peasants, these workers were kept separate and had to pass through an additional stage in the voting

[27] Ibid., p. 55.

[28] Cf., for example, the draft of Witte's January 9, 1906, report, requesting a three-week extension of the deadline for voter registration, TsGIA, f. 1544, op. dop. k 16 t., d. 21, ll. 293–94, and the ukase to this effect, l. 300 and ob.

[29] TsGAOR, f. 543, op. 1, d. 525, l. 2, and, with minor differences, "Iz rezoliutsii Nikolaia II," *Byloe* 12: 145; Lazarevskii, *Zakonodatel'nye akty*, pp. 247–48.

process; unlike their estate-based counterparts, they were not entitled to at least one Duma deputy per province. Witte had strenuously objected to such separate workers' representation in the confines of the August 6 law as arbitrary and insufficient. Though he failed, his criticism was well founded. Instead of estate or property criteria, the new law introduced occupational requirements, which in turn were circumscribed by the number of workers and the geographical location of a particular enterprise. Workers from small firms with fewer than fifty males were excluded altogether; above that level, smaller outfits tended to be overrepresented, as there was to be one elector for every shop and factory with between fifty and a thousand employees, and thereafter one elector for each additional thousand. All this was of little practical consequence, however, considering the low proportion of workers' electors in the provincial and town totals which effectively denied the workers any voice.

The new franchise, to be sure, was neither universal nor equal nor direct, but it was more inclusive than its predecessor.[30] The very emphasis on taxes accorded greater importance to an individual's productive capacity than before. Yet these conditions, while progressive, by definition excluded workers, precisely that social element most restive and in need of appeasement. Separate workers' representation must not be seen as a reversion to service estate principles akin to separate peasant representation; instead, it was a pragmatic, ad hoc response to the shortcomings of the property and tax-based system. Every precaution was taken lest such separate representation translate into a real political voice. Clearly, the workers did not enjoy the same reputation for conservatism and loyalty that the peasantry and the narod in general did. What is surprising is that the recent peasant disorders and the dire warnings of those who like Stishinskii had suffered sudden changes of heart had not yet shaken this reputation of the peasantry sufficiently to lead to any changes in the August 6 law. Not until the outcome of the first and second Duma elections and the experience of the two Dumas themselves did this high estimation change irrevocably.

[30] Unfortunately, precise figures on the expanded pool of eligible voters are not available. In addition to some workers, many nonworkers previously excluded received the right to vote, as property and tax minimums were abolished. In the landowners' curia, all private owners, not only those who could meet at least one-tenth of the full requirement, were entitled to elect plenipotentiaries in a preliminary meeting prior to the district assembly. Managers and lessors could participate, too, if they met the other requirements. In the townspeople's curia, the mere payment of tax, not the amount, determined one's right to vote. Finally, military personnel, although still excluded, for voting purposes could transfer their eligibility to their sons, if these, like all voters, were at least twenty-five years old. The remaining changes were relatively insignificant.

For the full text including all the addenda after December 11, 1905, see Lazarevskii, *Zakonodatel'nye akty*, pp. 668–789.

As Witte's vacillating conduct at the December conference in Tsarskoe Selo made clear, to say nothing of his still more recent conversion to the unrestrained use of force, he had become deeply concerned that the revolution might sweep away the existing political and social order. Contradictory impulses and conceptions ruled his thinking and behavior. He continued to subscribe, as did others, to the peasant monarchist illusion of a conservative and loyal narod that was tied to the person of the tsar and that would be the grateful beneficiary of the state bureaucracy's activist and interventionist reformism. This is why Witte supported a franchise that so obviously favored Russia's peasantry. This electoral law, moreover, was approved *after* the first serious disorders had racked the countryside, as the participants in the December conference knew all too well. Although his peasant monarchism had evidently survived intact for the time being, Witte also realized how dangerous the narod could be. Hence the misgivings that so perplexed his listeners in Tsarskoe Selo; hence, too, his increasingly shrill insistence on a governmental show of force. At the same time, in order to appease the narod and prevent still greater rural disturbances, he considered it necessary to make concessions that he would have ruled out in more normal circumstances. The franchise itself was such an attempt at appeasement—as would be his proposal for a partial expropriation of private lands.

THE STATE COUNCIL REFORMED

Witte's persistent anxieties notwithstanding, there could be little doubt that the worst of the revolutionary danger had passed by January 1906. With the revolution contained, if not defeated, and with the new legislative assembly appointed for the end of April, all energies could be turned toward implementing the reforms envisioned by the October acts: the institutional coordination of all government activity, the detailed formulation of a coherent program of government policies that would reshape society and the body politic, and the codification of recent conceptual changes through a revision of the State Duma and State Council charters as well as the Fundamental Laws of the Empire. The impending opening of the new Duma imparted a particular urgency to these tasks; otherwise the government would find itself face to face with the people's representatives without unity or a prepared program, and the legal revisions would become the plaything of public passions. Each of these imperatives, moreover, directly or indirectly entailed a particular definition of the autocrat's role. What follows is an attempt to bring into sharper focus these definitions and conceptual changes and to clarify the tsar's own positions and reactions in this process.

To consider the issue of State Council reform, Nicholas, on October

28, 1905, had asked Count Sol'skii to establish yet another Special Conference.[31] That body was to take its cue from Witte's report of October 17. This document had mentioned the great importance of "reforming the State Council on the basis of prominent participation by an elected element," so as to assure normal relations between the new State Duma and the existing State Council.[32] In something resembling a two-chamber Western legislature, the State Council was seen as the upper house and a conservative counterweight to a possibly radical and obstructionist Duma that might otherwise confront the monarch directly. An October 9 policy paper by Kryzhanovskii was still more explicit on this point. Hoping to avoid the overuse of the tsar's veto-power in those cases when the Duma's decisions would be unacceptable, Kryzhanovskii had written:

> Whatever the power of the executive and however deep the roots of this authority in the past life of the nation, political wisdom dictates that this power should be subjected to as few trials as possible in the petty instances and current affairs of legislation and administration. In the present circumstances of our state, which is experiencing both external events that place a heavy tax on the feelings of national pride and self-worth, and profound internal ferment marking the transition of the broad masses of the population from unconscious to conscious state life, the basic objective of our state structure ought to be the preservation of the Autocratic Authority of the Sovereign on the high level appropriate to it and its removal from the petty affairs of prosaic life and mutual clashes of social interests. The experience of both history and every-day life show that only the elevation and a certain remoteness of the Supreme Authority sustain its charm in the lower strata of the population.[33]

A reformed State Council on the same level as the State Duma and an integral part of the legislative process, so Kryzhanovskii's argument went, would help preserve the mystique and "charm" of autocratic power.

How was Nicholas going to react to this attempt at transforming or redefining his own role? Could his authority really be removed to "the high level appropriate to it" and still remain autocratic? According to autocratic ideology, the tsar transcended partisan and selfish interests, but he did not relinquish his right personally to resolve the conflict between them. If "the petty affairs of prosaic life and the mutual clashes of social interests" became the province of State Duma and Council, what would become of the tsar's role as personal arbiter? His power would be cur-

---

[31] Sol'skii's report of October 27, 1905, with Nicholas's resolution of October 28, TsGIA, f. 1544, op. dop. k 16 t., d. 16, ll. 111–12.

[32] Lazarevskii, *Zakonodatel'nye akty*, p. 155.

[33] The translation is Doctorow's, "Introduction of Parliamentary Institutions in Russia," pp. 215–16.

tailed and his mediating role institutionalized. Viewed in Weberian terms, the ruler's personal charisma would be routinized. The recent severe strains in the social fabric and the paralysis and disintegration of traditional bureaucratic authority had highlighted and exposed the person of the ruler. Lest the tsar lose his "charm" and legitimacy now that the mythical bureaucratic barrier between tsar and narod had all but vanished, a new screen had to be erected around him in the form of a counterbalancing two-chamber system.

While passage of the State Duma charter was a foregone conclusion, the exact dimensions of the State Council reform had still to be determined. After Count Sol'skii had submitted the conclusions of his Special Conference to Nicholas on February 6, 1906,[34] the tsar convened a conference at Tsarskoe Selo on February 14 and 16 in order to review any unresolved points and give final approval to the proposed changes. With few exceptions, the participants were the same as in December.[35]

To autocratic loyalists such as Count Ignat'ev, the remaking of the State Council into an upper chamber marked "already a decisive step towards a constitutional system, and this step can only be taken consciously." He felt obligated by his service oath to warn Nicholas not to go beyond what had been granted in the October Manifesto.[36] Echoing Kryzhanovskii's reasoning, Witte saw no grounds for concern, however. It would be the task of the State Council to serve as a "buffer" between Duma and tsar, a savior from the Duma's lack of restraint, guarantor of "the conservative system of government," and barrier to "all extreme views."[37]

Stishinskii, too, was disturbed by the institutionalization of the legislative process along Western lines. He attacked the proposal that there be as many elected members as there were appointed ones. If appointed members outnumbered elected members, Witte countered, the institution of the State Council would be discredited in the eyes of the public.

[34] Sol'skii's report, February 6, 1906, TsGIA, f. 1544, op. dop. k 16 t., d. 22, l. 113.

[35] The ministers of justice and agriculture had been replaced, and four other members were added on Sol'skii's recommendation; Sol'skii's report, February 12, 1906, ibid., d. 19, l. 2 and ob., 3 and ob.

[36] "Tsarskosel'skoe Soveshchanie. Protokoly sekretnogo soveshchaniia v fevrale 1906 g. pod predsedatel'stvom byvshego imperatora, po vyrabotke Uchrezhdenii Gosudarstvennoi Dumy i Gosudarstvennogo Soveta," Byloe 5–6 (November–December 1917): 293.

[37] The very election of 18 members from the provincial nobility, 6 from the Orthodox clergy, and 12 from trade and industry was going to assure a conservative makeup, Witte argued. In addition, of the 98 elected members, 34 were to represent the zemstvos, 22 those provinces without zemstvos, and 6 the universities and other institutions of higher learning. They would serve for nine years, with one-third of the membership to stand for election every three years. So as to assure the election of the "most stable" elements, the proposal raised the age and educational requirements that applied to Duma deputies; elected State Council members had to be graduates of secondary school and at least forty years old; ibid., pp. 293–94.

Though Witte later termed the issue "not very significant," six more participants spoke out in favor of numerical equality; five, among them Interior Minister Durnovo, opposed it openly. Eventually, Nicholas sided with the majority and the original plan.[38]

Another form of equality was at issue in the debate over whether a State Council veto could be overriden by a two-thirds Duma majority. This had been the position taken by two dissenters during the deliberations of Sol'skii's group. At the time, a lopsided majority of 25 to 2 had insisted that both chambers be granted equal rights; therefore, a bill rejected by either chamber would not be submitted to Nicholas nor could it be reintroduced without first being changed. Although Nicholas had already signaled his agreement with the majority,[39] Witte now chose to reopen the matter during the second meeting of the February conference in Tsarskoe Selo. Unless its veto could be overridden, Witte explained, the State Council would be seen as an aristocratic institution, one in which the peasants were not represented. It was they who had to have access to the tsar. Witte's peasant monarchist illusions made him forget his earlier warnings of a radical and obstructionist Duma and his praises of the State Council's buffer function. If the State Council were allowed to prevent a Duma bill from reaching the emperor's desk, Witte warned, then the peasants would conclude that the bureaucrats were once again separating them from their sovereign. The fact that Western systems required the approval of both houses was insufficient reason to adopt the same rule in Russia. Witte therefore suggested an amendment permitting the Duma to inform the tsar of its conclusions over the objections of the State Council. If the tsar agreed with the bill, he could order a minister to reintroduce it in the Duma.[40]

Witte's suggestion drew the ire of former Finance Minister Kokovtsev. Not only had the matter been settled already, he reminded Witte, but the proposed change would undermine the effectiveness and very purpose of the State Council. In a startling rejoinder, Witte accused Kokovtsev of seeking a constitution by insisting on copying the Western example of an upper house veto. At that point, the aged Count Palen, former minister of justice under Alexander II, interceded. Whether Witte agreed or not, Palen argued, the fact was that Russia had been governed constitutionally ever since the October Manifesto.[41] During a tea-break with Nicholas, Palen was still blunter in denouncing Witte's amendment: "But to say that you did not grant a constitution is to curry favor. You

[38] Ibid., pp. 294–95.
[39] He did question the prohibition against reintroducing in the same session projects that had been vetoed by either chamber or by the emperor.
[40] Ibid., pp. 305–6.
[41] Ibid., p. 306.

granted a constitution and must preserve it. Until now we have been ruined by bureaucratic omnipotence, but with the acceptance of the proposed measure we will sink into demagogic omnipotence."[42] Not so, replied Witte, for not a single university faculty would endorse Palen's definition of a constitution. After all, the tsar was introducing this system of his own free will, without compulsion and without having to swear an oath to the new order. The very opposition of the extreme parties only served to bear out his argument, Witte claimed.[43] Returning to the issue that had prompted this exchange, Witte pleaded that the psychology of the narod be taken into account. The unity of "God and Tsar!" implied that the narod should never be separated from its ruler.

Discussion on this point raged back and forth. Finally, Nicholas reaffirmed his earlier decision in favor of the majority.[44] Once again, as he had done in December during his audience with Witte and Kryzhanovskii, Nicholas had distanced himself from Witte's peasant monarchism. And consciously or not, by barring the suspension of a State Council veto by a two-thirds Duma majority, the tsar had in effect endorsed Kryzhanovskii's argument that the ruler be removed from the petty squabbles of partisan politics.

As for Witte's behavior, there was considerable truth in Palen's charge. Witte obviously knew how much Nicholas disliked the very word "constitution," to say nothing of its Western connotations. By accusing others of striving for a constitution or Western-style changes, Witte sought to discredit them and their arguments in the eyes of the tsar and get back into his good graces. As obvious as this opportunism was, however, it obscured the principles behind Witte's thinking.

The fact is that a constitutional system along Western lines, founded on an implied social contract and the delegation of authority by the sovereign people to their government, was not Witte's political ideal. Instead, the monarch was to be subject and to conform to the rules and laws of his own making. This Rechtsstaat ideal implied the delegation of authority from the ruler to his professional administrators and adjudicators, i.e., the bureaucracy headed by none other than Witte. The bureaucracy had to ascertain and be responsive to the needs of the people, of course, but without being responsible to them. In this sense, the bureaucratic administration shared in the mediating function of the autocratic ruler and could use his great power in order to effect changes.

Public opinion and popular representation played a crucial role in this scheme. Although they did not have the right to determine policy, they

[42] "Dnevnik A. A. Polovtseva," *KA* 4 (1923): 92.
[43] "Protokoly soveshchaniia v fevrale 1906 g.," pp. 306–7.
[44] Ibid., pp. 307–11.

served to publicize popular needs and problems, and thereby could strengthen the position of the bureaucracy vis-à-vis particularistic groups and institutions and sometimes even the emperor himself. Without a constituency of sorts, the bureaucracy would be left defenseless against the legal violations and encroachments of the autocrat and those anachronistic remnants.[45] Moreover, Witte was holding firmly to his faith in the goodness and loyalty of the peasant narod, despite the events of the past months.

Such a course was fraught with perils, of course. To pilot a reform-minded and interventionist bureaucracy between the Scylla of representative democracy, which would place them at the mercy of the mob, and the Charybdis of traditional autocracy, which delivered them into the clutches of arbitrary personal rule, demanded almost superhuman skills and talents, as Witte had already found out. The smooth functioning of the bureaucracy required restraints on the ruler's arbitrariness. Yet any popular restrictions on the powers and privileges of the emperor ultimately might also tie the hands of the bureaucracy and therefore were to be resisted. It is precisely for this reason that Witte had developed second thoughts about the rule that no law take effect without the approval of the two chambers; under these conditions, how could the tsar continue to issue administrative decrees, Witte wanted to know.[46] He also objected to the requirement that the tsar, in case of the Duma's dissolution, immediately set a date for its reconvocation within the next six months.[47] By the same token, Witte defended the procedures for issuing new laws at those times when the Duma was not in session as a necessary "stick in the corner."[48] To make his points, Witte was not averse to using the imagery and phraseology of autocratic ideology, which, to his mind at least, easily accommodated his conception of the modern bureaucratic state.

"LET YOUR POWERS BE UNLIMITED"

This conception emerged into full relief and was resisted by Nicholas during the reconsideration of Russia's Fundamental Laws in March and April 1906. Neither the October Manifesto nor Witte's report had made any mention of a possible revision of the Empire's basic laws. While this possibility may first have been raised during the deliberations of Sol'skii's

[45] According to Gurko, *Features and Figures*, pp. 450–51, Boris Glinskii made many of the same points in several articles he wrote for *Istoricheskii Vestnik* in 1912 or 1913, purportedly based on documents he had received from Witte.

[46] "Protokoly soveshchaniia v fevrale 1906 g.," p. 294.

[47] Draft of Duma Charter of February 16, 1906, with Witte's handwritten corrections, TsGIA, f. 1544, op. dop. k 16 t., d. 19, ll. 160–7 ob.

[48] "Protokoly soveshchaniia v fevrale 1906 g.," p. 295.

Special Conference on State Council reform in November, the actual redrafting process did not commence until January.[49] Despite alleged leaks "from Count Witte's circles and probably by himself,"[50] the public seems to have had little, if any, knowledge of the ongoing preparations. When the tsar ordered the latest draft of the basic statute reviewed by the Council of Ministers at the beginning of March, he stipulated that such review take place "under the condition of preserving full secrecy."[51]

Witte had already subjected the project to a withering critique that obviously came to guide the thinking of the Council of Ministers: "In my opinion, this project, on the one hand, contains several articles that it would be dangerous to permit and, on the other hand, does not contain those kinds of statements that under the new order of things appear absolutely necessary."[52] As before, he considered the distinction between laws and administrative decrees insufficient. Unless the tsar remained free to issue decrees without Duma and State Council approval, great complications were certain to ensue. Witte would later claim that without these criticisms and changes of the original draft, *"the state and its government* would have been politically castrated." But for his timely intervention, Witte insisted, the monarch, "voluntarily or, more correctly, unconsciously," for the second time since October 17 would have limited his power to a point where he would have commanded less than the French president and in some respects even less than the president of the Swiss Confederation.[53]

Whatever the validity of Witte's self-serving charge, there can be little doubt that the document that emerged from the ministerial deliberations was considerably less generous than its predecessor. Not only did Witte and the Council seek to define administrative decrees and executive regulations as distinct from laws so as to avoid any future conflict over such ticklish issues with the new Duma, but these attempts at clarification betrayed an unmistakable tendency to reserve for the government as many administrative prerogatives as possible. According to Witte, the functioning and regulation of all government agencies, the preservation of state security and public order, and the safeguarding of popular well-being all were to come within the purview of imperial ukases that did not require legislative approval. The conduct of foreign relations and military affairs, the imposition of emergency rule and the limitation of civil liber-

[49] For a detailed discussion of the exact circumstances surrounding this revision, cf. Verner, "Nicholas II and the Role of the Autocrat," p. 509 n. 196.
[50] At least, this was the charge made by Imperial Secretary Baron Ikskul' in his report of January 25, 1906; TsGAOR, f. 43, op. 1, d. 536, l. 136.
[51] Witte's report, March 2, 1906, TsGIA, f. 1276, op. 2, d. 7, ll. 1–2.
[52] Ibid.; also in "Iz arkhiva S. Iu. Vitte," *KA* 11–12 (1925): 115–16.
[53] Witte, *Vospominaniia*, 3:301; emphasis mine.

ties in such cases, the coinage of money, the disposition of imperial property, and the dismissal of government employees, including tenured
judges, were to be the exclusive preserve of the emperor, subject only to
budgetary review by the two chambers. Civil rights came under close
scrutiny, too. As for the political accountability of ministers, as distinguished from their responsibility under criminal and civil law, Witte
counseled against any details that might be misconstrued as sanctioning
legislative oversight. Instead, Witte proposed a general statement of
principle to the effect that the ministers bore collective and individual
responsibility for the general course of state administration before the
sovereign. Inasmuch as Russia's development was considered the accomplishment of its rulers—and their servitors, presumably—it was not to be
jeopardized by Duma interference.[54]

In early April the new draft received its final consideration at yet another Special Conference chaired by Nicholas. As Witte would explain at
the outset, there were good reasons for revising the Fundamental Laws,
even though the October acts had made no explicit mention of such a
possibility. For one, these acts and the reforms announced since then had
rendered some of the old Fundamental Laws obsolete. Many of the tsar's
rights, moreover, had to be defined for the first time in order to forestall
any infringement or alternative interpretation on the part of the Duma.
Once anchored in the Fundamental Laws, such prerogatives would be
effectively removed from the purview of the Duma, unless the tsar himself initiated a review. This was true for the budget rules, dynastic privileges, and other clauses of the Fundamental Laws as well. A complete
revision of these laws, as opposed to piecemeal amendments, would present the Duma with a fait accompli and thus avoid friction in the future.[55]

Sol'skii, too, argued for a complete revision of the Fundamental Laws,
though for different reasons. As chairman of the State Council and of a
Special Conference he had supervised many of the recent changes.
Hence he understood that the old laws had been "written under different
conditions; they were based on different principles. . . . The very principles of administration have changed. The Duma has been summoned
to legislate; it was granted a decisive voice." These new tenets had to be
incorporated into the Fundamental Laws, for "on [them] the state's existence is founded. Therefore, everything has to be corrected that does
not accord with the requirements of reality."[56]

---

[54] Ibid., 297–300; TsGIA, f. 1544, op. 1, d. 23, l. 412; cf., too, Doctorow, "Introduction
of Parliamentary Institutions in Russia," pp. 296–98.

[55] *Soveshchanie po peresmotru osnovnykh gosudarstvennykh zakonov. Protokoly zasedanii soveshchaniia, pod lichnym Ego Imperatorskago Velichestva predsedatel'stvom 7, 9,
11 i 12 aprelia 1906 goda* (St. Petersburg, 1906), pp. 5–7.

[56] Ibid., pp. 7–8.

At the heart of this reality, as everyone present knew only too well, was the proper definition of the tsar's power. The old Fundamental Laws had defined the Supreme Power as "autocratic and unlimited." The question whether this definition remained in force had exercised their minds ever since October. When Naumov had asked Witte at the end of their November 20 meeting whether tsarist autocracy continued "to exist in its full inviolability" after October, Witte had answered firmly and without hesitation: "Absolutely not."[57] Others, including Nicholas, had gone so far as to speak of a constitution.[58] In the Duma Charter of February 20, on the other hand, Nicholas had made an important and revealing revision: literally at the last minute, he had personally restored the appellation *samoderzhavnyi* (autocratic), but not *neogranichennyi* (unlimited).[59] Perhaps taking its cue from that act, the Council of Ministers now proposed to delete the modifier "unlimited" from the Fundamental Laws as well. As a memorandum accompanying the new draft explained, "autocratic" had always been synonymous with "unlimited"—which would have made the old definition redundant. Now, however, "autocratic" was to signify merely that the tsar had received power by God's grace, not by the will of the people, some convention, or another monarch.[60]

Nicholas was not to be so easily appeased. Had the tsar's power really ceased to be unlimited as a result of October? Identifying this question as the main issue before the conference, Nicholas admitted to considerable soul-searching and misgivings:

I have not ceased thinking about this problem since the project for a review of the Fundamental Laws came before My eyes for the first time. I have kept the project for a whole month and have continued to think about this question constantly since the Chairman of the Council of Ministers reported to Me on the revised project. All this time the thought has tormented Me, whether I have the right before My ancestors to change the boundaries of the power I received from them. The struggle within Me continues. I still have not arrived at a definitive conclusion. A month ago it seemed to Me easier to decide this question than it does now after long reflection when time demands a decision. During all this time I received and continue to receive every day scores of telegrams, addresses, requests from all ends and corners of the Russian land and from all sorts of estates of people. They convey to Me the touching feelings of loyal subjects, together with the plea not to limit My power and with gratitude for the rights granted by the Manifesto of October 17. Seeking to grasp the thinking of these people, I understand them as striving for the preservation

[57] Naumov, *Iz utselevshikh vospominanii*, 2:35–36.
[58] Cf. Golitsyn, "Vospominaniia" (Manuscript, REEACU), p. 162, and supra, p. 240.
[59] Duma charter with Nicholas's handwritten addendum, TsGAOR, f. 601, op. 1, d. 900.
[60] Liubimov, "Russkaia smuta," p. 455.

of the act of 17 October and the rights granted in it to My subjects, but not to go one step further and for Me to remain the Autocrat of all Russia.

I tell you sincerely, be assured, that if I were convinced that Russia wanted me to renounce my Autocratic rights, I would do this gladly for her good. The Act of 17 October was given by Me in a fully conscious way, and I have firmly resolved to carry it to its conclusion. But I am not convinced of the necessity under it to renounce the autocratic rights and to alter the definition of the Supreme power which has existed for 109 years in Article 1 of the Fundamental Laws. It is My conviction that on many grounds it is extremely dangerous to change this article and to adopt a new wording, even the one proposed by the Council of Ministers. If this is not done, it may give the impression of insincerity; they might say that this is a retreat from the promises made on October 17. I know and understand this. In any case, this rebuke must not be addressed to the government, but to Me personally. I assume all responsibility. Whatever happens and whatever they may say, they won't get Me to budge from last year's act and I won't retreat from it. I know that if article 1 remains unchanged, this will provoke alarm and attacks. But it must be understood from whom the reproach will come. It will come, of course, from the whole so-called educated element, the proletarians, the third element. But I am certain that 80 percent of the Russian people will be with Me, will offer Me support, and will be grateful to Me for such a decision. Just today I received a touching plea from Mogilev province not to renounce My rights, together with gratitude for the Manifesto of 17 October. The most important thing is to implement this Manifesto. . . . [T]he question of My prerogatives is a matter for My conscience, and I will decide whether it is necessary to leave the article as it is or to change it.[61]

In Nicholas's mind at least, the October Manifesto and autocracy were fully compatible. He refused to see any contradiction between the rights promised by the October acts and the absence of any limitations on the autocrat's personal power and prerogatives. While determined to uphold those promises, he was reluctant to change the traditional definition of his powers. The reforms owed their very origin to the tsar's autocratic and unlimited power, but could not possibly circumscribe it. Nicholas appeared to draw a distinction between the autocrat and his government, his actions and its policies; any criticism was to be directed at the ruler, not the government. It was as though the civil liberties and legislative participation announced in October were binding only on the government, but not on him personally. Nicholas was seeking refuge in the personalized and patriarchal conception of autocracy, while leaving others to invoke its institutionalized and impersonal counterpart.

The tsar's new-found resolve to see autocracy maintained coincided not

---

[61] *Soveshchanie aprelia 1906 goda*, pp. 28–29.

only with the waning of the revolutionary danger but also with a growing stream of loyal addresses and audience requests. As early as late October, Nicholas had referred to the "touching" messages of the "good people" that were urging him to preserve autocracy.[62] At the time, the imperatives of restoring order and of reform had taken precedence over the proper definition of the ruler's role. In several audiences with conservative noble delegations in December and early January, Nicholas repeatedly reaffirmed his unshakeable will to ensure the implementation of the liberties that had been granted in October.[63] During January, February, and early March, on the other hand, it was the inviolability of private property that would preoccupy the sovereign in his responses to petitions and delegations from the peasantry and nobility.[64] By the middle of February, the tsar was singing yet another tune, as he assured a delegation from Kazan that autocracy remained "as of old" and that he would not "tolerate any diminution of autocracy."[65] Any limitation of his power, Nicholas believed, would violate the sacred legacy of his ancestors and the expressed wishes of at least 80 percent of the Russian population. If Russia's good required such a momentous concession, he would grant it willingly, but the people had registered their opposition. Their sentiments clearly were instrumental in guiding his thinking, though not without considerable selection and rationalization on his part. He saw and heard what he wanted or what fit in with his preconceptions and predilections.

The overwhelming majority of these loyal messages came from peasants. The number of addresses and audience requests, already considerable in February, reached flood-level in March; the tsar had to order an end to such audiences on April 10 for simple lack of time. All of the messages affirmed the peasants' love and devotion to their "Little Father Tsar" and to "Little Mother Russia"; they denounced the "troubles" and the traitors' attempts to limit the tsar's autocratic power, calling on Nicholas to preserve it. Most expressed thanks for the manifestos of the past months, and some even stressed the need to convene the Duma immediately and to help the peasantry. Typically, one such address reminded the sovereign:

[62] Cf. supra, pp. 260–61.

[63] Cf. the diary entries of an exasperated Kireev: GLB OR, f. 126, d. 14, ll. 112, 121; see, too, TsGIA, f. 1276, op. 1, d. 49, ll. 18–19, and TsGIA, f. 516, op. 219/2728, d. 21, l. 608.

[64] TsGAOR, f. 601, op. 1, d. 1, l. 100, *Posluzhnii spisok*, January 18, 1906; TsGIA, f. 1276, op. 1, d. 49, l. 12, Draft of Nicholas's remarks to Prince Trubetskoi, the Moscow marshal of the nobility, on January 19, 1906; TsGAOR, f. 601, op. 1, d. 1, l. 101, February 2, 1906, Nicholas's comments before delegations of Tambov and Tula nobles; and ibid., l. 102, February 9, 1906, delegation from Vladimir nobility.

[65] GBL OR, f. 126, d. 14, l. 127, February 17, 1906.

Remember that You were put in Your place by the Lord God and that You are the Anointed before the Sacred Throne and that You, God's Anointed, are not free to renounce [autocratic power] and to take an oath [of allegiance], as you did to the one God, that is the will of the Lord God. Let Your power be unlimited, and the State Duma not deciding, but consultative.

Again and again, peasants called on Nicholas not to deliver them and Russia into alien, non-Orthodox hands, but to remain the defender of the Orthodox faith, a tsar in the fullness of his powers, "the single master of the Russian land." "You will defend us from the evil of untruth, by not permitting Your Orthodox narod to be put on the same level as the Jews." He was their intercessor, parent, provider, without whom "we cannot live." Only one word was needed and they would rally around the throne and protect it.[66] These then were the messages "from all ends and corners of the Russian land and from all sorts of estates of people" that had touched Nicholas and made him doubt the need to alter the traditional definition of the autocrat's power.

The tsar did not realize that these loyal sentiments were most certainly the outgrowth of a massive and well-coordinated campaign by local clergy, landowners, and government officials. Addresses from adjacent districts and townships as well as from provinces hundreds of miles apart, such as Vologda and Smolensk, contained many phrases and entire passages that were identical. The same historical and biblical allusions, the same quotations, the same bizarre or original ideas leave no doubt that large-scale collusion was at work here:

The Tsar will be elected only when the river Neva begins to flow uphill; let the dissatisfied loafers sit on the banks of the Neva and watch when it flows backwards, for then we will elect a tsar for them; but we do not need it, we have a sovereign from the House of the Romanovs and it is our wish that the Tsardom of the House of the Romanovs carry on from generation to generation.[67]

The ubiquitous references to prayer services, church teachings, the Orthodox faith, the tsar's role as God's Anointed and defender of the faith, and to the threat of non-Orthodox, non-Russian, and especially of Jewish groups suggests, moreover, that the clergy played a crucial role in initiating the campaign and supervising or undertaking the actual drafting of these messages. Involvement in this outpouring of loyal autocratic sentiments extended all the way to the minister of internal affairs, for the addresses really began to pile up after February 2, 1906, when Durnovo

[66] TsGIA, f. 1276, op. 1, d. 37 passim.
[67] This passage, for example, can be found in addresses from Smolensk and Kostroma guberniia, ibid., ll. 130, 167–68.

and Witte, with the tsar's blessing, agreed on a procedure for handling all requests for audiences.[68] On April 2, for example, Durnovo forwarded four petitions and several audience requests from Old Believers to the tsar with the following explanation: "the addresses, *in part corrected according to my instructions*, . . . still preserve their basic thought about the unshakeableness of Y.I.M.'s Autocratic Power."[69] The counterfeit and suspiciously unrepresentative nature of this wave of messages escaped Nicholas, however. Because they happened to confirm his own preferences, he took the pleas for the preservation of autocracy for bare coin.

"YOU, SOVEREIGN, DEIGNED TO LIMIT YOUR POWER"

It was clear to all attending the April conference in Tsarskoe Selo that the very fate of the reform process and of autocracy hung in the balance. At the center of the deliberations stood the nature of the autocrat's power. "With this question the whole future of Russia will be decided," Witte intoned.[70] While there was general agreement among the participants that the October acts had introduced a new and crucial distinction between administrative and legislative authority, they disagreed on whether the tsar's rights had been curtailed in one or both of these spheres. As it turned out, Nicholas was virtually alone in his insistence that the autocrat's power had been unaffected by the recent reforms.

Taking up the matter of the ruler's legislative prerogatives, Frish, who chaired the State Council's Department of Law, warned that the tsar could not simply reserve for himself, as he had just announced, the exclusive right to review or alter those parts of the Fundamental Laws concerning the imperial family and its possessions. The exclusion of the Duma and State Council in those instances was a violation of the principles laid down in the October Manifesto and in the legislation of February 20, Frish charged; it was "a direct retreat" that might even spark disorders. Those acts mandated Duma and State Council consideration of all legislative changes. On the other hand, the initiative and final approval for such alterations still remained with the monarch and thus precluded any unwanted revisions (8–9, 13–14). At least three other State Council members supported Frish's principled stand against exempting

[68] Ibid., l. 22.

[69] TsGIA, f. 1284, op. 241, d. 122, l. 67; emphasis mine.

[70] *Soveshchanie aprelia 1906 goda*, p. 30. All parenthetical page numbers in the text (pp. 303–7) refer to this source.

The extant proceedings of the four-day Special Conference take up a mere ninety-four pages, with wide line spacings to boot. Published in Tsarist Russia, the transcript was either incomplete or heavily excised. In vain do we look for any discussion of the infamous article 87, for example. Instead we have to search out lesser articles for even the slightest hint as to the thinking of the participants and the conceptions underlying their arguments.

any law from the Duma's purview, now matter how important or dear to the tsar's interests (11–12, 14–16).

Interior Minister Durnovo, on the other hand, preferred to leave any and all changes in the Fundamental Laws to the tsar. Such a rule would not violate the October Manifesto, as charged by Frish, but would be a much-needed addition: "the Act of 17 October is far from perfect and the whole rebellion arising after it was a consequence of this imperfection" (10–11). Ignoring this backhanded slap, Witte agreed with Nicholas that specific articles should remain the exclusive domain of the autocrat: "If you look at it from the point of view of the recently issued acts, then E. V. Frish is correct, but you have to take into consideration state needs, which are above logic." Better some dissatisfaction now than a general rebellion later (12–13). When it came to the primacy of state interests and the assertion of the state's power, Witte had little tolerance for constitutional niceties. Not surprisingly, State Council member Stishinskii sided with the tsar as well. Eventually, another ad hoc conference, consisting of five grand dukes, the court minister, and the imperial secretary, amended the project in conformance with Nicholas's wishes by excluding from Duma and State Council consideration those sections dealing with the imperial family (17).

The province of administrative responsibilities was separate from the tsar's legislative authority, according to Frish, but it, too, needed to be defined:

In this area the Sovereign Emperor acts independently and through subordinate organs. Until now everything has depended personally on the Sovereign, and therefore the vagueness existing in this regard did not present particular inconveniences. Now the power of the executive has to be delineated from the legislative power, so the Duma cannot interfere in the Supreme administration. Only the Fundamental Laws can reinforce this principle. (9–10)

Although he accepted the new distinction between the administrative and legislative spheres, former interior minister Goremykin took exception to Frish's position. The recent reforms had merely altered the procedure for issuing new laws and thus in effect had limited only the tsar's legislative power, Goremykin argued. No such restrictions applied to the "Supreme Power" in the administrative area. Either this power continued to be "unlimited" or it had to be defined precisely and comprehensively, a well-nigh impossible task: "The human mind cannot grasp this; it's impossible to foresee all displays of supreme government." In the absence of detailed provisions for every contingency, "if the word 'unlimited' is simply eliminated, it will be impossible to get out of difficult situations. Therefore the word should be dropped only when we determine escapes for all instances of state life. And since this is out of the question, it is best not to touch article 1 of the Fundamental Laws" (29–30). Despite the objections of nearly everyone present, Goremykin's observation was not without merit. The mere differentiation between legislative and administrative power was insufficient and would lead to conflict or paralysis, unless the exact dimensions of each were spelled out in detail.

Goremykin's distinction between the recently delimited legislative and the still unlimited administrative power of the autocrat was challenged by Witte. Since the Russian state was "governed on the firm basis of laws" according to the Fundamental Laws, Witte maintained, the "Supreme Power" in reality was "subordinate to the law and regulated by it"; in this sense, it had ceased to be unlimited with Alexander I. The autocrat's power had been restricted both in the legislative and the administrative sphere, Witte seemed to imply. If Nicholas considered it impossible, however, to renounce his unlimited power, then it would be best not to revise the Empire's basic statute. In that case, they should simply codify the recent changes and announce, lest the Duma turn into a constituent assembly, that the tsar alone could issue new ones. But Witte admitted to second thoughts. He claimed to be as "disturbed" now as he had been on October 17, unsure whether the proposed draft was really good enough. The contested article was indeed "imperfect." Perhaps it was dangerous to issue an imperfect law (30–31).

No such doubts beset the nine speakers that followed. Minister of Justice Akimov and one of his predecessors, Count Palen, while disclaiming any sympathy for the October Manifesto, agreed that with it the tsar's power indeed had been limited, at least in the legislative realm. "In my opinion," explained Palen,

> You, Sovereign, deigned to limit Your power. . . . [T]he word "unlimited" cannot remain. You only retained the power to stop a decision of the Duma and State Council that you find objectionable. When the legislative power does not belong in its entirety to the Emperor, the Monarch is limited. If you are to say "unlimited" now, this means to throw down the gauntlet, to establish irreconcilable hatred in the Duma.

So as to protect the tsar's rights and avoid conflict, one must say: "this is Mine, this is Yours" (32). State Council member Saburov took issue with Nicholas's long opening statement. The loyal addresses to which the tsar had referred came from the "dark people" who were ignorant of the disputed article. In no way should such sentiments be taken as proof that the October Manifesto could be reconciled with the notion of unlimited power. Rumors had it that the sovereign had renounced all of his rights. The assurance that Nicholas retained full administrative power would pacify the people. Nicholas's cousin, the Grand Duke Nikolai, pointed out that the October Manifesto had already left out the word "unlimited";

he was seconded by the tsar's uncle, the Grand Duke Vladimir, and two other speakers. Frish and Durnovo not only favored the proposed omission, but added that the sovereign no longer had the right under the terms of the October 17 and February 20 acts to change or revise the Fundamental Laws by himself. Only the initiative for such revisions belonged to the tsar (33–34).

Although Nicholas deferred his decision on the definition of his power, its outcome was virtually foregone. In spite of his earlier strong misgivings, he now bowed to the near-unanimity of his advisors. As a result, the word "unlimited" was not restored to the Council's draft of the Fundamental Laws. Only much later would it become clear that Nicholas had taken the advice of State Council member Stishinskii. While consenting to the editorial change, Stishinskii had insisted that the tsar preserve for himself the exclusive right of revision: "This is unlimited power. We must exclude only the word, but preserve the power." The fact was that "autocracy cannot be separated from unlimitedness" (35). In his heart Nicholas had indeed retained that right of revising the Empire's basic law when necessary.

Now that the autocrat's power was no longer unlimited, the Special Conference spent the rest of its time seeking to define the dimensions of this power and spell out its practical applications—just as Goremykin had predicted it should and would. How, for example, were ukases and decrees to be distinguished from laws, i.e., what orders could the tsar issue without first securing Duma and State Council approval? The debate on this particular question revealed a glaring lack of agreement (37–47).

Witte, in particular, wanted to reserve for the autocrat and his government as many privileges and powers as possible. In part, he hoped to reduce the chances of a future conflict between the Duma and the sovereign or his government. More importantly still, the outcome of the Duma elections had begun to shake his peasant monarchist beliefs. By the time the April conference convened, the first stage of these elections had already taken place, and Witte was clearly preparing for the worst. He spoke of the possibility of "a peasant, idealess Duma. . . . [T]he revolutionaries and the so-called intelligentsia will lead it by the reins, and this will be an insane asylum" (21). Anticipating just such an uncontrollable and recalcitrant Duma, Witte was eager to reduce its purview and thus its possible interference in government. He insisted, for example, that the holdings of the imperial family be expressly excluded from any discussion of private property that was likely to take place in the new Duma. While he did not wish to offend the legislature in any way by revoking past promises or unnecessarily limiting its freedom of action, he took great care to protect the government's freedom as well. He even went so far as to urge the removal of hitherto tenured judges, a proposal strongly opposed by Goremykin, Count Palen, and a minority in the Council of Ministers and eventually rejected by Nicholas (53–56, 59). Finally, Witte wanted to expand the emperor's emergency powers still further, so that he might "in extraordinary circumstances" issue ukases to prevent changes in the state order. While Goremykin and Durnovo appeared to side with Witte for once, many others objected to the plan as overly broad, subversive of the established order, and ultimately meaningless. "In the whole world there are no such laws that would anticipate a revolution," Akimov complained, and Nicholas had to agree (61–66).

A clause permitting the alienation of private property "for state and societal requirements" provoked a heated debate between Witte and his old nemesis Goremykin. The latter, we recall, had taken Witte's place after the closure of Witte's Conference on the Needs of Agricultural Industry in April 1905, and he was only a few days away from becoming Witte's successor once again, this time as the new chairman of the Council of Ministers. As might be expected from somebody with Goremykin's traditional bureaucratic outlook, he objected to societal needs as justification for property alienation. To eliminate that contingency, Witte answered, was to preclude the possibility of giving land to the peasants, if only for enclosure purposes. The Duma was sure to take up the matter. Such a prohibition would turn the Duma against the government; within two months the legislature would have to be dissolved and revolution would ensue. Launching a sharp personal attack on Goremykin, Witte doubted that the Duma would in fact grant private lands to the peasants; even if it did, however, the State Council was free to dissent and Nicholas could refuse to confirm such a measure. Emphasizing his experiences of the past six months, Witte explained that to prevent even a discussion of the matter, as Goremykin had urged, was to invite disaster (76–80).

What Witte did not say was that Goremykin's stand also tightened the perimeters of bureaucratic activism and interventionism. Clearly, Witte recognized the importance of the new chamber in airing society's grievances and in arriving at solutions acceptable to society and government alike. He did not wish to muzzle or emasculate the new legislature. At the same time, he was mindful of the need for strong central authority and bureaucratic initiative. This path was fraught with risks and uncertainties, so much so that Witte had begun to lose confidence and to waver. Although he would later point to this disagreement as one of the factors leading to his resignation request,[71] temporarily at least he emerged victorious. After Durnovo and Frish endorsed the original wording on the alienation of private property as fully consistent with existing civil law, the tsar agreed to retain it.

[71] Witte, *Vospominaniia*, 3:303–4.

Throughout the proceedings, Nicholas comes across as moderate and sensible. He certainly recognized the momentousness of the occasion as well as the significance of the proposed changes. As a rule, he heeded the strict legalistic arguments of Frish, Sol'skii, Palen, or Akimov. Spasskii-Odynets, Witte's "press-secretary," would later describe the tsar during these deliberations as more liberal and better attuned to the country's political mood than Witte.[72] Durnovo, disturbed by the ease with which Nicholas appeared to be yielding his privileges at the conference, depicted his imperial master as "the kind of person who, when asked for his last shirt, will take it off and give it away."[73] In a certain sense, both men were correct. Nicholas, whether in December, February, or April, had resisted many of Witte's more extreme demands for the expansion and increased use of governmental powers; he had repeatedly cast his first minister's dire warnings to the wind. And the equanimity with which Nicholas assented to the formal limitation of his own power after first making known his grave reservations was indeed remarkable. Yet neither example must be taken as evidence of a sudden liberal turn of the tsar's mind. Instead, Nicholas was demonstrating his utter estrangement from the role envisioned for him by Witte in the legal reforms and in everyday practice. Thus, it was not only Witte's personal qualities or his failure to restore order promptly, but also his conception of government and its implications for Nicholas that were responsible for the tsar's waning trust in his first minister.

THE GOVERNMENT'S VISIONARY PROGRAM

Witte's day-to-day management of the government, his attempt at unifying the administration mechanically and programmatically, served as a constant reminder to Nicholas of how much his position had changed, or would change if those efforts were successful. Here is how Witte, in a supplement to the government's *Sel'skii Vestnik*, sought to define his own role for the paper's rural readership:

> It is more beneficial for the State order itself that one man stand at the head of the highest executive forces of the State, whom the Sovereign and the State Duma can hold accountable for how he carries out the will of the tsar and the narod. This highest minister, in turn, would have power over the other ministers subordinate to him, and would instruct them as to how state matters need to be carried out.

To remind his ministerial colleagues of their obligations to the Council and to him under the terms of the October 19 legislation on government

[72] Spasskii, "Vospominaniia," pp. 292–93.
[73] Kryzhanovskii, *Vospominaniia*, p. 75n.

unification, Witte had this pamphlet forwarded to all ministers.[74] Six weeks later he sent them a more explicit reminder,[75] and, in yet another letter to Durnovo, he threatened to invoke his right to be present at the ministers' personal audiences with the emperor[76]—all without any evident backing from Nicholas. Even when Witte complained to the tsar directly about the lack of ministerial solidarity and cooperation, he elicited little sympathy.[77]

Nicholas's reaction to a March 7 article in *Russkoe Gosudarstvo*, the new government paper founded by Witte, exemplifies the resentment he felt at seeing his own role belittled: "Scandalous! How could such an article appear?" The passage that had provoked the tsar's particular displeasure read: "The government, after issuing the Manifesto of October 17, may turn out to be unequal to this act, but that does not diminish its significance one iota." Judging by the question mark in the margin, Nicholas objected especially to the first part of this statement. Witte, while vigorously defending the contents and writer of the piece, conceded that the phrase should have read: "The government during whose term the Supreme Manifesto was issued."[78] Evidently, Nicholas was outraged at seeing the government, not the ruler, credited with the authorship of the manifesto. At the same time, his alienation from the kind of government represented by Witte was so great that he did not object to having its integrity impugned.

Similarly, Witte's determination to formulate a comprehensive and coherent legislative program for reorganizing society could bring little comfort to Nicholas, for it confronted him with conceptions that signified the institutionalization of the impersonal state power and the aggrandizement of activist bureaucratic government at the expense of the tsar's personal role. The need for such a program had first been pointed out in early December by Finance Minister I. P. Shipov, a close associate of Witte's. Government unity was not simply a matter of mechanical coordination, Shipov had argued, but had also to reflect a consensus on how to meet the demands of the population. A program based on homogeneous principles and worked out in detail had to be readied before the Duma opened in order to influence its deliberations and to preserve the government's authority before the new chamber. Such a program would

[74] TsGIA, f.1276, op. 1, d. 36, ll. 40–49.

[75] Witte's letter to all ministers, January 20, 1906, TsGIA, f. 1276, op. 1, d. 36, l. 56.

[76] Witte's letter to Durnovo, February 5, 1906, ibid., l. 57.

[77] Cf. Witte's letter to Nicholas, February 12, 1906, Witte Collection, REEACU. In the words of Minister of War Rediger, "the unity of the government was purely external"; "Zapiski A. F. Redigera o 1905 g.," *KA* 45 (1931): 90. Cf., too, the accounts of Spasskii, "Vospominaniia," pp. 15 and 21; Mendeleev, "Svet i teni," pp. 96–97; or the letter from Minister of Education Count Ivan Tolstoi to Witte, November 24, 1905, Witte Collection, REEACU.

[78] Witte's report of March 9, 1906, TsGAOR, f. 543, op 1, d. 234, ll. 1–4.

guarantee that the government's representatives spoke with one voice to the people's representatives.

Until now the Council of Ministers had been primarily preoccupied with political as opposed to socioeconomic issues, Shipov continued. Various agencies had embarked on preliminary preparations, to be sure, but Shipov wanted the ministers to discuss in detail the future direction of government policy, in particular, specific measures to effect a thorough reform of socioeconomic relations, without which the country could not return to peace and quiet. Such policies included, above all, "the social-economic organization of the laboring masses, i.e., of the peasant population and the working class," as well as the problem of rural and urban self-government, tax, pension, and school reform, and, finally, the Jewish question. Only a logical, comprehensive, and detailed program could compel the public and its representatives to come to terms with the government's views on these all-important issues.[79] Witte clearly sympathized with Shipov's recommendations, which were very much in keeping with the ideas that Witte had advanced in October. The implementation of these ideas, just as Shipov had contended, went beyond "mere" political reform; it entailed the complete overhaul and restructuring of social relationships at the hands of a modern, activist bureaucracy. Nothing less was Witte's goal.

Two weeks later, on January 24, the Council of Ministers met to consider Shipov's memorandum. The ministers agreed that such a program should be prepared in order to support the government's authority, weld its members into a united whole, and direct the Duma's activity "along a definite, business-like course." They reaffirmed the centrality of the peasant problem, for its manner of resolution would determine both the legal structure of local life and Russia's economic future. With work on the economic aspects of this problem already underway, the Ministry of the Interior should immediately consider its legal dimensions as well. Any legal reform, in turn, was bound up with other important issues, such as an overhaul of local administration, zemstvo affairs, the judiciary, and the tax system.

Ultimately, of course, everything depended on whether the peasants remained a separate estate. Communal landownership was clearly the distinguishing feature of peasant existence; the peasant world would maintain its insular identity as long as allotments continued to exist. The ministers explained that the Ministry of Internal Affairs had already begun to draft laws that would permit the peasants to leave the commune. The resulting class of small peasant proprietors could not be kept isolated as a separate estate, all the more so since the peasants had been sum-

---

[79] I. I. Shipov's memorandum, n.d., TsGIA, f. 1276, op. 1, d. 47, ll. 2–4.

moned to participate in the nation's affairs. Moreover, if economic reasons were to dictate the abolition of communal landholding, then one also had to proceed to a local zemstvo unit below the district (uezd) level and to non-estate organs of local self-government that would put an end to the peasantry's administrative and judicial isolation. The ministers agreed with Witte's defunct Special Conference on the Needs of Agricultural Industry that the volost' court, a peasant institution on the township level, be replaced by an all-estate court that would be independent of the administration and part of the judicial system. To maintain a special court not based on universal laws and to preserve administrative supervision (opeka) in the form of the Land Captains was to contradict these other reforms.[80]

This, in brief, was the remarkable vision of a universalistic society liberated of all particularistic restrictions, the vision toward which Witte's Special Conference had been groping before running afoul of imperial opposition, the vision with which Witte and his cabinet hoped to confront and win over the Duma—if Nicholas so agreed. Indeed, in the six weeks leading up to the Duma opening, the Council of Ministers discussed and approved proposals that would have gone a long way toward realizing that ambitious scheme: Shipov's tax reform plans, which stipulated the equalization of the direct tax burden with a view toward helping the non-propertied masses, the introduction of a 4 percent income tax, a 40 percent increase in the tobacco tax, and indirect contingency taxes;[81] judicial reforms that included, among other things, the abolition of the volost' court and the abrogation of the judicial functions of the land captains, with the void to be filled by locally elected justices of the peace;[82] and educational innovations, such as universal and compulsory primary education strictly supervised by the Ministry of Education, an expansion of secondary education and vocational training, and native-language instruction for non-Russians.[83]

[80] Other reforms addressed by the Council of Ministers included the passport issue and the Jewish question. "Memoriia Soveta Ministrov," January 24, 1906, TsGIA, f. 1276, op. 2, d. 4, ll. 12–16 (printed copy). The original was reviewed by Nicholas on February 2, 1906.

[81] "Memoriia Soveta Ministrov," March 7, 1906, ibid., ll. 56–62; ministerial project, dated January 31, 1906, ll. 18–39.

[82] "Memoriia Soveta Ministrov," April 8, 1906, ibid., ll. 98–100; ministerial project, dated March 31, 1906, ll. 77–91.

[83] "Memoriia Soveta Ministrov," December 30, 1905 and January 24, 1906, TsGIA, f. 1276, op. 1, d. 145, ll. 6–7. Still other proposals were submitted to the Council of Ministers by the Ministry of Communication on March 23, 1906, TsGIA, f. 1276, op. 2, d. 4, ll. 65–75; the Ministry of Trade and Industry on April 14, 1906, ibid., ll. 102–41; the Ministry of Finance on April 6, ibid., l. 172; the Ministry of War on April 10, 1906, ibid., ll. 202–3.

THE INVIOLABILITY OF PRIVATE PROPERTY

These steps, however, were secondary to and predicated on a solution of the age-old peasant land problem. No other task was as difficult, daunting, and urgent, if only because of the perceived danger of continued peasant unrest. By early January Witte had confidently ruled out the possibility of renewed revolutionary disturbances in Russia's cities and towns, with the conceivable exception of the Caucasus, Poland, and the Baltic provinces, where national and ethnic strains played an aggravating role; yet his optimism did not extend to the countryside. Indeed, agrarian disorders, in the opinion of Witte and the Council of Ministers, had only just begun, and still larger and more frequent outbreaks could be expected in the spring unless preventive measures were taken. In his January 10 report to Nicholas, Witte distinguished between short-term, negative actions to bring about the immediate pacification of the countryside, and long-term, structural policies that aimed at changing the underlying conditions.[84]

As an example of positive, long-term measures, the ministers mentioned the November 3, 1905, manifesto. The October Manifesto had only been a week old when Goremykin and Budberg, whose own manifesto draft had lost out to Witte's, had warned Nicholas that the grant of political liberties would do little, if anything, for Russia's peasantry. While other social groups were celebrating, the two claimed, the majority of the population was saying to itself: "All these blessings were granted to the lords, intelligenty, kulaks, and others, and must be beneficial to them, if they cause so much joy, but what is there for us? Pay taxes, starve as before, and wait for two birds in the bush!" To prevent the narod from acting out their dissatisfaction, the two authors urged the cancellation of redemption payments before the new Duma had a chance to demand it. The tsar had been very receptive to these suggestions and their implied criticisms of the week-old reform acts. In his October 31 rescript directing the Council of Ministers to discuss the Goremykin-Budberg proposal, he expressed regret that the October 17 Manifesto had ignored the peasants and their needs. Although the publication of a second manifesto a mere two weeks after the first might appear like a

---

Only the first of these was taken up by the Council on April 14, before Witte's resignation put a halt to this process.

[84] As for the first category, the Council of Ministers had discussed and recommended specific steps to strengthen the land police, make better use of military forces, and improve the efficiency of judicial organs and local administrators; copy of Witte's report, January 10, 1906, Witte Collection, REEACU, and Semennikov, *Revoliutsiia 1905 goda*, pp. 45–54. Notations in the margin and pencil markings indicate that Nicholas took an intense interest in the matter.

belated correction of an oversight made in haste, Nicholas conceded that "the matter is of prime importance, of course, and in my opinion incomparably more essential than those civil liberties granted Russia a few days ago. . . . The correct and gradual establishment of the peasantry *on the land* will guarantee Russia genuine domestic calm for many decades."[85] Three days later Nicholas announced the phasing out of all redemption payments, which were to be cut in half as of January 1, 1906, and end by January 1, 1907. At the same time he instructed the Peasant Land Bank to acquire more private lands and to make them available to needy peasants on more generous terms.[86]

In his January 10 report Witte recommended that further measures altering existing relations in the countryside, including controversial changes of property rights, be left to the Duma to decide. To this end the government should draft a legislative project and then notify the inquiring and agitated public that the agrarian question would be the Duma's first order of business.

One such project had been drawn up by Minister of Agriculture Kutler in early November and called for the forcible alienation of some private lands with compensation for the owners. As if to play down the importance of this particular proposal, which had already become the target of an anonymous bureaucratic memorandum that had found favor with Nicholas,[87] Witte hastened to add that it was one of several tentative projects that had provoked serious disagreements in the Council discussions. In the end a sharply divided Council of Ministers had decided to defer a final discussion until a Special Conference of various agency representatives could consider Kutler's project and any other that might be presented.

According to Witte, the critics of the project subscribed to the "principled view of the sacredness of the notion of property," warning of the dangerous threat to the state if that important tenet were abandoned. The peasants, they contended, would not be satisfied until they had obtained all privately held land; even then each peasant's share would increase only marginally and crop yields would decline. Denying any connection between land shortages and agrarian disorders, Kutler's opponents instead blamed the unrest on the peasants' proclivity for violence and mischief. Therefore, external measures to reestablish order and improvements in the peasantry's cultural conditions should take precedence over land reform.

The supporters of Kutler's proposal, on the other hand, attributed the

---

[85] The relevant archival documents, which I was unable to see, are discussed in Iu. B. Solov'ev, *Samoderzhavie i dvorianstvo v 1902–1907 gg.* (Leningrad, 1981), pp. 192–93.

[86] The original of the manifesto is to be found in TsGAOR, f. 601, op. 1, d. 1031, ll. 1–2.

[87] *Agrarnyi vopros v Sovete Ministrov (1906 g.)* (Moscow, 1924), pp. 63–64.

peasants' cultural backwardness to their sheltered rural existence and isolation from other estates. The close relationship between disorders and the peasants' mental and spiritual development pointed to the shortcomings of the Orthodox clergy and the church-run schools. Such improvements could only happen gradually. Lack of peasant restraint and the absence of coercive power alone did not account for the agrarian disturbances. The agrarian question existed both in reality and in the consciousness of the peasants who were faced with steadily rising land prices and shrinking allotments. In many localities these holdings were simply too small. Numerous communications from the peasantry testified to their strongly held beliefs that they had acquired rights to their rented lands through their rent payments, the aggregate of which far exceeded the actual value of the land. Given such an outlook, it might be more profitable for the landlords to yield some of their land while retaining the rest, as they had done in 1861. Otherwise they might lose all of it under more unfavorable circumstances or be required to pay a progressive income tax which would rule out large holdings of land in the future.

Although Witte had sought to defuse the emotional explosiveness of the issue—and protect himself—by presenting the arguments of both sides as objectively as possible, Nicholas would not be swayed. Taking note of the diagnosis presented by Kutler's opponents, the tsar wrote in red pencil: "Private property *must* remain inviolable." And opposite the description of Kutler's plan, he added: "I do not approve."[88] On January 18 Nicholas reaffirmed his position in front of a peasant delegation from Kursk: "Any property right is inviolable: what belongs to the landlord, belongs to him; what belongs to the peasant, belongs to him. Always remember that the right of ownership is sacred and must remain inviolable."[89]

Other reactions, though equally negative, were still more emphatic—and colorful. From Denmark, where she had learned of the inclusion of crown and cabinet lands among those suggested for alienation, the dowager empress railed against *"those swine* [who] want to take away . . . *the personal and private rights* of the emperor and his family."[90] A petition from southern Russian landowners to Nicholas, which made the rounds of St. Petersburg in January, warned of the grave threat "from the quarters of the all-powerful representatives of the government who worked out legislative projects and issued prescriptions and circulars containing all the destructive force of socialist heresies." The anonymous authors invoked Nicholas's promise contained in his April 10, 1905, ukase that

[88] Semennikov, *Revoliutsiia 1905 goda*, pp. 45–54.
[89] Solov'ev, *Samoderzhavie i dvorianstvo*, p. 197.
[90] "Perepiska Nikolaia II i Marii Fedorovny," *KA* 22 (1927): 188–89, January 16, 1906.

"all private property is inviolable and [that] it is the very first obligation of the government to protect it from illegal encroachments, and even more so, from violence." This promise had apparently "been forgotten by the radical members of Count Witte's cabinet." Rumors allegedly confirmed by Witte himself had it that "a legislative proposal prepared by one of the closest associates of Count Witte, the Active State Counsellor Kutler," stipulated maximum norms of private landownership and called for the obligatory expropriation of all private lands exceeding those norms.

The implementation of Kutler's project, the petition warned, would constitute not only "an unprecedented attack on the vast class of landowners loyal to your throne," but it would harm the peasantry and the Treasury; indeed, it would deliver a death blow to Russian culture. In actual fact, if not in law, all land cultivated in Russia was in the use of peasants. The "so-called agrarian question is only an invention of the revolutionaries and dreamer-bureaucrats unfamiliar with the real life of the countryside." Was it any wonder, the petitioners asked, that voices were being heard in society claiming that "the utopian legislative projects of Count Witte's Cabinet" were designed to carry the revolution into the countryside and thus to bring about the political transformation desired by the revolutionary parties now that they had failed in the cities? Any doubts as to the inviolability of private property were also bound to harm Russia's financial standing abroad. The government's intentions had created unrest and raised the specter of famine: many landowners were purportedly hesitant to sow and plant in the fear that they might lose their lands, while many peasants were refusing to work in the expectation that they would receive title to the lands free of charge. In conclusion, the petition called on Nicholas to affirm publicly the inviolability of private property and to change "the present government, personified by its head, Count Witte," which did not command the confidence of the country: "All of Russia awaits Your Majesty's replacement of this despotic dignitary by a person with firmer state principles and more experience in selecting reliable state servitors worthy of the people's trust."[91]

This attack on Witte and his agrarian policies understandably provoked the first minister. Although the petition had been printed in Kiev and relayed to Witte by his minister of communication, Witte was convinced that it had been initiated by the so-called "Black Hundreds of the State Council." It would be a waste of time to inquire into the exact identity of the authors and initiators of the document, Witte wrote to Nicholas on February 2, for it was well known that its views were those of Count A. P. Ignat'ev, Stishinskii, Shtiurmer, Goremykin, Abaza, or any other

[91] Witte Collection, REEACU.

member of that "crowd." This "honorable group," instead of openly pursuing power at considerable risk to its members, had preferred to act behind the scenes, Witte alleged, by spreading all sorts of lies in the salons of Petersburg and through loyal press organs, professors, and other means. Nicholas, however, could not muster much sympathy for his first minister; "the count is angry" was his only recorded reaction.[92]

If Witte was angry at such criticism, it was because Nicholas had given every indication of heeding it by demanding Kutler's dismissal. "Isn't it time to think about a replacement for Kutler?" he asked Witte on January 26.[93] Witte wrote back the same day, defending Kutler as "a gifted person, extremely hardworking, knowledgeable, resourceful, irreproachably honest, and loyal to Y.I.M." To be sure, his project for land reform lacked common sense; indeed, Witte claimed to have told him that as soon as he saw it. According to Witte, Kutler himself had confessed that he considered his proposal harmful and extreme. After hesitating for a long time, with no other solution in sight, Kutler had asked that it at least be discussed in the Council of Ministers, where everybody spoke out against it. A new project was in preparation now under Kutler's supervision, and Witte had made sure that opposing views would be represented.

If the peasants did not receive at least part of the private lands on favorable terms, Kutler had argued, they would simply end up taking it all. "I do not share this opinion," Witte hastened to add, "but I understand its psychology." Only a few weeks ago, before the revolution had been put down for good, he had heard the most conservative people express such opinions. Adjutant General Dubasov, upon returning from his forcible pacification of Kursk province, had told Witte openly that unless the government was prepared to grant the peasants half of the private lands now, they would take all of them later. Very conservative landlords had written Witte the same. Kutler's had been a political mistake that was perfectly understandable under the influence of the revolutionary events; as to "his thoughts and character there is not the slightest danger whatsoever for state life." Witte therefore did not consider it "useful" to replace Kutler now, especially since no suitable successor was in sight.[94]

Contrary to Witte's assertions, Kutler had not come up with his proposal on his own but had been ordered or at least encouraged to do so by Witte. Kutler had had considerable misgivings about the project from the outset and was not its main advocate. If he insisted on a Council review, it was to air these doubts. In his own words, "I received orders from

[92] Ibid., and Semennikov, *Revoliutsiia 1905 goda*, p. 57.
[93] Nicholas's handwritten note, without addressee, TsGAOR, f. 543, op. 1, d. 525, l. 2.
[94] Witte's report, [January 26, 1906], ibid., ll. 3–6.

Witte and had to comply, especially since we now have a unified government. Now that the project has failed, however, everybody repudiates all responsibility and says that it was entirely Kutler's idea."[95] Thus Witte's spirited defense of Kutler vis-à-vis Nicholas was as much the product of his own guilty conscience at seeing a scapegoat made of an honorable and talented associate as it was the result of his concern with Kutler's personal fate. In fact, he continued to fight for Kutler, even after the tsar had categorically refused to change his mind.[96]

No matter how much distance he might have been trying to put between himself and Kutler, Witte, in defending his associate, was also defending his own opinions. Beyond personal considerations, he was deeply worried, as we have seen, by the problem of public order. Kutler's dismissal not only meant a general rebuff for the man who had appointed him but would also signal the failure of any immediate attempt at relieving peasant land hunger, so closely identified was Kutler's name in the eyes of the public and of Witte's critics with the possible expropriation of private lands. In his report, Witte cautioned Nicholas that the revolution was not over and that the peasants' interests ought not to be ignored:

> If it was dangerous and, from the state's point of view, criminal to advocate under the influence of fear that the peasants be given a part of the private land no matter what might happen, then in my conviction it would be just as dangerous to yield to those desires that began to appear primarily in noble circles after the suppression, though not the destruction, of the revolution. Now a different kind of talk has arisen: "The peasants should not be given anything, bayonets are all that is needed, all this is only childish mischief, all damages must be reclaimed from them, they must pay more for our land," etc. This path will not lead to anything good either. In general political terms, the peasants' interests must be accorded first priority, they no longer ought to be considered, in K. P. Pobedonostsev's expression, half-persons, and it must be kept in mind that while Russia might survive without us, she will perish without the tsar and the peasantry.[97]

In fighting for Kutler, Witte was also betraying his fears of future agrarian disorders.

For much the same reason, Witte proposed that every peasant wishing

[95] Kokovtsov, *Out of My Past*, p. 100, and Liubimov, "Russkaia smuta," pp. 258–59. For a detailed discussion of this case and the supporting evidence, see Verner, "Nicholas II and the Role of the Autocracy," p. 500 n. 175.

[96] Nicholas's letter to Witte, January 29, 1906, and Witte's letter to Nicholas, February 2, 1906, Witte Collection, REEACU.

[97] Witte's report, [January 26, 1906], TsGAOR, f. 543, op. 1, d. 525, ll. 3–6.

to take his allotment out of the communally held lands be granted this right now that the redemption payments had been abolished:

> A resolution of these two questions, i.e., the recognition of the allotment lands as the property of the owners and the establishment of a procedure for the peasants' departure from the communes, together with a separation of the parcels from the land now owned communally, might have, in the opinion of the Council, a beneficial influence on the peasants' legal consciousness, instilling in the peasants healthier views on somebody else's right of ownership.

Accordingly, a commission of agency representatives, originally headed by the notorious Kutler, was asked to draw up a suitable project.[98] Like the controversial Kutler proposal, this measure went to the heart of Witte's agrarian reconstruction plans; he considered the measure necessary for economic as well as political reasons, in order to ward off still greater rural disturbances. Unlike the Kutler plan, however, it appeared to be perfectly consistent—indeed, it appeared logically to follow from—the tsar's insistence on the inviolability of private property. Once peasants had secured private title to their holdings, they could be expected better to respect the property rights of others.

As with some of the proposals on subsidiary issues, Nicholas initially went along with this suggestion not out of any real sense of conviction, but because it had not yet entered the decisive stage and, if necessary, could still be stopped. Before being introduced into the Duma, each project presumably would have to be cleared by the tsar, and Nicholas might well have known that Witte would no longer be around by then. In fact, when Witte insisted that independent, separate, personal, and unified property rights be granted to the peasants even before the Duma convened in order to shield the issue from demagoguery, he found himself stymied. At a preliminary conference of State Council members on March 18, 1906, Ignat'ev, Stishinskii, Goremykin, Semenov, and others—i.e., precisely those people whom Witte had branded as the Black Hundreds of the State Council—opposed his plan on the rather hypocritical grounds that the issue was best left to the Duma where the peasants themselves had a voice. As a result, the project was rejected by a vote of 21 to 17.[99]

All winter Nicholas had harped on the inviolability of private property—indeed, this had been the cause of Kutler's downfall—yet an extension of this principle to the communal peasantry was still considered premature, if not outright unpalatable. The effect was, of course, the preservation of the status quo. As recently as March 11 the tsar had asked

[98] Semennikov, *Revoliutsiia 1905 goda*, pp. 45–54.
[99] "Dnevnik A. A. Polovtseva," *KA* 4 (1923): 96–97, March 18, 1906.

a peasant delegation from half a dozen provinces to remind their brothers back home "that all property is inviolable and that the narod will prosper only through long and persistent labor as long as everyone, no matter what estate he belongs to, is certain that his property is inalienable."[100] The tsar conveniently ignored the fact that millions of Russian peasants did not yet enjoy such inalienable property rights. To Nicholas and people of Goremykin's ilk, the inviolability of private property was instead synonymous with the continued isolation of the peasant estate. In this sense, the universalist principle of property ownership was applied selectively for regressive, particularistic purposes, as a euphemism for the defense of noble landed interests.

A PARTING OF THE WAYS

This, then, was the role that Nicholas had chosen for himself when confronted with the rival conceptions of Witte's administration: Henceforth he would act as the legalistic defender of private property and public order, removed from the everyday workings of the impersonalized bureaucratic state apparatus.

If any further proof is needed, it is to be found in the final revisions of the new Fundamental Laws after the conclusion of the April conference in Tsarskoe Selo. Trepov had taken it upon himself to submit the latest draft to a commission of prominent liberals belonging to the new Constitutional-Democratic ("Kadet") Party. By April 18 they had prepared a thorough critique that found the project a perversion of the October Manifesto. Not only were the promised civil liberties laced with exceptions and qualifications, the Kadet critics contended, but the draft served to defend the interests of the highest bureaucrats: "Like before, all responsibility before God, history, and the narod remains with the sovereign emperor, the ministers answer neither for the course of policy nor for the general direction of their activity nor for the illegal actions of their agencies." The people's respect for authority would increase if the ministers countersigned all laws and thereby assumed responsibility. Any and all violations of civil rights, moreover, had to be prosecuted. Most importantly, the Kadet critique insisted on the clear separation of the ruler and his government:

> Standing above changing moods and parties and outside the policies pursued by them, the Sovereign must be the incarnation of the idea of unity and of the greatness of the empire, of truth and well-being in his land. The mistakes of

[100] TsGIA, f. 1291, op. 122–1906, d. 41, ll. 5. On Nicholas's orders, these remarks subsequently were telegraphed to all governors and disseminated by them in print editions of up to 100,000 copies, ll. 1–2, 50.

temporary leaders must not serve as a source of distrust or dislike for the Supreme power. "The King," English law says, "can do no evil." With these words, the English express the idea that members of the government, not the King, answer for any untruth or mistake.[101]

Evidently some of these suggestions struck a responsive chord in Nicholas, for he saw to it that they were incorporated into the draft.[102] Though the final version that was made public on April 23, 1906, four days before the convocation of the Duma, did not come close to meeting all of the Kadet criticisms, it certainly did not ignore them. Among the changes made were restrictions on the tsar's authority over administrative personnel, reductions in the scope of imperial ukases precisely as suggested by the Kadets, the elimination of offensive budget rules, and the ministerial countersignature of imperial acts.[103] Nicholas, it would appear, had every intention of being a good legalistic monarch along the lines of the English model: "The King reigns, but does not rule." This new attitude was a measure not of any newly acquired taste for constitutionalism but of Nicholas's distance from the conceptions represented by Witte and by the recent reforms in the state order.

The effect of the Fundamental Laws was to codify the reforms and the promised civil liberties of the past months. The new legislative chambers were confronted with a fait accompli that they could undo only with the emperor's prior permission and subsequent approval. In seeking to define, no matter how broadly or imprecisely, the tsar's prerogatives in the areas of general administration, foreign affairs, the military, and the budget, the new Fundamental Laws explicitly and implicitly recognized for the first time that the autocrat's power was no longer unlimited. In theory at least, the new codex integrated the office and person of the autocrat into the new "legal order" that Witte had affirmed as his goal in his October report. In this sense, the revised statute ratified a conceptual change that was light-years removed from the traditional formulations of autocratic ideology, yet fell far short of the vision that had inspired it. Nicholas's own conceptions and their influence on autocratic practice, moreover, did not necessarily accord with these changes. Nothing dramatized these discrepancies better than Witte's departure on the eve of the Duma's opening.

As early as late January, Witte seems to have resigned himself to put-

---

[101] In addition, the Kadets demanded greater powers of inquiry, appropriation, and financial review for the new legislature. As for a further revision of the Fundamental Laws, a two-thirds majority should be able to *request* it; if the tsar agreed, any changes would have to be approved by a two-thirds majority as well; memorandum by Kovalevskii et al., April 18, 1906, *KA* 11–12 (1925): 116–20.

[102] TsGIA, f. 1544, op. dop. k 16 t., d. 25, l. 221; draft with his corrections, ll. 222–28.

[103] Doctorow, "Introduction of Parliamentary Institutions in Russia," p. 315.

ting his house in order and to preparing for the new Duma era and an orderly transition of power to his successor, whoever he might be. On January 29, 1906, the very day that Kutler's fate was sealed once and for all, Witte informed the tsar of his intention to compile a chronicle of events. Relying on the growing number of papers, journals, pamphlets, and public pronouncements, such a chronicle would serve to provide a clear picture of the election campaign and results, Witte explained. More importantly still, it could serve as a historical record illuminating the birth and development of political life in Russia.[104] So important was this matter to Witte that, when Nicholas refused, he asked to be relieved of his responsibilities as chairman of the Council of Ministers and from any dealings with the State Duma.[105] Mystified by Witte's insistence, Nicholas had no choice but to give in, though not without a reprimand of sorts: "In my opinion, the role of the Chairman of the Council of Ministers must be confined to unifying the activity of the Ministers; all executive work remains the responsibility of the ministries concerned. But if you nonetheless consider it necessary personally to lead the compilation of the work proposed by you, then I agree to your original proposals."[106] Apparently Witte had begun to look back on the events of the past months and wanted to record his role for posterity while he still had a chance to influence its writing. His resignation threat demonstrated how strongly he felt about this matter and how he had begun to divorce himself from the ultimately disappointing and unsuccessful role of first minister.[107]

On April 14, less than forty-eight hours after the last session of the Special Conference, Witte asked the tsar to relieve him from his duties. Nicholas accepted the resignation request the very next day. Without awaiting the official results of the second stage of the Duma election on April 14, Witte already knew what the outcome would be. On March 30, four days after the first electoral stage, Witte had predicted a hostile Duma, which he blamed on Durnovo's unnecessarily cruel and repressive measures. His own protests to Nicholas had been of no use, Witte complained to Polovtsev. Durnovo had continued his coercive actions long after the worst of the revolutionary danger had passed with the successful suppression of the Moscow uprising, for which Witte claimed considerable credit. Villified by left *and* right, unable to justify Durnovo's actions before the Duma, he would have no choice but resign before it

[104] Witte's report, January 29, 1906, Witte Collection, REEACU.

[105] Witte's report, January 31, 1906, TsGAOR, f. 543, op. 1, d. 537, l. 2.

[106] Nicholas's resolution of February 2, 1906, on report of January 29, after it apparently had been resubmitted, Witte Collection, REEACU.

[107] In his memoirs Witte says nothing about this curious episode; Witte, *Vospominaniia*, 3:217.

opened. Even more importantly, he was in need of rest, as his nerves were completely "shot." By his own admission, he was getting no more than two hours' sleep a night and could not even open a letter without his hands starting to tremble. If he went before the Duma in such a state, he might lose his mind or commit some unpardonable stupidity. Either Justice Minister Akimov or State Controller Filosofov would be suitable successors.[108]

Elaborating on those complaints, Witte's resignation letter to the tsar in effect amounted to a seven-count indictment of Nicholas's failure to support him and his policies. (1) "I feel crushed by the general baiting and so nervous that I will be unable to maintain the composure required in the position of Chairman of the Council of Ministers, especially in the new circumstances." (2) The actions of the minister of internal affairs and of a number of local administrators in the last two months since the suppression of the revolution had been irresponsible and had supposedly led to the election of extremists to the Duma as a form of protest. (3) He and Durnovo could not appear in the Duma together. He would have to remain silent on all questions concerning government actions that had been carried out without his knowledge or even against his expressed wishes, "since I did not possess any executive authority." Nor would he be able to support Durnovo's explanations. (4) Taking note of the lack of agreement and unity in the Council of Ministers and among "influential circles" on some of the most important problems, such as the peasant, Jewish, and confessional questions, he did not want to have to defend ideas that did not correspond to his own convictions, in particular the extreme conservative views that Durnovo had incorporated into his "political credo." (5) If ideas such as those propounded by Count Palen and Goremykin on the peasant issue and on government policy in general were to prevail, then those individuals should be given the opportunity to implement them and bear the responsibility. (6) "In the course of six months I was the object of persecution by everyone screaming and writing in Russian society, and subjected to systematic attacks by extremist elements with access to Your Imperial Majesty." The revolutionaries and liberals had criticized him for his firm measures and his adherence to his oath of office, while the conservatives had held him personally responsible for all the policy changes since Sviatopolk-Mirskii. Most harmful and damaging of all had been the "nobles and higher servitors who naturally always had and will have access to the tsar, and therefore inevitably raised and will raise doubts about the actions and even intentions of politicians disliked by them." (7) With the Duma about to open, the government could either seek to reach agreement or pursue "extreme measures." In the first

---

[108] "Dnevnik A. A. Polovtseva," KA 4 (1923): 97–99.

case, a cabinet change would facilitate the task; in the second, Witte would only be an obstacle and focus of criticism from the right.

There were still other reasons, Witte added, but those listed were sufficient. "I would have made this request much earlier," Witte concluded, "as soon as I noticed that my position . . . had been shaken, but I did not think that I had the right to do this while Russia's financial situation gave rise to such serious fears."[109] He had felt obligated to prevent a financial collapse and to ward off a situation that would allow the Duma to extract concessions, "concessions corresponding to the goals of the parties, but not to the benefit of the whole state, inseparably linked with the interests of Your Majesty." Now, with the financial solvency of the empire assured for the foreseeable future and with the Duma about to open, Witte felt free to take his leave.[110] Although he later would claim to have accomplished all that he had set out to do,[111] he could do no more, given his defeat on the agrarian question, the unfavorable electoral outcome which had shaken his peasant monarchist illusions, his mental exhaustion, and Nicholas's disenchantment. Unlikely to receive the emperor's backing or to find support in a hostile Duma, his position had become utterly untenable.

Witte's letter of resignation coincided with his report on the success of the international loan subscription.[112] The actual loan agreement had been concluded on April 3. Exactly two weeks later, Witte could inform the tsar that the first part of the loan had been floated, with the remainder sure to be subscribed to by the April 25 deadline.[113] Never one to show false modesty, Witte took full responsibility for the success.[114] Witte had indeed been instrumental in securing the loan, even though the actual negotiations in Paris involved ex-Minister of Finance Kokovtsev who would later claim the main credit. Witte had put out the initial feelers in Paris and Berlin upon his return from Portsmouth in September 1905, and he stayed in close touch with French and German bankers and his negotiators during the two negotiating rounds in December and March. The first round ran aground because of Franco-German tensions over Morocco and concern in foreign financial circles over domestic unrest in Russia. In fact, the implementation of the promised reforms—in

[109] This passage is at odds with a claim in Witte's memoirs that he offered his resignation in February after realizing that Nicholas had been preparing to dispense with his services. Supposedly both Nicholas and Trepov asked him to stay on at least until the conclusion of the foreign loan and the convocation of the Duma; *Vospominaniia*, 3:217.

[110] Original of Witte's resignation letter, Witte Collection, REEACU; copy, TsGAOR, f. 543, op. 1, d. 537, ll. 4–6. See, also, Witte, *Vospominaniia*, 3:304.

[111] Witte, *Vospominaniia*, 3:95–96.

[112] TsGIA, f. 1276, op. 1, d. 87, l. 402.

[113] Witte's report, April 17, 1906, ibid., l. 403.

[114] Witte, *Vospominaniia*, 3:96.

particular, the convocation of the Duma—came to be seen as essential prerequisites for the return of domestic peace and stability, without which the French government circles and investors would be unwilling to risk their capital. Equally important, Witte was able to persuade Nicholas to throw Russia's support behind France in the latter's diplomatic confrontation with Germany.[115]

From the tsar's as well as Witte's point of view, the loan negotiations may have been all that stood between Witte and his release. In accepting Witte's resignation, Nicholas let it be known that he considered the conclusion of the loan Witte's major accomplishment during his tenure as chairman of the Council of Ministers: "The satisfactory conclusion of the loan constitutes the best page of your activity. It is a great moral success of the government and a guarantee for the future tranquility and peaceful development of Russia. It is clear that the prestige of our motherland stands high in Europe." Although Nicholas could not refuse to bestow praise where it was due, his compliment could scarcely have been more backhanded, for he passed over in silence virtually all the remaining facets of Witte's brief but frenetic term. Indeed, the only mention of the reforms and events that form the focus of this chapter was negative:

> How matters will turn out after the opening of the Duma—only God knows. But I do not look at the near future as bleakly as you do.
>
> It seems to me the Duma turned out so extreme not as a result of the repressive measures of the government, but due to the latitude of the electoral law of December 11, the inertia of the conservative masses of the population, and the total abstention of all authorities from the election campaign, which does not happen in other states.

In the end, Witte was left with the tsar's lukewarm gratitude for his valiant efforts:

> I thank you sincerely, Sergei Iulevich, for your devotion to me and for your diligence which you displayed as far as possible in that difficult position which you occupied for six months in especially trying circumstances. I wish you rest and restoration of your strength. Grateful to you. Nikolai[116]

[115] For a more detailed history of the loan negotiations, see "K peregovoram Kokovtsova o zaime v 1905–1906 gg.," *KA* 10 (1925): 3–37; many of the original documents, including Witte's reports on the progress of the December and March talks, Kokovtsev's telegrams, etc., can be found in TsGIA, f. 1276, op. 1, d. 87. For Witte's and Kokovtsev's accounts, see Witte, *Vospominaniia*, 3:95–96, 219–53, and Kokovtsev, *Iz moego proshlago*, 1:89–90. Both Spasskii, "Vospominaniia," p. 49, and Liubimov, "Russkaia smuta," pp. 431–32, side with Witte.

[116] Nicholas's letter to Witte, April 15, 1906 (original and copy), Witte Collection, REEACU.

In his official rescript of April 22, the tsar attributed Witte's resignation to his failing health,[117] but the fact is that Nicholas had lost all confidence in his first minister. So complete was his dislike for Witte that he honored him for his services only most perfunctorily and never again appointed him to a government post. Although Witte retained his seat in the State Council and thus an opportunity to criticize the government's policies, he never received the ambassadorship that Nicholas had allegedly promised him at the time of his resignation, nor would the tsar deign to meet Witte's final wish of passing on his title to his step-grandson.[118]

[117] Imperial Rescript to Witte, April 22, 1906, Witte Collection, REEACU.

[118] Witte's letters to Nicholas, October 18, 1908 and undated last letter before his death, TsGAOR, f. 601, op. 1, d. 1204, ll. 3, 6–7.

CHAPTER X

The Constitutional Autocrat

NICHOLAS, in describing his April 17 audience with Witte's successor-to-be, spoke of asking Goremykin to "form a new ministry." The phrase, to be found in the tsar's diary,[1] had a constitutional ring to it, echoing the cabinet unification of the past fall. More importantly still, it was a measure of Nicholas's new distance from the business of government, though not necessarily of any new-found constitutional sympathies on his part.

Some of the comments greeting Goremykin's appointment singled out his inertia and lack of new ideas. As an autocratic servitor of long standing, he appeared to be a symbol of the *ancien régime* and thus a singularly inappropriate choice to ring in a new era.[2] Actually, Goremykin's passivity and lack of originality might have been a real advantage in this instance. Not only did it reflect the tsar's own remoteness and unwillingness to interfere, but it made Goremykin more likely to yield to the momentum of the bureaucratic reform process and to continue his predecessor's policies. With the exception of his stand on the agrarian question, this is precisely what happened.

The political program that Goremykin presented to the tsar two days after his appointment committed itself to the course charted by Witte. The choice was between a return to the old forms of state life, Goremykin explained, and a continuation along the lines of the August 6 and October 17 manifestos and subsequent reforms. Flatly ruling out "the path of reaction," he argued that the idea of popular participation in legislative work had taken deep roots among all strata of the Russian people. In view of the universal hatred of the bureaucratic system, any attempt to water down that principle or to do away with it altogether would imperil monarchical authority itself. Fears of just such interference might well have influenced the electoral outcome, Goremykin suggested, and they would continue to be exploited by those hostile to the government.

On the other hand, Goremykin insisted, nothing, not even an oppositional majority, could deter his government from carrying out its most important obligation, the restoration and maintenance of order. Goremykin did not expect the new Duma to cooperate on this score, given its lack of experience, the absence of a consensus, and the shortcomings of

---

[1] TsGAOR, f. 601, op. 1, d. 249, April 17, 1906.
[2] Cf. Golitsyn, "Vospominaniia" (manuscript, REEACU), p. 197.

the electoral law, which had crowded out reliable local elements in favor of radical and rootless intelligenty. Even under the best of circumstances, it probably would still be an unruly and fractious affair. To dissolve such a Duma, however, was to make martyrs of the government's enemies. Such an extreme step should only be taken "if the Duma usurps power not belonging to it and turns into a constituent assembly." Such an outcome was unlikely in Goremykin's eyes as long as the Kadets cared to maintain their public standing. Barring such an eventuality, the Duma should be left to ruin its prestige and reveal its impotence.[3]

Despite the change of personnel, the general direction of the ship of state would not change. Standing outside the new state order, apart from government and Duma alike, Nicholas was content for the time being to let them continue on their charted course—as long as the protection of private property and the preservation of public order were assured. Here Nicholas could rely on Goremykin to hold firmly to the inviolability of private property. At the recently concluded Special Conference, Goremykin had clashed vehemently with Witte over the very issue of forcible property alienation. This stand was bound to have made a favorable impression on a tsar who had come to identify order with the sanctity of property.[4]

The belief in the absolute inviolability of private property was, of course, irreconcilable with Witte's modern bureaucratic version of autocracy, in which state interests took priority over individual property interests. Nicholas's retreat into the preservation of order and property indicates just how much he had distanced himself from this particular form of autocratic government. The new bureaucratic state with the Duma, revamped State Council, and reformed Council of Ministers was alien to him. Instead of heeding Witte's suggestions for an amelioration of the peasantry's land hunger, Nicholas had come to identify with his nobles and their concerns: the maintenance of public safety and the protection of their real estate. That stand in turn slighted the property interests of the Russian peasantry and thus spelled the death knell for the notion of peasant monarchy, the mystical union of tsar and narod. In this sense, Nicholas's position also diverged from the traditional patriarchal interpretation of autocracy, which affirmed that union and treated the entire realm as the tsar's votchina or patrimony.

The tsar's new hands-off approach was evident in how the new minis-

---

[3] Goremykin's report, April 19, 1906, f. 543, op. 1, d. 520, ll. 22–25.

[4] Witte went so far as to label Goremykin's stand at the recent Special Conference a program that Goremykin had no choice but to fulfill. Witte saw his disagreement with Goremykin as the "ladder" to Goremykin's success with Trepov's aid, while Mendeleev more generally spoke of behind-the-scenes intrigues by Goremykin, Krivoshein, and the Trepov brothers; Witte, Vospominaniia 3:303–4, and Mendeleev, "Svet i teni," pp. 94–96.

ters were selected after Witte's resignation, for it was Goremykin, not Nicholas, who appears to have had the decisive voice. He ignored several names suggested by the tsar, among them Nicholas's candidate for the all-important Ministry of Internal Affairs, Lifland governor Zvechuntsov, in whose place Goremykin presented Saratov governor Stolypin as a fait accompli.[5] Stolypin was a newcomer to the St. Petersburg political and social scene, though not a total stranger to the tsar. Thanks in part to his own and Trepov's promotional efforts, Stolypin had recently received Nicholas's attention and gratitude for his firmness and personal courage in dealing with disorders in Saratov.[6] His nomination therefore met with the tsar's approval. A few months later, Nicholas would even sing Goremykin's praises for enlisting Stolypin's invaluable services: "how I have come to love him and respect him. Old Goremykin gave me *good* advice in pointing him out as the *only* one. I thank him for that."[7]

When the tsar received Stolypin in Goremykin's presence on April 25 to make the formal offer, he encountered considerable misgivings in the minister-to-be. To put a governor from Saratov opposite a formidable and well-organized Duma opposition was to condemn the new ministry to failure, Stolypin argued. It would be better to appoint a man who could command influence and authority in the Duma and preserve order. Rejecting a ministry based on an accidental Duma majority, Nicholas insisted that Stolypin accept. The governor then proceeded to lay out his program, reminding the tsar that he was speaking in the presence of Goremykin "as Premier" and asking for Nicholas's approval. After several questions, the tsar agreed. Once again, Stolypin prayed to be spared after having bared his soul; only if commanded would he undertake the assignment. Nicholas was silent for a moment and then—all too prophetically in view of Stolypin's eventual assassination by a police agent—ordered him to make the ultimate "self-sacrifice" for Russia's benefit. In

[5] Goremykin's report, April 19, 1906, TsGAOR, f. 543, op. 1, d. 199, ll. 1–3. Naumov, *Iz utselevshikh vospominanii*, 2:88, confirms that Stolypin was appointed at Goremykin's "initiative and insistence."

Goremykin evidently objected to the tsar's candidate for the Ministry of Communications as well. In lieu of any guidance from Nicholas, he also took it upon himself to put State Council member Stishinskii in charge of agriculture and land management, with the capable and more experienced Krivoshein at his side. Both men belonged to the anti-Witte camp. Stishinskii, moreover, and the new procurator-general, Prince A. A. Shirinskii-Shikhmatov, a protégé of Pobedonostsev's, had been among the most vocal adherents of traditional autocratic conceptions during the conferences of the past months.

[6] Stolypin's report to the MIA of January 29, 1905 (copy), with Nicholas's resolution of February 28, 1905, TsGAOR, f. 102, op. 166, d. 19, ll. 33–47 ob; Trepov's report, August 6, 1905, in Semennikov, *Revoliutsiia 1905 goda*, pp. 99–103.

[7] Nicholas's letter to Maria Fedorovna, October 11, 1906, TsGAOR, f. 642, op. 1, d. 2328, ll. 17–20, and "Perepiska Nikolaia II i Marii Fedorovny (1905–1906gg.)," *KA* 22 (1927): 204.

parting, the tsar firmly pressed Stolypin's hand with both of his. With tears in everyone's eyes, the new minister in turn kissed the tsar's hand and said: "I obey you." As Stolypin wrote to his wife, the die had been cast; he had become "the first constitutional minister of internal affairs in Russia." He held no illusions, however, about the difficulties and conflicts awaiting him in the Duma. As for Goremykin, he had promised not to interfere; their relations were most pleasant, Stolypin claimed.[8]

While Stolypin's letter remained silent about the details of his program, it demonstrated that he recognized both the importance of the Duma and the need to maintain order. The two went hand in hand. Only by influencing and enlisting the Duma could the second objective be achieved. The composition and agitated state of mind of the new legislative chamber made that a difficult, if not impossible task; still he would try.

The audience with Nicholas allowed a first glimpse into Stolypin's human qualities and diplomatic talents, with which he impressed people of different persuasions and, above all, Nicholas: his apparent candor and humility, sensitivity to form, his charm and almost old-fashioned politeness. In this regard, Stolypin presented a vivid contrast to the abrasive, openly ambitious, arrogant, and disdainful Witte. Even if they disagreed with Stolypin, people were much slower to take offense. Kryzhanovskii, his closest collaborator, saw Stolypin's significance not in the originality or creativity of his legislative reforms, all of which had been inherited from his predecessors, but in the psychological realm instead, in his ability to reconcile different members and segments of society with autocracy.[9]

Even allowing for some exaggeration in this last statement, there can be no doubt that individuals of radically different persuasions saw in Stolypin what they wanted. For example, both A. I. Izvol'skii, the new liberal minister of foreign affairs, and crusty General A. A. Kireev, autocratic traditionalist par excellence, claimed to have discovered one of their own in Stolypin.[10] After meeting the new minister for the first time, Kireev was beside himself with joy: "He produces a *splendid* impression, a gentleman of the old school, *sensible*, well-disposed, understands the situation. God be with him! He paid me [a number of] compliments. . . . our opinions are *very* close."[11] Another visit more than five months later

[8] Stolypin's letter to his wife, April 26, 1906, TsGIA, f. 1662, op. 1, d. 231, ll. 87–88, 103–4.

[9] Kryzhanovskii, *Vospominaniia*, pp. 209–21 gives a very sensitive and insightful portrait of Stolypin.

[10] Doctorow, "Introduction of Parliamentary Institutions in Russia," p. 335, makes this point and describes some of the same personal qualities.

[11] GBL OR, f. 126, d. 14, l. 148, May 20, 1906.

confirmed Kireev's excellent impressions: "A *real* gentleman! (And that is important!)."[12] This sense of propriety and courtliness would stand Stolypin in good stead; it certainly helps account for his success in dealing with a tsar who put great stock in the formal and the ritual, in appearances and orderliness.

THE FIRST DUMA

Mirroring British customs, the formal opening of the Duma with the emperor's speech from the throne demonstrated the extent to which Nicholas seemed to have become a legalistic monarch, divorced from the actual business of governing. When its chairman S. A. Muromtsev informed Nicholas of the Duma's request to have a special delegation present the official Duma response to the speech, Nicholas refused to receive them, asking that the address be sent instead.[13] Presumably, to receive the delegation would have meant to continue old practices; the government, not the tsar, was the proper recipient for the Duma's address. In keeping with this new approach, Goremykin delivered the government's response on May 13, 1906.[14]

Distinguishing between the Duma's grievances concerning legislative matters and those affecting the order of state administration, Goremykin pledged the government's full cooperation on those concerns that did not transcend the Duma's legislative purview. He rejected outright all demands for a revision of the new Fundamental Laws. Proposals for making ministers responsible to the legislature, abolishing the State Council, and broadening the Duma's powers were not the prerogative of the Duma. Goremykin then presented the Duma with a legislative agenda of his own. He announced his intention to introduce projects for the reform of secondary schools and of higher educational institutions based on the principle of self-government. Proposals for universal elementary education were currently in preparation; these were to involve "societal forces" as much as possible. Goremykin also singled out measures to strengthen zakonnost'. Local court reform—simplifying the organization of the courts, speeding up their disposition of cases, and bringing them closer to the population—would constitute an important step in this direction. Measures concerning the civil and criminal liability of officeholders would leave no doubt that the government's representatives were subject

[12] Ibid., l. 192, November 5, 1906.

[13] Sergei Muromtsev's report, May 5, 1906, TsGAOR, f. 543, op. 1, d. 530, l. 1; see, too, "Iz rezoliutsii Nikolaia II," *Byloe* 12 (June 1918): 142.

[14] The draft presented to the tsar on May 12 had Goremykin speaking on behalf of the Council of Ministers. Nicholas struck the phrase and replaced it by "government" throughout the speech, TsGAOR, f. 543, op. 1, d. 520, ll. 2–8.

to the law as well. In an attempt to distribute the tax burden more equitably, he promised to present an income tax proposal and review some indirect taxes. Finally, he envisioned a reform of the much-resented laws on internal passports.[15]

This program was little more than a vague and selective restatement of Witte's program, with one important exception: the land question. The use of state and church lands and the forcible alienation of privately owned lands to satisfy the peasants' land hunger, as demanded by the Duma, was utterly unacceptable, Goremykin declared. Not only did these private lands include those already purchased by peasants themselves, as Nicholas had pointed out, but

> the government cannot recognize the right of landownership for some and at the same time take it away from others. Nor can the power of the state deny in general the right of private landownership, without at the same time denying all property rights. In the whole world and at all stages in the development of civic life the principle of the inalienability and inviolability of property constitutes the cornerstone of popular well-being and societal development, the fundamental tenet of state being, without which the very existence of the state is inconceivable.

Instead, the land question could be solved legally through means at the government's disposal. Having categorically rejected any transfer of privately owned and state-held lands to the peasants, Goremykin nonetheless acknowledged the need for far-reaching reforms in order to overcome the separation of the peasant estate and to unite it with other estates with regard to both civil rights and administrative and judicial organization. This desegregation would include lifting restrictions on the peasants' rights to their allotment lands, though Goremykin said nothing about the dissolution of the commune. The government was also to assist the peasantry in improving cultivation techniques and land management. To alleviate land hunger the government would distribute vacant state lands, render assistance through the offices of the Peasant Land Bank, and encourage migration to Asia.

These were the very issues on which the battle between the government and the Duma was soon joined. After rejecting Goremykin's response as insufficient and calling for his replacement by a ministry enjoying the confidence of a Duma majority,[16] the new chamber proceeded with its own agenda. Most importantly, it drafted a peasant land reform bill that included the forcible alienation of private property. This provision was utterly unacceptable to Goremykin's cabinet, to say nothing of

---

[15] Ibid.

[16] Stolypin's report of May 13, 1906, TsGIA, f. 1328, op. 2, d. 15, l. 38 and ob.

Nicholas, who had come to see himself as the defender of private property and who had appointed Goremykin with this very goal in mind. Even if the Council of Ministers had been differently inclined, they would not have gotten their way with the tsar, as both Witte and Kutler had found out not long ago.

Lest there be any doubt, on June 20 the Council of Ministers reiterated its position on the agrarian question. Forcible expropriations of the sort envisioned by the Duma were to the peasants' own disadvantage, the statement claimed. Instead, the government planned to make available to needy peasants all empty lands under state control as well as those sold voluntarily by private landowners, presumably through the Peasant Land Bank. This was, of course, the position Goremykin had taken in mid-May; it also echoed the platform adopted at the First Congress of the United Nobility in late May. Denouncing the forcible alienation of private lands as "the first step toward the victory of the idea of socialism which rejects all forms of property," the plenipotentiaries of twenty-nine provincial noble assemblies had called for the purchase of land through the Peasant Bank, resettlement of peasants on empty state lands, and the transfer from communal landholding to private ownership.[17] The affinity between the nobility's interests and Nicholas's own concerns on this matter, as expressed by Goremykin, could hardly have been more striking.

The outcome, of course, was foregone. If the Duma members insisted on broadcasting their demands for a redistribution of land and for other radical reforms, Goremykin told Polovtsev, the government had no choice but to dissolve the Duma; before convening it anew, it should seek to influence the elections through all available means. If the new Duma proved equally uncooperative, it, too, would have to be dissolved and a new electoral law issued.[18] Even though Goremykin would soon find himself without the power to influence events, his forecast proved to be chillingly accurate.

Only the timing remained to be decided. First, the Duma had to be given enough time to discredit itself in the eyes of the moderate public.[19] A full month elapsed before the Duma was finally dissolved on July 9, 1906. This interval was filled with events of the most curious sort, in particular, various consultations between members of the government and representatives of society about the possibility of including public men in the cabinet or of making it a Kadet ministry altogether. These negotiations involved Stolypin and Izvol'skii on the government's side

[17] Chermenskii, *Burzhuaziia i tsarizm*, pp. 287–88.

[18] "Dnevnik A. A. Polovtseva," *KA* 4 (1923): 114.

[19] As Polovtsev found out, this is the strategy that the Council of Ministers proposed to Nicholas, ibid., pp. 115–16, June 13, 1906. Cf., too, Doctorow, "Introduction of Parliamentary Institutions in Russia," pp. 329–31.

and Shipov, Miliukov, Muromtsev, Trubetskoi, and others as spokesmen for society. Some of the same public men also were negotiating with D. F. Trepov, the palace commandant. Whereas the first set of talks apparently had the tsar's personal backing, the second conceivably did not. Nor were the objectives the same, though it is not entirely certain what they were. Izvol'skii may have hoped to moderate the behavior and demands of the Duma by saddling the Kadets with the responsibility for preserving public order. Others, such as Stolypin, may have seen such a step only as a stopgap measure of having someone else do the dirty work of dissolving the Duma. Trepov, in turn, was accused of hoping for still greater disorganization and unrest under a Kadet ministry in order to dramatize the need for some form of military dictatorship.[20] Some of these negotiations resumed even after the dissolution of the Duma, but finally came to an end in an atmosphere of mutual suspicion and recrimination. After going so far as to receive N. N. L'vov and A. Guchkov, Nicholas was left with "the deep conviction that they are not suited to be ministers now. They are not men of action [dela], i.e., of state administration, particularly L'vov."[21]

Wherever the truth may lie, the entire episode illustrates the extent to which Nicholas had distanced himself from the role of the autocrat and was willing to play the quasi-constitutional monarch. For a short while, it appears, he was even willing to contemplate the idea of a ministry composed of Constitutional Democrats. Although he would later deny ever having been serious about the whole venture, the fact remains that the tsar at least had knowledge of some of these talks and that he was prepared to see the government and the new chamber reach some sort of accommodation—as long as private property and public order were protected.

The Second Duma

Despite the most unsettling experience of the First Duma with its unacceptable demands for radical reform, the dissolution of this assembly of "unworthies" did not bring any change either in Nicholas's role or in the electoral law. Much to his own surprise, Goremykin found himself dis-

---

[20] Kireev reports rumors of such negotiations on June 26, 1906, GBL OR, f. 126, d. 14, l. 158. For details on the talks, see Izwolsky, *Recollections*, pp. 183–95, 215; and Kokovtsov, *Out of My Past*, pp. 146–49, or *Iz moego proshlago*, 1:196–97, 204–8. Chermenskii, *Burzhuaziia i tsarizm*, pp. 286–87, 290–93, 295–97, 325–26, draws on these and other accounts by Miliukov and Koni. The talks are one of the main subjects of Startsev, *Russkaia burzhuaziia i samoderzhavie*, pp. 70–130.

[21] Chermenskii, *Burzhuaziia i tsarizm*, pp. 325–26.

missed, together with the body he had sought to control.[22] The unceremonious way in which he was relieved of his duties was reminiscent of constitutional practices.[23] In fact, one of the reasons for his ouster may have been his inability to accept the notion of a united ministry, in particular his continued practice of involving the tsar in daily decision making and of expecting Nicholas to take the initiative. Reportedly it was just such hesitation on Goremykin's part that had been responsible for some of the delay between the decision in principle to dissolve the Duma and its implementation more than a month later.[24] Nicholas therefore turned to Stolypin, who was ready to act on his own. Indeed, Stolypin's very first act as chairman of the Council of Ministers was to secure the dismissal of two ministers whose continued presence was deemed incompatible with the idea of a united ministry and its reform plans. True to his new role, Nicholas granted that Stolypin was perfectly within his rights to do so.[25]

Similarly, the decision not to revise the electoral law and to fix a date for the opening of the Second Duma indicated the tsar's willingness to abide by constitutional practices. Despite the fact that a large number of the autocratic faithful appealed to Nicholas to change the law in a more conservative direction,[26] he went along with the recommendations of his government to eschew such a revision in favor of active electioneering, i.e., a concerted government effort to influence the election outcome. As Stolypin admitted, the current law was flawed, a hybrid of property and nonproperty criteria, "based on the mistaken notion of the peasants as the most reliable pillar of the existing political order." Unlike Witte before him, Stolypin was not under the spell of peasant monarchist illusions. Furthermore, the franchise slighted Russians living in the border regions, and gave the urban electorate twice as many electors as their share in the general population, Stolypin pointed out. Yet he cautioned against any revision of the franchise. In contrast to Western Europe, in Russia the struggles for political liberties and for social transformation were occurring simultaneously. Since the majority would vote for anyone promising an improvement in their material existence, measures had to be undertaken forthwith to improve social and economic conditions. Barring any wholesale disenfranchisement of large segments of the popula-

[22] "Dnevnik Polovtseva," *KA* 4 (1923): 117, July 10, 1906.

[23] GBL OR, f. 126, d. 14, ll. 163–64, July 12, 1906.

[24] According to Kokovtsov, *Out of My Past*, p. 146, "Goremykin let it be understood that he could do nothing until we received direct orders from the Emperor. Stolypin . . . felt that the tsar was rather dissatisfied with Goremykin's lack of decision and was waiting only for the government to take a definite decision." This was also the impression that Kokovtsev gained from his weekly audiences with Nicholas.

[25] Kokovtsev, *Iz moego proshlago*, pp. 214–15.

[26] E.g., Shvanebakh's memorandum, June 17, 1906, TsGAOR, f. 543, op. 1, d. 515, ll. 26–31; or memorandum, signed by several conservatives, ibid., ll. 49–54.

tion, only such an improvement offered any real guarantee for a more cooperative and conservative Duma.[27]

It is this argument that explains the haste with which Stolypin proceeded to implement his agrarian reform program through the use of Article 87—which granted the government broad legislative emergency powers when parliament was not in session—before the Second Duma even had been convened. Beginning with measures to expand the pool of land available to the Peasant Bank and to ease the terms under which peasants could obtain mortgages, the legislation-by-proclamation culminated in the November 9, 1906, ukase, according to which "any householder who holds allotment land by communal right may at any time demand that the parts of this land accredited to him be deeded to him as personal property."[28] While the reform broke down the barriers between communal and private landholding by allowing peasants to acquire private title to their allotments and to enclose them subject to certain restrictions, this legislation stayed well within the bounds established by Nicholas—the inalienability and inviolability of private property rights. The legal integration and physical separation of communal land and the weakening of the peasant estate's isolation were designed to affirm the primacy of private property.

The renewal of urban terrorism and rural unrest in the summer and early fall of 1906 not only added urgency to the problem of agrarian reform but also revived concern about public order. Indeed, fears for the personal safety of the emperor and his family during this time made them virtual prisoners in Peterhof; these fears haunted them even on their annual fall excursion to the Finnish isles where the imperial yacht, accompanied by a small flotilla of mine sweepers and other naval vessels, frequently had to change its moorings.[29] Stolypin was himself the target of a terrorist bomb that destroyed his home, seriously injured his children, and killed almost twenty petitioners. Plots against Nicholas, the Grand Duke Nikolai, Trepov, and others were discovered.[30] Other targets were less fortunate.

[27] Stolypin's report on Duma electoral law, TsGAOR, f. 601, op. 1, d. 912, ll. 11–25. Nicholas reviewed it on July 15, 1906. According to Doctorow, "Introduction of Parliamentary Institutions in Russia," pp. 337–38, it was Kryzhanovskii who drew up this report by late May.

Goremykin's report of July 19, 1906, which took stock of his tenure, echoed most of these conclusions, though it did not rule out any revision of the franchise; TsGAOR, f. 543, op. 1, d. 520, ll. 11–21.

[28] Geoffrey A. Hosking, *The Russian Constitutional Experiment. Government and Duma 1907–1914* (Cambridge, Mass., 1973), p. 65.

[29] Nicholas's letter to Maria Fedorovna, September 13, 1906, "Perepiska Nikolaia i Marii Fedorovny," *KA* 22 (1927): 200; GBL OR, f. 126, d. 1, ll. 181–82, September 10–11, 1906.

[30] Describing the arrest of the suspected ringleaders, Nicholas wrote to his mother on August 30, 1906, "But you'll understand my feelings, dear Mama—not to be able to go out

This breakdown of domestic peace led to various countermeasures, above all the notorious ukase of August 19, 1906, establishing special courts that liberally doled out death sentences and thus earned Stolypin the sobriquet of "bloody hangman." The label was not entirely deserved. During his tenure as governor in Saratov he had shown himself reluctant to resort to such extreme force and had expressed relief when all responsibility for possible bloodshed had passed to the new governor-general appointed by Nicholas.[31] One of his first actions as head of the Council of Ministers had been to advise all provincial and local officials to show discipline and firmness, but not to exceed the limits of law and moderation.[32] By August 1906 Stolypin evidently felt that he had no choice but to adopt extraordinary measures. Public order was gravely threatened; had he himself not just barely escaped assassination? More importantly still, he undoubtedly knew that the maintenance of order was uppermost in the tsar's mind. Stolypin's position very much depended on his ability to restore domestic peace, something that even the best-laid reform plans could not hope to accomplish. In the short run, at least, more direct and forceful measures were required.

While such actions might have reassured the tsar and propertied interests, they did nothing to produce a more pliable or cooperative Duma.[33] Despite the government's active intervention through administrative pressure, financial support for acceptable candidates and sympathetic press organs, and the judicial disqualification of opposition candidates, the elections of September–October 1906 resulted in a Duma more polarized than its predecessor. The big winners were the right and still more so the left, largely at the expense of the Kadets. Long before the new Duma convened on February 20, 1907, it was clear that it would not moderate its demands and that a renewed clash between the government and the people's representatives was inevitable. At that point this Duma, too, would have to be dissolved. Unlike the first time, however, another election under the old franchise would be out of the question. Indeed, preparations for a new electoral law began in the fall of 1906, months before the Second Duma's first meeting.

Again, once the actual decision to dissolve had been made by late

---

on horseback or to go beyond the gate, no matter where. And this in one's own home, in always peaceful Peterhof!! I blush as I write to you about this, both from shame for our motherland and from annoyance that such a thing could happen near Petersburg itself!" "Perepiska Nikolaia i Marii Fedorovny," *KA* 22 (1927): 198.

[31] Stolypin's letters to his wife, TsGIA, f. 1662, op. 1, d. 231, ll. 43–44, October 15, 1905; ll. 45–46, October 16, 1905.

[32] Stolypin's report, July 11, 1906, TsGIA, f. 1328, d. 17, ll. 34–35 ob.

[33] In his letters to the dowager empress, Nicholas expressed his delight at the "sobering" effects of the new measures; "Perepiska Nikolaia i Marii Fedorovny," *KA* 22 (1927): 202, September 27, 1906.

March–early April 1907, only the timing of the dissolution remained in doubt. Naturally, it was the question of land reform and of public order that provoked the break; the culpability of Social Democratic deputies in their contacts with members of the St. Petersburg garrison and the controversy over their immunity from prosecution were nothing more than a pretext manufactured by the government.[34] If there was one additional element that may help explain Nicholas's impatience at seeing the dissolution carried out, it was the offense he took at what he considered the Duma's insolent behavior.[35] In impugning the integrity of the army, for example, the Duma had committed an unforgivable breach of form that may have weighed almost as heavily in the tsar's mind as their disagreements on matters of substance.[36]

THE JUNE 3RD SYSTEM

The so-called June 3 coup d'état, which terminated the Second Duma and proclaimed a new electoral law, did not reflect a change in Stolypin's conception of autocratic government, although the revised franchise produced a pronounced shift to the right and raised at least the possibility of a government majority in the Duma. In the words of Kryzhanovskii, assistant minister of internal affairs and principal author of the new franchise, its purpose was

> to tear the State Duma from the hands of the revolutionaries, to adapt it to the historical institutions, to bring it into the state system. . . . To try, on the basis of the new law, to distill from Russia's chaos those elements in which there lived a feeling for the Russian state system, and to create out of these [elements] the Duma as an organ for the reeducation of society.[37]

Even during the first two Dumas, Stolypin had firmly adhered to his belief in bureaucratic initiative and interventionism in order to construct a more rational and efficient social and administrative structure. He had not been prepared to relinquish to the representatives of society the right to determine the country's affairs. In fact, the Duma was very much a part of this modern state apparatus, at once a necessary and a complicat-

---

[34] Kokovtsev, *Iz moego proshlago*, 1:271–72, says so, too.

[35] For some of Nicholas's comments about the Second Duma, see his correspondence with Mariia Fedorovna, "Iz perepiski Nikolaia i Marii Romanovykh v 1907–1910gg.," *KA* 50–51 (1932): 175–76, March 1, 1907; p. 177, March 18, 1907; pp. 179–80, March 29, 1907.

[36] Kokovtsev, *Iz moego proshlago*, 1:260–65, describes Zubatov's speech on April 17 as a real turning point, after which Nicholas impatiently waited for the government to dissolve the Duma.

[37] This quotation from Hosking, *Russian Constitutional Experiment*, p. 44, has been slightly revised.

ing element. The Duma represented one side of the quasi-constitutional equation that excluded the tsar in his traditional autocratic role. No matter how constraining its presence may have seemed, the Duma gave Stolypin and his bureaucratic government space to maneuver. Without the Duma there would have been no need for a united ministry or for a first minister who controlled its policies by directing, persuading, manipulating, cajoling, ordering, or firing ministers and Dumas alike. The new system made Stolypin the effective head of government. If it were not for the Duma which had to be tamed and for his own withdrawal from government and state, Nicholas might well have dispensed with Stolypin's services.

At the same time, the Duma was to give visible expression to the idea of a Russian nation that animated Stolypin. The fact that the first two Dumas, with their sizable contingents of non-Russian elements representing border areas and ethnic minorities, did not live up to this idea had been yet another reason for dissolving these chambers and revising the franchise so as to exclude precisely those alien and politically suspect constituencies. This aspect of the electoral revision and Stolypin's so-called nationalist policies went beyond the cynical use and manipulation of chauvinist slogans in order to rally a majority in the Duma; it was bound up with Stolypin's vision of nationhood integrating bureaucracy and society in a strong national state. His experience as a Russian landowner and appointed marshal of the nobility in the ethnic and religious heterogeneity of the western provinces had sensitized him to the national, i.e., peculiarly Russian, features of the state and culture to which he belonged.[38] Russian nationhood as a unifying principle joined the unific symbolism of the autocrat's person. This dimension was particular to Stolypin and thus marked a departure from Witte's purely technobureaucratic ideal of statehood.

Nothing better illustrates Stolypin's conception of government and its relationship to Duma and society than the dissolution of the First Duma, the coup d'état snuffing out the Second, and his use of the notorious article 87. With these acts he asserted his claim to lead and to assume ultimate responsibility and hence demonstrated his unwillingness to brook any determined opposition, interference, or competing claims. Stolypin's view of the law was utilitarian at best; if it did not serve his purpose, it had to be ignored. Whenever his leadership and the primacy of modern bureaucratic government were drawn into question, he showed scant regard for constitutional niceties, to the point of ruthlessness. Here Stolypin made no distinctions between the elected representatives of the Duma and the appointed half of the State Council. The opposition of the

---

[38] On this last point, cf. ibid., p. 22.

State Council's right wing to either local administrative reform or the introduction of zemstvos into the western provinces, for example, was as unacceptable as the Duma's lack of cooperation on the agrarian question or on matters of public order had been. If anything, such recalcitrance was less acceptable, for appointed State Council members were expected to support the government and not surrender to their own petty ambitions and jealousies or the intrigues and machinations of reactionary circles that might even include the emperor himself.

If June 3, 1907, did not mark a break in Stolypin's conception of government, neither did it signal a change in Nicholas's exercise of his role. Once again, the tsar refused to go along with those who felt that the coup d'état had not gone far enough and that the Duma should be reduced to a consultative assembly or be closed indefinitely while the sovereign took charge.[39] Occasionally, Nicholas would interfere with some of Stolypin's policies, but much of this reaction was visceral, as in his response to Stolypin's attempt to liberalize laws on Jews in December 1906.[40] In such instances narrow prejudices triumphed over any formal or external norms of conduct. These, however, were the exceptions that confirmed the rule: the appearance of a detached, noninterventionist, legalistic, formalistic monarch standing on the outside. Stolypin's sense of purpose, tactical ability, and diplomatic skills alone do not explain his relative political longevity and success. Without Nicholas's trust and toleration of Stolypin and his willingness, however temporary, to abide by the newly established conventions of the united ministry and the Duma the arrangement never could have succeeded.

Stolypin's policies had to meet two crucial conditions, of course, that went to the heart of Nicholas's role: the maintenance or restoration of order and the protection of private lands. Taking a personal interest, the tsar backed Stolypin directly and strongly in these two areas. Not coincidentally, it is here that Stolypin was most successful. His agrarian reform in defense of private property not only became, in Hosking's words, "the keystone of the June 3rd alliance" between the government, the Octobrists, the Duma right wing, the State Council, and the United Nobility but also proved to be the only area of unanimous agreement.[41] Nicholas's support clearly made the difference.

By contrast, when Nicholas tacked most closely to the noninterven-

[39] P. Kh. Shvanebakh, "Zapiski sanovnika. Politika P. A. Stolypina i Vtoraia Gosudarstvennaia Duma," Golos minuvshego, no. 1–3 (January–March 1918): 127–38; Kireev's letter to Nicholas, July 4, 1907, TsGAOR, f. 601, op. 1, d. 2374, ll. 1–3, and GBL OR, f. 126, 21(2), d. 6, ll. 9–13.

[40] Stolypin's letter to Nicholas, December 10, 1906, Byloe 5 (November 1917): 3–4; Kokovtsev, Iz moego proshlago, 1:236–38.

[41] Hosking, Russian Constitutional Experiment, pp. 59, 64, 72.

tionist course and left Stolypin to fend for himself, as in the case of the Western zemstvo bill or the reorganization of local courts and administration, the prime minister ran into trouble. These planned reforms had been in the making for many years, some going back to the Kakhanov Commission of the late 1870s and early 1880s. They represented the working out of the modern bureaucratic blueprint for the autocratic state and society.[42] The fact that these proposals now resurfaced not only revealed the vacuum created by the revolution but also showed how Nicholas had made his exit from this modern bureaucratic version of autocratic government. Giving the impression of being a legalistic monarch, he was washing his hands of everything and letting the government proceed as it saw fit. Laissez-faire, however, did not mean that Nicholas wholeheartedly approved of these measures or that he was prepared to do battle for them against their enemies. The rightist faction within the State Council therefore felt free to oppose the government and the Duma whenever Nicholas failed to make his position known or when he was rumored to be in disagreement with the government. To Stolypin's evident exasperation, Nicholas was content to leave several of the proposed reforms to their own fates and did not appear unduly upset when these measures were crippled or blocked by the Duma or State Council. After all, such was the risk of popular representation in legislative affairs. As a result, every major piece of legislation, except for the agrarian reforms, became the target and victim of such conservative resistance.

On the Western zemstvo bill, for example, Nicholas told the State Council members that they were free to vote according to conscience, whereupon the national curiae—separate and unequal representation based on nationality—went down to defeat on March 4, 1911.[43] As this example reveals, the tsar's demonstrative distance from the government made for serious instability, depriving Stolypin of invaluable support in his confrontations with an untractable State Council and a less than sympathetic Duma right wing. The issue itself had been relatively noncontroversial until it became the vehicle for intrigues directed against Stolypin. Holding the tsar indirectly responsible, Stolypin threatened to resign unless the two ringleaders of the State Council right were banished and the legislature was prorogued for three days to permit passage of the Western zemstvo bill pursuant to Article 87. Nicholas suggested that the bill be passed through the Duma again, whereupon he would personally see to its approval by the State Council, but Stolypin would not hear of it. If the tsar really backed the bill, as he now claimed, then

---

[42] For a detailed discussion of these reform plans and their entire history, see Francis W. Wcislo, *The Dilemmas of Reforming Rural Russia* (forthcoming).

[43] Hosking, *Russian Constitutional Experiment*, pp. 133–34.

it should be implemented forthwith. After several days of agonized reflection, Nicholas capitulated to all of Stolypin's demands.[44] Whatever one's views of this unsavory episode, which did much to damage Stolypin's standing in the eyes of his nominal Duma allies and of the tsar, if Nicholas is to be faulted, his crime was one of omission rather than commission.

Although the June 3rd system had been designed to produce a cooperative Duma representing the conservatism of its property-owning constituencies, its effect had been to grant a virtual political monopoly to the landed nobility. The stranglehold of some thirty thousand gentry families on the Empire's political affairs certainly did not reflect the actual constellation and aspirations of society or, for that matter, Stolypin's intentions, yet it corresponded perfectly to the tsar's own priorities and predilections. From his point of view, there was no need to intervene in the affairs of government. The result was a legislative stalemate that preserved the status quo and eventually allowed the gentry to withdraw into its own cultural, psychological, and political isolation.[45]

CONCLUSION

The events of the First Russian Revolution had confronted Nicholas II with both changing and antithetical conceptions of autocracy and the autocrat's role. The choices facing the tsar reflected the crisis of the Russian body politic, its ideological divisions, social challenges, and political transformation.

On the one hand, there was the personalized pre-Petrine notion of rulership resting on the union of tsar and narod, of the all-powerful monarch who heard out his loyal and faithful subjects through some sort of consultative mechanism. Part of this view was the myth of an alien bureaucracy of German origin which formed a wall between ruler and ruled, pursuing its own selfish interests by choking off communication and intercepting or distorting the tsar's personal grants of mercy and favor. Such a conception was obviously irreconcilable with the institutionalization of authority, as it was hostile to the bureaucracy's superordinate pretensions and reforms. Ideally, bureaucrats were little more than the executors of the tsar's personal will, his *prikazchiki* (pre-Petrine administrators) or personal agents—or, more realistically, miniature tsars.

This interpretation of autocracy did not have to exclude the notion of legality, or zakonnost', as Sviatopolk-Mirskii, the most prominent proponent of the notion of Legal Autocracy, would argue in the fall of 1904.

[44] Ibid., pp. 135–38.

[45] For a multifaceted consideration of the June 3rd system and its pernicious effects, see Leopold H. Haimson, ed., *The Politics of Rural Russia* (Bloomington, Ind., 1979).

Laws were necessary to assure the execution of the tsar's will and to contain the arbitrary tendencies of the bureaucrats. Indeed, according to this view, it was the very absence of such laws or the failure to observe them that had allowed the bureaucracy to interpose itself between tsar and people and to become an end in itself. The potential for conflict is self-evident, of course. The ruler was the source of those laws; yet he remained free to change or ignore them, thus undermining the very authority of the law. Inasmuch as the tsar was not bound by the rules of his own making, neither were his agents who participated in the formulation of those laws.

As for popular representation, it, too, could serve to contain a self-aggrandizing bureaucracy by apprising the autocrat of his subjects' needs and thus breaking down the wall between ruler and ruled. The people's voice could only be advisory, however, never binding. Standing above all selfish, particular interests and not bound by accidental majorities, the tsar was at liberty to choose between different opinions or to reject them altogether. The zemskie sobory of the sixteenth and particularly of the early seventeenth century were widely perceived to have been such consultative assemblies speaking for the Russian land and demonstrating the unity of tsar and narod. Hence the adherents of autocratic omnipotence who were critical of the bureaucratic reforms of 1905–6 often argued their cause in terms of early seventeenth-century precedents and concepts, real or imagined.

Their bureaucratic opponents, on the other hand, subscribed to a conception of autocracy that had its roots in the Petrine reforms, but that had evolved considerably under the impact of recent events. This was the institutionalized, impersonal notion of autocracy that identified the bureaucracy with the tsar's superordinate vantage point. Together they stood above society—itself a notion altogether missing from the original interpretation of autocracy—molding and controlling while taking care to heed its legitimate needs and grievances. Russia's latest and gravest crisis demonstrated that the Petrine service state founded on a hierarchy of juridically defined estates was an anachronism. Taking its place was the modern bureaucratic state in which an interventionist professional bureaucracy administered, if not fashioned (according to clearly defined and consistent rules) a society of classes based on the universal criterion of property-ownership. To the extent that this society was still encrusted with the atavistic strictures of the service estate system, it was the bureaucracy's task to remove them—as, for example, in the case of the isolated peasantry.

This alternative conception included the notions of legality and of popular representation, too. Laws and regulations were the cement holding together the bureaucratic state. Not only the bureaucracy and society, but the tsar himself was subject to these rules. Without such a legal order, the bureaucracy's primacy and leadership was threatened from above and below. By granting the population a legislative instead of a mere consultative voice, the bureaucracy both recognized the legitimacy of societal interests and sought to strengthen its own position vis-à-vis the ruler. At no time did it abdicate to the people's representatives its claims to lead and control; it no more wished to be the simple executor of the popular will than it cared to implement the tsar's personal caprices. This was the vision that inspired Witte, who, moreover, laid claim to leading this modern bureaucratic state himself.

Prodded by his advisors and buffeted by events, Nicholas had formally endorsed a number of such different conceptions in succession. Regardless of what measures he approved or which interpretation of autocracy he appeared to embrace, however, he did so with profound reservations. Nicholas constantly seemed to be acting against his own better judgment, even when that judgment itself was unknown or in doubt.

Given his instinctive predilections and his fealty to the sacred memory of that strapping incarnation of autocratic omnipotence, Nicholas felt emotionally drawn to the example of Alexander III yet lacked a clear sense of what his father's role had been. As a result, others invested this role with their own personal interpretations and, exploiting Nicholas's emotional vulnerability, sought to convince him that their views were correct. Through the efforts of Interior Minister Sipiagin and his patron Meshcherskii, for example, Alexander's role in retrospect was identified—incorrectly—with the pre-Petrine paternalistic conception. Witte, on the other hand, argued at the height of the revolutionary crisis that Alexander III himself would have undertaken the reforms recommended by Witte. Indeed, even those who regarded the pre-Petrine model as an anachronism unsuited to Russia's current needs often tried to bolster their own, more modern notions by resorting to the language and imagery of seventeenth-century autocracy.

By virtue of his personality and upbringing, however, as everyone including Nicholas himself knew only too well, he was temperamentally unsuited for being a personally imposing ruler like Alexander III. Instead, he identified with Michael, the meek founder of the Romanov dynasty who had been overshadowed by the forceful presence of his own father, Filaret; like Michael before him, Nicholas named his only son "Alexis." When Kireev and others appealed to the strong centralizing role inherent in the paternalist conception of autocracy, asking Nicholas to be the strong personal ruler who cut through the web of bureaucratic intrigues and self-gratification in order to restore the mystical union with his people, they failed to stir him to action. Nicholas might go on insisting on the theoretical unlimitedness of his power, but he was not prepared to practice what he preached. Eventually he would even accede to the theoretical limitation of his power.

Nicholas's inability to synthesize and internalize a coherent conception of his role made for distance and disillusionment. He acted the role without conviction and thus undermined the faith of autocratic loyalists of all persuasions, to say nothing of the public at large. At the same time, such poor acting encouraged others to put forth and act on their own convictions and political demands, as we have seen. He went through the motions and tried to compensate for the lack of substance by adhering to its formal aspects. Incapable of filling the pre-Petrine autocratic role, he instead dressed himself and his court in seventeenth-century garb, as happened at the 1903 court ball. Empty ritual and formal routine, i.e., the orderly progression of the visible details of physical life, became a substitute for the essential. As in Russian iconography, form was to represent essence.

The external, formal functions with which Nicholas had come to equate his position included, of course, the bureaucratic routine, the endless series of ministerial reports and audiences that were a firm and unchanging part of his daily rhythm. Nicholas resented this routine and as a result grew still more alienated. All the while a formal sense of duty commanded him to submit to this burdensome schedule. In fact, the more onerous the obligations, the more convinced he became that he was carrying out his autocratic duties. Small wonder, considering the externality of his role and of his notion of duty, that Nicholas should exhibit not only a profound religious fatalism, but a feeling of being punished by Providence. Evidently the exercise of his responsibilities implied, indeed required, great suffering. This idea of divinely ordained punishment pervaded Nicholas's correspondence with his mother and his wife. It came to the fore at critical junctures, whenever he was left with no choice but to do something personally unpalatable; witness his conversations with Ermolov prior to the issuance of the Bulygin Rescript, for example, or the events leading up to the October Manifesto.

Seeking refuge in exterior forms and observances, Nicholas gave new meaning to the term "trappings." Time and again, he left the impression of being trapped by administrative practices and differing ideological formulations. As events were spinning out of control, the structures of autocratic administration and autocratic ideology constrained and determined his actions. Incapable of asserting himself in any sustained fashion, hemmed in by structures external to him, he would periodically revolt against these strictures, lashing out verbally and even screwing up his courage to act decisively. But invariably he could not sustain this act of rebellion and would back down. Aware of his own impotence, he described himself to his wife as "your little huzzy with no will."

Even though Nicholas felt still less affinity for the bureaucratic conception of autocracy, it was precisely his willingness to submit to an onerous routine and his need for external order of any kind that made him vulnerable to bureaucratic overtures and manipulations, as long as these did not violate his sense of propriety and orderliness. Since many, if not most, proposals for reform were generated by the bureaucracy, where they often lay dormant for years, the tsar did not have to take the initiative or enunciate an active conception of his own. He simply had to respond and approve the drafting, consideration, and implementation of such suggestions when circumstances so demanded.[46] If Nicholas could be convinced through the "logic" of events or argument, that any contemplated measures followed inevitably from previous promises or precedents, or were consonant with autocratic principles (such as the unlimitedness of the supreme power) or were required for the preservation or restoration of public order, then he was likely to go along with them. The formal contributions of these reforms to form and order were as important as their material effects.

Imperial approval or tolerance did not signify that Nicholas had embraced the conceptions and assumptions underlying such reforms. His relationship to the bureaucratic notion of autocracy, which itself was continuing to evolve, was no less formal, externalized, and distant than his attitude toward any other interpretation. Obeying rules external to him, Nicholas did not care to intervene in bureaucratic practices and decisions or to provide the centralizing role that was needed in times of crisis, both in terms of policy-making and of administrative coordination. The revolution severely undermined, at times even destroyed, bureaucratic authority and added to the institutional rivalries and disarray that had contributed to the chaos in the first place. Instead of alleviating such disorganization, Nicholas only compounded it by establishing a still greater number of ad hoc institutions and by circumventing bureaucratic channels and authorities through his use of personal agents. At the same time, he did not want to see anyone else assume this coordinating function; this reluctance may well help explain his growing animosity toward Witte, who sought to play just such a role.

While Witte's scheme of the modern bureaucratic state may have had the advantages of internal logic and consistency, these features were readily apparent only to its proponents. This vision found plenty of detractors among more traditionally oriented high-ranking servitors and circles well-connected at court. Equally significant is the fact that society,

[46] Cf. Daniel Field's description of Alexander II's role in the Emancipation process, *The End of Serfdom. Nobility and Bureaucracy in Russia, 1855–1861* (Cambridge, Mass., 1976), passim.

too, was by no means uniformly enthusiastic about the proposed changes. To many the reforms that grew out of this conception were but cosmetic improvements or, worse, deliberate deceptions designed to mask the continuing arbitrariness and irresponsibility of the autocratic bureaucracy. Still others interpreted such reforms in ways that were favorable to society but clearly unacceptable from the modern bureaucratic vantage point. Inasmuch as Witte's scheme neither allowed for the kind of independence, initiative, and leadership desired by society nor won the unanimous backing of courtiers and bureaucrats, it only exacerbated the disintegration of authority and contributed to disorder.

The fact that order and quiet did not return with the announcement of the bureaucratically inspired reform measures only heightened the tsar's disaffection from the role implicit in those reforms. As a result, he grew still more distrustful toward Witte. Witte, in turn, shaken by the continuing unrest and the emperor's mounting suspicions, appeared to depart from his course and came to insist on maximizing the power and initiative of the government vis-à-vis the new Duma. Hoping to protect the bureaucratic state from incursions by society and to preserve its freedom to control and manipulate, Witte favored a broad definition of the tsar's right to issue administrative decrees. Nicholas, however, drew the line here.

Identifying the ambitious and untrustworthy Witte with the newly reformed state order, Nicholas wanted to have as little as possible to do with either. It is not that he was prepared to become the personal ruler that autocratic traditionalists had implored him to be. For the time being, that was clearly out of the question. With the Duma about to convene, the tsar could not go back on his own word lest he provoke still greater disorders. The promised reforms had to go forward. By the same token, by April 1906 Nicholas, unlike Witte, was not interested in expanding the government's prerogatives or in providing it with escape-hatches from Duma control; it might as well be subject to the legislature or at least dependent on it. Surrendering his identification with government, or at any rate the kind of government represented conceptually and personally by Witte, Nicholas acted as though he were ready to become a legalistic monarch.

His withdrawal did not indicate a real conversion to constitutional principles, of course, but instead bespoke his reservations about them. In this sense the prescribed distance between a constitutional ruler and his government, best captured by de Tocqueville's dictum of the king who reigns, but does not rule, was a welcome cover for Nicholas: it masked his internal distance from government much better than any previous role had done. His misgivings expressed themselves through heightened suspicions of his bureaucratic servitors, and Witte was their first victim.

These reservations also should have made Nicholas more receptive to the appeals of those urging him formally to renounce or at least tacitly abandon the role envisioned in the reforms of 1905–6. In the short run, his refusal to do so in any official way testified to Stolypin's diplomatic and political skills and to the absence of any personal alternative.

For all of Stolypin's talents and successes, however—his attention to form and convention, his restoration of order, and his handling of the Duma—they served merely to delay but not to prevent Nicholas's rebellion against the constraints against which he felt himself to be chafing. The fact is that Nicholas's very identification with his nobles rendered him vulnerable to their pleas that he play a more traditional, active role once again. This identification revealed just how much he had distanced himself from the role of the constitutional autocrat. Hence he was more likely to heed the nobles' appeals when it suited him. His inability to internalize a consistent conception of the autocrat's role made such a change probable. After withdrawing from government, the state, and its institutions to the point where they confronted him as something external and alien, Nicholas was now free to revolt against that state. He may even have felt psychologically compelled to do so.

The first open expression of his growing resentment against his role first came as early as 1909 during the naval staffs' imbroglio, when Nicholas apparently suggested a revision of Article 48 along lines reminiscent of the tsar's traditional function as arbiter. In the case of disagreements between Duma and State Council, Nicholas asked that both bills be submitted to him so he could confirm one of them, return them for a second reading, or let the matter rest altogether.[47] Although nothing came of the idea, similar reactions characterized Nicholas's behavior toward Stolypin at the height of the controversy over the Western zemstvo bill; not for the first time, they were held in check by Stolypin's blunt talk and threat of resignation. According to Stolypin the tsar believed that "I [Stolypin] have overshadowed him as though I stand between him and the country."[48]

Two years after Stolypin's assassination in September 1911, this smoldering resentment finally burst out into the open (in the fall of 1913), when Nicholas yielded to the suggestions of his minister of internal affairs, N. A. Maklakov, and of Meshcherskii, the editor of *Grazhdanin*, and contemplated his own coup d'état against the Duma and the Council of Ministers. In the wake of the massive strikes and protests unleashed

---

[47] TsGAOR, f. 601, op. 1, d. 823, l. 9. Although undated, at the top appear two addenda in Nicholas's handwriting: "1909" and "About changing Article 87."

[48] Cf. Stolypin's summary of his conversation with Nicholas, [March 5, 1911], TsGIA, f. 1662, op. 1, d. 325, ll. 1–2. Nicholas's note to Stolypin, TsGAOR, f. 601, op. 1, d. 1125, ll. 53–54.

by the Lena gold field massacre of March 1912, relations between government and the recently elected Fourth Duma had deteriorated to the point where the Council of Ministers had begun to boycott the Duma sessions. Although Nicholas approved of the ministers' action, he was not satisfied. Growing disenchanted with the insufficiently forceful and uncompromising conduct of Finance Minister Kokovtsev, Stolypin's successor as chairman of the Council of Ministers, he leant a sympathetic ear to those hoping to oust Kokovtsev, dissolve the Duma, and reduce its legislative role to a consultative one.

On October 14, 1913, while Kokovtsev was engaged in important loan negotiations abroad, Maklakov made his move. The interior minister warned the tsar, who was on vacation in the Crimea, that the mood of the factory workers and "the so-called intelligentsia" in St. Petersburg was agitated and that the Duma, with its members returning from their summer recess in order to do battle with the government, would "sharply raise the temperature of society." With the tsar's permission, Maklakov wanted to issue a government declaration calling the Duma to its senses and threatening it with dissolution if it did not mend its destructive ways and if it failed to cooperate in ensuring the welfare of the motherland. Should the Duma respond to such a threat with a storm of indignation, "that will only hasten the denouement which seems scarcely avoidable." While the authorities were prepared to handle any public manifestations of such an explosion, Maklakov asked Nicholas to sign two undated ukases, one dissolving the Duma and the other declaring a "state of extraordinary protection" in the capital.[49] Before the tsar had even had a chance to respond, Maklakov took up the matter with a rump session of the Council of Ministers on October 17 and secured their endorsement. Considering "a significant part of the Duma circles, even from relatively moderate parties, to be in an extreme oppositional mood," the three ministers forwarded the necessary papers for the tsar's signature.[50]

In his reply of October 18, the tsar not only approved of Maklakov's proposed declaration to the Duma, but added that it was long overdue. Given the element of surprise, it was bound "to clear the atmosphere and force Mr. Rodzianko [the Duma chairman] and his dreamers to bite their tongues." He also agreed with Maklakov's contingency plans. Still unaware that some of the ministers, claiming to speak for the Council of Ministers, had already acted on their own, he instructed the interior minister to discuss the drafting of the two ukases with the Council's acting chairman. In conclusion, the tsar added a proposal of his own:

[49] V. P. Semennikov, ed., *Monarkhiia pered krusheniem 1914–1917* (Moscow-Leningrad, 1927), pp. 93–94.

[50] TsGIA, f. 1276, op. 20, d. 68, ll. 48–50, "Osobyi zhurnal Soveta ministrov 17 Oct. 1913," signed by Kharitonov, Shcheglovitov, and Maklakov; l. 51, undated ukase.

I also consider it necessary and beneficial for the Council of Ministers to discuss immediately my longstanding idea of changing the article of the Duma charter, according to which a bill lapses whenever the Duma does not accept the amendments of the State Council and fails to confirm the bill. Since we do not have a constitution, that is utterly senseless!

Presenting the opinions of both the majority and the minority to the Emperor for his selection and confirmation will be a good way of returning to the previous tranquil course of legislative activity and will be in the Russian spirit to boot.[51]

Moreover, after receiving the recommendations of the ministerial rump council on October 23, Nicholas insisted that the convocation of a new Duma be "considerably delayed." He signed the undated Duma dissolution edict, which, contrary to law, left open the date for new elections and instead promised that it would be announced later.[52] Presumably such a delay would make it possible to alter the Duma statute in a consultative direction. Exactly eight years earlier Nicholas had dubbed the October Manifesto a constitution; denying its very existence, he now was conspiring to erase its most important provisions.

As it turned out, Maklakov lost his nerve in the face of opposition from his colleagues. The overwhelming majority of those ministers who were present at a October 21 meeting disapproved of Maklakov's proposed ultimatum; not only would such a step provoke the Duma still further, but it should not be taken in the absence of the most senior ministers, Kokovtsev, Krivoshein, and Sabler. After all, it was the chairman of the Council and not the minister of internal affairs, its most junior member, who was responsible for Duma affairs. Maklakov therefore did not even tell his colleagues of Nicholas's October 17 letter but merely intimated that the tsar in principle had recognized such a declaration by the minister of internal affairs as a possibility. In such circumstances, a consideration of the majority/minority opinion issue would have been out of the question, Maklakov informed Nicholas the following day.[53] Upon his return from abroad Kokovtsev personally protested to Nicholas about Meshcherskii's editorial insinuations and Maklakov's recent intrigues. He demanded that the principle of collective consultation and decision making be observed by all ministers, especially the interior minister.[54]

Although the coup had come to naught, it did nothing to stem Nicholas's growing rebelliousness against the restrictions of his "constitutional" role. Kokovtsev was dismissed as chairman and finance minister on Jan-

[51] Semennikov, *Monarkhiia pered krusheniem*, pp. 91–92.
[52] TsGIA, f. 1276, op. 20, d. 68, ll. 48–51.
[53] Semennikov, *Monarkhiia pered krusheniem*, pp. 94–95.
[54] Hosking, *Russian Constitutional Experiment*, pp. 202–3.

uary 30, 1914, and the chairmanship was divorced from any ministerial portfolio, with the aged Goremykin stepping into the breach once again. Angered by the Duma's and State Council's failure to pass laws desired by his government, Nicholas even revived his proposal for reducing the two chambers to their August 6, 1905, consultative status. On June 18, 1914, at the end of the Duma's second session, he personally sought to enlist the support of the assembled ministers in the cause of restoration, but to no avail. Except for Maklakov, they were unanimous in their opposition and the tsar backed down once again.[55] Then war broke out and exposed the bankruptcy of Russian autocracy for all the world to see.

Long before that point was reached, however, the regime had all but ceased to function—paralyzed from within and besieged from without. Time and again Nicholas had failed to make his peace with the quasi-constitutional role prescribed by the reforms of 1905–6 and repeatedly upheld by his ministers, yet he had also proved incapable of asserting himself against those same bureaucrats with another role of his own choosing. In the end, he would leave the bureaucracy to its own devices and escape to the front as commander of his army. On February 8, 1917, Nicholas returned to his original idea once more, asking Maklakov, who had been dismissed from his post in 1915, to draft the necessary papers for a dissolution and revamping of the Duma.[56] This time the revolution intervened and there was nothing left for Nicholas to do but to resign with evident relief from the position that for more than twenty-two years he had occupied so unwillingly and yet so stubbornly.

[55] *Padenie tsarskogo rezhima*, 2:437–38, and 3:133–34. About the preceding compare, too, the valuable detailed account in V. S. Diakin et al., *Krizis samoderzhaviia v Rossii 1895–1917* (Leningrad, 1984), pp. 526–34.

[56] Cf. Maklakov's letter to Nicholas, February 9, 1917, Semennikov, *Monarkhiia pered krusheniem*, pp. 97–98.

Glossary

boiar', boyar — boyar, noble of high rank
bunt — peasant rebellion, jacquerie
Duma, duma — representative assembly, council
Gosudar' Imperator — Sovereign Emperor (formal title)
gosudarstvo — state
gosudarstvennost' — state system, state principle
guberniia — province
intelligent — member of the intelligentsia
narod — simple people, folk
obshchestvo — civil society, educated public
opeka — administrative supervision
oprichnina — Ivan IV's personal realm of terror
pravda — truth/justice
prikaz — pre-Petrine administrative department
Pugachevshchina — eighteenth-century peasant war, synonym for chaos, i.e., "Pugachev Affair"
Rus' — ancient name for Russia
samoderzhavie — self-rule, autocracy
-shchina — suffix, usually with names: -Affair
smuta, smutnoe vremia — Time of Troubles preceding Romanov dynasty
soslovie, sosloviia — service class(es) or estate(s)
Tsar' Batiushka — Little Father Tsar (popular appellation)
uezd — district
ukaz — ukase, tsarist decree
vlast' — power/authority
voevoda, voievoda — pre-1775 governor, tsarist agent
volost' — township composed of several villages
votchina — patrimony, hereditary possession
vsepodanneishii doklad — "most humble report" to the tsar
zakon — law
zakonomernost' — conformance with law, regularity
zakonnost' — legality
zemlia — land, the Russian lands
zemskii sobor, zemskie sobory — Assembly(ies) of the Land
zemstvo — limited rural self-government
zemtsy — elected members of the zemstvos

PERIODICALS

Grazhdanin — Citizen
Moskovskiia Vedomosti — Moscow News
Novoe Vremia — New Time
Osvobozhdenie — Liberation
Pravitel'stvennyi Vestnik — Government Herald
Russkii Vestnik — Russian Herald
Russkiia Vedomosti — Russian News
Russkoe Gosudarstvo — Russian State
Sel'skii Vestnik — Rural Herald

Select Bibliography

A. ARCHIVES

Tsentral'nyi Gosudarstvennyi Arkhiv Oktiabr'skoi Revoliutsii (TsGAOR)

fond 102:   Departament politsii
fond 543:   Tsarsko-Sel'skii Aleksandrovskii Dvorets
fond 568:   V. N. Lamzdorf
fond 586:   V. K. Pleve
fond 595:   D. N. Trepov
fond 601:   Nikolai II
fond 640:   Aleksandra
fond 642:   Imperatritsa Mariia Fedorovna
fond 644:   Pavel Aleksandrovich
fond 648:   Sergei Aleksandrovich
fond 652:   Vladimir Aleksandrovich
fond 653:   Petr Nikolaevich
fond 660:   Konstantin Konstantinovich
fond 668:   Mikhail Aleksandrovich
fond 671:   Nikolai Nikolaevich
fond 681:   Aleksei Aleksandrovich
fond 859:   A. A. Budberg
fond 1001:   A. Mosolov

Tsentral'nyi Gosudarstvennyi Istoricheskii Arkhiv SSSR (TsGIA)

fond 40:   Ministerstvo Torgovli i Promyshlennosti
fond 381:   Ministerstvo Zemledeliia
fond 446:   Ministerstvo Putei Soobshchenii
fond 472:   Ministerstvo imperatorskago dvora. Kantseliariia
fond 476:   Ministerstvo imperatorskago dvora. Gofmarshal'skaia chast'
fond 516:   Kamer-fur'erskie zhurnaly (*KFZ*)
fond 563:   Komitet Finantsov
fond 575:   Ministerstvo Finantsov. Glavnoe upravlenie neokladnykh sborev
fond 583:   Ministerstvo Finantsov. Osobennaia kantseliariia po kreditnoi chasti
fond 744:   Ministerstvo Prosveshcheniia
fond 797:   Ober-Prokuror Sviateishago Sinoda. Kantseliariia
fond 922:   V. I. Glazov
fond 1263:   Komitet Ministrov
fond 1276:   Sovet Ministrov
fond 1282:   Ministerstvo Vnutrennikh Del. Kantseliariia
fond 1284:   Ministerstvo Vnutrennikh Del. Departament Obshchikh Del
fond 1328:   Ministerstvo Vnutrennikh Del. Shefskie vsepoddanneishie zapiski
fond 1405:   Ministerstvo Iustitsii

fond 1412: Kantseliariia E.I.V. po priniatiiu proshenii
fond 1544: Soveshchaniia obrazovannye pri Gosudarstvennom Sovete dlia ob-
            suzhdeniia voprosa o gosudarstvennykh preobrazovaniiakh
fond 1574: K. P. Pobedonostsev
fond 1591: Osoboe Soveshchanie o vyiasnenii prichin, kotorye priveli Rossiiu k
            vooruzhennomu stolknoveniiu s Iaponiei
fond 1622: S. Iu. Witte
fond 1626: I. L. Goremykin
fond 1662: P. A. Stolypin

Gosudarstvennaia Biblioteka im. V. I. Lenina, Otdel Rukopisei (GBL OR)
fond 126:   Kireevy

Gosudarstvennaia Publichnaia Biblioteka im. M. E. Saltykova-Shchedrina, Otdel Rukopisei
fond 354:   D. F. Kobeko
fond 443:   V. I. Losev
fond 760:   N. S. Tagantsev
fond 781:   I. I. Tolstoi

Bakhmetev Archive, formerly Russian and East European Archive, Columbia University (REEACU)

Girs, A. F. "Vospominaniia byvshago ofitsera Sv. Gv. Preobrazhenskago Polka i Minskago Gubernatora A. F. Girsa o svoikh vstrechakh s Gosudarem Imperatorom Nikolaem II." Unpublished manuscript.

Golitsyn. "Vospominaniia." Unpublished manuscript.

Liubimov, D. N. "Russkaia smuta nachala deviatisotykh godov. 1902–1906. Po vospominaniiam, lichnym zapiskam i dokumentam." Unpublished manuscript.

Mendeleev, P. P. "Svet i teni v moei zhizni (1864–1933). Obryvki vospominanii." Unpublished manuscript.

Spasskii-Odynets, A. A., "Vospominaniia." Unpublished manuscript.

Witte Collection.

International Law Library, Harvard University (ILLHU)

Gosudarstvennoe Pravo. Materialy.

Materialy i zapiski, razoslannye Chlenam Komiteta Ministrov dlia razsmotreniia p.p. 1, 2, 4, 5 i 8 Vysochaishago ukaza 12 Dekabria 1904 goda.

Materialy i zapiski, razoslannye Chlenam Komiteta Ministrov dlia razsmotreniia p. 6 Vysochaishago ukaza 12 Dekabria 1904 goda.

Materialy i zapiski, razoslannye Chlenam Komiteta Ministrov na zasedaniia 25 Ianvaria, 1, 8, 15 i 22 Fevralia i 1 i 8 Marta 1905 goda dlia razsmotreniia p. 6 Vysochaishago ukaza 12 Dekabria 1904 goda.

Materialy i zapiski razoslannye Chlenam Komiteta Ministrov na zasedaniia 15, 22 i 23 Marta, 5 i 6 Aprelia 1905 goda po delu o poriadke vypolneniia p. 7 Vysochaishago ukaza 12 Dekabria 1904 goda v otnoshenii k 9 zapadnykh gubernii.

Materialy, zapiski i memorii Soveta Ministrov po delu o primenenii Ukaza 18 Fevralia 1905 goda. Uchrezhdenie Gosudarstvennoi Dumy i Polozhenie o vyborakh.

Ob"edinenie deiatel'nosti ministrov.
Pravitel'stvennye Akty, vol. 1.
Predpolozheniia vysshago pravitel'stva o privlechenii izbrannykh ot naseleniia lits k zakonosoveshchatel'noi deiatel'nosti.
Zhurnaly Soveta Ministrov 1906.

B. Dissertations

Bennet, D. J., Jr. "The Idea of Kingship in 17th Century Russia." Ph.D. diss., Harvard University, 1967.

Doctorow, G. S. "The Introduction of Parliamentary Institutions in Russia, 1905–1906." Ph.D. diss.—preliminary version, Columbia University, 1976.

Koroleva, N. G. "Sovet Ministrov Rossii v gody pervoi russkoi revoliutsii." Kandidatskaia dissertatsiia, Moscow, 1971.

Macey, D.A.J. "The Russian Bureaucracy and the 'Peasant Problem.' The Pre-History of the Stolypin Reforms, 1861–1907." Ph.D. diss., Columbia University, 1976.

Ostrovskii, A. V. "Tret'eiunskii perevorot 1907 g." Kandidatskaia dissertatsiia, Leningrad, 1976.

Stepanskii, A. D. "Gosudarstvennyi Sovet v period revoliutsii 1905–07 gg." Kandidatskaia dissertatsiia, Moscow, 1965.

Taranovski, T. "The Politics of Counter-Reform: Autocracy and Bureaucracy in the Reign of Alexander III, 1881–1894." Ph.D. diss., Harvard University, 1976.

Verner, Andrew M. "Nicholas II and the Role of the Autocrat during the First Russian Revolution, 1905–07." Ph.D. diss., Columbia University, 1986.

C. Contemporary Newspapers and Journals

Grazhdanin
Moskovskiia Vedomosti
Novoe Vremia
Pravitel'stvennyi Vestnik
Russkiia Vedomosti
Russkii Vestnik

D. Published Documents

"Agrarnoe dvizhenie v 1905 g. po otchetam Dubasova i Panteleeva." KA 11–12 (1925): 182–92.

Agrarnyi vopros v sovete ministrov (1906). Part 4 of *Materialy po istorii krest'ianskikh dvizhenii v Rossii*, ed. V. V. Veselovskii, V. I. Pichet, and V. M. Friche. Moscow-Leningrad, 1924.

"Iz arkhiva S. Iu. Vitte." KA 11–12 (1925): 107–43.

"Bezobrazovskii kruzhok letom 1904 g." KA 27 (1926): 70–80.

"Bor'ba S. Iu. Vitte s agrarnoi revoliutsii." KA 31 (1928): 81–102.

Boylen, Joseph O. "The Tsar's 'Lecturer-General.' W. T. Snead and the Russian Revolution of 1905 with Two Unpublished Memoranda of Audiences with the

Dowager Empress Marie Fedorovna and Nicholas II." *Georgia State College School of Arts and Sciences Research Papers*, no. 23 (July 1969).

"Iz bumag D. F. Trepova." *KA* 11–12 (1925): 448–66.

"Iz chernovykh bumag K. P. Pobedonostseva." *KA* 28 (1926): 203–7.

"9–e ianvariia 1905 g." *KA* 11–12 (1925): 1–25.

"Dnevnik A. A. Bobrinskogo (1910–1911 gg.)" *KA* 27 (1926): 127–50.

"Dnevnik A. A. Polovtseva." *KA* 3 (1923): 75–172; 4 (1923): 63–128.

"Dnevnik A. N. Kuropatkina." *KA* 2 (1922): 5–117; 5 (1924): 82–101; 7 (1924): 55–69; 8 (1925): 70–100; 68 (1935): 65–96; 69–70 (1935): 101–26.

Dnevnik A. S. Suvorina. Ed. M. Krichevskii. Moscow-Petrograd, 1923.

"Dnevnik Borisa Nikol'skogo." *KA* 68 (1934): 55–97.

"Dnevnik kn. Ekateriny Alekseevny Sviatopolk-Mirskoi za 1904–1905 gg." *Istoricheskie zapiski* 77 (1965): 236–93.

Dnevnik Imperatora Nikolaia II. Berlin, 1923.

"Dnevnik I. Ia. Kopostovtsa, sekretaria grafa S. Iu. Vitte vo vremia portsmutskoi mirnoi konferentsiia iiul'–sentiabr 1905 goda." *Byloe* 7 (January 1918): 180–222; 8 (February 1918): 110–46; 9 (March 1918): 58–85; 12 (June 1918): 154–82.

"Iz dnevnika Konstantina Romanova." *KA* 43 (1930): 92–115; 44 (1931): 126–51; 45 (1931): 112–29.

"25 let nasad. Iz dnevnika L. Tikhomirova." *KA* 38 (1930): 20–69; 39 (1930): 47–75; 40 (1930): 59–96; 41–42 (1930): 103–47.

"Iz dnevnika L. Tikhomirova. 1907." *KA* 61 (1933): 82–128; 72 (1935): 120–59; 73 (1935): 170–90; 74 (1936): 162–91; 75 (1936): 171–84.

"Dokladnaia zapiska departamenta politsii predsedatel'iu soveta ministrov S. Iu. Vitte." *KA* 9 (1925).

"Doklady S. Iu. Vitte Nikolaiu II." *Byloe* 3 (March 1918): 3–10.

"Doklady S. Iu. Vitte Nikolaiu II." *KA* 11–12 (1925): 144–58.

"Doklady V. N. Kokovtsova Nikolaiu II." *KA* 11–12 (1925): 1–25.

"Dokumenty o khodynskoi katastrofe 1896 g." *KA* 76 (1936): 31–48.

"Finansovoe polozhenie tsarskogo samoderzhaviia v period russko-iaponskoi voiny i I russkoi revoliutsii," *Istoricheskii arkhiv*, no. 2 (1955).

Gosudarstvennye akty osvoboditel'noi epokhi. St. Petersburg, 1906.

Gosudarstvennye akty ot ukaza 12 dek. 1904 g. do ukaza 11 dek. 1905 g. St. Petersburg, 1906.

Gosudarstvennyi Sovet. *Otchet gosudarstvennago soveta*. St. Petersburg, 1904–6.

———. *Stenograficheskie otchety*. Sessia 1–2. St. Petersburg, 1906–7.

———. *Vsepoddanneishii otchet predsedatelia Gosudarstvennago Soveta*. St. Petersburg, 1904–7.

"Graf S. Iu. Vitte i Nikolai II v oktiabre 1905 g." *Byloe* 4 (1925): 107.

"K istorii agrarnoi reformy Stolypina." *KA* 17 (1926): 81–90.

"K istorii borby samoderzhaviia s agrarnym dvizheniem v 1905–1907 gg." *KA* 78 (1936): 128–60.

"K istorii karatel'nykh ekspeditsii v Sibiri." *KA* 1 (1922): 329–43.

"K istorii 'Krovavogo Voskreseniia' v Peterburge." *KA* 68 (1935): 41–64.

"K istorii manifesta 6 avgusta 1905 g." *KA* 14 (1926): 262–70.

"K istorii manifesta 17 oktiabria 1905 goda." *Byloe* 14 (1919): 108–11.

"K istorii manifesta 17 oktiabria." *KA* 4 (1923): 411–17.

Komitet Ministrov. *Svod Vysochaishikh otmetok po vsepoddanneishim otchetym general-gubernatorov, gubernatorov*. St. Petersburg, 1904–6.

——. *Zhurnaly Komiteta ministrov po ispolneniiu ukaza 12 dekabria 1904 g.* St. Petersburg, 1905.

"Konets russko-iaponskoi voiny (Voennoe soveshchanie 24 maia 1905 g. v Tsarskom Sele)." *KA* 28 (1928): 182–204.

"Krest'ianskoe dvizhenie 1905 goda." *KA* 9 (1925): 66–93.

Kuz'min-Karavaev, V. D. *Iz epokhi osvoboditel'nago dvizheniia*. St. Petersburg, 1907.

Lopukhin, A. A., "Doklad Direktora departamenta politsii Lopukhina Ministru vnutrennikh del o sobytiakh 9-go ianvaria." *Krasnaia Letopis'*, no. 1 (1922): 330–38.

"Manifest 17 Oktiabria." *KA* 11–12 (1925): 39–106.

Ministerstvo vnutrennikh del. *Materialy po uchrezhdeniiu Gosudarstvennoi Dumy*. St. Petersburg, 1905.

"Iz neizvestnoi perepiski imp. Aleksandra III i Nikolaia II s kn. V. P. Meshcherskim." *Sovremenniia Zapiski* 70 (1940): 165–88.

"Nikolai Romanov o anglo-burskoi voine." *KA* 63 (1934): 124–26.

"Nikolai Romanov o revoliutsionnym dvizhenii v armii v 1905 g." *KA* 41–42 (1930): 215–20.

"Nikolai II v 1905 g. (Po reskriptam, rezoliutsiiam i telegrammam)." *KA* 11–12 (1925): 433–39.

"Nikolai II i Finlandiia." *KA* 27 (1927): 225–33.

"Nikolai II—'imperator kafrov'." *KA* 69–70 (1935): 241–56.

"Obuzdanie revoliutsionnoi deiatel'nosti stolichnoi i provintsial'noi periodicheskoi pechati v 1906 g." *KA* 2 (1922): 280.

Padenie tsarskogo rezhima po materialam Chrezvychainoi Komissii Vremennogo Pravitel'stva. Ed. P. E. Shchegolev, 5 vols. Leningrad, 1925.

"K peregovoram Kokovtsova o zaime v 1905–1906 gg." *KA* 10 (1925): pp. 3–37.

"Perepiska N. A. Romanova i P. A. Stolypina." *KA* 5 (1925): 102–8.

"Perepiska Nikolaia II i Marii Fedorovny (1905–1906 gg.)." *KA* 22 (1927): 153–209.

Perepiska Vilgel'ma II s Nikolaem II. Ed. M. N. Pokrovskii. Moscow, 1923.

"Perepiska S. Iu. Vitte i A. N. Kuropatkina v 1904–1905 gg." *KA* 19 (1926): 64–82.

"Perepiska Vitte i Pobedonostseva (1895–1905)." *KA* 30 (1928): 89–116.

"Iz perepiski Nikolaia i Marii Romanovykh v 1907–1910 gg." *KA* 50–51 (1932): 161–93.

"Iz perepiski Nikolaia Romanova s V. A. Romanovym." *KA* 17 (1926): 219–22.

"Iz perepiski P. A. Stolypina s Nikolaem Romanovym." *KA* 30 (1928): 80–88.

"Pervye shagi russkogo imperializma na Dal'nem Vostoke (1888–1903 gg.)." *KA* 52 (1932): 34–124.

"Petitsiia literatorov Nikolaiu II v 1895 g." *KA* 20 (1927): 237–40.

"Iz pisem gen. N. N. Levasheva A. N. Kuropatkinu." *KA* 25 (1926): 212–22.

"Pisma I. I. Vorontsova-Dashkova Nikolaiiu Romanovu (1905–1915 gg.)." *KA* 26 (1928): 97–126.

"Pisma Nikolaia II Dubasovu." *KA* 11–12 (1925): 440–42.

"Pisma S. Iu. Vitte k D. S. Sipiaginu (1900–1901 gg.)." *KA* 18 (1926): 30–40.

"Pismo kn. E. N. Trubetskogo Nikolaiu Romanovu po povodu rospuska I Gos. dumy." *KA* 10 (1925): 300–4.

"Pismo V. K. Pleve k A. A. Kireevu." *KA* 18 (1926): 201–3.

Pokrovskii, M. N., ed. *1905. Materialy i dokumenty.* Vol. I: *Agrarnoe dvizhenie v 1905–1907 gg. Materialy i dokumenty.* Ed. S. M. Dubrovskii and B. Grave. Moscow-Leningrad, 1925.

Polnoe sobranie rechei Imp. Nikolaia II, 1894–1906. St. Petersburg, 1906.

"Portsmut." *KA* 6 (1924): 3–31.

"Poslednye Romanovy o 'liberalizme' i konstitutsionnom stroe." *KA* 22 (1927): 250–57.

Pridvornyi kalendar'. St. Petersburg, 1888–1917.

"Proekt zakhvata Bosfora v 1896 g." *KA* 47–48 (1931): 50–70.

"Proekt manifesta o sobytiiakh 9 ianvaria." *KA* 11–12 (1925): 26–38.

Rabochii vopros v komissii V. N. Kokovtsova. ed. B. A. Romanov. Moscow, 1926.

Raeff, Marc, ed. *Plans for Political Reform.* Englewood Cliffs, N.J., 1966.

Revoliutsiia 1905–1907 gg. v Rossii. Dokumenty i materialy. Ed. A. M. Pankratova et al. Moscow, 1957.

Romanov, B. A., ed. *Russkie finansy i evropeiskaia birzha v 1904–1906 gg. Sbornik dokumentov.* Moscow-Leningrad, 1924.

"Iz rezoliutsii Nikolaia II." *Byloe* 12 (June 1918): 142–47.

"Iz rezoliutsii Nikolaia Romanova." *KA* 58 (1934): 130–32.

"Russko-germanskii dogovor 1905 g. zakliuchennyi v B'erke." *KA* 5 (1924): 5–49.

Sbornik rechei Stolypina, proiznesennykh v zasedaniiakh Gosudarstvennago soveta i Gosudarstvennoi dumy (1906–1911gg.). St. Petersburg, 1911.

The Secret Letters of the Last Tsar: Being the Confidential Correspondence between Nicholas II and His Mother Dowager Empress Maria Feodorovna. New York, 1938.

Semennikov, Vladimir Petrovich. *Nikolai II i velikie kniaz'a (rodstvennye pisma k poslednomu tsariu).* Leningrad, 1925.

———. *Revoliutsiia 1905 goda i samoderzhavie.* Moscow, 1928.

"S. Iu. Vitte, frantsuskaia pressa i russkie zaimy." *KA* 10 (1925): 36–40.

Shvanebakh, P. Kh. "Zapiski sanovnika (politika P. A. Stolypina i Vtoraia Gosudarstvennaia Duma)." *Golos minuvshego* 1–3 (January–March 1918): 115–38.

Soveshchanie dlia obsuzhdeniia prednachertanii, ukazannykh v Vysochaishem reskripte 18 fevralia 1905 goda. Avg. 1–8. 1905. Protokoly zasedanii soveshchaniia, pod lichnym Ego Imperatorskago Velichestva predsedatel'stvom. St. Petersburg, 1905.

Soveshchanie dlia razsmotreniia predpolozhenii Soveta Ministrov o sposobakh osushchestvleniia Vysochaishikh predukazanii vozveshchennykh v punkte 2 Manifesta 17 Oktiabria 1905 goda. 5, 7 i 9 dekabria. Protokoly zasedanii so-

veshchaniia, pod lichnym Ego Imperatorskago Velichestva predsedatel'stvom.
St. Petersburg, 1905.

Soveshchanie po peresmotru osnovnykh gosudarstvennykh zakonov. Protokoly zasedanii soveshchaniia, pod lichnym Ego Imperatorskago Velichestva predsedatel'stvom. 7, 9, 11 i 12 aprelia 1906 goda. St. Petersburg, 1906.

Sovet ministrov. *Materialy po uchrezhdeniiu Gosudarstvennoi dumy 1905 g.* St. Petersburg, 1905.

Sovet ministrov. *Osobyi zhurnal.* 6 June 1906–December 1907.

Das Tagebuch des letzten Zaren. Berlin, 1923.

"Trepovskii proekt rechi Nikolaia II k rabochim posle 9 ianvaria 1905 g." *KA* 20 (1927): 240–42.

"Tsarizm v bor'be s revoliutsionnoi pechat'iu v 1905 g." *KA* 105 (1941): 140–55.

"Tsarskosel'ske Soveshchaniia. Protokoly sekretnogo soveshchaniia v fevrale 1906 g. pod predsedatel'stvom byvshego imperatora po vyrabotke Uchrezhdenii Gosudarstvennoi Dumy i Gosudarstvennogo Soveta." *Byloe* 5–6 (November–December 1917): 289–318.

Tsentrarkhiv. *Pis'ma K. F. Pobedonostseva k Aleksandru III.* Ed. M. Pokrovskii. 2 vols. Moscow, 1925.

"Vil'gelm II o russko-iaponskoi voine i revoliutsii 1905 g." *KA* 9 (1925): 56–65.

Vinogradoff, Igor. "Some Russian Imperial Letters to Prince V. P. Meshchersky (1839–1914)." *Oxford Slavonic Papers* 10 (1962): 105–58.

"S. Iu. Vitte, frantsuskaia pressa i russkie zaimy." *KA* 10 (1925): 36–40.

Zakonodatel'nye akty perekhodnago vremeni (1904–1908gg.). Ed. N. I. Lazarevskii. 3d ed. St. Petersburg, 1909.

"Zapiska Glazova o ianvarskom soveshchanii." *KA* 11–12 (1925): 28–37.

"Zapiski A. F. Redigera o 1905 g." *KA* 45 (1931): 86–111.

"Zapiski A. S. Ermolova." *KA* 8 (1925): 49–69.

"Zapiski F. A. Golovina." *KA* 19 (1926): 110–49.

E. Published Memoirs

Alexander, Grand Duke. *Once a Grand Duke.* New York, 1932.

Aleksandr Mikhailovich, V. K. *Kniga vospominanii.* Paris, 1933.

Bogdanovich, A. V. *Tri poslednikh samoderzhtsa.* Moscow-Leningrad, 1924.

Bompard, M. *Mon Ambassade en Russie, 1903–1908.* Paris, 1937.

Bok, M. P. *Vospominaniia o moem otse P. A. Stolypine.* New York, 1953.

Fabritskii, S. S. *Iz Proshlago. Vospominaniia fligel'-ad'iutanta Gosudaria Imperatora Nikolaia II.* Berlin, 1926.

Gilliard, Pierre. *Thirteen Years at the Russian Court.* New York, 1921.

Gurko, Vladimir Iosifovich. *Features and Figures of the Past: Government and Opinion in the Reign of Nicholas II.* Stanford, 1939.

———. *Tsar i Tsaritsa.* Paris, 1927.

Gavril Konstantinovich, V. K. *V mramornom dvortse.* New York, 1955.

Iswolsky, Alexander. *Recollections of a Foreign Minister.* Garden City, N.Y., 1921.

Kizevetter, A. *Na rubezhe dvukh stoletii.* Prague, 1929.

Kokovtsev, V. N. *Iz moego proshlogo,* vol. 1. Paris, 1933.

360 · Select Bibliography

Kokovtsev, V. N. *Out of My Past.* Ed. H. H. Fisher. Stanford, 1935.
Krivoshein, K. A. *A. V. Krivoshein (1857–1921). Ego znachenie v istorii Rossii nachala XX veka.* Paris, 1973.
Kryzhanovskii, S. E. *Vospominaniia.* Berlin, n.d. [1938].
Liubimov, D. N. "Gapon i 9 ianvaria." *Voprosy istorii,* no. 8 (1965).
Mamontov, V. I. *Na gosudarstvennom sluzhbe.* Tallinn, 1926,
Meshcherskii, V. P., *Moi vospominaniia.* St. Petersburg, 1912.
Mosolov, A. A. *At the Court of the Last Tsar; Being the Memoirs of A. A. Mosolov, Head of the Court Chancellery, 1900–1916.* London, 1935.
Naumov, A. N. *Iz utselevshikh vospominanii, 1868–1917.* New York, 1954–55.
Obolenskii, A. V., *Moi vospominaniia i razmyshleniia.* Brussels, 1961.
"Otryvki iz vospominanii D. N. Liubimova (1902–1904 gg.)." *Istoricheskii Arkhiv,* no. 6, 1962.
Shipov, D. N. *Vospominaniia i dumy o perezhitom.* Moscow, 1918.
Surguchev, I. D. *Detstvo Imperatora Nikolaia II.* Paris, 1952.
Tagantsev, N. S. *Perezhitoe.* Vol. 1: *Uchrezhdenie Gosudarstvennoi Dumy v 1905–1906 gg..* Petrograd, 1919.
Voeikov, V. N. *S tsarem i bez tsaria. Vospominaniia poslednego dvortsogo komendanta Gosudaria Imperatora Nikolaia II.* Helsinki, 1936.
"Vospominaniia V. B. Lopukhina. Liudi i politika (konets XIX–nachala XX v.)." *Voprosy istorii* 51, no. 9 (1966).
Witte, S. Iu. *Vospominaniia.* 3 vols. Moscow, 1960.

F. CRITICAL LITERATURE

Anderson, Perry. *Lineages of the Absolutist State.* London, 1974.
Armstrong, J. A. *The European Administrative Elite.* Princeton, N. J., 1973.
———. "Old-Regime Governors: Bureaucratic and Patrimonial Attitudes." *Comparative Studies in Society and History* 14, no. 1 (1972): 2–29.
Ascher, Abraham. *The Revolution of 1905.* Stanford, 1988.
Aufhauser, Joh. B. "Die Sakrale Kaiseridee in Byzanz." in *Studies in the History of Religions.* Vol. 4: *The Sacred Kingship.* Leiden, 1959.
Avrekh, A. Ia. *Stolypin i Tret'ia Duma.* Moscow, 1968.
———. *Tsarizm i tret'eiunskaia sistema.* Moscow, 1966.
Barsov, E. V. *Drevne-russkie pamiatniki sviashchennago venchaniia tsarei na tsarstvo v sviazi s grecheskimi ikh originalami s istoricheskim ocherkom chinov tsarskogo venchaniia v sviazi s razvitiem idei tsaria na Rusi.* Moscow, 1883.
Besançon, H. *Le Tsarevich Immolé.* Paris, 1967.
Black, J. L. *Nicholas Karamzin and Russian Society in the Nineteenth Century. A Study in Russian Political and Historical Thought.* Toronto, 1975.
Bocock, Robert. *Ritual in Industrial Society.* London, 1974.
Byrnes, Robert F. *Pobedonostsev. His Life and Thought.* Bloomington, Ind., 1968.
Carlton, Charles. *Royal Childhoods.* London, 1986.
Chermenskii, E. D. *Burzhuaziia i tsarizm v Pervoi Russkoi Revoliutsii.* 2d ed. Moscow, 1970.

Cherniavsky, Michael. *Tsar and People. Studies in Russian Myths*. New York, 1969.

Conroy, M. S. "Stolypin's Attitude toward Local Self-Government." *Slavonic and East European Review* 46 (1968): 446–62.

Dal', V. *Poslovitsy russkogo naroda*. Moscow, 1957.

Danilov, F. (Dan). "Obshchaia politika pravitel'stva i izmeneniia v gosudarstvennyi stroi k nachalu XX veka." *Obshchestvennoe dvizhenie v Rossii v nachale XX veka*, vol. 1. St. Petersburg, 1909, pp. 422–82.

Davidovich, A. M. *Samoderzhavie v epokhu imperializma*. Moscow, 1975.

Diakin, V. S., et al. *Krizis samoderzhaviia v Rossii, 1895–1917*. Leningrad, 1984.

Diatlova, N. P., and R. Iu. Matskina. "Obzor fonda 'Soveta ministrov (TsGIA SSSR v L)." *Arkheograficheskii ezhegodnik za 1958 god*, pp. 233–56.

Doctorow, G. S. "The Fundamental State Laws of 23 April 1906." *Russian Review* 35, no. 1 (January 1976): 33–52.

———. "The Government Program of 17 October 1905." *Russian Review* 34, no. 2 (April 1975): 123–36.

Dubrovskii, S. M. *Stolypinskaia zemel'naia reforma. Iz istorii sel'skago khoziaistva i krest'ianstva Rossii v nachale XX veke*. Moscow, 1963.

Emmons, Terence. *The Formation of Political Parties and the First National Elections in Russia*. Cambridge, Mass., 1983.

Enden, M. N. "The Roots of Witte's Thought," *Russian Review* 29, no. 1 (January 1970): 6–24.

Erikson, Erik H. *Young Man Luther. A Study in Psychoanalysis and History*. New York, 1958.

Ermolov, V. *Tsar' i narod*. St. Petersburg, 1906.

Eroshkin, N. P. *Istoriia gosudarstvennykh uchrezhdenii dorevoliutsionnoi Rossii*. 3d ed. Moscow, 1983.

Field, Daniel. *The End of Serfdom*. Cambridge, Mass., 1976.

———. *Rebels in the Name of the Tsar*. Boston, 1976.

Firsov, N. N. "Aleksandr III. Lichnaia kharakteristika chast'iu po ego neizdannym dnevnikam." *Byloe* 29 (1925): 90–104.

———. *Nikolai II. Opyt lichnoi kharakteristiki*. Kazan, 1929.

Florovskii, Georgii. *Puti Russkago Bogosloviia*. Paris, 1937.

Frankland, N. *Imperial Tragedy: Nicholas II, Last of the Tsars*. New York, 1961.

Friedrich, Carl J. *Tradition and Authority*. New York, 1972.

Grunwald, Constantin de. *Le tsar Nicolas II*. Paris, 1965.

Haimson, Leopold H. *The Russian Marxists and the Origins of Bolshevism*. Boston, 1953.

———. ed. *The Politics of Rural Russia*. Bloomington, Ind., 1979.

Halpern, Ben. " 'Myth' and 'Ideology' in Modern Usage." *History and Theory* 1 (1960): 129–49.

Hammer, D. P. "Russia and the Roman Law." *Slavic Review* 16, no. 1 (1957): 1–13.

Harcave, Sidney. *First Blood. The Russian Revolution of 1905*. London, 1964.

Harris, Nigel. *Beliefs in Society. The Problem of Ideology*. London, 1968.

Hocart, A. M. *Kingship*. London, 1969.

Hocart, A. M. *Kings and Councillors. An Essay in the Comparative Anatomy of Human Society.* Chicago, 1970.

Hosking, Geoffrey A. *The Russian Constitutional Experiment. Government and Duma 1907–1914.* Cambridge, 1973.

Hull, Isabel V. *The Entourage of Kaiser Wilhelm II 1888–1918.* Cambridge, 1982.

Ilovaiskii, D. I. *Kratkie ocherki russkoi istorii. Kurs starshago vozrasta.* 9th ed. Moscow, 1868.

———. *Rukovodstvo k russkoi istorii. Srednyi kurs.* 44th ed. Moscow, 1916.

Iusefovich, B. *Samoderzhavie ili Gosudarstvennoe Samoupravlenie?* Kiev, 1904.

Kaiser, Robert G. *Russia. The People and the Power.* New York, 1976.

Kantorowicz, E. H. *The King's Two Bodies. A Study in Medieval Political Theology.* Princeton, N.J., 1957.

Kazanskii, P. E. *Vlast' vserossiiskago imperatora; ocherki deistvuiushchago russkago prava.* Odessa, 1913.

Khomiakov, D. A. *Samoderzhavie. Opyt' skhematicheskago postroeniia etogo poniatiia.* N.p., 1903.

Kizevetter, A. A. "Imperator Nikolai I kak konstitutsionnyi monarkh." *Istoricheskie ocherki.* Moscow, 1912.

Klapp, O. E. *Ritual and Cult. A Sociological Interpretation.* Washington, D.C., 1956.

Korkunov, N. M. *Russkoe Gosudarstvennoe Pravo.* 2 vols. St. Petersburg, 1910.

———. *Ukaz i zakon.* St. Petersburg, 1894.

Koroleva, N. G. "Reforma Soveta Ministrov Rossii v 1905 godu (po dokumentam TsGIA SSSR)." *Sovetskie Arkhivy*, no. 1 (1972): 85–88.

Lazarevskii, N. I. *Lektsii po russkomu gosudarstvennomu pravu.* 2d ed. 2 vols. St. Petersburg, 1910.

Levin, A. "Russian Bureaucratic Opinion in the Wake of the 1905 Revolution." *Jahrbücher für die Geschichte Osteuropas* 11 (1963): 1–12.

Lichtheim, G. "The Concept of Ideology." *History and Theory* 4, no. 2 (1965): 164–95.

Lincoln, W. Bruce. *Nicholas I. Emperor and Autocrat of All the Russias.* Bloomington, Ind., 1978.

Maistre, Joseph de. *The Works of Joseph de Maistre.* Ed. Jack Lively. New York, 1965.

Mannheim, Karl. "Das konservative Denken." *Archiv für Sozialwissenschaft und Sozialpolitik* 57 (1927): 68–142, 470–95.

Massie, Robert K. *Nicholas and Alexandra.* New York, 1967.

Matskina, P. Iu. "Ministerskie otchety i ikh osobennosti kak istoricheskii istochnik," *Problemy arkhivovedeniia i istochnikovedeniia.* Leningrad, 1964, pp. 209–26.

Mehlinger, H. D., and J. M. Thompson. *Count Witte and the Tsarist Government in the 1905 Revolution.* Bloomington, Ind., 1972.

Miliukov, P. N. *Glavniia techeniia russkoi istoricheskoi mysli.* Moscow, 1898.

———. *Russia and Its Crisis.* New York, 1962.

Morrill, D. C. "Nicholas II and the Call for the First Hague Conference." *Journal of Modern History* 46 (1974): 296–313.

Neubauer, Helmut. *Car und Selbstherrscher. Beiträge zur Geschichte der Autokratie in Russland*. Wiesbaden, 1964.

Oldenburg, S. S. *Last Tsar. Nicholas II, His Reign and His Russia*. Trans. Leonid I. Mihalap and Patrick J. Rollins. 4 vols. Gulf Breeze, Fla., 1975–77.

———. *Tsarstvovanie Imperatora Nikolaia II*. Belgrade, 1939.

Pipes, Richard. "Karamzin's Conception of the Monarchy." *Russian Thought and Politics. Harvard Slavic Studies* (Cambridge, Mass.) 4 (1957): 35–58.

———. *Karamzin's Memoir on Ancient and Modern Russia*. Cambridge, Mass., 1959.

Plamenatz, John. *Ideology*. New York, 1970.

Pobedonostsev, Konstantin P. *Reflections of a Russian Statesman*. Ann Arbor, Mich., 1965.

Presniakov, A. E. "Samoderzhavie Aleksandra II," *Russkoe proshloe*, no. 3, (1923).

Rieber, A. J. "Alexander II: A Revisionist View." *Journal of Modern History* 43, no. 1 (1971): 42–58.

Rogger, Hans. "The Formation of the Russian Right 1900–1906." *California Slavic Studies* 3 (1964): 66–94.

Sablinsky, Walter. *The Road to Bloody Sunday*. Princeton, N.J., 1976.

Schaeder, H. *Moskau, das dritte Rom*. Hamburg, 1929.

Semenov, P. N. *Samoderzhavie kak gosudarstvennyi stroi*. St. Petersburg, 1906.

Shanin, Teodor. *The Roots of Otherness: Russia's Turn of Century*. Vol. 1: *Russia as a "Developing Society."* Vol. 2: *Russia, 1905–07: Revolution as a Moment of Truth*. New Haven, Conn. 1986.

Sidel'nikov, S. M. *Agrarnaia reforma Stolypina*. Moscow, 1973.

———. *Obrazovanie i deiatel'nost' Pervoi Gosudarstvennoi Dumy*. Moscow, 1962.

Simonova, M. S. *Krizis agrarnoi politiki tsarizma nakanune pervoi rossiiskoi revoliutsii*. Moscow, 1987.

———. "Agrarnaia politika samoderzhaviia v 1905 g." *Istoricheskie zapiski* 81 (1968).

———. "Politika tsarizma v krest'ianskom voprose nakanune revoliutsii 1905–1907 gg." *Istoricheskie zapiski* 75 (1965).

Snow, G. E. "The Kokovtsev Commission: An Abortive Attempt at Labor Reform in Russia in 1905," *Slavic Review* 31, no. 4 (1972): 780–96.

Solov'ev, Iu. B. "Nachalo tsarstvovaniia Nikolaia II i rol' Pobedonostseva v opredelenii politicheskogo kursa samoderzhaviia." *Arkheograficheskii ezhegodnik za 1972 god*. Moscow, 1974.

———. *Samoderzhavie i dvorianstvo v 1902–1907 gg*. Leningrad, 1981.

Startsev, V. I. *Russkaia burzhuaziia i samoderzhavie v 1905–1917 gg*. Leningrad, 1977.

Stepanskii, A. D. "Reforma Gosudarstvennogo Soveta v 1906," *Trudy Moskovskogo Gosudarstvennogo Istoriko-Arkhivnogo Instituta* 20 (1965).

Sternheimer, Stephen. "Administering Development and Developing Administration: Organizational Conflict in Tsarist Bureaucracy, 1906–1914." *Canadian-American Slavic Studies* 9, no. 3 (Fall 1975): 277–301.

Szeftel, M. "The Form of Government of the Russian Empire prior to the Constitutional Reforms of 1905–6." *Essays in Russian and Soviet History.* Ed. J. H. Curtiss. New York, 1963, pp. 105–19.

———. "The Legislative Reform of August 6, 1905 (The 'Bulygin Duma')." In *A. Marongiu. Mélanges.* Palermo, 1967, pp. 127–84.

———. "Nicholas II's Constitutional Decisions of October 17–19, 1905, and Sergei Witte's Role." In *Album J. Balon.* Namur, 1968.

———. *The Russian Constitution of April 23, 1906. Political Institutions of the Duma Monarchy.* Brussels, 1976.

Therborn, Göran. *The Ideology of Power and the Power of Ideology.* London, 1980.

Tikhomirov, L. A. *Monarkhicheskaia Gosudarstvennost'.* Buenos Aires, 1968.

Topitsch, Ernst, et al. *Ideologie. Herrschaft des Vorurteils.* Munich, 1972.

Valdenberg, V. *Drevnerusskie ucheniia o predelakh tsarskoi vlasti. Ocherki russkoi politicheskoi literatury ot Vladimira Sviatago do kontsa XVII veka.* Petrograd, 1916.

Walsh, Warren B. "The Romanov Papers: A Bibliographic Note," *The Historian* 31, no. 2 (February 1969): 163–72.

Walzer, Michael, ed. *Regicide and Revolution. Speeches at the Trial of Louis XVI.* New York, 1974.

Weber, Max. *From Max Weber: Essays in Sociology.* Ed. H. H. Gerth and C. Wright Mills. New York, 1958.

———. *The Theory of Social and Economic Organization.* Ed. Talcott Parsons. New York, 1964.

Weissman, Neil B. *Reform in Tsarist Russia. The State Bureaucracy and Local Government, 1900–1914.* New Brunswick, N.J., 1981.

Wesson, Robert G. *The Imperial Order.* Berkeley, Calif., 1967.

Westwood, J. N. *Russia Against Japan, 1904–05. A New Look at the Russo-Japanese War.* Albany, N.Y., 1986.

Wittfogel, K. A. *Oriental Despotism. A Comparative Study of Total Power.* New Haven, Conn., 1957.

Yaney, George L. "Law, Society and the Domestic Regime in Russia in Historical Perspective," *American Political Science Review* 59 (June 1965): 380–86.

———. *The Systemization of Russian Government. Social Evolution in the Domestic Administration of Imperial Russia, 1711–1905.* Urbana, Ill., 1973.

Zaionchkovskii, P. A. *Krizis samoderzhaviia na rubezhe 1878–1880 gg.* Moscow, 1964.

———. *Rossiiskoe samoderzhavie v kontse XIX stoletiia.* Moscow, 1970.

Zakharova, L. G. "Krizis samoderzhaviia nakanune revoliutsii 1905 goda." *Voprosy istorii,* no. 8 (1972).

Zavalishin, S. *Gosudar' Imperator Nikolai II Aleksandrovich; sbornik pamiati 100-letiia so dnia rozhdeniia.* New York, 1968.

Index

Abaza, A. M., 108n

absolutism, 74–75, 80–81

Akimov, M. G., 271, 322; at April 1906 conference, 305, 307, 308

Aksakov, I. S., 84

Alekseev, E. I., 59, 68

Aleksei Alexandrovich (grand duke), 62, 137, 206

Aleksei Mikhailovich (Alexis) (tsar), 73, 232, 343

Aleksei Nikolaevich (Alexis) (tsarevich), 107, 119n, 175, 343

Alexander I, 19, 100, 119, 305

Alexander II: reforms of, 71, 82, 85, 88, 94, 98, 119, 125, 126

Alexander III, 70, 76, 98, 138; bureaucracy under, 53, 82, 128; illness and death of, 7, 34–36, 37, 102; and Nicholas, 12, 13, 18, 25, 28, 40n, 88, 343; and zemstvos, 105. See also Nicholas II

Alexander Mikhailovich (grand duke), 7, 19n, 34, 142, 173, 206, 222

Alexandra Fedorovna (Alix), 12, 60, 69, 228, 231; and Kireev, 194, 201, 215; relationship of, with Nicholas II, 31–34, 35–37, 38, 39, 62, 114; religiosity of, 30–31, 32, 33–34, 37, 39; and surrender of Port Arthur, 146–47; and Sviatopolk-Mirskii, 124

Aristotle, 74

Assembly of the Land. See zemskii sobor

authority: personalized versus institutionalized, 51, 52, 53, 54–56, 78, 79–80, 81–82, 86–87, 88–89, 239, 242, 245, 341. See also vlast'

autocracy: conflicting conceptions of, 78–81, 83, 91, 144–45, 213, 245, 320, 341; crisis of, 3, 70–71, 341; definitions of, 72–73, 112; evolution of, 73–75, 97–98, 99–100; and history, 97–100, 101–2; ideology of, 4–6, 45, 70, 71, 72, 75–77, 78, 96, 180, 214, 216, 220, 228, 232, 286, 292, 344; inviolability of, 208, 214, 216; modern bureaucratic conception of, 79, 96, 141, 187–88, 245, 295–96, 337–39,

340, 342–43; and *narod*, 89–93; and notion of Legal Autocracy, 78, 83, 96, 119, 126–27, 128, 140, 341–42; organicist conception of, 78–79, 87, 96, 97–100; paternalist conception of, 78, 95–96, 125, 126, 245, 270, 341, 343; and popular representation, 112, 113, 118–19, 121, 132–33, 134, 137, 138–39, 202, 203, 205, 209, 213–16, 342–43; and society, 78, 93–94, 96, 188, 190–91, 199, 208, 214, 229–30, 232–33, 243, 342, 343; structure of, 45, 69. See also tsar

autocrat. See tsar

Benckendorf, P. K. (count), 67

Bennet, Douglas J., 73, 74

Bezobrazov, A. M., 68, 69, 108n

Birilev, A. A., 60

Black Hundreds, 247, 315, 318

Bloody Sunday, 152–53, 157–58; events leading to, 148–49, 150–52; official response to, 157–67; society's response to, 157, 167–68

Bobrikov, N. I., 106

Bobrinskii, A. A., 205, 209, 210; at December 1905 conference, 283, 284

Borki: railway disaster at, 36, 240

Budberg, A. A. (baron), 236, 238, 239, 263, 312–13

Bulygin, A. G., 58, 63, 156–57, 200, 219, 221, 226; and February 18 rescript, 175, 181, 182, 184, 198–200, 212; and Nicholas II, 189–91, 192, 198, 200. See also Duma, Bulygin

Bunge, N. Kh., 21, 42

bureaucracy: dependent on tsar's favors, 53–55; disunity in, 54–57; myth and criticisms of, 80–84, 85–86, 90, 162–63, 180, 216, 270, 293, 341–42; Nicholas II's attitudes toward, 26, 28–29, 59, 61, 65–67, 69, 82, 145, 155, 168, 185; superordinate pretensions of, 190–91, 198; Witte's faith in, 251–52, 291, 295–96; workings of, 45–49, 50–53, 54–55, 185, 198

Studies of the Harriman Institute

Soviet National Income in 1937 by Abram Bergson, Columbia University Press, 1953.

Through the Glass of Soviet Literature: Views of Russian Society, Ernest Simmons Jr., ed., Columbia University Press, 1953.

Polish Postwar Economy by Thad Paul Alton, Columbia University Press, 1954.

Management of the Industrial Firm in the USSR: A Study in Soviet Economic Planning by David Granick, Columbia University Press, 1954.

Soviet Politics in China, 1917–1924 by Allen S. Whiting, Columbia University Press, 1954; paperback, Stanford University Press, 1968.

Literary Politics in the Soviet Ukraine, 1917–1934 by George S. N. Luckyj, Columbia University Press, 1956.

The Emergence of Russian Panslavism, 1856–1870 by Michael Boro Petrovich, Columbia University Press, 1956.

Lenin on Trade Unions and Revolution, 1893–1917 by Thomas Taylor Hammond, Columbia University Press, 1956.

The Last Years of the Georgian Monarchy, 1658–1832 by David Marshall Lang, Columbia University Press, 1957.

The Japanese Thrust into Siberia, 1918 by James William Morley, Columbia University Press, 1957.

Bolshevism in Turkestan, 1917–1927 by Alexander G. Park, Columbia University Press, 1957.

Soviet Marxism: A Critical Analysis by Herbert Marcuse, Columbia University Press, 1958; paperback, Columbia University Press, 1985.

Soviet Policy and the Chinese Communists, 1931–1946 by Charles B. McLane, Columbia University Press, 1958.

The Agrarian Foes of Bolshevism: Promise and Defeat of the Russian Socialist Revolutionaries, February to October, 1917 by Oliver H. Radkey, Columbia University Press, 1958.

Pattern for Soviet Youth: A Study of the Congresses of the Komsomol, 1918–1954 by Ralph Talcott Fisher, Jr., Columbia University Press, 1959.

The Emergence of Modern Lithuania by Alfred Erich Senn, Columbia University Press, 1959.

The Soviet Design for a World State by Elliot R. Goodman, Columbia University Press, 1960.

Settling Disputes in Soviet Society: The Formative Years of Legal Institutions by John N. Hazard, Columbia University Press, 1960.

Soviet Marxism and Natural Science, 1917–1932 by David Joravsky, Columbia University Press, 1961.

Russian Classics in Soviet Jackets by Maurice Friedberg, Columbia University Press, 1962.

Stalin and the French Communist Party, 1941–1947 by Alfred J. Rieber, Columbia University Press, 1962.

Sergei Witte and the Industrialization of Russia by Theodore K. Von Laue, Columbia University Press, 1962.

Ukranian Nationalism by John H. Armstrong, Columbia University Press, 1963.

The Sickle under the Hammer: The Russian Socialist Revolutionaries in the Early Months of Soviet Rule by Oliver H. Radkey, Columbia University Press, 1963.

Comintern and World Revolution, 1928–1943: The Shaping of Doctrine by Kermit E. McKenzie, Columbia University Press, 1964.

Weimar Germany and Soviet Russia, 1926–1933: A Study in Diplomatic Instability by Harvey L. Dyck, Columbia University Press, 1966.

Financing Soviet Schools by Harold J. Noah, Teachers College Press, 1966.

Russia, Bolshevism, and the Versailles Peace by John M. Thompson, Princeton University Press, 1966.

The Russian Anarchists by Paul Avrich, Princeton University Press, 1967.

The Soviet Academy of Sciences and the Communist Party, 1927–1932 by Loren R. Graham, Princeton University Press, 1967.

Red Virgin Soil: Soviet Literature in the 1920's by Robert A. Maguire, Princeton University Press, 1968; paperback, Cornell University Press, 1987.

Communist Party Membership in the U.S.S.R., 1917–1967 by T. H. Rigby, Princeton University Press, 1968.

Soviet Ethics and Morality by Richard T. DeGeorge, University of Michigan Press, 1969; paperback, Ann Arbor Paperbacks, 1969.

Vladimir Akimov on the Dilemmas of Russian Marxism, 1895–1903 by Jonathan Frankel, Cambridge University Press, 1969.

Soviet Perspectives on International Relations, 1956–1967 by William Zimmerman, Princeton University Press, 1969.

Krondstadt, 1921 by Paul Avrich, Princeton University Press, 1970.

Class Struggle in the Pale: The Formative Years of the Jewish Workers' Movement in Tsarist Russia by Ezra Mendelsohn, Cambridge University Press, 1970.

The Proletarian Episode in Russian Literature by Edward J. Brown, Columbia University Press, 1971.

Labor and Society in Tsarist Russia: The Factory Workers of St. Petersburg, 1855–1870 by Reginald E. Zelnik, Stanford University Press, 1971.

Archives and Manuscript Repositories in the USSR: Moscow and Leningrad by Patricia K. Grimsted, Princeton University Press, 1972.

The Baku Commune, 1917–1918 by Ronald G. Suny, Princeton University Press, 1972.

Mayakovsky: A Poet in the Revolution by Edward J. Brown, Princeton University Press, 1973.

Oblomov and his Creator: The Life and Art of Ivan Goncharov by Milton Ehre, Princeton University Press, 1973.

German Politics Under Soviet Occupation by Henry Krisch, Columbia University Press, 1974.

Soviet Politics and Society in the 1970's, Henry W. Morton and Rudolph L. Tokes, eds., Free Press, 1974.

Liberals in the Russian Revolution by William G. Rosenberg, Princeton University Press, 1974.

Famine in Russia, 1891–1892 by Richard G. Robbins, Jr., Columbia University Press, 1975.

In Stalin's Time: Middleclass Values in Soviet Fiction by Vera Dunham, Cambridge University Press, 1976.

The Road to Bloody Sunday by Walter Sablinsky, Princeton University Press, 1976; paperback, Princeton University Press, 1986.

The Familiar Letter as a Literary Genre in the Age of Pushkin by William Mills Todd III, Princeton University Press, 1976.

Russian Realist Art. The State and Society: The Peredvizhniki and Their Tradition by Elizabeth Valkenier, Ardis Publishers, 1977.

The Soviet Agrarian Debate by Susan Solomon, Westview Press, 1978.

Cultural Revolution in Russia, 1928–1931, Sheila Fitzpatrick, ed., Indiana University Press, 1978; paperback, Midland Books, 1984.

Soviet Criminologists and Criminal Policy: Specialists in Policy-Making by Peter Solomon, Columbia University Press, 1978.

Technology and Society under Lenin and Stalin: Origins of the Soviet Technical Intelligentsia by Kendall E. Bailes, Princeton University Press, 1978.

The Politics of Rural Russia, 1905–1914, Leopold H. Haimson, ed., Indiana University Press, 1979.

Political Participation in the USSR by Theodore H. Friedgut, Princeton University Press, 1979; paperback, Princeton University Press, 1982.

Education and Social Mobility in the Soviet Union, 1921–1934 by Sheila Fitzpatrick, Cambridge University Press, 1979.

The Soviet Marriage Market: Mate Selection in Russian and the USSR by Wesley Andrew Fisher, Praeger Publishers, 1980.

Prophecy and Politics: Socialism, Nationalism, and the Russian Jews, 1862–1917 by Jonathan Frankel, Cambridge University Press, 1981.

Dostoevsky and The Idiot: *Author, Narrator, and Reader* by Robin Feuer Miller, Harvard University Press, 1981.

Moscow Workers and the 1917 Revolution by Diane Koenker, Princeton University Press, 1981; paperback, Princeton University Press, 1986.

Archives and Manuscript Repositories in the USSR: Estonia, Latvia, Lithuania, and Belorussia by Patricia K. Grimsted, Princeton University Press, 1981.

Zionism in Poland: The Formative Years, 1915–1926 by Ezra Mendelsohn, Yale University Press, 1982.

Soviet Risk-Taking and Crisis Behavior by Hannes Adomeit, George Allen and Unwin Publishers, 1982.

Russia at the Crossroads: The 26th Congress of the CPSU, Seweryn Bialer and Thane Gustafson, eds., George Allen and Unwin Publishers, 1982.

The Crisis of the Old Order in Russia: Gentry and Government by Roberta Thompson Manning, Princeton University Press, 1983; paperback, Princeton University Press, 1986.

Sergei Aksakov and Russian Pastoral by Andrew A. Durkin, Rutgers University Press, 1983.

Politics and Technology in the Soviet Union by Bruce Parrott, MIT Press, 1983.

The Soviet Union and the Third World: An Economic Bind by Elizabeth Kridl Valkenier, Praeger Publishers, 1983.

Russian Metaphysical Romanticism: The Poetry of Tiutchev and Boratynskii by Sarah Pratt, Stanford University Press, 1984.

Ruling Russia: Politics and Administration in the Age of Absolutism, 1762–1796 by John P. LeDonne, Princeton University Press, 1984.

Insidious Intent: A Structural Analysis of Fedor Sologub's Petty Demon by Diana Greene, Slavica Publishers, 1986.

Leo Tolstoy: Resident and Stranger by Richard Gustafson, Princeton University Press, 1986.

Workers, Society, and the State: Labor and Life in Moscow, 1918–1929 by William Chase, University of Illinois Press, 1987.

Andrey Bely: Spirit of Symbolism, John Malmstad, ed., Cornell University Press, 1987.

Government and Peasant in Russia, 1861–1906: The Prehistory of the Stolypin Reforms by David A. J. Macey, Northern Illinois University Press, 1987.

The Making of Three Russian Revolutionaries: Voices from the Menshevik Past, edited by Leopold H. Haimson in collaboration with Ziva Galili y García and Richard Wortman, Cambridge University Press, 1988.

Revolution and Culture: The Bogdanov-Lenin Controversy by Zenovia A. Sochor, Cornell University Press, 1988.

A Handbook of Russian Verbs by Frank Miller, Ardis Publishers, 1988.

1905 in St. Petersburg: Labor, Society, and Revolution by Gerald D. Surh, Stanford University Press, 1989.

Iuzovka and Revolution. Volume 1, *Life and Work in Russia's Donbass, 1869–1924* by Theodore H. Friedgut, Princeton University Press, 1989.